SILVER BURDETT & GINN
SOCIAL STUDIES

Geography of States and Regions

Theodore Kaltsounis
Professor and Associate Dean, College of Education
University of Washington, Seattle, Washington

SILVER BURDETT & GINN
MORRISTOWN, NJ • NEEDHAM, MA

Atlanta, GA • Cincinnati, OH • Dallas, TX • Menlo Park, CA • Deerfield, IL

SERIES AUTHORS

W. Frank Ainsley Jr., Associate Professor of Geography, University of North Carolina at Wilmington

Val E. Arnsdorf, Former Professor, College of Education, University of Delaware, Newark, Delaware

Herbert J. Bass, Professor of History, Temple University, Philadelphia, Pennsylvania

Richard C. Brown, Former Professor of History, State University of New York College at Buffalo

Patricia T. Caro, Assistant Professor of Geography, University of Oregon, Eugene, Oregon

Kenneth S. Cooper, Professor of History, Emeritus, George Peabody College for Teachers, Vanderbilt University, Nashville, Tennessee

Gary S. Elbow, Professor of Geography, Texas Tech University, Lubbock, Texas

Alvis T. Harthern, Professor of Early Childhood Education, West Georgia College, Carrollton, Georgia

Timothy M. Helmus, Social Studies Instructor, City Middle and High School, Grand Rapids, Michigan

Bobbie P. Hyder, Elementary Education Coordinator, Madison County School System, Huntsville, Alabama

Theodore Kaltsounis, Professor and Associate Dean, College of Education, University of Washington, Seattle, Washington

Richard H. Loftin, Former Director of Curriculum and Staff Development, Aldine Independent School District, Houston, Texas

Mary Garcia Metzger, Dean of Instruction, Dowling Middle School, Houston, Texas

Clyde P. Patton, Professor of Geography, University of Oregon, Eugene, Oregon

Norman J.G. Pounds, Former University Professor of Geography, Indiana University, Bloomington, Indiana

Arlene C. Rengert, Associate Professor of Geography, West Chester University, West Chester, Pennsylvania

Robert N. Saveland, Professor of Social Science Education, University of Georgia, Athens, Georgia

Edgar A. Toppin, Professor of History and Dean of the Graduate School, Virginia State University, Petersburg, Virginia

GRADE-LEVEL CONTRIBUTORS

Elizabeth A. Barnes, Teacher, Attwood Elementary School, Lansing, Michigan

Gary A. Brown, Teacher, Renton Park Elementary School, Renton, Washington

Jean Gallie, Teacher, St. Mary of Celle, Berwyn, Illinois

Holly Gambill, Teacher, Gifted Program, Steed Elementary School, Midwest City, Oklahoma

Edward Graivier, Teacher, Highland Elementary School, Hazel Crest, Illinois

Phyllis H. Morelock, Teacher, Sam Houston Elementary School, Maryville, Tennessee

Lula Parran, Teacher, Huntington Elementary School, Huntington, Maryland

CONTENTS

4 Plains Regions

MAPS (continued)

Atlas

GRAPHS

TIME LINES

DIAGRAMS

TABLES

FACTS ABOUT STATES AND COUNTRIES

PEOPLE AND PLACES

USING SKILLS

The Earth—Our Home

This year you will be studying the different regions of the earth. One of the best ways to study the earth is by using maps. Maps can show all or part of the earth. Maps can also help you find out how to get from one place to another.

Have you ever used a map to plan a trip or a vacation? There are many exciting places to visit in the United States. The family in the photograph below is using a road map to plan a trip from their home in Georgia to Walt Disney World in Orlando, Florida. The map they are using will show them which roads to travel on to get to Orlando. The map will also show them places they can visit while on their trip.

Maps can help people in many ways. People sometimes use maps to plan trips. Maps help people find their way from one place to another.
■ Can you think of other ways that maps can help people?

Maps will also help you to not get lost. The Girl Scouts in this picture are using a map to plan out a walking route before they enter the woods. If they plan carefully and then follow their route properly, they will not get lost.

Walking and hiking trips need careful planning. Maps of an area can help people do their planning.
■ What other forms of information are the girls using?

Pilots often use landmarks on the ground as a guide.
■ Do you think your school might be a landmark? Why?

Maps are even important to people who travel above the earth. Marilyn flies a small plane on her job. Before a flight, she plans her trip with a special map called an aeronautical (ar ə nôt′ i kəl) chart. The chart has landmarks, such as bridges, highways, towns, and rivers. It also shows airports. Marilyn draws a line on the chart to show the route she wants to fly.

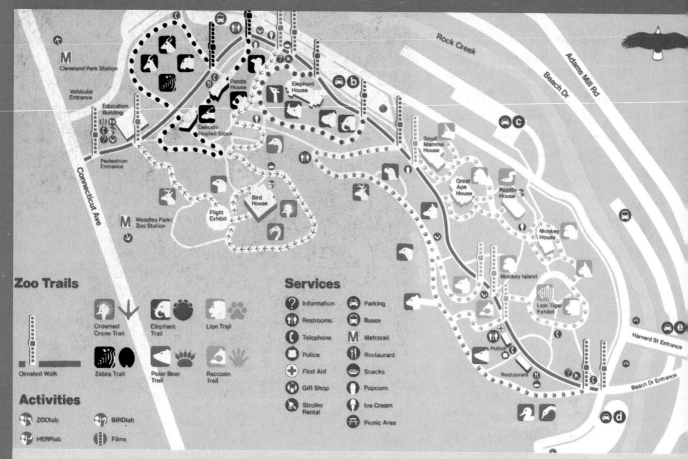

The map of the National Zoo in Washington, D. C., shows the various trails, activities, and services at the zoo.
■ How many trails are shown under the *Zoo Trails* key?

There are many other times when you will find it helpful to read maps. For example, suppose you were visiting a zoo and you wanted to find certain animals. A map of the zoo would help you find the location of the animals that you are looking for.

Maps can even help you when you are going to a baseball game. Suppose you and your family had tickets to see the New York Yankees play against the Kansas City Royals at Yankee Stadium in New York City. By using a map like the one shown here, you would be able to tell where in the stadium your seats are located.

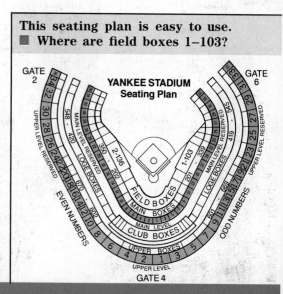

This seating plan is easy to use.
■ Where are field boxes 1–103?

4

Maps are not only used to plan special trips or when visiting special places. There are many different uses for maps. For example, you may use a map to find a certain classroom in your school. Or you may even draw your own map to show a friend how to get to your house. The people in this photograph are in a shopping mall. The map they are looking at will help them find certain stores. Can you think of any other ways that people use maps every day?

Maps of shopping malls show the many stores that make up the mall. These maps help people find the stores that they want to shop in.
■ What is this mall called?

A graph, like a map, is a special kind of drawing. These students are looking at a circle graph.
■ Why, do you think, is it called a circle graph?

THE EARTH'S SURFACE

Land   Water

Another way to learn about the earth is by studying graphs. Graphs can give us a lot of different information that we cannot get from a map. The children in the photograph to the left are studying a graph. It shows how much of the earth is made up of land and how much is made up of water. During your study of social studies this year, you will be using many maps and graphs to help you learn about the regions of the earth.

1 Using Maps and Globes

Learning About the Earth

In what ways is a globe like a model of the earth?

VOCABULARY

astronaut	continent
sphere	history
globe	geography
ocean	

Where Do You Live?   How would you answer if someone asked you where you live? Would you give the name of the street on which you live? Or would you simply say that you live somewhere on the earth? Of course,

both answers would be correct. Your street is part of the earth. You do live on the earth. In fact the earth is the home of all people. Only **astronauts**, or people who journey in outer space, can leave the earth for a long period of time. But even they must return to the earth. (Words in heavy type are in the Glossary at the end of the book.)

High Above the Earth   Have you ever dreamed about being an astronaut? Would you like to fly in a

Both the photograph taken from space and the globe show the earth.
■ What do the different colors in the photograph taken from space show?

spaceship, high above the earth? The first picture on page 6 shows what the earth looks like from space.

The earth is a **sphere**. That means it is round, like a ball. If you look at a ball, you can see only half of it at a time. Therefore you can see only half of the earth at one time.

A Model of the Earth   As the picture shows, the earth is made up of land and water. The picture of the **globe** at the bottom of page 6 will help you see more clearly the difference between land and water. A globe is a model of the earth. It shows the shapes of the earth's land and water.

Oceans and Continents   About two thirds of the earth is made up of water. The largest bodies of water are called **oceans**. There are four oceans. They are the Atlantic, Pacific, Indian, and Arctic oceans.

Only about one third of the earth is made up of land. This land is divided into **continents**. A continent is a very large body of land. There are seven continents. They are Asia, Australia, Africa, Europe, Antarctica, South America, and North America. Asia is the largest continent, Australia is the smallest.

Countries   For us the most important continent is most likely North America. Do you know why? There are more than 170 countries on the earth. Our country, the United States of America, is on the continent of

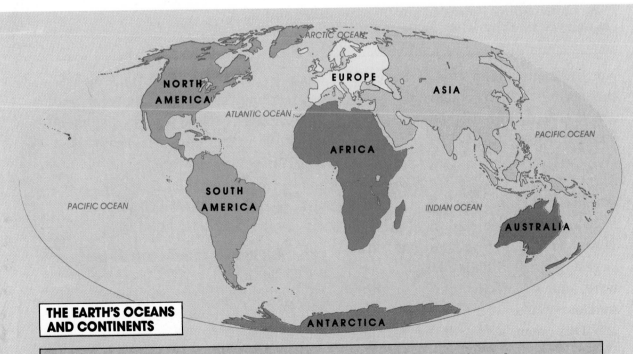

THE EARTH'S OCEANS AND CONTINENTS

The photograph and the map show that the surface of the earth is made up of land and water.
■ **Can you name the earth's seven continents and four oceans?**

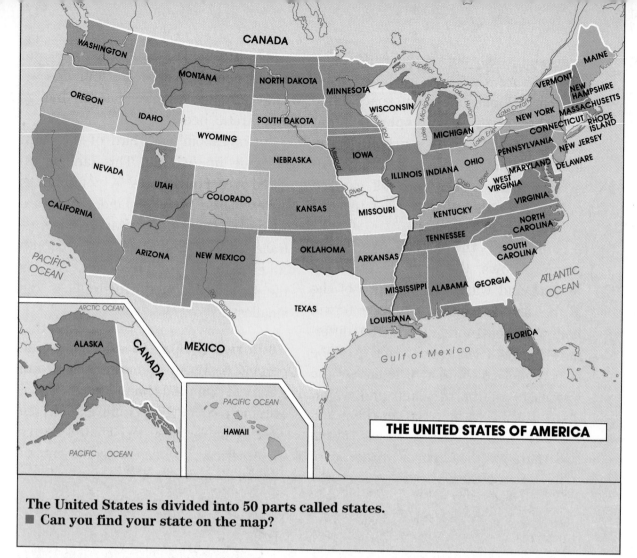

The United States is divided into 50 parts called states.
■ **Can you find your state on the map?**

North America. The United States is the second largest country in North America. Only our neighbor Canada is larger.

States Our country is divided into 50 parts. Each part is called a state. In which state do you live? Alaska, Texas, and California are our three largest states. Rhode Island, Delaware, and Connecticut are our three smallest states.

This year you will be learning about many of the states in our country, as well as about some of the other countries on the earth. You will be learning about the **history** and **geography** of these places. History is the study of the past. History is filled with interesting stories about people and events. Geography is the study of how people use the earth.

CHECKUP
1. What is a globe?
2. Name the four oceans.
3. What is a continent?

4. **Thinking Critically** Why, do you think, is the study of history and geography important?

Finding Your Way on a Map

How can maps help you learn about the earth?

VOCABULARY

map	east
boundary	west
border	North Pole
north	South Pole
south	compass rose

Boundary Lines   There are many tools that will help you learn about the earth. **Maps** are among the most important tools you can use. A map is a special kind of drawing. Look at the map at the bottom of page 7. It shows the earth's continents and oceans. Which oceans touch North America? What country is shown on the map on page 8?

A **boundary** is a line that separates one state or country from another. States and countries **border**, or touch, one another at the boundary. Sometimes a boundary is called a border. Name the states that share a boundary with your state. Do any countries share a boundary with your state?

The Language of Maps   Have you ever wanted to go somewhere but have not known how to get there? Or have you ever been in an amusement park, looking for a special ride? If so,

The city of Memphis, Tennessee borders on the Mississippi River. On the other side of the Mississippi is Arkansas. The Mississippi River forms part of the boundary of ten states.
■ Using the map on the opposite page, name the eight other states that border on the Mississippi River.

maps would have been a big help to you. As you already know, maps show you where things are. They also can tell you how far places are from one another. Maps can give you important and interesting facts. To find these facts on maps, you must first learn the language of maps. It is a simple language.

Directions Before learning where things are on a map, you must first learn about directions. There are many ways to tell where something is. You could say that something is *up* or *down*. You might say it is *above* or *below*. You might also say it is to the *left* or to the *right*. Or it might be *in* something else or *on* something else.

You have probably used these direction words many times. There are four other special direction words you should learn. They describe the main directions on a map. They are **north**, **south**, **east**, and **west**.

North is the direction toward the **North Pole**. The North Pole is the most northern place on the earth. The boy in the picture below is pointing to the North Pole on the globe. Look at the other picture on this page. The girl in this picture is pointing to the **South Pole**. The South Pole is the most southern place on the earth. It is at the opposite end of the earth from the North Pole. South is the direction toward the South Pole. North and south are opposite one another.

The North Pole and the South Pole are opposite each other.
■ **To which pole is the boy in the photograph on the left pointing to?**

If you face north, south is behind you.
■ In which direction is the girl
pointing with her right hand?

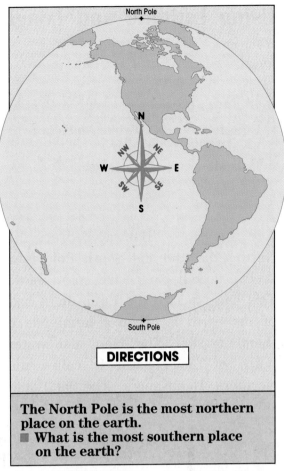

DIRECTIONS

The North Pole is the most northern
place on the earth.
■ What is the most southern place
on the earth?

East and west are the other two main directions. They too are opposite one another. If you face north, east will be on your right. West will be on your left.

Sometimes a drawing like the one on the map above is used to show where north, south, east, and west are on a map. This drawing is called a **compass rose**. It is also called a direction finder. The letters *N, E, S,* and *W* stand for north, east, south, and west. Sometimes we need to find places that are in between two of the four main directions. The other letters on the drawing show us where

these in-between directions are. *NE* stands for northeast. Northeast is between north and east. What do you think the other letters stand for? What direction is between north and west? Find all the in-between directions on the map above.

CHECKUP

1. How can maps help you learn about the earth?
2. Name the four main directions.
3. What is a compass rose?
4. **Thinking Critically** Make a list of the kinds of maps that you may have used.

11

Using Latitude and Longitude

How can lines of latitude and longitude be helpful in finding places on a map?

The Equator　Halfway between the North Pole and the South Pole is a special line. It circles the entire earth. This line is called the **Equator**. A half of the earth is called a **hemisphere** (hem′ ə sfir). The land and water north of the Equator is called the Northern Hemisphere. The land and water south of the Equator is called the Southern Hemisphere. The continent on which we live is in the Northern Hemisphere. Find both the Northern Hemisphere and our continent on the map below.

Latitude　The Equator is a line of **latitude**. All the lines that run *across* the map are called lines of latitude. Those between the Equator and the North Pole are called lines of north latitude. Those between the Equator and the South Pole are called lines of south latitude.

　The Equator is the most important line of latitude. All other lines of

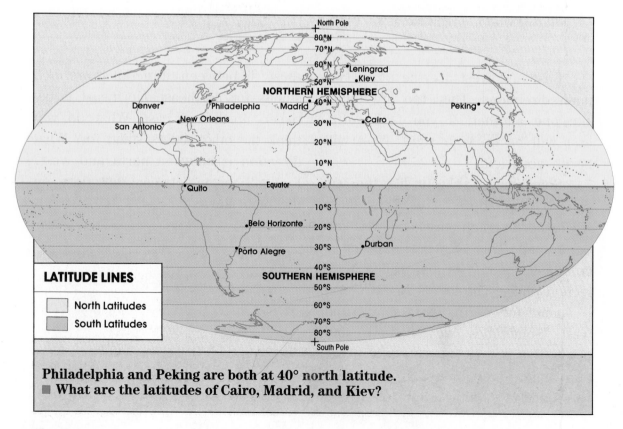

Philadelphia and Peking are both at 40° north latitude.
■ **What are the latitudes of Cairo, Madrid, and Kiev?**

12

latitude measure distances north or south of the Equator. These distances are measured in degrees. The symbol for degrees is °. The Equator is numbered 0° latitude. By using these lines it is easier to find places.

Prime Meridian Lines of **longitude** are another set of lines drawn on maps. These lines run from the North Pole to the South Pole. There is one special longitude line. It is called the **Prime Meridian** (me rid′ ē ən). It is numbered 0° longitude. All other longitude lines measure distances east or west of the Prime Meridian. The Prime Meridian passes through Greenwich, England.

The Prime Meridian divides the earth in half from east to west. The land and water west of the Prime Meridian is called the Western Hemisphere. The land and water east of the Prime Meridian is called the Eastern Hemisphere.

Look at the map below. Put your finger on the line of longitude marked 75° W. Move your finger until you come to the city of Philadelphia. You will see that Philadelphia is found at 75° west longitude. Look back at the map on page 12. Notice that Philadelphia is also found at 40° north latitude. To tell someone where Philadelphia is, you would say that it is at 40° north latitude and 75° west

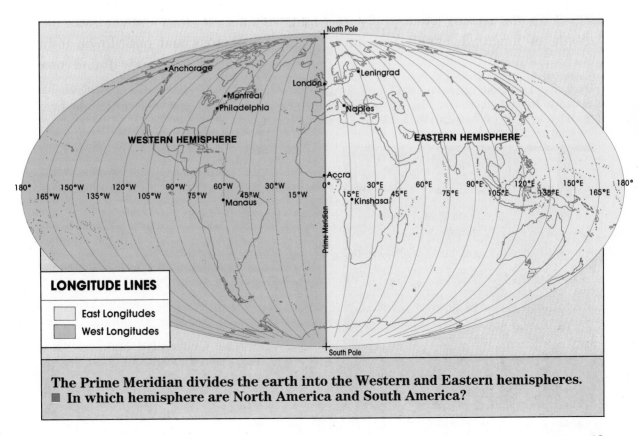

The Prime Meridian divides the earth into the Western and Eastern hemispheres.
■ **In which hemisphere are North America and South America?**

longitude. Leningrad is also shown on both maps. How would you tell someone where Leningrad is found?

Using a Grid   If you know the latitude and longitude of a place, you can find it on a map by using the **grid**. A grid is a system of crossing lines that form boxes. Crossing latitude and longitude lines are a grid. But sometimes the places you are looking for are not found exactly at the point where two lines cross. When this happens, you have to **estimate**, or figure out *about*, where those places are. Look at the map of Michigan on the next page. You will see that Flint is very close to 43° north latitude. It also is located very close to 84° west longitude. Now find Lansing. It is not exactly on any line of latitude or longitude either. You have

to estimate its latitude and longitude. Lansing is between 42° north latitude and 43° north latitude. It is nearer to 43° north latitude. So it would be close enough to say that Lansing is at 43° north latitude. It is also between 84° west longitude and 85° west longitude. So you would be close enough if you said that it was at 85° west longitude. Figure out the latitudes and longitudes for Detroit, Grand Rapids, and Marquette (mär ket′).

Notice that the crossing lines of latitude and longitude form boxes. At the top of the map, you will see the numbers *1, 2, 3, 4, 5, 6, 7,* and *8.* Along the left-hand side of the map, you will see the letters *A, B, C, D, E,* and *F.* Put a finger on the letter *C.* Put a finger of your other hand on the number *3.* Now move both fingers, one across and one down, until they meet. You have now found box *C-3.* You will see that J.W. Wells State Park and Escanaba are both in box *C-3.* This is another way of finding places on maps. Road maps often help you find places in this way. What state park is in box *B-2*? What cities are found in box *F-5*?

Park workers use maps to help visitors to the park.
■ **Why are maps helpful to park visitors?**

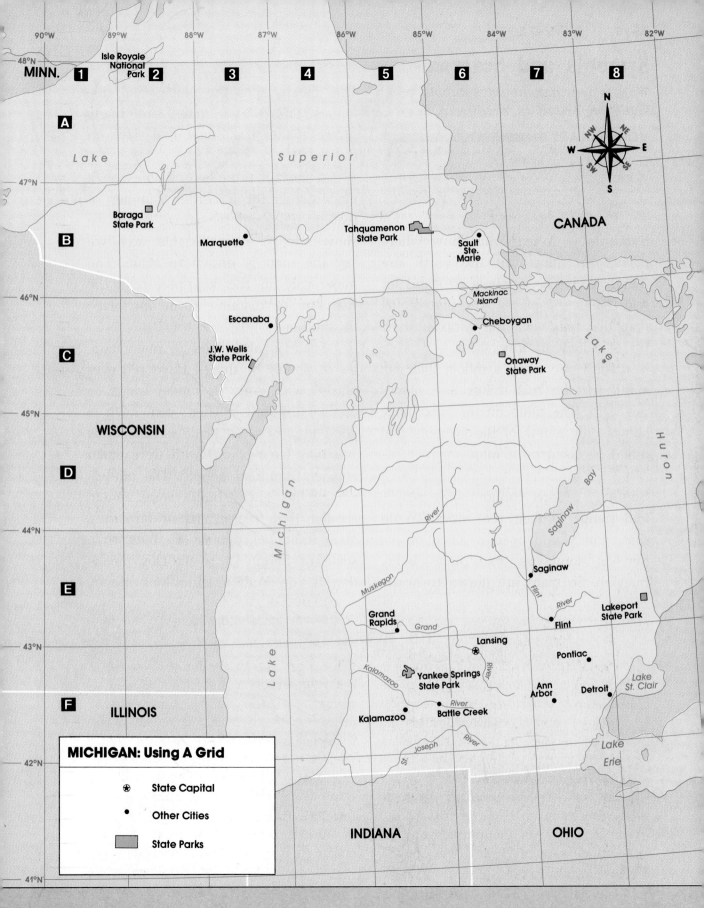

MINN.

1 2 3 4 5 6 7 8

A

Lake *Superior*

Isle Royale
National
Park

CANADA

B

Baraga
State Park

Marquette

Tahquamenon
State Park

Sault
Ste.
Marie

*Mackinac
Island*

CANADA

Escanaba

Cheboygan

C

J.W. Wells
State Park

Onaway
State Park

WISCONSIN

D

Lake

Michigan

Saginaw

Bay

Lake

Huron

E

Muskegon

River

Saginaw

Grand
Rapids

Grand

Flint

River

Lakeport
State Park

Flint

Lansing

Pontiac

Kalamazoo

Yankee Springs
State Park

River

Ann
Arbor

Detroit

*Lake
St. Clair*

F ILLINOIS

Kalamazoo

Battle Creek

River

MICHIGAN: Using A Grid

⊛   State Capital

•   Other Cities

◼   State Parks

St. *Joseph* *River*

Lake

Erie

INDIANA

OHIO

Grid boxes help you locate places on a map.
◼ In which grid box will you find the city of Pontiac?

Symbols and Scale

Why is learning about symbols and scale important in reading a map?

VOCABULARY

symbol	**scale**
key	

Symbols A map can show where places or things on the earth are found. Maps use **symbols** to stand for real things and places. The part of the map that tells what the symbols stand for is called the **key**.

There are many symbols that can stand for the real things and places on earth. The table on the next page shows only a few of the symbols that might be used on a map.

Scale Maps cannot show places and things in their real sizes. To do that, you would need a piece of paper as large as the place being mapped. So maps are drawn to **scale**.

This means that the places and distances shown on maps are many times smaller than their real sizes on the earth.

A certain number of inches on a map stands for a certain number of feet or miles on the earth. When we show size or distance this way, we say the map is drawn to scale. The map scale in the key box tells the real size or distance from one place to another.

Scale is also used to make copies of people or things. Have you ever played with dolls or model trains or model airplanes? Then you have a good idea of what scale is. The dolls you may have played with were much smaller than real people. The models you may have built were much smaller than real trains or airplanes. Many model airplanes are built to a scale of about 50 to 1. This means that if you built a 1-foot-long model,

THE METRIC SYSTEM

On page 19 you will find the words *1 inch stands for about 50 miles. (One centimeter stands for about 32 kilometers.)* Centimeters and kilometers are units of measure in the metric system.

The metric system is a way of measuring area, distance, weight, capacity, and temperature. This system is used in all major countries except the United States. In the future, you will be using more of the metric system.

To get you ready for this change, both American and metric measurements are given in this book. Each measurement used in our country is followed by the metric measurement that is about equal to it. Miles are changed to kilometers (km), inches to centimeters (cm), feet or yards to meters (m), acres to hectares (ha), pounds to kilograms (kg), and degrees Fahrenheit (°F) to degrees Celsius (°C).

MAP SYMBOLS

REAL PLACE OR THING

SYMBOL

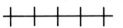

SYMBOL

SYMBOL

SYMBOL

NAME

Railroad

NAME

Road

NAME

City

NAME

Trees

REAL PLACE OR THING

SYMBOL

SYMBOL

SYMBOL

SYMBOL

NAME

Airport

NAME

River

NAME

House

NAME

Oil

17

you would know that the length of the real airplane was 50 times 1 foot, or 50 feet.

Make believe that you are in an airplane flying over a football field. The football field would probably look like the drawing below. This drawing was made to a scale in which 1 inch stands for 20 yards. The drawing is 6 inches long. So the total length of a real football field is 120 yards, or 6 groups of 20 yards ($20 + 20 + 20 + 20 + 20 + 20 = 120$). How wide is a real football field?

Map Distance and Earth Distance
The scale line on a map shows how much an inch (centimeter) on the map stands for in real distance on the earth. A map can be drawn to many different scales. Look at the three maps on the bottom of page 19. Each

This girl is putting together a model of a rocket.
■ Do you think the model in this picture looks like a real rocket?

On the football field below, 1 inch stands for 20 yards.
■ How many yards is it between each vertical line on the football field?

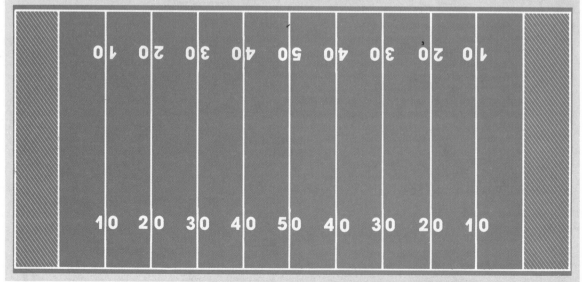

map shows the state of New Jersey. But each map is drawn to a different scale.

Put a ruler under the scale line of the map on the left. You will see that 1 inch stands for about 50 miles. (One centimeter stands for about 32 kilometers.) On this map how many inches (cm) is it in a straight line from Newark to Atlantic City? If you measured correctly, your answer should be about 2 inches (5 cm). To find out how many miles (km) it is

from Newark to Atlantic City, you would multiply 2 x 50 (5 x 32).

Go through the same steps with the other two maps of New Jersey. You will find that the number of inches (cm) to miles (km) changes from map to map. However, when you use the scale for each map to figure miles (km) on the earth's surface, the distance from Newark to Atlantic City stays the same. Use the scale to find out the distance between Trenton and Vineland.

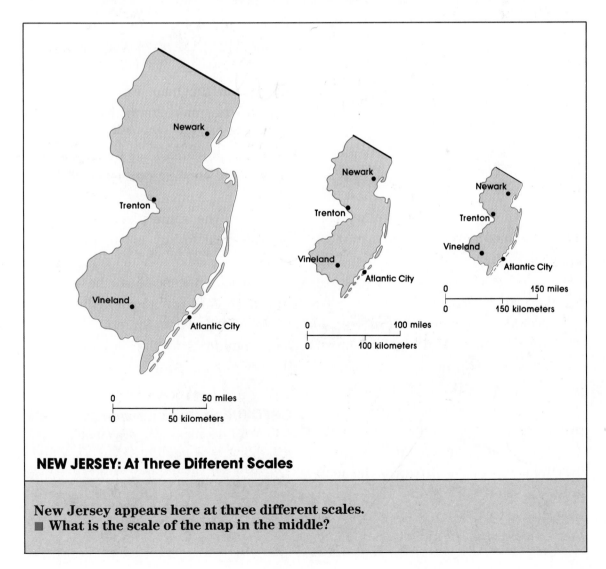

NEW JERSEY: At Three Different Scales

New Jersey appears here at three different scales.
■ What is the scale of the map in the middle?

This photograph of Giants Stadium in East Rutherford, New Jersey was taken from an airplane directly overhead.
■ **Why, do you think, is this photograph called a "bird's-eye view?"**

A Bird's-eye View Earlier you learned that a map is a special kind of drawing. Symbols, scale, directions, and a grid system are some of the things that make maps special. Another is that a map shows how the earth looks from straight overhead. A map is a bird's-eye view of a part of the earth. A map shows what a bird would see if it looked straight down on the earth from high in the sky. You would see what a bird sees if you were in an airplane looking down on the earth. The higher the airplane flies, the more of the earth you would see. If you went up high enough, you could see about one half of the earth.

The photograph on the next page was taken from an airplane. The map below it shows the same place as in the photograph. Find some shapes in the photograph. Find those same shapes on the map. Find some buildings in the photograph. Now find the buildings on the map.

Find a symbol on the map. Look at the key to find out what the symbol means. Notice that the symbol is shown in the same place on the map as the real thing is in the photograph.

Look at the scale in the key box. Use it to find out the length and the width of the swimming pool. Are there more buildings to the east or west of the swimming pool?

CHECKUP
1. Why do maps need symbols?
2. What is a map key?
3. Why are maps drawn to scale?

4. **Thinking Critically** What type of symbols would you need to use on a map of your neighborhood?

The map below is of the same area as the photograph above.
See how the symbols stand for real things.
■ Can you find the basketball courts in the photograph and on the map?

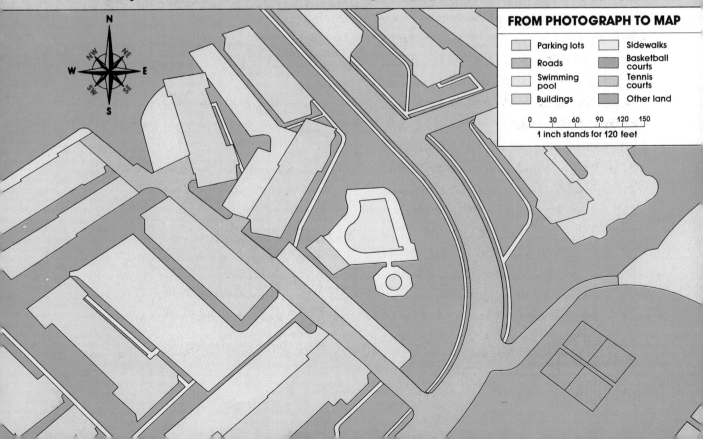

FROM PHOTOGRAPH TO MAP

Parking lots   Sidewalks

Roads   Basketball
courts

Swimming
pool   Tennis
courts

Buildings   Other land

0   30   60   90   120   150

1 inch stands for 120 feet

Contours and Elevation

How do contour lines show elevation on a map?

Contour Lines   You learned earlier that the earth is made up of land and water. Some parts of the land are more than 5 miles (8 km) above the level of the earth's seas, or oceans. **Contour lines** are a good way to show the height of the land. All points along one contour line are exactly the same distance above the level of the sea.

To measure your own height, you would measure the distance from your base, the bottom of your feet, to the top of your head. The earth's hills and mountains are also measured from base to top. The base for all the earth's hills and mountains is the level of the sea.

Find **sea level** (0 feet) on the drawing of the island on page 23. The island is high and rugged. In some places it rises sharply from the sea. The lines drawn onto the island are contour lines. They are labeled sea level (0 feet), 100 feet (30 m), 200 feet (61 m), and 300 feet (91 m). All the points along one contour line are the

In some places, high mountains are found right along a coastline. Such places clearly show that the base of mountains and hills is the level of the sea.
■ What things can you find at sea level in this picture?

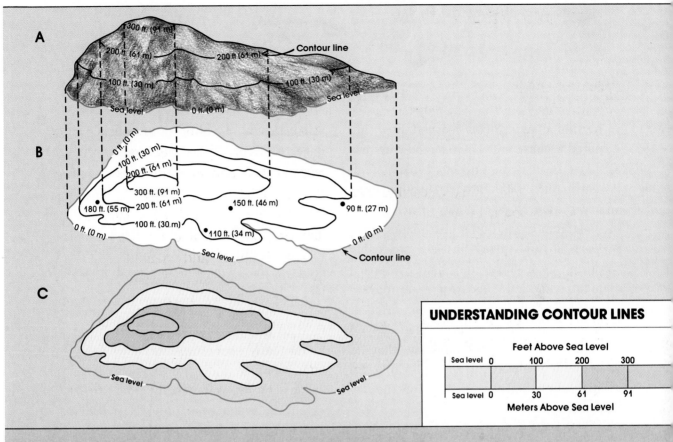

A

300 ft. (91 m)
200 ft. (61 m)
Contour line
200 ft. (61 m)
100 ft. (30 m)
100 ft. (30 m)
Sea level
Sea level
0 ft. (0 m)

B

0 ft. (0 m)
100 ft. (30 m)
200 ft. (61 m)
300 ft. (91 m)
180 ft. (55 m)
200 ft. (61 m)
150 ft. (46 m)
90 ft. (27 m)
100 ft. (30 m)
0 ft. (0 m)
110 ft. (34 m)
0 ft. (0 m)
Sea level
Contour line

C

Sea level
Sea level

UNDERSTANDING CONTOUR LINES

	Feet Above Sea Level		
Sea level 0	100	200	300
Sea level 0	30	61	91
	Meters Above Sea Level		

On drawing A, find the contour line marked 200 feet (61 m).
Place your finger on the same contour line on drawing B.
■ **What is the height of the land shown in purple?**

same distance above the level of the sea.

On the drawing marked A, find the contour line that shows an elevation of 100 feet (30 m). Then find the same contour line on drawing B.

On drawing A, find the contour line marked 300 feet (91 m). Place your finger on the same contour line on drawing B. Notice on drawing B that the elevation of some places that fall between the contour lines are given. For example between the contour lines marked 100 feet (30 m) and

200 feet (61 m), three points are marked. One is 110 feet (34 m), another is 150 feet (46 m), and a third is 180 feet (55 m). It would be very hard to read a map if we marked all the elevation points of the land this way.

Often color is added between contour lines to show the different elevations. Look at drawing C. Color has been added between the contour lines. Notice the part of the island shown in yellow on this drawing. The elevation of this area is between 100

23

Living in Space

In this chapter, you learned how important maps are. Learning how to use maps is also an important part of an astronaut's job. But astronauts must learn many other things. One of the most important things astronauts must learn is how to live in their spaceship during their flight into space. A space flight sometimes lasts for many days.

Living in space is much different from living on the earth. There is no air in space, and we all know that no one can live without air to breathe. So spaceships must carry air for the astronauts.

In space, people and objects lack weight. They float in the air inside a spaceship if they are not held down. To keep from floating, the astronauts must hang on to handles in the spaceship or must be held down by straps or ties. In the first small spaceships,

astronauts were strapped to couches in order to sleep. In today's larger spaceships there is a special place set aside for sleeping. The astronauts work themselves into packages that are something like sleeping bags. The packages are attached to the spaceship so that they will not float in the air.

A spaceship must carry enough food to last for the length of the flight. In the early spaceships there was very little room, so food was made as small as possible. It was usually freeze-dried —that is, water was removed from it and it was frozen.

Meals on today's spaceships are easier to prepare and eat. Food is still small in size, but it is warmed up in a galley, or kitchen. Water is provided for drinking and for washing.

The astronauts wear special suits to protect themselves. There are many dangers in space flights. One danger is the speed of the takeoff. A rocket lifts a spaceship into the air at a speed that may reach 17,000 miles per hour (28,000 km per hour). The sudden speed puts great pressure on the bodies of the astronauts.

Over the last 25 years, much has been learned about living in space. This information will make possible more exploration of space in the years ahead.

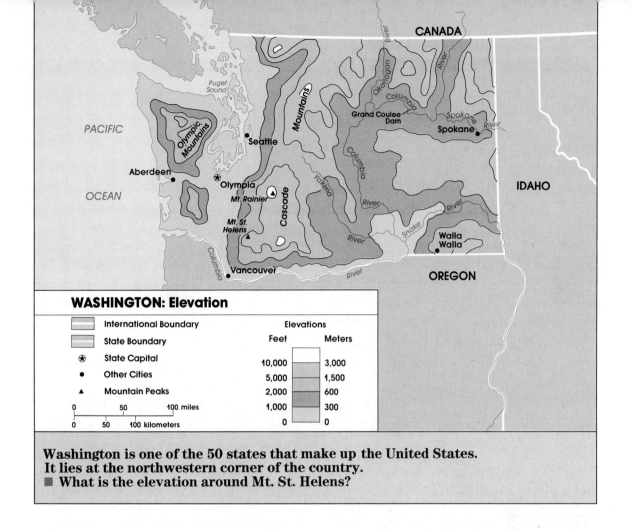

WASHINGTON: Elevation

	International Boundary
	State Boundary
✳	State Capital
•	Other Cities
▲	Mountain Peaks

Elevations	
Feet	Meters
10,000	3,000
5,000	1,500
2,000	600
1,000	300
0	0

0   50   100 miles
0   50   100 kilometers

Washington is one of the 50 states that make up the United States. It lies at the northwestern corner of the country.
■ **What is the elevation around Mt. St. Helens?**

and 200 feet (30 and 61 m) above sea level. What is the height of the land shown in green? What is the height of the land shown in pink? What color is used to show sea level?

A Relief Map   Maps that use different colors to show the range between contour lines are often called **relief maps**. Sometimes they are called physical maps. This kind of map shows the **elevation** of the land. Elevation is the distance above sea level. The map above shows elevations for the state of Washington.

The state capital of Washington is Olympia (ō lim pē ə). Can you find Olympia on the map? What color is used to show the elevation of land around Olympia? Find this color in the key. You will see that this color stands for 0 to 1,000 feet (0 to 300 m). What is the elevation of the land around Seattle? What is the elevation of Mt. Rainier?

CHECKUP
1. What are contour lines?
2. To find the elevation of a place, what point do we measure from?
3. What are relief maps?
4. **Thinking Critically** Why, do you think, is it necessary to show elevation on some maps?

25

Using Parts of This Book

CONTENTS

This book has many special parts to help you in social studies this year. The first of these parts is the Contents. This tells you how the book is divided into units and chapters. Turn to the Contents at the front of the book. Answer the following questions.

1. What is the name of Unit 4?
2. Name the chapters in Unit 4.

INDEX

Another helpful part of the book is the Index. It tells you the numbers of the pages on which various topics are discussed. Turn to the Index, starting on page 384. Use the Index to answer the following questions.

1. Which pages would you turn to if you wanted to read about pulp mills?
2. On what pages would you find information about Denver, Colorado?
3. On what pages would you find oasis? Sugarcane?

GLOSSARY

The Glossary is another important part of this book. The Glossary is arranged alphabetically, like the Index, and defines all the key social studies words. These are the words found in the boxes at the beginning of each lesson. Turn to the Glossary starting on page 378. Answer the following questions.

1. What is a desert?
2. What is an astronaut?

GAZETTEER

Another part of the book arranged alphabetically is the Gazetteer. It gives information about many places—cities, mountains, rivers, and other geographical features. For many of these places, the Gazetteer also gives latitude and longitude. The page number at the end of each definition directs you to a map that shows where the place is. Turn to the Gazetteer, starting on page 368, and answer the following questions.

1. What is the latitude and longitude of Chicago, Illinois?
2. Where does the Danube River start?

ATLAS

The Atlas is a special collection of maps. In the Contents you will find a list of the maps included in the Atlas. These maps give information on the location of physical features, boundaries of countries, and cities. Turn to the physical map of Africa on page 360, and answer the following questions.

1. What is the elevation, in meters, of most of the land around Lake Victoria?
2. Into what ocean does the Zaire River flow?

Turn to the political map of South America on page 359, and answer these questions.

1. What is the national capital of Chile?
2. To which country do the Falkland Islands belong?

CHAPTER 1 REVIEW

MAIN IDEAS

1. Globes are like a model of the earth because they show the shapes of the earth's land and water.
2. Maps can give you important information and interesting facts about the earth.
3. Lines of latitude and longitude form grids for locating places on the earth.
4. Symbols on maps stand for real things and places.
5. Scale helps us draw maps showing places and distances many times smaller than their real sizes.
6. On relief maps, or physical maps, contour lines show the height of the land. All points along one contour line are exactly the same distance above sea level.

VOCABULARY REVIEW

Match these terms with the definitions. Use a separate sheet of paper.

a. astronauts	**f.** hemisphere
b. oceans	**g.** key
c. map	**h.** symbol
d. North Pole	**i.** Equator
e. compass rose	**j.** globe

1. The latitude line numbered 0°
2. A special kind of drawing of all or part of the earth
3. People who journey into outer space
4. The part of the map that tells what the symbols stand for
5. The largest bodies of water on earth
6. A model of the earth
7. A drawing that is used to show where north, south, east, and west are on a map
8. Used to show places and things on maps
9. The most northern place on the earth
10. Half of the earth

CHAPTER CHECKUP

1. What are the names of the seven continents of the world?
2. What are the names of the lines that are drawn on maps to help us find places?
3. How does a map show what the symbols mean?
4. **Thinking Critically** Compare and contrast the uses of maps and globes.

APPLYING KNOWLEDGE

1. On a piece of graph paper, draw five vertical lines about 1 inch (3 cm) apart. Then draw five horizontal lines, about 1 inch (3 cm) apart, across the vertical lines. Label the vertical lines numbers *1* through *5* and the horizontal lines letters *A* through *E*. Then complete the following.
   a. Draw a symbol for a house where line *A* and line *2* intersect.
   b. Draw a symbol for a school where line *C* and line *1* intersect.
   c. Draw a symbol for a flower where line *B* and line *5* intersect.
   d. Draw a symbol for a lake where line *E* and line *3* intersect.
   e. Draw a symbol for a supermarket where line *D* and line *4* intersect.

   Be sure to put a key box in the lower left-hand corner of your map to explain all of your symbols. Then, on a separate sheet of paper, make up five questions concerning your map.

2 Learning From Graphs, Diagrams, and Photographs

Using Graphs

How can graphs be used for learning about the earth?

VOCABULARY

pictograph	bar graph
pie graph	line graph

Drawings To Compare Things   The map below shows how much rain falls in different parts of the United States in a year. But it does not show how much falls in one place in a given month. This kind of information can be shown more clearly on a graph. A graph, like a map, is a special kind of drawing. Graphs use pictures, circles, bars, and lines to compare things.

Pictographs   There are four kinds of graphs. One of the simplest is called a **pictograph**. A pictograph

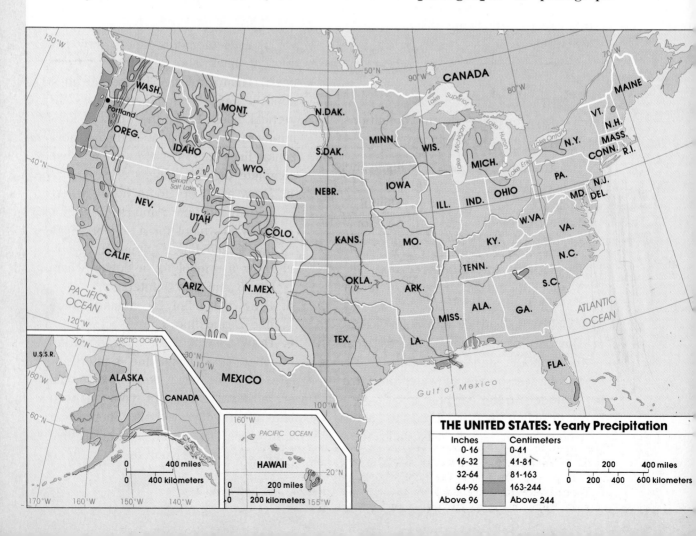

THE UNITED STATES: Yearly Precipitation

Inches	Centimeters
0-16	0-41
16-32	41-81
32-64	81-163
64-96	163-244
Above 96	Above 244

uses small symbols or pictures. On the pictograph at the bottom of this page, each raindrop stands for 1 inch (2 1/2 cm) of rain. The letters along the bottom show the months of the year. The numbers along the left side of the graph show the number of inches of rain received. The numbers along the right side of the graph show the number of centimeters of rain received. At the top is the title of the graph. It gives the name of the city that the graph is about. The name of the city is Portland. Portland is a city in the state of Oregon.

If you look at the graph you will see that six raindrops are shown for the month of January. This means that during January, Portland receives an average of 6 inches (15 cm) of rain. Add all the raindrops shown for all the months. You will then know how much rain Portland receives in 1 year.

Pie Graphs   A second kind of graph is called a **pie graph**. A pie graph is used to show the parts of a whole. In Chapter 1 you learned the names of the earth's seven continents. In the pie graph on page 30, the circle stands for the whole land area of the earth. You will see that the circle is divided into seven pieces. Each piece stands for a continent.

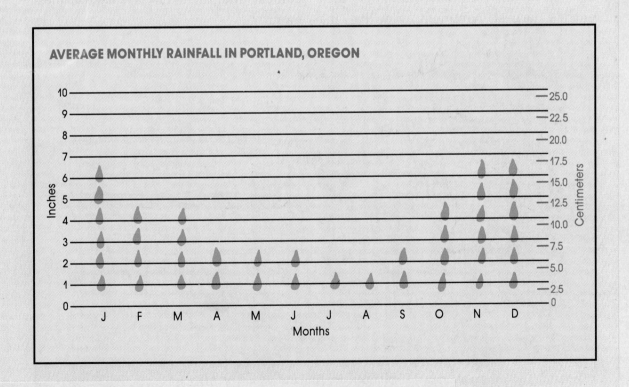

AVERAGE MONTHLY RAINFALL IN PORTLAND, OREGON

The map to the left shows the average yearly rainfall for the entire United States. But to find the average rainfall for one city, a pictograph, like the one above, would be more helpful.
■ Would you use the map or pictograph to find out how much rain Portland gets in one month?

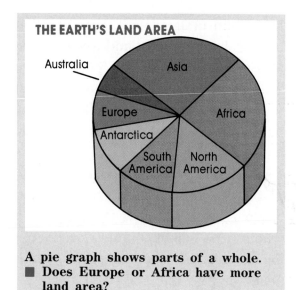

THE EARTH'S LAND AREA

A pie graph shows parts of a whole.
■ Does Europe or Africa have more land area?

Look at the piece where the name Antarctica appears. You can see that Antarctica makes up about one tenth of the earth's land surface. The largest piece is for Asia. Asia is the earth's largest continent. We live in North America. What part of the whole circle do you think represents North America?

Bar Graphs   One of the most useful kinds of graphs is a **bar graph**. A bar graph shows information by using bars. A sample of the kind of information best shown on a bar graph is given below.

The first thing you should do when you read a bar graph is to read the title. This graph is about temperatures in New York City. If you look at the graph, you will see that the average December temperature is 36°F (2°C). What is the average temperature for July? January is New York's coldest month. What is its warmest month?

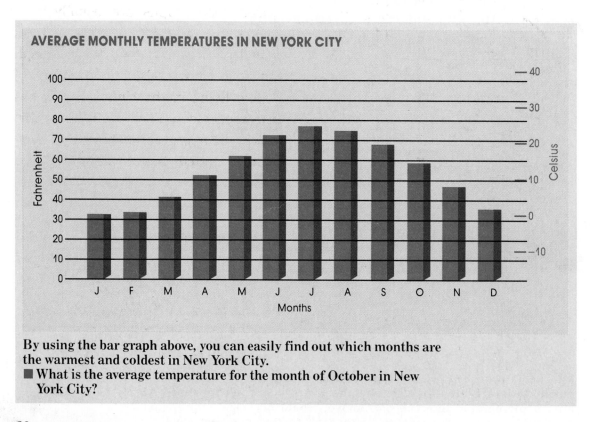

AVERAGE MONTHLY TEMPERATURES IN NEW YORK CITY

By using the bar graph above, you can easily find out which months are the warmest and coldest in New York City.
■ What is the average temperature for the month of October in New York City?

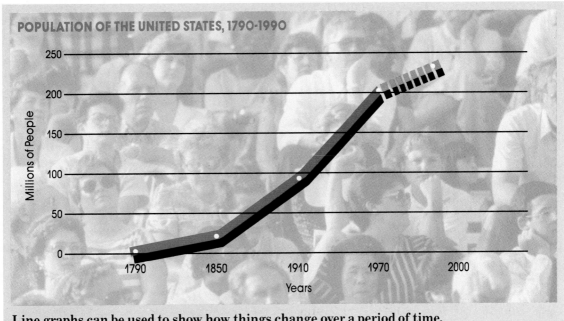

POPULATION OF THE UNITED STATES, 1790-1990

Millions of People

250
200
150
100
50
0

1790   1850   1910   1970   2000

Years

Line graphs can be used to show how things change over a period of time.
■ **About how many people were living in the United States in 1850?**

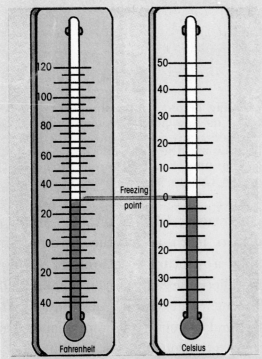

The Fahrenheit thermometer has been used for many years in our country, but the metric system uses the Celsius thermometer.
■ **What is the freezing point on the Celsius thermometer?**

Line Graphs The last kind of graph we will discuss is called a **line graph**. Line graphs are usually used to show how things change over a period of time. Look at the line graph above. It shows how the number of people living in the United States has increased since 1790. What does this graph show you about the population of the United States from 1900 to 1985?

CHECKUP

1. What kind of graph uses pictures or symbols?
2. What is a pie graph used to show?
3. What is the difference between a bar graph and a line graph?

4. **Thinking Critically** Compare the ways the four types of graphs studied in this lesson can be used.

Photographs and Diagrams

How can you use photographs, drawings, and diagrams to study about the earth?

VOCABULARY

picture dictionary	peninsula
canyon	plain
coast	plateau
delta	river
gulf	sea
harbor	valley
island	diagram
lake	axis
mountain	

Looking at old photographs can show us how people looked and dressed many years ago.
■ How are the people's clothes in this photograph different from the clothes we wear today?

Photographs   A photograph is another important source of information. Sometimes looking at a photograph is the best possible way of getting information. Old photographs can show what people looked like, what kind of clothing people wore, and how people worked and played. Photographs can also show us what buildings and streets looked like. We can use old pictures to see how much things have changed over the years.

Study the two photographs on page 33. They show the same place at two different times. The photograph on the top of page 33 was taken around 1900. The photograph on the bottom was taken in 1986. Tell what kind of change has taken place by carefully looking at these two photographs. Without these two pictures it would take a great number of words to describe the changes.

A Picture Dictionary   Another way to learn about the earth is by using a **picture dictionary**. A picture dictionary gives you pictures or drawings and written descriptions of land and water of different shapes. On pages 34 through 37 is a picture dictionary of important landforms and water forms that you will be studying throughout the year. Study them carefully.

These photographs, taken about 80 years apart, are of the same
street in Philadelphia, Pennsylvania.
■ What are some of the differences between the two photographs?

Canyon

A **canyon** is a very deep valley with very steep sides. Canyons are formed by running water that cuts into the ground over thousands of years. The best known canyon in the United States is the Grand Canyon in Arizona.

Continent

A **continent** is, as you learned in Chapter 1, a very large body of land on the earth's surface. There are seven continents: Africa, Antarctica, Asia, Australia, Europe, North America, and South America. One of the continents is shown at the right. To find out the name of this continent, turn to the map on page 7.

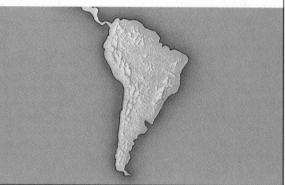

Coast

A **coast** is land next to a large body of water. In Chapter 10 you will read about the coasts of the states of Maryland and Louisiana.

Delta

A **delta** is a piece of land formed by mud and sand that settles from water flowing out of the place where the river ends. The soil of a delta usually makes rich farmland.

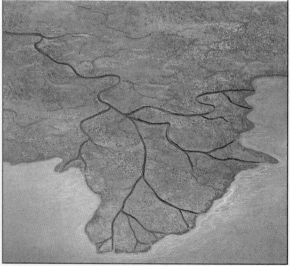

Gulf

A **gulf** is a part of an ocean or a sea that pushes inland. The Gulf of Mexico is shown on the map below. It is off the southern shore of the United States.

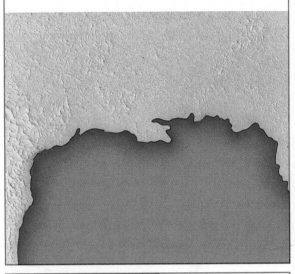

Island

An **island** is a body of land that has water all around it. It is smaller than a continent. The largest island in the world is Greenland. Locate Greenland on the map on pages 350–351.

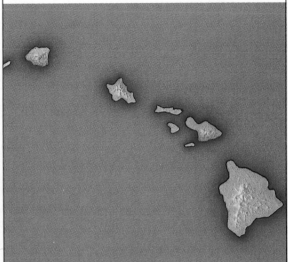

Harbor

A **harbor** is a protected body of water. It is often protected by an arm of land lying between the harbor and a larger body of water, such as an ocean or a sea. Cities and towns have often grown up beside harbors.

Lake

A **lake** is a body of water with land all around it. Lakes can be found in all parts of the world. Find the large lake in the state of Utah on the map of the United States on pages 354–355. This lake is called the Great Salt Lake.

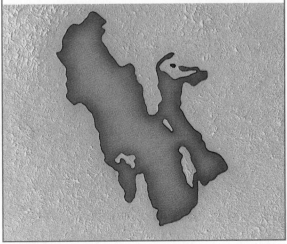

Mountain

A **mountain** is a piece of land that rises steeply from the land that is around it. The top of a mountain is usually peaked or round. Mountains cover one fifth of the earth's surface.

Peninsula

A **peninsula** is a strip of land with water nearly all the way around it. It is connected to a main body of land. The peninsula outlined below is the state of Florida. Locate Florida on the map of the United States on pages 354–355.

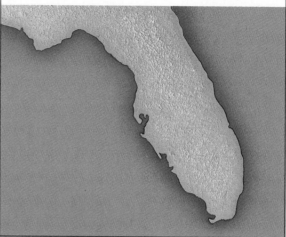

Ocean

An **ocean** is a very large body of salt water. There are four oceans: the Pacific Ocean, the Atlantic Ocean, the Indian Ocean, and the Arctic Ocean. Locate these four oceans on the map on page 7.

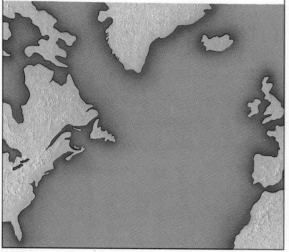

Plain

A **plain** is an almost level, often treeless piece of grassy land that stretches for miles and miles.

Plateau

A **plateau** is a raised, level piece of land. It covers a large area. Some plateaus are only a few hundred feet high. Others are several thousand feet high.

Sea

A **sea** is a large body of salt water, but it is not as large as an ocean. The sea that reaches most of the way across the map below is the Mediterranean (med e te rā' nē en) Sea. It is the largest sea in the world.

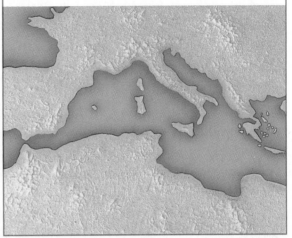

River

A **river** is a long, narrow body of water that flows through the land. A river most often begins as a small stream. In Chapters 5 and 8 you will learn about the world's two biggest rivers, the Amazon (am' e zon) and the Nile. The two largest rivers in the United States are the Missouri River and the Mississippi River.

Valley

A **valley** is a long, low place between hills or mountains. There is often a stream or river in a valley. There are cities and towns in many valleys.

Diagrams Another special kind of drawing is a **diagram**. A diagram is not meant to show exactly what something looks like. It is meant to explain how something works or why something happens. The diagram below explains several things about the earth and the sun.

The diagram shows how the earth moves on its path around the sun. It takes the earth about 365 days to make this journey. On the diagram the earth is shown at four different places on its path.

The diagram also shows what causes day and night. At the same time that the earth moves around the sun, the earth is turning on its **axis** every 24 hours. The earth's axis is an imaginary line running through the earth between the North Pole and the South Pole. As the earth turns, it is day on the side of the earth that is toward the sun. On the other side of the earth it is night.

The diagram shows, too, what causes the seasons — spring, summer, fall, and winter. Look carefully once more at the diagram. The earth, you will note, is always tilted on its axis. At the right side of the diagram you will see the position of the earth on December 22. Follow the arrows from the sun to the earth. Where the

Some diagrams, like the one below, help to explain why something happens.
■ **What is this diagram explaining?**

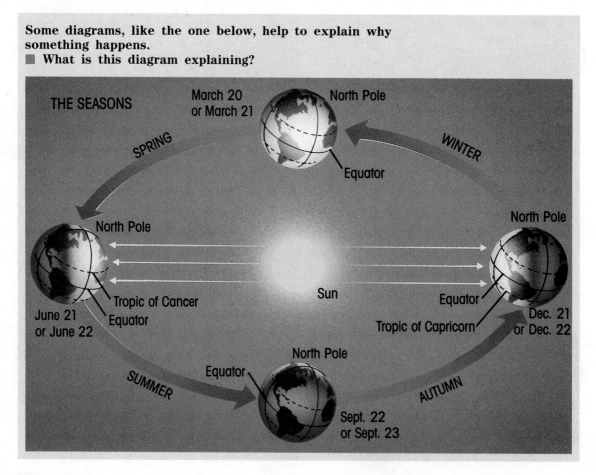

THE SEASONS

March 20 or March 21 · North Pole · Equator

SPRING

WINTER

North Pole · Tropic of Cancer · Equator · June 21 or June 22

Sun

North Pole · Equator · Tropic of Capricorn · Dec. 21 or Dec. 22

SUMMER · Equator · North Pole · Sept. 22 or Sept. 23 · AUTUMN

sun's rays are striking straight down, it is mostly below the Equator, isn't it? Because of the earth's tilt, the Southern Hemisphere is getting more direct sunlight. The ground gets more heat with direct sunlight. Therefore the Southern Hemisphere is receiving more heat at this time of year than the Northern Hemisphere is. Because the Southern Hemisphere is receiving more heat, it is summer there. It is winter in the Northern Hemisphere, which is receiving less heat.

As it moves on its path around the sun, the earth reaches — on June 22 — the point shown at the left side of the diagram. Now it is the Southern Hemisphere that is tilted *away* from the direct rays of the sun. The Northern Hemisphere is now tilted *toward* the sun. In which hemisphere is it summer on June 22?

Look at the photographs to the right. Both were taken in the month of December. The photograph on the top was taken in New York City. The photograph on the bottom was taken in Sydney, Australia. Australia is in the Southern Hemisphere. As you know, it is summer in the Southern Hemisphere in December; at the same time it is winter in the Northern Hemisphere. How would these two photographs differ if they were taken in June?

What causes the seasons could have been explained with words alone. But the diagram made this much easier to understand, didn't it?

December is usually cold and snowy in New York City (above), but in Sydney, Australia (below) it is sunny and warm.
■ Why is the weather in these two cities so different?

WHEEL

WATER

The diagram above explains how a waterwheel works.
■ Why is the moving water important in making a waterwheel work?

How Does It Work? As you already know, some diagrams help to explain how things work. Above is a diagram of how a waterwheel works.

The force of running rivers and streams turns the large waterwheel. The moving waterwheel then provides the power to turn the grinding stone in the gristmill. A gristmill is a place where grain is made into flour. Flour is needed to make foods like bread and cakes. Have you ever seen a waterwheel work? If not, the diagram above will help you get a better idea of how one works.

You will use other diagrams in this book. They will help you understand how a certain thing works or what makes something happen.

To Help You Learn In the chapters that follow, you will learn about the world we live in. You will make use of all the learning tools described in Chapters 1 and 2. Maps, graphs, diagrams, and photographs — as well as words — will help you learn about the different regions of the United States and other parts of the world.

CHECKUP
1. What information can you get from looking at old photographs?
2. What is a picture dictionary?
3. What is a diagram?
4. **Thinking Critically** What kinds of photographs would you include in a photograph album titled "My Family History"?

Using a Time Line

ORDERING EVENTS

We often cannot understand events unless we know the order in which they happen. Thinking clearly about time is an important skill.

Below is a list of steps in preparing fresh orange juice. However, the steps are not in the order in which they take place. List the steps in the right order.

a. Selling the oranges in the store
b. Packing the oranges in boxes
c. Squeezing the oranges at home
d. Sending the oranges to market
e. Picking the oranges from trees

DRAWING TIME LINES TO SCALE

Making a list in which events are placed in the right order is one way of being clear about time. Another way is through a time line. A time line, like a map, is drawn to scale. On a map, 1 inch equals a certain distance on the earth. On a time line, 1 inch equals a certain amount of time.

Look at the time line below. It is 4 inches long. It begins in 1780 and ends in 1980. Each inch on the line stands for 50 years. The time line shows when each of four famous Americans became President of the United States.

George Washington	1789
Abraham Lincoln	1861
Theodore Roosevelt	1901
Franklin D. Roosevelt	1933

You can see that the first inch of the time line runs from 1780 to 1830. The first event that goes on the time line is Washington's becoming President. This date is much closer to 1780 than to 1830, isn't it? We place a dot on the line where we think the date 1789 should be. Then we write above the dot Washington's name. In the same way, we place the other dots and names.

SKILLS PRACTICE

Here is a list of important events in American history for your time line.

Declaration of Independence is signed	1776
Civil War begins	1861
Erie Canal opens	1825
United States Constitution becomes law	1788

1. First, decide what years your time line will cover. In this case you might have your time line run from 1770 to 1870. If you do this, how many years will the time line include? Then decide what the scale will be and how long your time line will be.
2. After you draw your line, add dates in the proper places. Put a dot in the right place for each event. Then label each event above the correct dot.

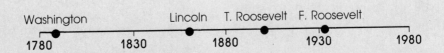

Washington   Lincoln   T. Roosevelt   F. Roosevelt

1780   1830   1880   1930   1980

CHAPTER 2 REVIEW

MAIN IDEAS

1. Graphs help us learn about the earth by giving us specific information about the earth.
2. Four types of graphs are pictographs, pie graphs, bar graphs, and line graphs.
3. Photographs can be useful by showing us what people and places looked like at an earlier time.
4. A picture dictionary gives pictures or drawings and a written description of land and water of different shapes.
5. Diagrams explain how a thing works or why something happens.

VOCABULARY REVIEW

Match the terms with the definitions. Use a separate piece of paper.

    a. pie graph
    b. picture dictionary
    c. axis
    d. pictograph
    e. diagram

1. Explains how things work or why something happens
2. An imaginary line running through the earth between the North Pole and the South Pole
3. A graph that is used to show parts of a whole
4. Gives pictures or drawings and a written description of land and water of different shapes
5. A simple type of graph that uses small symbols or pictures

CHAPTER CHECKUP

1. What type of graph is used to show how things change over a period of years?

2. What type of graph is used to show the parts of a whole?
3. What kind of information can you get from a photograph?
4. **Thinking Critically** Study the two photographs on page 33. Then on a sheet of paper, make a chart comparing the two photographs. Information on the chart should include the following: what has remained the same in the two photographs, what changes have taken place, why you think these changes have been made. Discuss your answers with your classmates.
5. **Thinking Critically** If you were asked to take a picture of your favorite place in your community, what would the picture show?

APPLYING KNOWLEDGE

1. Draw a diagram showing how a seed grows into a flower. Be sure to include all the steps, from the planting of the seed to the blooming of the flower. Remember to show that a seed needs plenty of water and sunshine to grow into a flower. Review the section on diagrams on pages 38–40, if necessary.
2. Make a bar graph showing the amount of time you spent doing homework during the last 5 days of school. At the bottom of the graph, write the days of the week. On the left side of the graph, label the following periods of time: 1/2 hour, 1 hour, 1 1/2 hours, 2 hours. Then fill in the bars for each day.
3. Draw a pie graph showing how many boys and girls there are in your class.

SUMMARIZING UNIT 1

REVIEWING VOCABULARY

1. ocean   The four largest bodies of water on the earth are called oceans. Can you name the earth's four oceans?

2. continent   The earth's land is divided into large bodies of land, called continents. How many continents are there and what are their names?

3. map   Maps are special drawings of the earth. How can maps help you learn about the earth?

4. pictograph   A pictograph uses small symbols or pictures to compare things. What are the names and uses of the other kinds of graphs that you learned about in Chapter 2?

5. diagram   Diagrams are different from pictures or drawings because diagrams do not show exactly what something looks like. What does a diagram show?

EXPRESSING YOURSELF

1. How would you feel?   Imagine that you are an astronaut making your first space flight. Explain how you feel as your space ship is about to take off.

2. Who would you rather be?   A historian is a person who studies history, a geographer studies geography. Would you rather be a historian or a geographer?

3. In your opinion   In your opinion, which are more important, maps or graphs?

4. Thinking like a geographer   How do you know the earth is round?

5. What if . . .?   What if you were given the choice of living in a place where the season never changes. Which season would you choose?

Forest Regions

Have you ever visited a forest? A forest is a large area covered with trees. Among the trees are bushes, vines, and other plants. It is shady beneath the trees, and the air is fresh. Birds, animals, and insects make their homes in the forest. Many people hike through or camp in a forest to look at its beauty. Other people work in the forest to protect it from fires and pollution. Many other workers help to make the forest's natural resources available to us. A natural resource is something useful to people and supplied by nature.

Campers enjoy their lunch in an opening of the forest in Colorado's Rocky Mountain National Park.
■ How would you describe this campsite?

Fires are a great danger to the life of a forest.
■ Is this a dangerous job?

Three kinds of forests are deciduous (left), coniferous (right), and tropical (middle).
■ **Which forest trees shed their leaves every year?**

Not all forests are alike. One type of forest has trees that shed their leaves every year. Such trees are called deciduous. The leaves of deciduous trees are usually broad, so these trees are also called broadleaf trees. Another type of forest has trees that do not shed their leaves. The leaves are not broad but are shaped like needles. These trees are called coniferous because they bear cones. Since these trees stay green all year round, they are also called evergreen trees. A third type of forest is a tropical forest. Tropical forests lie on both sides of the Equator. The tropics extend from about 23° north latitude to about 23° south latitude. Most trees in a tropical forest do not shed their leaves. Therefore, these trees are evergreens. But they also have broad leaves. Because of this, these trees are called broadleaf evergreens.

Forests are valuable in many ways. We get lumber from forests. Lumber is used in making houses, furniture, and baseball bats. Of course, not all trees are made into lumber.

Many things are made of wood. These men are making baseball bats.
■ Have you ever used this kind of bat?

Maple trees produce a sap that is made into maple syrup. The sap is often collected in buckets.
■ What color does the sap appear to be?

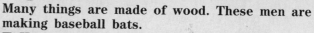

Many people use wood from trees to heat their homes and cook their food. Also, some wood from trees is used to make paper. Other forest products include maple syrup, charcoal, and cork for bottle stoppers and bulletin boards.

Forests can be found all over the world. Look at the map of the world's forest regions, below. Locate the Soviet Union and the Amazon Basin on the map. You will learn more about the forests in the Soviet Union and the Amazon Basin in Chapter 5.

Many people think that the continent of Africa is covered with thick forests called jungles. But only one fifth of the continent is forested. Africa's forests are located in the Zaire Basin, in parts of western Africa, and on the island of Madagascar, located off Africa's east coast. What kind of forests are found in Africa?

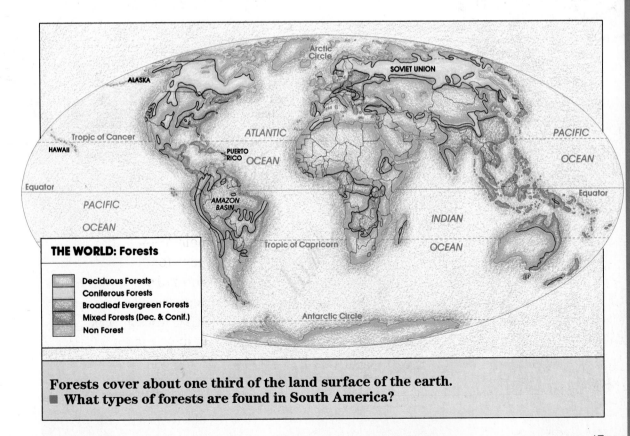

THE WORLD: Forests

- Deciduous Forests
- Coniferous Forests
- Broadleaf Evergreen Forests
- Mixed Forests (Dec. & Conif.)
- Non Forest

Forests cover about one third of the land surface of the earth.
■ **What types of forests are found in South America?**

Much of Southeast Asia is made up of broadleaf evergreen forests. Southeast Asia includes the countries of Vietnam, Indonesia, the Philippines, and Thailand.

The largest forests in Europe are found in the northern part of the continent. In Finland, thick forests cover about two thirds of the land. Other forests are located in central and southern Europe.

In some Asian forest regions, elephants are used to carry logs.
■ How is the elephant picking up the log?

Large forests cover some parts of Europe. This farm is in Germany's Black Forest.
■ Would you like to live on a farm in a forest region?

48

This logger stands on a log raft as he guides logs down the Fraser River in Canada.
■ What is he using to guide the logs?

The map on page 47 shows where forests are located in North America, South America, Australia, and Africa. What types of forests are found on these four continents? Six of the world's seven continents have forests. Only the continent of Antarctica is without forests.

Africa has large tropical forests. This tropical forest is in the country of Zimbabwe.
■ Why are these trees called evergreens?

The map below will help you locate forested areas in the United States. If you look at the states of Oregon, California, and Washington, you will see large areas of coniferous forests. These forests include fir, hemlock, spruce, and cedar trees. These three states are our leading lumber-producing states.

Great forests once covered most of America. In the warmer parts of the country, there were huge deciduous forests. In the colder parts there were big coniferous forests. In between there were mixed forests of broadleaf and evergreen trees.

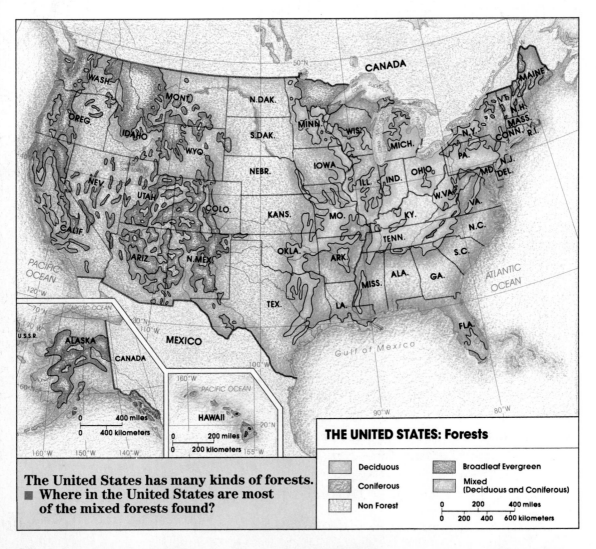

THE UNITED STATES: Forests

Deciduous

Coniferous

Non Forest

Broadleaf Evergreen

Mixed
(Deciduous and Coniferous)

| 0 | 200 | | 400 miles |
| 0 | 200 | 400 | 600 kilometers |

The United States has many kinds of forests.
■ **Where in the United States are most
of the mixed forests found?**

Today the busy seaport city of Boston stands where there was once a large forest.
■ Do you see any trees in this view of Boston?

The world's largest tree, known as the General Sherman, grows in the Sequoia National Park in California.
■ Can you find the people in the picture?

Most of the northeastern part of the United States was forest at one time. Now the Northeast has large cities, like New York City, Philadelphia, and Boston. The first white settlers cut down many trees. They built their homes with wood and cleared fields for farming. They used wood as fuel for heating their houses and for cooking. As people moved west, more trees were cut down. Forests were destroyed to make farmland and to make room for highways and railroads.

There are still many forests today. One third of the United States is covered with forests. Are there any forests near where you live? If so, what kind are they?

3 Alaska—A Land Of Plenty

A State of Variety

Why is Alaska called a state of variety?

VOCABULARY

natural resource	refuge
Arctic Circle	climate
strait	lumber
permafrost	hydroelectric
tundra	power

Something for Everyone The word *Alaska* means "big land." This is a very good description of our largest state. Alaska is twice as large as our second largest state, Texas. Alaska has high mountains, large forests, and wide plains. There are about 3 million lakes in Alaska. Alaska has more national parkland than any other state. It is the home of Mount McKinley, the tallest mountain peak in North America. Mount McKinley is more than 20,000 feet (6,096 m) high. That is almost four miles (6.5 km) high! There are 19 other mountain peaks in Alaska that rise above 14,000 feet (4,267 m).

There are many **natural resources** and a variety of climates in the state of Alaska. Natural resources are things useful to people and supplied by nature. The people who live in Alaska come from all parts of the United States and other parts of the world. In this chapter you will be studying about the land and about the people who make up this great state.

Where is Alaska Located? Alaska is one of the two states in the United States that do not share a border with another state. To the east, Alaska borders Canada. Northern Alaska borders the Arctic Ocean. This is the only part of the United States that is above the **Arctic Circle**. The Arctic Circle is a special line of latitude. It is located at 66 1/2° north of the Equator. It is usually cold in the land north of the Arctic Circle. The Bering Sea forms Alaska's western border. Alaska's Little Diomede Island is located only about 2 1/2 miles (4 km) east of Big Diomede Island, which is part of the Soviet Union. Both of these islands are located in the Bering Strait. A **strait** is a narrow strip of water that connects two larger bodies of water. The Bering Strait connects the Arctic Ocean and the Bering Sea. Locate the Bering Strait on the map on page 55. Alaska's southern coast borders the Gulf of Alaska and the Pacific Ocean.

Alaska has large forests, many lakes, and high mountains. Mount McKinley, shown above, is the highest mountain in North America.
■ Why, do you think, is Alaska called a state of variety?

Mountains and Plains If you look at the map of Alaska, you will see that the state is divided by three mountain ranges. A mountain range is a group of connected mountains. There are the Coast Ranges around the Gulf of Alaska. Northwest of the Coast Ranges is the Alaska Range. In the northern part of the state is the Brooks Range. All three ranges have some high mountains. Do you have any mountains in your state?

As the map shows, there is a large plain between the Alaska Range and the Brooks Range. It is called the Yukon Basin. The Yukon River flows through this large plain. Large sections of the Yukon Basin are always frozen. This frozen land is called **permafrost**. Also, there are thousands upon thousands of lakes throughout the Yukon Basin. Parts of the basin flood often because the water from the rain and snow cannot get through the permafrost.

One sixth of Alaska is north of the Brooks Range. This is a large area of lowlands. This part of Alaska is closest to the North Pole. Most of it is always frozen. These lowlands are called the **tundra**.

Plants of the tundra do not grow very high. This is because of the strong winds that blow all year and the cold temperatures in the winter. The Arctic National Wildlife Range is located in the tundra. It is the largest wildlife **refuge** in the United States, covering 13,000 square miles (33,670 sq km). Each of nine whole states in the United States is less than 13,000 square miles (33,670 sq km) in size. A refuge is a place that protects people or animals. The Arctic National Wildlife Range is home to such animals as the caribou (kar′ ə bü), grizzly bear, Dall sheep, and many different kinds of birds. Locate this refuge on the map on page 55.

Alaska's Climate **Climate** is made up of a region's precipitation, wind, and temperature over a long period of time. When we think of Alaska's climate, we think of snow, ice, and cold weather. For the most part this is true. But there are also some places in Alaska where the weather is not so cold. The entire coast of southern Alaska around the

Grizzly bears, which live mainly in Alaska and western Canada, have thick, wooly fur.
■ How are grizzly bears able to live in Alaska's cold climate?

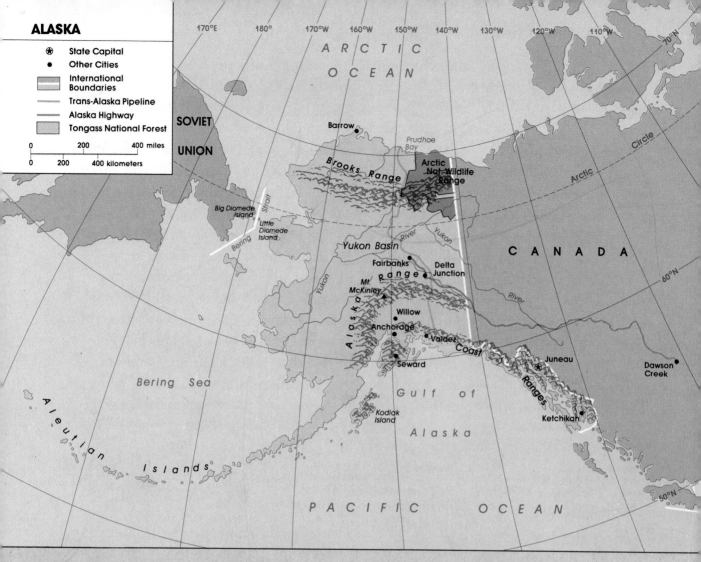

ALASKA

⊛ State Capital
• Other Cities
▨ International Boundaries
⎯ Trans-Alaska Pipeline
⎯ Alaska Highway
▨ Tongass National Forest

0   200   400 miles
0   200   400 kilometers

170°E   180°   170°W   160°W   150°W   140°W   130°W   120°W   110°W   70°N

ARCTIC OCEAN

SOVIET UNION

Barrow

Prudhoe Bay

Brooks Range

Arctic Nat. Wildlife Range

Arctic Circle

Big Diomede Island

Little Diomede Island

Bering Strait

Yukon Basin

River

Yukon

CANADA

60°N

Fairbanks

Delta Junction

Range

Mt. McKinley

Yukon

River

Willow

Anchorage

Valdez

Coast

Seward

Juneau

Dawson Creek

Bering Sea

Gulf of

Ranges

Kodiak Island

Alaska

Ketchikan

Aleutian Islands

50°N

PACIFIC OCEAN

Alaska is the largest state in the United States.
■ **What is the capital of Alaska?**

Gulf of Alaska has a mild climate. This area also gets around 60 inches (152 cm) of rain a year. Rain is very important to forests. Without rain there would be no forests, because trees need a lot of water to grow tall.

To the north the weather gets colder. Also, there is less rain. In the Yukon Basin the weather changes a lot between summer and winter. It can get warm in the summer and very cold in the winter.

A very interesting thing happens in Alaska's tundra region. During the winter, this region receives almost no sunlight. But during the summer months, this part of Alaska has sunlight almost all the time. The reason is that at the North Pole the sun does not set at all from the end of March to the end of September. From September to March the sun does not rise. Night lasts for six months and day lasts for six months. As you move away from the North Pole, the sun does rise and set during each 24-hour period.

Natural Resources   Alaska has been called the state of the future. This is because it has many natural resources. Some of Alaska's natural resources are gold, oil, natural gas, coal, silver, and zinc.

Alaska's forests are also a natural resource. As you know, forests provide wood for **lumber** and paper. Lumber is trees that have been sawed into boards, beams, and other forms of wood. Later in this chapter you will learn more about the importance of Alaska's forests.

Another important natural resource in Alaska is water. There are many streams, rivers, and lakes in Alaska. Some of the rivers are used to produce electricity. How can rivers do this? In Chapter 1, you studied the diagram of how a waterwheel works. Well, electric power is made in much the same way. The power of the river turns a wheel that drives a machine that makes electric power. Electric power made in this way is called **hydroelectric power**. Electric power lights buildings, runs machines in homes and factories, and does many other things. Alaska's largest hydroelectric power plant is near the city of Juneau (jü′ nō).

As shown in the diagram below, a hydroelectric power plant uses the power of falling water to make electricity.
■ What is the name of the building where the electricity is made?

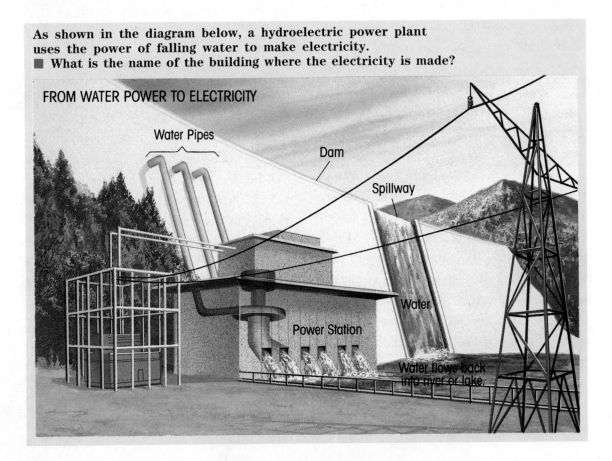

FROM WATER POWER TO ELECTRICITY

Water Pipes

Dam

Spillway

Water

Power Station

Water flows back into river or lake.

Alaska is bordered by water on three sides. Many kinds of fish are caught in Alaska's coastal waters as well as in its rivers, lakes, and streams.

We know that Alaska is a state that is rich in natural resources. Yet we do not know exactly how rich it is. Some people believe that there are many natural resources that have not yet been discovered. Many of these resources are believed to be buried deep beneath the frozen ground or found deep in the forests.

Alaska's Forests Forests in Alaska cover about one third of the state's land. This is a lot of forests. Some of Alaska's largest forests are located along the southeastern coast. The largest national forest in the United States is located in this part of Alaska. The Tongass National Forest, covering over 5 million acres (over 2 million ha), makes up most of southeastern Alaska. Locate the Tongass National Forest on the map on page 55. Large forests are also found in the middle of the state.

Forests are important to Alaska. They provide homes for many animals and make beautiful recreation areas. Trees from forests are used to make lumber and paper.

It is difficult to reach many of Alaska's forests. There are only a few roads in the state, and the cold weather makes it difficult to build more. Some people want to keep the

Many people enjoy eating Alaskan king crab legs. King crabs are one of many kinds of fish caught in Alaskan waters.
■ What kind of job do you think the man in the photograph has?

forests as they are. These people do not want to see Alaska's forests made available to tourists or to big lumber companies. Other people realize that these forests have many valuable products. Whatever happens in the future, forests will continue to be an important part of Alaska.

CHECKUP

1. List Alaska's natural resources.
2. What are the names of Alaska's three mountain ranges?
3. Where are some of Alaska's largest forests located?
4. **Thinking Critically** What does the climate in Alaska have to do with the locations of the state's forests?

Alaska's Forest Industry

How is wood from Alaska's forests used to make paper?

VOCABULARY

logger	barking drum
felling	grinder
bucking	groundwood pulp
skidding	renewable resource
pulp mill	seedling

Industry Improves Industry and manufacturing in Alaska depend on the state's natural resources. Since Alaska became a state in 1959, industry and manufacturing have improved. One of the most important industries in Alaska is the making of forest products. The most important forest product that is made in Alaska is paper.

In the Forests Before trees can be used to make paper, they must first be taken out of the forests. The people who do this are called **loggers**. Before cutting a tree, they must decide where it should come down. In the direction in which they want the tree to fall, they cut a wedge-shaped piece from the trunk, close to the ground. Then they cut through the trunk with a chain saw.

Have you ever seen a chain saw? The teeth of the saw are an endless chain. The chain saws that are used

Sometimes, loggers must cut a large tree into smaller pieces before it can be taken out of the forest.
■ How can you tell that this logger is concerned with safety?

by loggers are powered by gasoline engines. Loggers do not talk of "cutting" a tree. **Felling** a tree is the way they say it.

Removing the limbs is the next step. Loggers used to do this with axes. Now it is usually done with chain saws. The tree trunk, many feet long, is then cut into shorter pieces. Sawing the trunk into logs is called **bucking**.

If the ground is quite level, tractors may drag the logs to a loading area. This is called **skidding**. On rough ground, long cables may be used to pull the logs. The cables run to an engine through pulleys on a high metal pole or on the upper trunk of a tall tree. In the roughest places, helicopters are sometimes used to lift logs and carry them to loading areas. At the loading area, the logs are transported to a **pulp mill**. Pulp mills turn logs into pulp, which is needed to make paper.

At the Pulp Mill   One of the largest pulp mills in the world is located in Ketchikan (kech′ i kan). Turn to the map on page 55 and find Ketchikan in southeastern Alaska. This mill employs more than a thousand people. Half of them work in the mill and half work in the forest. The wood for this mill comes from the Tongass National Forest.

As soon as logs reach the pulp mill, they are cut into smaller sections and carried into large drums,

Helicopters are sometimes used to get logs out of the forest.
■ How else are logs taken out of the forest?

At a pulp mill, logs are turned into pulp.
■ What is pulp used for?

called **barking drums**. Each drum looks like an oversized barrel, 45 feet (13 m) long and 25 feet (7 m) around. Inside the drums, the logs tumble around, rubbing against each other and against the sides of the drums. This helps remove the bark from the logs.

The clean logs are then fed into **grinders**, which grind them into tiny pieces. These pieces are mixed with water and bleach and passed through screens to separate the large and small pieces of wood. To make good paper, the large pieces of wood are removed. The finished product is called **groundwood pulp**. The groundwood pulp is then fed into a paper machine.

Making Paper   A paper machine is several hundred feet long. The mushy pulp goes in one end and paper comes out the other end. Inside the machine, the pulp is spread in thin layers. As the layers of pulp move through the paper machine, they are dried and pressed into a solid sheet of paper. Finally, the paper is pressed to the desired thickness, dried again with steam-heated rollers, and wound into large rolls.

Think of all the things you use that are made from paper. Schoolbooks, notebooks, napkins, tissues, and newspapers are just a few. Maybe the paper of this book or the paper you will be writing on was made in Alaska.

After paper is made, it is put into large rolls like the one above.
■ **Why, do you think, is paper put into rolls rather than into flat sheets?**

Renewing the Forests   With so much wood used each year, one might think that someday all the forests will be cut down. However, forests are a **renewable resource**; that is, they are something of value that can be replaced. New trees can be grown to replace those that were cut down.

New forests are usually planted in places where all the trees have been cut. First the ground must be made ready for planting. Brush must be removed. Sometimes the whole area is plowed. **Seedlings** are then planted. These are small young trees that have been grown from seed. Seedlings are planted either by hand

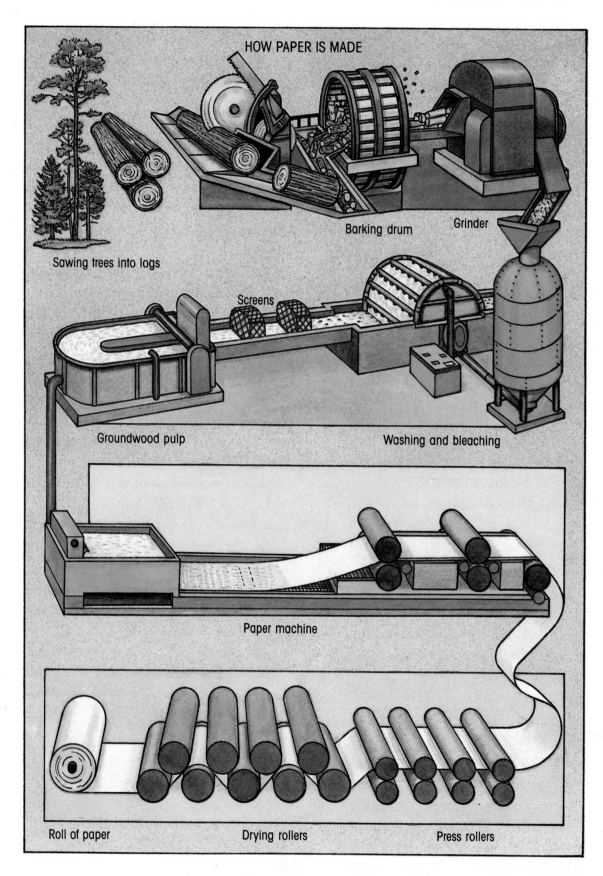

HOW PAPER IS MADE

Sawing trees into logs

Barking drum

Grinder

Screens

Groundwood pulp

Washing and bleaching

Paper machine

Roll of paper

Drying rollers

Press rollers

Fighting a forest fire is a difficult and dirty job.
■ **What fire-fighting equipment does the woman above have?**

Protecting the Forests   Fire and disease are the worst enemies of forests. Fires are started by careless people or by lightning. They destroy thousands of trees. It takes many people to fight forest fires. Diseases can kill trees quickly. Sometimes insects, birds, and squirrels carry diseases from one tree to another. Whole forests can be wiped out within a few months.

To keep forests healthy, diseased trees should be destroyed. Trees can sometimes be saved if they are sprayed with something that attacks the disease. It is a hard job to control the diseases of trees.

Other Forest Products   Paper is not the only product made from Alaska's forests. There are also a number of sawmills in the state. At a sawmill logs are cut into lumber.

Alaska's forest industry is very important. It provides thousands of jobs for Alaskans and many products that are used by people in all the United States and throughout the world.

or by machine. Lumber companies have special places called nurseries where they grow seedlings.

The new trees are given plant food called fertilizer every five years to make them grow faster. At times the growing forest is thinned out. Some trees grow faster than others. Smaller trees are cut to allow the bigger ones to grow even faster. It takes between 30 and 60 years for the trees to grow big enough to cut.

CHECKUP
1. What are people who take trees out of a forest called?
2. What is a pulp mill?
3. What are seedlings used for?
4. **Thinking Critically** Explain how paper is made from its beginnings as a tree in the forest to the finished product that comes out of the paper machine.

62

Other Industries in Alaska

What are Alaska's other major industries?

Alaska's Fishing Industry   Alaska's fishing industry is very important to the state. Some of the best **fisheries** in the world are found in the waters in and around Alaska. A fishery is a place for catching fish. Thousands of people work on boats that catch fish or in plants that put fish in cans or process it in other ways.

The most important catch to the Alaskan fishing industry is the salmon. Salmon are very interesting fish. They are born in streams or rivers, then travel to the ocean. Salmon stay in the ocean for a few years until they are ready to lay their eggs. To do this, the salmon leave the ocean and travel back upstream to where they were born. Salmon are usually caught by net and are sold fresh, frozen, smoked, or canned. Many people also enjoy fishing for salmon and other kinds of fish in Alaska as a recreational activity. Crabs, scallops, smelts, and herring eggs are also parts of Alaska's fishing industry.

Farming in Alaska   Alaska has very little farming. The cold climate in Alaska means that the time for growing crops is very short. Most of Alaska's farms are near the cities of Anchorage (Ang' kə rij) and Fairbanks. Farmers in Alaska grow barley, hay, oats, and potatoes. They also raise some livestock.

Most Alaskan farming is done near Anchorage and Fairbanks. This farm is located south of Anchorage.
■ What, do you think, are the farmers in this picture doing?

Alaskan farmers produce only 10 percent of what the people need. The other 90 percent has to come from outside Alaska. Most of the farm products reach Alaska by boat from Seattle, Washington. It is a long trip, and it costs a great deal of money. That is why people in Alaska pay more money for food than those who live in other parts of the United States.

Mining in Alaska   Some scientists believe that Alaska has as much coal as the rest of the United States combined. Great amounts of other natural resources aré also found in Alaska. All of these are important. But the discovery of oil in Alaska has become especially important to people all over the United States. In 1968, drilling for oil began in northern Alaska. The Prudhoe (prüd' ō) Bay oil field is Alaska's chief oil-producing area.

Can you find Prudhoe Bay in northern Alaska on the map on page 55? Hundreds of people work there to get the oil from the ground. They send the oil all the way to Valdez (val dēz), in southern Alaska. Find Valdez on the map. Many more people work in Valdez loading the oil into special large ships. These ships are called **oil tankers**. They take the oil to other states to be **refined**. *Refine* means "to improve or make pure." We use refined oil for many things, such as running our automobiles and heating our homes.

Transporting the oil from Prudhoe Bay to Valdez was a big problem. This is a distance of about 800 miles (about 1300 km). It is covered with permafrost and by large rivers, streams, and two mountain ranges. Finally, it was decided to build a long pipeline between the two places. The oil would move from Prudhoe Bay through the pipeline to Valdez. This pipeline is called the **Trans-Alaska Pipeline**. The Trans-Alaska Pipeline took many years to build. But it has been worth the time and the hard work because it has made more oil available to the United States and other countries.

In some places, building the Trans-Alaska Pipeline was very difficult.
■ How is this piece of the pipeline being held in place?

Many tourists to Alaska take in the beautiful scenery at Glacier Bay National Park.
■ **From looking at the photograph above, can you tell why people like to visit Glacier Bay National Park?**

Tourism in Alaska Thousands of tourists visit Alaska each year. Most of them go to Alaska during the summer to admire the beautiful scenery, to hunt, or to fish. About one fourth of the land in Alaska is part of the National Park System. This land is protected by the government in Washington, D.C. One of Alaska's national parks, Denali (də näl′ ē) contains Mount McKinley. Other Alaskan national parks include Glacier Bay National Park and Lake Clark National Park.

Tourists can now travel by car to Alaska by using the Alaska Highway. The Alaska Highway is a 1,523 mile (2,451 km) road that connects Dawson Creek in British Columbia, Canada, and Fairbanks in Alaska.

Most people still go to Alaska by airplane or by ship. From mid-May to October each year, cruise ships sail to Alaska from other states in the United States and from Canada. In the comfort of the cruise ships, tourists come to see the beautiful land and to visit Alaska's cities along the coast.

CHECKUP
1. What fish is the most important catch to Alaska's fishing industry?
2. How is oil transported from Prudhoe Bay to the city of Valdez?
3. In which of Alaska's national parks can Mount McKinley be found?
4. **Thinking Critically** Which of the four industries mentioned in this lesson would you most like to work in?

The People of Alaska

Why have many people over the years decided to live in Alaska?

VOCABULARY

population density	**Aleut**
Eskimo	**igloo**

Alaska's First People Even though Alaska is our largest state, not many people live there. Today only about 525,000 people live in the state of Alaska. Alaska ranks last of all 50 states in **population density**. Population density tells how crowded a place is. To find the population density of a place, we divide the number of people by the land area. Alaska has a population of about 525,000 and a land area of 570,000 square miles (1,478,458 sq km). This means that Alaska has a population density of less than 1 person per square mile (less than 1 person per sq km). By comparison, New Jersey, our most crowded state, has a population density of about 1,027 people per square mile (397 people per sq km). Of course, each square mile of Alaska does not have only 1 person. Some parts of the state have many more people per square mile. Other parts of Alaska have no one living in them.

No one knows exactly when or how the first Alaskans came to Alaska. Some scientists believe that it was many thousands of years ago. At that time a strip of land about 50 miles (80 km) long joined Asia and North America. The first Alaskans may have walked across this strip of land looking for good hunting grounds. This strip of land is now covered by the Bering Strait. These first Alaskans were called Indians.

Today, relatives of these Indian groups are still living in Alaska. Two of the best known are the **Eskimos** (es′ kə mōz) and the **Aleuts** (a lüts′). The Eskimos live in the northern and western part of Alaska. They are also known as Inuits (in′ yə wəts), which

The blanket toss was started by Eskimo hunters who were looking for animals.
■ How do you think the blanket toss helped the hunters find animals?

means "people." The Aleuts are mainly found on the islands that bear their name—the Aleutian Islands. Other smaller Indian groups live in south-eastern and central Alaska.

Some Eskimos still live by using what they find around them for food and shelter. They hunt in the forests for wild animals. They eat the meat and use the skins to make warm clothes. Sometimes, while hunting, the Eskimos live in **igloos** (ig′ lüz). These small houses are made out of blocks of ice. The igloo protects the Eskimos from wind and snow. To travel from one place to another, some Eskimos still use sleds pulled by teams of dogs.

But life for most Eskimos and other Indian groups living in Alaska is much different today than it was many years ago. They live in houses, drive cars, buy their food and clothes in stores, and watch television. These Alaskans now live in much the same way as people who live in other parts of the United States.

After Alaska became a state in 1959, the United States took over all the land. Some relatives of the first Alaskans felt that they deserved some of the land. In 1971, they were given 40 million acres (16 million ha) of land. Owning this land is important to these people. They are able to use their land for hunting and fishing. Also, they must be paid for any natural resources taken from their land. This land allows these Indian groups

These Eskimo children are climbing on a large whale bone. Eskimos once hunted whales in the waters off Alaska.
■ Why, do you think, did Eskimos hunt for whales?

Some Eskimos build igloos to live in during hunting trips.
■ What is an igloo made of?

67

In the year 1899, gold was discovered near the city of Nome, Alaska. Thousands of Americans rushed to Alaska to look for gold.
■ The men in the photograph above are working at a gold mine in Nome. Do you think the photograph was taken in the summer or winter?

A. G. Simmer/Alaska Historical Library

to keep a part of their past. At the same time, this land is helping them prepare for their future.

Other People Come To Alaska In 1741, two men exploring the northern part of the Pacific Ocean for the country of Russia became the first Europeans to see Alaska. Many Russians started to come to Alaska to hunt animals and to trade furs. Russia controlled Alaska until 1867, when the United States bought Alaska from Russia.

The first Americans came to Alaska to catch animals for fur, to

fish, and to look for gold. But most of these people usually did not stay very long in Alaska. They took from Alaska what they wanted and then would leave. Some people became rich by selling the things they took home from Alaska. It was not until after 1945 that large numbers of Americans became aware of Alaska's richness and beauty, and decided to make it their home.

Today, Alaskans are very proud of their state. They work together to improve it and make it a better place to live. Some Alaskans choose to live in the wilderness, but most Alaskans

The History of Alaska

In 1741, a Danish sea captain sailing with a Russian explorer became the first people from Europe to land in Alaska. These men took back to Russia the furs from sea otters. Soon, Russian hunters and traders began traveling to Alaska. By 1784, Russia had made the first European settlement in Alaska, on Kodiak Island.

From 1799 to 1867, the country of Russia governed Alaska. On March 30, 1867, the United States bought Alaska from Russia. Secretary of State William Seward agreed to pay $7,200,000, or about 2 cents per acre (5 cents per ha), to Russia for Alaska. Not many Americans thought this was a good buy. Alaska was thought to be a frozen piece of land, of little use to anyone except hunters, trappers, and people who fish. Some Americans nicknamed Alaska *Seward's Folly* and *Seward's Icebox*.

For several years Americans paid little attention to this new land. But in 1880, something happened that changed Alaska forever. Gold was discovered in the area around the present-day city of Juneau. Thousands of people came pouring into Alaska in hopes of finding gold. More gold was discovered near the city of Nome in 1899 and near the city of Fairbanks in 1902. These discoveries made Alaska more attractive to many Americans.

Alaska became the forty-ninth state in the United States on January 3, 1959. The new state struggled throughout the 1960s. In 1964, a major earthquake hit Alaska, and in 1967, a large flood in Fairbanks caused a great amount of damage. But in 1968, the discovery of oil at Prudhoe Bay changed Alaska's outlook. The future of Alaska is bright. Today, more people than ever before are discovering the beauty of Alaska.

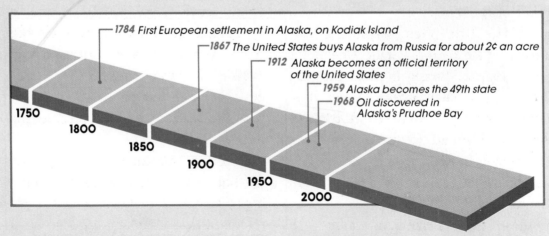

1784 First European settlement in Alaska, on Kodiak Island
1867 The United States buys Alaska from Russia for about 2¢ an acre
1912 Alaska becomes an official territory of the United States
1959 Alaska becomes the 49th state
1968 Oil discovered in Alaska's Prudhoe Bay

1750 1800 1850 1900 1950 2000

live in or near cities and towns. Life for most of these people is much like life in cities and towns in other parts of the United States.

Alaska's Major Cities   The three largest cities in Alaska are Anchorage, Fairbanks, and Juneau. Fairbanks is in the middle of the state, in the Yukon Basin. Its population is about 23,000 people. The University of Alaska is located in Fairbanks.

Anchorage and Juneau are on the southern and southeastern coasts. Juneau has a population of about 20,000 people. It is the capital of the state.

Anchorage is the largest city in the state, having a population of almost 235,000 people. Almost half of the people in Alaska live in the Anchorage area. Anchorage is a modern city, with apartment buildings, hotels, and office buildings. It is also a trade and transportation center. Alaska's most important port is in Anchorage.

About 40 miles (64 km) north of Anchorage is the town of Willow. In 1974, the people of Alaska voted to move the capital of the state from Juneau to Willow. Alaskans wanted their capital to be closer to where most of the people live. But at the present time, no final plans have been made to move the capital to Willow. Some Alaskans now feel that with the improved methods of transportation available, it is no longer necessary to move the state's capital city.

Traveling in Alaska   Traveling in the state of Alaska is difficult. There are very few highways and only one railroad line. The frozen ground and the mountains make it difficult to build more. Can you find Seward on the map of Alaska? It is located on the southern coast. The only railroad line in the state starts in Seward and goes north to Anchorage. From there it goes all the way to Fairbanks.

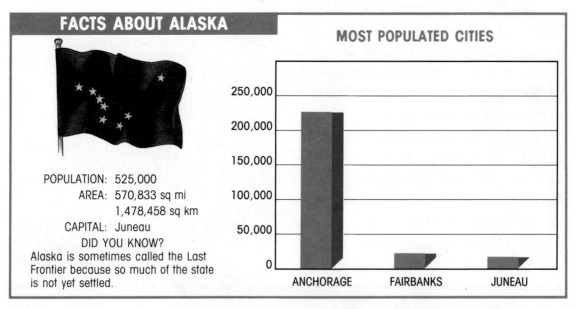

FACTS ABOUT ALASKA

POPULATION: 525,000
AREA: 570,833 sq mi
1,478,458 sq km
CAPITAL: Juneau
DID YOU KNOW?
Alaska is sometimes called the Last Frontier because so much of the state is not yet settled.

MOST POPULATED CITIES

(bar graph with vertical axis marked 0, 50,000, 100,000, 150,000, 200,000, 250,000; horizontal axis labeled ANCHORAGE, FAIRBANKS, JUNEAU)

The modern city of Anchorage, Alaska's largest city, is an important trade and transportation center.
■ How can you tell from this photograph that Anchorage is a modern city?

Many villages in Alaska are very far from others. Sometimes it is difficult for people in these villages to get food or medical supplies. In the last few years, small airplanes have been flying to these villages from larger towns. The airplanes land on small airstrips or on frozen lakes.

Alaska's transportation connections with the outside world are constantly improving. Airplanes fly every day to London, Tokyo, and major cities throughout the United States. Also, a ferryboat goes back and forth between Alaska and Seattle, Washington. A great many ships carry products in and out of Alaska's ports. Anchorage is the largest trading center in Alaska. Most of the things the people of Alaska need come through Anchorage. Also, most of the products that Alaskans sell to others leave from Anchorage. Fairbanks, the state's second largest city, is also an important trading center in the state of Alaska. Improvements in Alaska's industries and trade as well as the state's natural beauty and many resources truly make our forty-ninth state a land of plenty.

CHECKUP

1. How do scientists believe people first got to Alaska?
2. What are the names of the two best known Indian groups still living in Alaska?
3. In what year did the United States buy Alaska from Russia?
4. What is the name of Alaska's largest city?
5. **Thinking Critically** How is life for some Eskimos living in Alaska different from most other people living in the state?

What is a Dictionary?

A dictionary is a book that contains the words of a language. A dictionary tells several things about these words. The spelling and the meaning of each word are given. The respelling shows you how to pronounce, or say, a word. It divides the word into parts, called syllables, and identifies the sounds of the letters.

The words are listed in alphabetical order. This helps you find the words easily. It also makes it possible for you to easily check the spelling of a word.

When you see a word that you do not know, you can find the meaning of the word in a dictionary. If you do not know how to use a word, a dictionary can help.

Answer the questions below by using the dictionary entries.

SKILLS PRACTICE

1. Write the respelling of the word *ancestor.*
2. How many syllables are there in the word *climate?*
3. Write a sentence using the first definition of the word *strait.*

an ces tor (an'ses'ter), **1** person from whom one is descended, such as one's great-grandparents: *Their ancestors came to America in 1812.* **2** the early form from which a species or group is descended: *Dinosaurs and snakes have the same ancestors.*

cli mate (klī' mit), **1** the kind of weather a place has. Climate includes conditions of heat and cold, moisture and dryness, clearness and cloudiness, wind and calm. **2** region with certain conditions of heat and cold, rainfall, wind, sunlight, etc.: *to live in a dry climate.* **3** condition or feeling that exists at some time: *The climate of public opinion favored tax reforms.* *n.*

strait (strat), **1** a narrow channel connecting two larger bodies of water: *The Strait of Gibraltar connects the Mediterranean Sea and the Atlantic Ocean.* **2** OLD USE. narrow; limited; confining. **3** straits, *pl.* difficulty; need; distress: *be in desperate straits for money.* **1,3** *n.* **2** *adj.* —**strait' ly,** *adv.* —**strait' ness,** *n.*

Some students say, "If I cannot spell a word, how can I look it up in a dictionary?" Usually you can spell a word close enough to search and find it in the dictionary. Use a dictionary to correct the misspelled words listed below. The misspelled part is underlined. Write the correct spellings on a piece of paper.

SKILLS PRACTICE

1. iglu
2. populasion
3. barc
4. hidroelectric
5. tondra
6. resourse
7. seadling
8. toorist
9. dencity
10. plente

CHAPTER 3 REVIEW

MAIN IDEAS

1. Alaska is the largest state in the United States. It has high mountains, large forests, wide plains, and many natural resources.
2. Alaska's climate ranges from mild in the south to very cold in the north.
3. Alaska's natural resources include coal, gold, oil, natural gas, silver, zinc, water, and forests.
4. Alaska's Tongass National Forest is the largest national forest in the United States.
5. Most of the wood from Alaska's forests is made into pulp, which is needed to make paper.
6. Along with forest products, other industries in Alaska include fishing, farming, mining, and tourism.
7. Over the years, people from all over the United States and the world have made Alaska their home because of the region's beauty and many natural resources.

VOCABULARY REVIEW

Fill in the blanks with the word or words that best completes the sentence. Use a separate sheet of paper.

1. _____ is the combination of a region's precipitation, wind, and temperature over a long period of time.
2. People who take wood out of the forest are called _____ .
3. To make groundwood pulp, logs are put through the _____ to grind them into small pieces.
4. The _____ moves oil from Alaska's Prudhoe Bay to the city of Valdez.

5. Ships that take oil to be refined are called _____ .

CHAPTER CHECKUP

1. Name the four bodies of water that border Alaska to the north, south, and west.
2. What is Alaska's most important forest product?
3. What is a renewable resource?
4. In which city do almost half of Alaska's people live?
5. **Thinking Critically** Imagine that you are going to Alaska in 1900 to look for gold. Make a list of 10 items that you would take with you on your trip.
6. **Thinking Critically** List some reasons why you would or would not like to live in Alaska.

APPLYING KNOWLEDGE

1. Create a poster that would make people want to take a vacation in Alaska. Your poster should include pictures or drawings and a written description of the many sites in Alaska that a tourist can visit.
2. Below are the average January and July temperatures for the cities of Barrow, Anchorage, and Juneau.

	January	July
Barrow	$-15°F(-26°C)$	$39°F(4°C)$
Anchorage	$12°F(-11°C)$	$58°F(14°C)$
Juneau	$24°F(-4°C)$	$56°F(13°C)$

Make two bar graphs that show this information. Find each of these cities on the map of Alaska on page 55. What can you tell about Alaska's climate from studying the graphs and the map?

4 Hawaii and Puerto Rico

Exploring a Tropical Forest

What are tropical forests like?

VOCABULARY

tropics	creeper
rain forest	humid
canopy	

Our Newest State Hawaii (hə wī′ ē) is different from other states in the United States in several ways. It is the only state that is not on the mainland of North America. Hawaii is made up of a chain of more than 100 islands. It became a state in 1959, just 8 months after Alaska became a state. So Hawaii is the newest of our 50 states. It is also the state that is farthest south.

Locate the state of Hawaii on the map below. It is in the Pacific Ocean. The Pacific Ocean is the largest ocean in the world. It may surprise you that the islands that make up Hawaii stretch for about 1,500 miles (2,410 km) — half the distance from California to New York. Many of the islands are tiny and few people live on

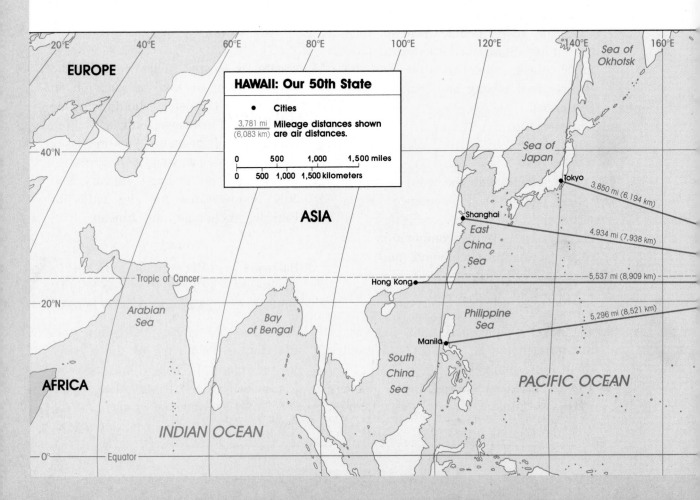

any of these smaller islands. The state nearest to Hawaii is California, about 2,400 miles (3,860 km) away. Find the city of Los Angeles on the map. Los Angeles is in the state of California. How many miles is it from Honolulu (hon əl ü′lü), Hawaii's capital city, to the city of Los Angeles?

Hawaii is such an interesting state that millions of tourists from all over the world visit it every year. Most of them come from the United States mainland. These tourists travel thousands of miles to get to Hawaii. Look at the map to find out how many miles people living in New York would have to travel if they wanted to take a vacation in Honolulu.

Tourists go to Hawaii to enjoy the beauty and variety of the state. For example there are steep mountains and flat sandy beaches. There are small, quiet villages and the busy modern city of Honolulu. There is lots of sunshine and lots of rain. There are dry areas and wet tropical forests. These forests are much different than the forests in Alaska that you studied about in Chapter 3.

Visiting a Tropical Forest There are not many places in the United States where tropical forests are found. That is because most tropical forests are found around the Equator, between about 23° north latitude and

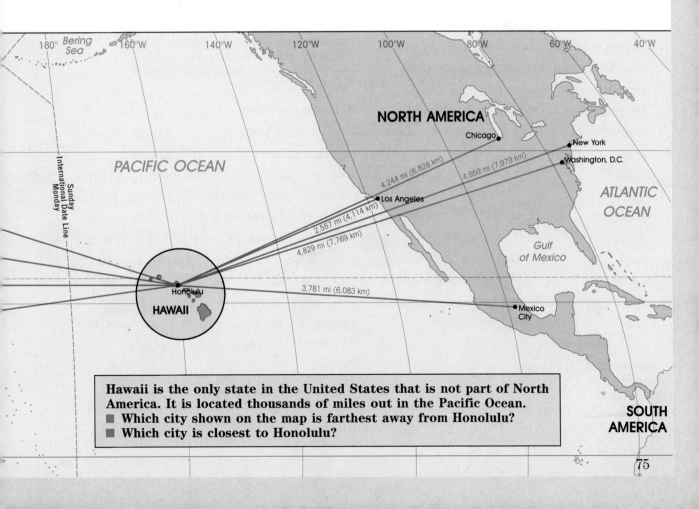

Hawaii is the only state in the United States that is not part of North America. It is located thousands of miles out in the Pacific Ocean.
■ Which city shown on the map is farthest away from Honolulu?
■ Which city is closest to Honolulu?

about 23° south latitude. This region is known as the **tropics**. Tropical forests are also called **rain forests** because so much rain falls there. Most of the United States is not in the tropics. But the state of Hawaii and the island of Puerto Rico (pwer′ tə rē′kō) are. However, even if you never get a chance to visit a tropical forest, we can all make believe. Let's take a make-believe trip to a large tropical forest.

A Large Green Blanket   To get to our tropical rain forest, we must take an airplane ride. Flying over the tropical forest, we look down and see something that looks like a great big green blanket. What we are actually looking at are the top branches and leaves of the tallest trees. This green blanket is called the **canopy** (kan′ ə pē). It looks the same all year round because these trees are broadleaf evergreens. The leaves on broadleaf evergreen trees stay green all year round.

Entering the Forest   Once our airplane has landed, we must travel by boat up a river and into the forest. From the boat the forest looks like a thick green wall. In some places this wall is 200 feet (60 m) high.

After docking our boat along the riverbank, we begin to cut a path into the forest, using knives and axes. Inside, the forest becomes more open. Before us are tree trunks of all sizes.

Rain forests are woodlands of trees and bushes that stay green all year.
■ Why do so many trees and bushes grow in a rain forest?

It is hard to walk because the ground is soft and wet, like a sponge. Many tree roots are above the ground.

On the upper branches of the canopy, little flowering plants have taken root. Hanging down from these branches are vines and growing things that look like ropes. These ropelike vines are known as **creepers**. Have you ever watched Tarzan on television, as he swung from one tree to another? He swung on creepers like these.

An Exciting Visit   Our visit inside the tropical forest does not last very long. Tropical forests can be very exciting but also very scary places! The light is dim because the dense canopy blocks out the sunshine. You can hear the sounds of many animals, but you cannot see too many of them because of the thick trees and bushes. It is quite hot. The air is **humid** (hyü′ mid), that is, very damp. Insects, especially mosquitoes, fly all around us. On the moist ground, we can see snakes, spiders, anteaters, and lizards.

As we return home, we think back on our exciting visit. We had the chance to see some strange plants and beautiful flowers. We have seen brightly colored birds and different kinds of animals. We now know how different life is in a tropical forest.

Tropical Forests Around the World
In the tropics the sun at noon is almost straight overhead all year round. That is why the weather is hot in most tropical places.

Not all of the land in this region we call the tropics is covered with trees. As you know, trees need a lot of rain to grow. Some lands in the tropics do not have enough rain for trees. Only grass may grow in those dry places.

The forests in the tropics are mainly made up of broadleaf evergreen trees. Broadleaf evergreen forests can also be found outside the tropics. Look at the map on page 47. Broadleaf evergreen forests can be found in southern Florida, even though the state of Florida is not in the tropics.

As you know, in the United States, only the state of Hawaii and the island of Puerto Rico are in the tropics. In the pages that follow, we shall learn about the land and people of Hawaii and Puerto Rico.

In some places in a rain forest, brightly colored flowers stand out among the trees and bushes.
■ What colors are in these flowers?

CHECKUP
1. In what ocean is Hawaii located?
2. What is another name for a tropical forest?
3. What parts of the United States are in the tropics?
4. **Thinking Critically** Describe what a visit to a tropical forest would be like.

The Land Of Hawaii

What is Hawaii's land and climate like?

VOCABULARY

volcano	leeward side
trade wind	sandalwood
windward side	lava

Hawaii's Climate   The temperature in Hawaii changes very little between summer and winter. It is mild and comfortable all year round.

The rainfall differs from one island to another. The island that has the most rain is Kauai (Kou′ ī). Like the other islands of this state, Kauai rises from the bottom of the Pacific Ocean. It was created millions of years ago by **volcanoes** under the ocean. A volcano is an opening in the earth from which steam and other gases, stones, ashes, and melted rock pour out from time to time. Kauai rises to high, steep mountain peaks. One of the highest is Mount Waialeale (wī äl ā äl′ ā). The average rainfall at the top of this mountain is 450 inches (1,125 cm) a year. It is one of the rainiest places in the world. The rains make plants and trees grow rapidly. With all its greenery, Kauai is known as the Garden Island.

Some of the most beautiful birds in the world live on the island of Kauai. The reason for this has to do with two other animals — the rat and the mongoose. About 100 years ago, mongooses were brought in from the country of India to get rid of the many rats found on the islands. But along with eating rats, a mongoose also eats birds and bird eggs. The people of Kauai would not allow the mongooses on their island. As a result, today there are certain kinds of birds that can only be found on the island of Kauai.

Why It Rains   The rain that falls on the islands of Hawaii is brought by the **trade winds**. These are ocean winds that always blow in one direction, usually toward the Equator. The trade winds that blow across Hawaii come from the northeast. That is why

HAWAII

Forest	✳ State Capital
National Parks	• Other Cities

0   50   100 miles
0   50   100 kilometers

The largest of the more than 100 islands that make up the state of Hawaii are shown on the map above.
■ **On which island is Honolulu located?**

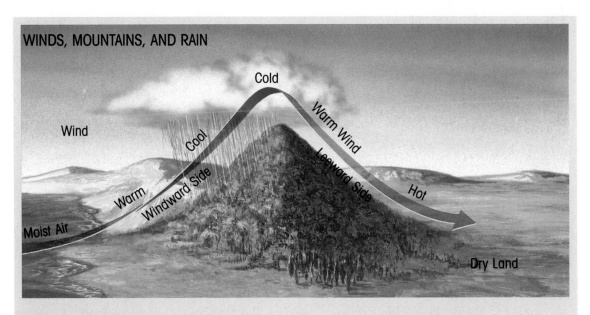

WINDS, MOUNTAINS, AND RAIN

Cold

Wind

Warm Wind

Cool

Leeward Side

Warm

Windward Side

Hot

Moist Air

Dry Land

This diagram helps to explain how mountains affect Hawaii's rainfall.
■ **Do winds rise up the windward or up the leeward side of a mountain?**

the northeast side of the mountains in Hawaii is called the **windward side**. The side directly opposite is called the **leeward side**.

As they come near the islands the winds pick up moisture from the ocean. The mountains force the air to go higher. As the air cools off, part of its moisture turns into rain. More rain falls on the windward side of the mountains than on the leeward side.

After the air goes over the mountains, it has very little moisture. That is why it does not rain as much on the leeward side of mountains. In fact the whole leeward side of each island in Hawaii is mostly dry. The diagram above shows how the moist air turns into rain and then moves toward the leeward side.

Much of the rain that falls on Kauai comes down on high ground in the eastern part of the island. Here, there is a rain forest. The trees are close to each other and very tall. Moss grows on the trunks of the trees. Leafy plants cover the ground. Fog often hangs over the forest.

Forests In Hawaii   Years ago, Hawaii had large forests. In these forests were many **sandalwood** trees. Sandalwood is a fragrant, oily wood used for carving ornaments and decorations. Much of this wood was sold in China, where it was highly prized. The sale of sandalwood caused many forests to be destroyed. Other forests on the islands were cut to make room for farmland.

Hawaii still has several tropical forests. They are located below the mountain peaks of the five largest islands. Even outside large cities like

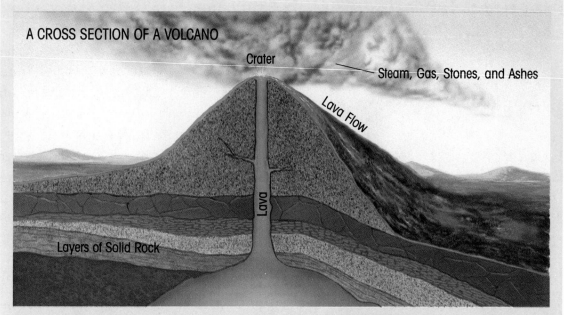

A CROSS SECTION OF A VOLCANO

Crater

Steam, Gas, Stones, and Ashes

Lava Flow

Lava

Layers of Solid Rock

This diagram explains how a volcano erupts. Lava, or melted rock, is forced through a vent at the top of the volcano.
■ What else, besides lava, is forced out of a volcano?

Honolulu, one can find some thick, beautiful forests.

The few remaining tropical forests are valued for their beauty. These forests are in two national parks. They are the home of rare birds and plants that are found almost nowhere else in the world.

Mountains and Volcanoes As mentioned earlier, the Hawaiian Islands were created millions of years ago by volcanoes. Today, you can still see the volcano craters on the mountain peaks. A crater looks like a huge bowl. It is through the center of this crater that the **lava** comes out. Lava is melted rock that is very hot. As it comes out of an active volcano, lava flows down the sides of the mountains and burns everything in its way.

When the lava cools off, it turns into rocks and soil. Years later, plants can grow on ground covered with hardened lava.

Most of the volcanoes in Hawaii are no longer active. But on the big island of Hawaii, there are two active volcanoes. Both volcanoes are in the Hawaii Volcanoes National Park. You can find this national park on the map on page 78.

CHECKUP

1. What is a volcano?
2. Explain why it rains more on the windward side of a mountain.
3. What is the wood from sandalwood trees used for?
4. **Thinking Critically** Summarize what you have learned about Hawaii's land and climate.

Living in Hawaii

How do people live and work in Hawaii?

VOCABULARY

sugarcane   plantation

Hawaiians Yesterday and Today

It is thought that the earliest settlers of Hawaii came from other islands in Polynesia (pol ə nē′ zhə) in big canoes about a thousand years ago. But it was not until 1778 that people in Europe and the United States found out about the islands. In that year an English sea captain named James Cook landed on the islands and found about 300,000 people living there.

Today about 1,083,000 people live in the state of Hawaii. They come from many different backgrounds. The Polynesians were followed by Chinese and Japanese. Many people from the United States mainland have made their homes in Hawaii. People from many other countries have also made their homes in Hawaii. The people of all these different backgrounds are proud of the way they live and work together in their state.

More than three fourths of the people of Hawaii live in and around the city of Honolulu on the island of Oahu (ə wä′ hü). As you know, Honolulu is Hawaii's capital. Many people in Honolulu work in the tourist industry. Many others have jobs on army, navy, and air force bases not far from Honolulu.

Life Outside the City

Away from Honolulu, there are many small rural villages. One such village is Hana, on the eastern part of the island of Maui (mou′ ē). Look at the map on page 78 to find this island. Like many other villages in Hawaii, Hana is on the coast. A sandy beach protects the village from big waves. Behind the beach are the slopes of steep mountains covered with thick tropical forests. In earlier times the people of Hana made a living by fishing in the ocean and hunting in the forest. Some of the people still live that way. Others work at farming or in the tourist industry.

These Hawaiian children are learning about their state.
■ In what ways is their classroom like your classroom?

The people of Hawaii are very friendly. In villages like Hana, they enjoy having visitors at their festivals. At such times the village people take part in sports and games. One of the high points is the roasting of a wild pig. The pig is killed and covered with leaves. It then is buried among hot rocks. The next day, everyone feasts on the delicious meat.

Today many village people fear that their quiet way of life may be in danger. They see more hotels being built on the beaches. They see the

Honolulu's Waikiki Beach, with its modern hotels, attracts many tourists. ■ What kind of boats do you see?

spreading cities, such as Honolulu. Hawaii's government says that it will not let the old ways die out. It has taken steps to protect the land and the remaining forests.

Sugarcane Farming   Fifty years ago, about half of Hawaii's people worked on farms. Not nearly that many work on farms today. Yet certain kinds of farming are still very important.

Sugarcane is an important crop. It is the plant from which we get sugar. Sugarcane is grown on **plantations**. These are large farms that usually raise only one kind of crop.

To plant a cane field, the workers cut small pieces of sugarcane and put them in the ground. The pieces then take root. In a year or two, the plants are 15 feet (4 1/2 m) high and ready for harvest.

The first step in harvesting is to set the cane fields on fire. The fire burns the leaves from the main stem of the cane. Workers then cut the cane and load it on trucks bound for the sugar mill.

At the mill the sugarcane is washed, cut into small pieces, and crushed. The juice that is squeezed out is heated to remove water.

After a number of other steps, sugar is produced. At this point it is a yellowish-brown color. It has to be treated further before it becomes the white food that we use to sweeten things.

HOW SUGAR IS MADE

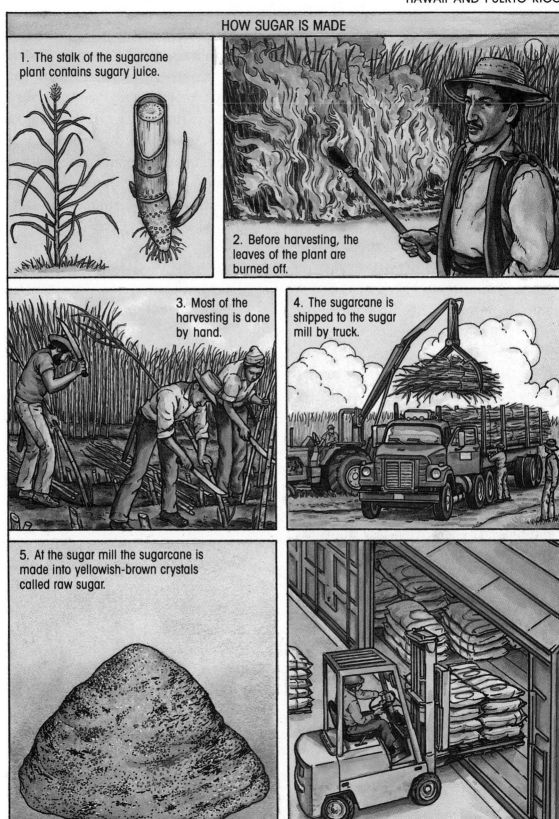

1. The stalk of the sugarcane plant contains sugary juice.

2. Before harvesting, the leaves of the plant are burned off.

3. Most of the harvesting is done by hand.

4. The sugarcane is shipped to the sugar mill by truck.

5. At the sugar mill the sugarcane is made into yellowish-brown crystals called raw sugar.

6. The raw sugar is shipped to be sold or to be made into white sugar.

Growing Pineapples The next time your family uses a can of pineapple, take a close look at the label. The pineapple probably came from Hawaii. It may have been grown on the island of Lanai (lə nī′). This island is called the Pineapple Island. The island is owned by a company that produces pineapples. To find Lanai, look at the map on page 78.

On top of each pineapple fruit is a bunch of small leaves called the crown. When the crown is placed in the soil, it grows into a new plant. It takes from 14 to 20 months for a new plant to bear fruit. Most pineapple plants weigh between 4 and 8 pounds (2 and 4 kg).

Pineapples are usually harvested by hand. After the fruit is picked, new sprouts grow from the bottom of the plants. They then bear a second crop of fruit. A third crop can be grown, but after that the fields are replanted.

Lanai is not the only island on which pineapples are grown. Several other islands of Hawaii also have pineapple plantations. Pineapple ranks next to sugarcane as Hawaii's most important crop.

Other farm products include coffee, rice, bananas, and vegetables. There are also cattle and dairy farms on the islands.

A Hawaiian Vacation Hawaii is a favorite vacation spot for tourists. Most tourists come to Hawaii by airplane from the United States mainland. Other visitors come from Japan. Hawaii's biggest industry is giving tourists the services they need. Many Hawaiians work in the hotels where visitors stay. Many others work in restaurants and shops. Most tourists come to Honolulu, on the island of Oahu, but many of them also visit other islands.

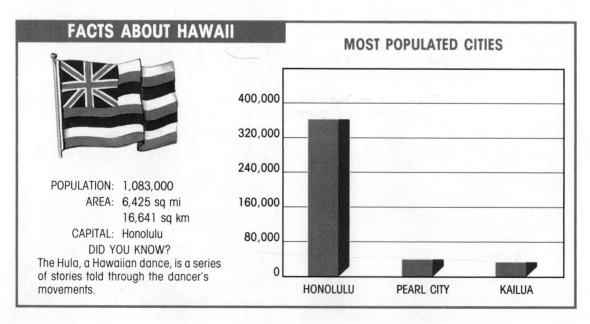

FACTS ABOUT HAWAII

POPULATION: 1,083,000
AREA: 6,425 sq mi
16,641 sq km
CAPITAL: Honolulu
DID YOU KNOW?
The Hula, a Hawaiian dance, is a series of stories told through the dancer's movements.

MOST POPULATED CITIES

400,000
320,000
240,000
160,000
80,000
0

HONOLULU   PEARL CITY   KAILUA

The History of Hawaii

On January 18, 1778, Captain James Cook of the British navy landed on one of the Hawaiian Islands. It was from Captain Cook's landing that the world found out about this beautiful land. At the time of Cook's landing, Polynesians lived on the island. After Cook returned to England, other traders and settlers from Europe traveled to Hawaii.

For many years each of the islands had its own government. Then, in 1810 a king of one of the Hawaiian Islands became ruler of all the islands. That is how Hawaii was ruled for the next 90 years. By 1820 many countries, including the United States, opened up trade with Hawaii. Hawaii's sugar and pineapple industries were started at that time.

In 1893 some of the Americans living in Hawaii organized a revolt against the Hawaiian government. As a result a new government was formed.

It wanted Hawaii to become part of the United States. That happened in 1900, when Hawaii became a territory of the United States.

The Hawaiian Islands became very important to the United States. Many ships and planes stopped there while crossing the Pacific Ocean. Also, United States military bases were set up on Hawaii. It was the United States naval base at Pearl Harbor, Hawaii, that was attacked by Japan on December 7, 1941. This attack forced the United States to enter World War II.

On August 21, 1959, Hawaii became the fiftieth state in the United States. Since becoming a state, Hawaii has continued to grow. Honolulu is a major trading center. United States military bases are still located on the islands. Hawaiian sugar and pineapple are still important crops. More and more tourists are continuing to discover the beauty of Hawaii.

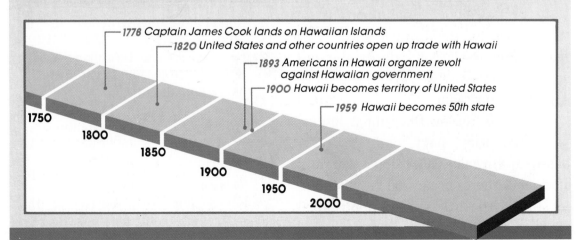

1778 Captain James Cook lands on Hawaiian Islands
1820 United States and other countries open up trade with Hawaii
1893 Americans in Hawaii organize revolt against Hawaiian government
1900 Hawaii becomes territory of United States
1959 Hawaii becomes 50th state

1750 1800 1850 1900 1950 2000

The U.S.S. *Arizona* Memorial at Pearl Harbor, Hawaii, honors those who died in the Japanese attack there on December 7, 1941.
■ Do you see the outline of the ship that is partly below water?

Protecting Our Country The state of Hawaii is very important to the defense of the United States. Far out in the Pacific, it guards the air and sea lanes that lead to North America from Asia.

For this reason the United States has large army, navy, and air force bases in Hawaii. The troops that are stationed there bring much business to stores. The bases also supply jobs for many of Hawaii's people.

CHECKUP

1. About how many people live in Hawaii today?
2. How is life in Hawaiian villages different from life in a large city like Honolulu?
3. What two important crops are grown on Hawaiian plantations?
4. Why is Hawaii important to the defense of the United States?
5. **Thinking Critically** What kind of job dealing with tourism in Hawaii would you like to have?

The Land and People of Puerto Rico

What is it like to live in Puerto Rico?

An Island in the Atlantic   In some ways, Puerto Rico is like Hawaii. Each is about the same distance from the Equator. Trade winds from the oceans blow across both. Many of the kinds of plants and trees that are found in Hawaii also grow in Puerto Rico.

There are differences, too. Hawaii and Puerto Rico are far apart, in different oceans. As you know, Hawaii is in the Pacific Ocean. Puerto Rico is in the Atlantic Ocean. Hawaii is one of our 50 states. Puerto Rico is not a state. But Puerto Rico has many of the same laws that we have. Puerto Ricans also are American citizens. If Puerto Ricans wish to, they might someday ask to have their island become the fifty-first state.

Puerto Rico's Location   Look at the map on page 350. You will see that Puerto Rico is one of the islands of the West Indies. It is about 1,000 miles (1,600 km) from Florida. Puerto Rico's southern coast is on the Caribbean (kar ə bē′ ən) Sea. This sea is part of the Atlantic Ocean.

Many people who go to Puerto Rico fly from Miami in southern Florida. If you draw an imaginary line between Miami and Puerto Rico, the line will go alongside the islands of Cuba and Hispaniola. (See the lower map on page 350.) These islands and Puerto Rico are in a line. They are the peaks of a huge mountain range rising from beneath the sea.

Puerto Rico is about 100 miles (160 km) long and 35 miles (56 km) wide. A line of hills rising to mountains runs from east to west along the center of Puerto Rico. The land is low along the coast of the island. That is where most of Puerto Rico's cities are. The largest city is San Juan (san wän′), the capital.

This waterfall is located in a rain forest in Puerto Rico.
■ **Have you ever seen a waterfall?**

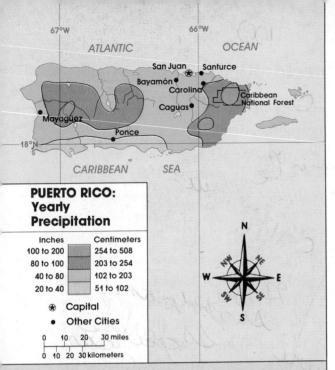

Some parts of Puerto Rico receive much more rain than do other parts of the island.
■ **How much yearly precipitation does the Caribbean National Forest get?**

A Large Rain Forest Driving south from San Juan, one soon comes to the Caribbean National Forest. Visitors to this large rain forest can get a good idea of what much of Puerto Rico looked like years ago. Here, trees grow close together and are hung with vines. Beneath them are smaller trees and bushes. Ferns sometimes grow 30 feet (9 m) high. Parrots and other birds fly from tree to tree. Tree frogs chirp. On the damp forest floor is a tangle of mosses and ferns. Have you ever seen **orchids** (ôr′ kidz), perhaps in a flower shop? These beautiful flowers grow wild in the rain forest.

Do you remember why there are tropical forests in Hawaii? They grow in Puerto Rico for the same reason. The climate is mild. The temperature

changes very little between summer and winter. It averages about 76° F (24° C). Trade winds from the Atlantic dump their moisture as they rise over the central highlands. Rainfall varies, but in the Caribbean National Forest it totals about 180 inches (450 cm) a year.

Fighting Erosion Until about 100 years ago, most of Puerto Rico was covered with thick tropical forests. At that time, only about 75,000 people lived on the island. Then the population began to grow. People cleared the forests to make room for farms. They used the timber for buildings. In time the great forests that once covered the island were almost destroyed.

Cutting the forests created a problem. At times it rains very hard in Puerto Rico. When it does, streams

Parrots are brightly colored birds.
■ **What color shows most on this bird?**

88

After a mud slide in 1985 near the city of Ponce, Puerto Rico, the mud covered homes and killed hundreds of people.
■ What can cause a mud slide?

of water run down the hills and mountain slopes. Without trees to keep the soil in place, the water washes the soil away. This is called **erosion** (i rō′ zhən). When the soil is washed away, the land is not good for growing crops.

Sometimes during a period of heavy rain, the soil will wash away very quickly. This is called a mud slide. Mud slides can be very dangerous. Houses can be covered with mud and destroyed. People can get hurt or killed if they are not warned soon enough about a mud slide. In October 1985 the area around the city of Ponce (pôn′ sā), Puerto Rico, was hit with a very serious mud slide. In a period of only two days, about 15 inches (38 cm) of rain fell. This large amount of rain caused mud slides that covered many homes and killed hundreds of people.

To stop erosion the government has had millions of new trees planted. As the roots grow, they absorb water and hold the soil in place. But stopping erosion is not easy. It takes a long time to raise a new forest.

A Large Population Puerto Rico is a very crowded island. More than 3 million people live there today. Most of them are of Spanish background. There are also many people of African and mixed backgrounds. Spanish is the language of most of the people of Puerto Rico.

For many years, almost all Puerto Ricans made a living by working the land. They had small plots and farmed with hand tools. They could not raise much. Most farm families were very poor.

As the population grew, life became even harder. There was not enough farmland for everyone to make a living. So the government set out to bring new industries to Puerto Rico. At the same time, farmers were taught to make better use of the land.

Farming in Puerto Rico Sugarcane has long been the most important crop in Puerto Rico. As in Hawaii, it is grown mostly on big plantations.

A lot of water is needed to make sugarcane grow. The northern part of Puerto Rico gets plenty of rain, but the southern part does not. In the south the plantation owners have built canals and pipelines to bring water to the fields. This is called **irrigation**.

The planting and harvesting of sugarcane are done in much the same way as in Hawaii. Many people work in the cane fields. Much of the cane is grown on hilly land and must be cut with hand tools. It is then taken to the sugar mill for processing.

Coffee beans, tobacco, bananas, pineapples, and a variety of vegetables are also grown in Puerto Rico. But not enough is produced to feed the large population of the island. Most fruits and vegetables have to be brought into the island from the mainland United States.

Industry in Puerto Rico Farming is not as important as it used to be in Puerto Rico. Over the past 40 years, the government has built up manufacturing. Many different products are made in the factories. Among these products are clothing, shoes, machinery, paint, chemicals, and

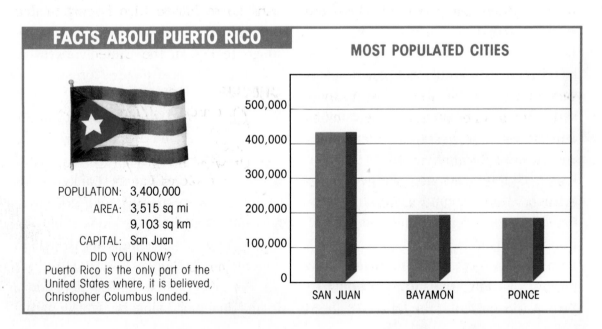

FACTS ABOUT PUERTO RICO

POPULATION: 3,400,000
AREA: 3,515 sq mi
9,103 sq km
CAPITAL: San Juan
DID YOU KNOW?
Puerto Rico is the only part of the United States where, it is believed, Christopher Columbus landed.

MOST POPULATED CITIES

	SAN JUAN	BAYAMÓN	PONCE
Population	~425,000	~190,000	~185,000

Over one million people visit the island of Puerto Rico each year.
■ **Which water shown is coastal water?**

medicines. In fact, so many medicines are made in Puerto Rico that it is sometimes called the Pill Capital of the World.

As in Hawaii, tourism is a major industry in Puerto Rico. The mild climate, sandy beaches, and friendly people attract many visitors. There are some beautiful hotels near the beaches.

The capital city of San Juan is one of the places that most tourists visit. It is one of the oldest cities started by Europeans in the Americas. It was founded in 1521, long before the first European settlements in what is now the mainland of the United States.

A Bright Future Many Puerto Ricans are better off than they were 50 years ago. However, it is still hard for some to make a good living. There are not enough jobs for the number of people living on the island. To seek a better life, many Puerto Ricans have moved to the mainland United States. Large numbers live in New York City, Chicago, and Miami. In Puerto Rican neighborhoods in these cities, one can hear Spanish spoken on the streets. The signs in the stores are printed in Spanish, and one can hear Spanish music.

The Puerto Rican government is trying to make life better for its people. One thing shows that it is having some success. Many Puerto Ricans who left their island are moving back. In recent years, more people have been returning to Puerto Rico than have been leaving this island in the West Indies.

People from Cuba and other neighboring island nations are also moving into Puerto Rico. Many Cubans go to Puerto Rico hoping to find a better life or hoping for a chance to go to live in the United States.

CHECKUP

1. What are the differences and similarities between Hawaii and Puerto Rico?
2. Of what background are most of the people of Puerto Rico?
3. What is Puerto Rico's most important crop?

4. **Thinking Critically** What kinds of jobs in Puerto Rico depend on the land and climate of the island?

Understanding a Legend

STORIES HANDED DOWN

Do you know what a legend is? It is a story handed down through the years. It may or may not be true. Sometimes these old stories tried to explain things that people did not understand.

An old Hawaiian legend tried to explain why summer days in Hawaii are longer than winter days. According to the legend, it was not always like this. All days used to be alike and all were short. The legend explains why summer days are longer.

AN OLD HAWAIIAN LEGEND

A Hawaiian boy named Ma-ui noticed how fast the sun moved and how short the days were in winter. He asked his grandmother what he could do about it.

Grandmother told Ma-ui to get 16 ropes, the strongest ever made, and make a trap for the sun. Ma-ui set out the ropes and watched as the first ray of light, the first leg of the sun, came over the mountain. It was caught in one of the ropes. Then the other rays of light came. These were the other legs of the sun. All were caught.

Soon there was a big fight between the sun and Ma-ui. The heat of the sun was terrible. But Ma-ui fought the sun with a magic stone ax. Finally the sun gave up and agreed to do whatever Ma-ui wanted.

Ma-ui said that the sun must not hurry across the sky so fast. The sun promised to move slowly for 6 months of the year. The days would be longer. People would have more time for fishing and farming.

It was also agreed that the sun could travel just as fast as ever during the other 6 months of the year. During that time, of course, the days would still be short. After these agreements had been reached, Ma-ui let the sun go free.

SKILLS PRACTICE

Ever since that time, the legend says, summer days in Hawaii have been longer than winter days. Now complete the following activity.

1. What would be a good title for this legend?
2. Did Ma-ui want to make the days longer or shorter? Why?
3. How did he trap the sun?
4. In the big fight, what was the sun's weapon? What was Ma-ui's weapon? Who won the fight?
5. What agreement did Ma-ui and the sun make?
6. We said earlier that a legend may or may not be true. Do you think this legend is true?

Take a sheet of paper and answer question 6 in a paragraph. Before you write your answer, you may want to look back at the diagram on page 38. Can you find there a different reason why days differ in length between summer and winter?

CHAPTER 4 REVIEW

MAIN IDEAS

1. Tropical forests grow near the Equator.
2. Tropical forests receive a lot of rain, are covered with broadleaf evergreen trees, and the air is very humid.
3. Hawaii's climate changes very little between summer and winter. It is mild and comfortable all year round.
4. Hawaii is made up of a chain of islands in the Pacific Ocean. Forests and mountains are found on the islands.
5. Many Hawaiians work on sugar and pineapple plantations, in the tourist industry, or on United States military bases.
6. Most Hawaiians live in or around the city of Honolulu. But there are some Hawaiians that remain living in small rural villages.
7. The land of Puerto Rico was at one time covered with large tropical forests. Most of these forests have since been cleared to make way for farmlands and buildings.
8. Some Puerto Ricans still work on sugarcane plantations or in sugar mills. But today most Puerto Ricans work in factories.

VOCABULARY REVIEW

Match these terms with the definitions. Use a separate sheet of paper.

a.	canopy	f.	sugarcane
b.	irrigation	g.	erosion
c.	creepers	h.	plantation
d.	humid	i.	volcano
e.	tropics	j.	trade winds

1. The washing away of soil
2. Bringing water to farm fields
3. The top of a tropical forest
4. Very damp
5. An opening in the earth from which gases and melted rock pour out from time to time
6. Ocean winds that usually blow toward the Equator
7. Vines hanging down from trees
8. The region near the Equator
9. The plant from which we get sugar
10. A large farm that usually raises only one kind of crop

CHAPTER CHECKUP

1. What is our newest state?
2. Where are the tropics located?
3. What is Hawaii's largest industry?
4. What city is Puerto Rico's capital?
5. How is sugar produced in Hawaii and Puerto Rico?
6. **Thinking Critically** Would you like to live in a tropical forest?
7. **Thinking Critically** Compare and contrast Hawaii and Puerto Rico.

APPLYING KNOWLEDGE

1. Imagine that you are a piece of sugarcane about to be planted. Write a descriptive paragraph explaining the steps that will lead to your becoming the refined sugar that we use to sweeten things.
2. Prepare a chart of similarities and differences between Hawaii and Puerto Rico. On the chart, list the following categories: location, climate, forests, farming, and industry. Then provide information on each category for both Hawaii and Puerto Rico.

5 The Soviet Union and the Amazon Basin

Forests In the Soviet Union

What are some important physical features of the Soviet Union?

VOCABULARY

ethnic group

The World's Largest Country   The full name of the Soviet Union is the Union of Soviet Socialist Republics. It is also called Russia. The Soviet Union is the largest country in the world. From east to west the Soviet Union is about 6,000 miles (9,600 km) wide. All of the land in the countries of the United States, Canada, and Mexico could easily fit inside the borders of the Soviet Union.

The Soviet Union stretches across two continents. Part of this country is in Europe, and part is in Asia. Find the Ural (yur′ əl) Mountains on the map on page 362. The Urals form part

of the boundary between the continents of Europe and Asia. The Ural Mountains are not high mountains. Another mountain range also forms a part of the boundary between the two continents. These mountains are called the Caucasus (kô′ kə ses) Mountains. They are located between the Black and Caspian seas. The Caucasuses are much higher mountains than the Urals. Can you find the Caucasus Mountains on the map on page 362?

There are other mountains in the southern and eastern parts of the Soviet Union. But much of the country is quite flat. Some of the level lands are on plateaus. If you do not remember what a plateau is, look back at page 37.

The Tundra   The Soviet Union is farther north than almost all of the United States. In the far north is the tundra. Only mosses, grasses, and other small plants grow in this cold region, where there is snow for more than half of the year.

During the short summers, geese nest on the tundra. Reindeer graze there, and seals sun themselves on rocks along the coast. But very few people live so far north.

South of the tundra a large area of forests runs from east to west across the Soviet Union. The northern part of this forest belt is made up of spruce, fir, and other coniferous trees. Farther south, broadleaf trees grow. Most of the forests are east of

Fast trains, such as this Trans-Siberian Express, carry passengers throughout the Soviet Union, the largest country in the world.
■ Why, do you think, are trains important in the Soviet Union?

the Ural Mountains, in a region called Siberia (sī bir′ ē ə).

Also located in Siberia is the world's deepest lake. From the surface to the lake floor, Lake Baikal (bī kal′) measures more than 1 mile (1.6 km) at its deepest point. Lake Baikal holds one fifth of the world's fresh water. Many forms of animal life that are found in Lake Baikal are found nowhere else in the world. For example, do you know what a nerpa (nėr′ pə) is? It is a cute little seal with a silvery coat. Nerpas can only be found in Lake Baikal.

An Important Resource The forests are one of the Soviet Union's most important resources. Over the years the forests have supplied a great deal of timber. Until recent times, almost all of the buildings in the Soviet Union were made of wood. People used wood as fuel for heating their houses and for cooking. Yet, today, there are still great forests that have hardly been touched.

One reason there are so many untouched forests is that it is hard to move the timber after it is cut. In most wooded areas of the Soviet Union there are no railways and few roads. In such places, lumbering is usually done in the winter. Then, tractors can pull sleds of logs over snow-covered trails. The logs may be piled on a riverbank. After the ice melts, the logs are pushed into the river and are floated to a sawmill. There they are cut into lumber.

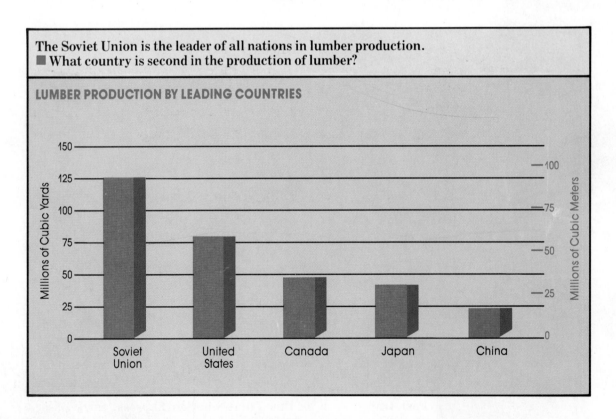

The Soviet Union is the leader of all nations in lumber production.
■ What country is second in the production of lumber?

LUMBER PRODUCTION BY LEADING COUNTRIES

Millions of Cubic Yards
150
125
100
75
50
25
0

Millions of Cubic Meters
100
75
50
25
0

Soviet Union   United States   Canada   Japan   China

Helicopters are sometimes used in logging operations. This pine forest is located in Siberia, south of the tundra.
■ What is the wide snow-covered trail being used for?

The forests are important, too, for the fur-bearing animals that live in them. Among these animals are beaver, mink, fox, and ermine. In a country so far north, furs are used for making warm clothing.

The Soviet People   About 286 million people live in the Soviet Union. Only the countries of China and India have more people. Most of the Soviet people live west of the Ural Mountains, in the European part of the country.

The Soviet Union has many **ethnic groups.** An ethnic group is made up of people who share the same language and customs. There are more than 90 different ethnic groups in the Soviet Union. Many different languages are spoken. However, Russian is the official language for the whole country.

CHECKUP

1. From east to west, about how many miles does the Soviet Union cover?
2. What is the name of the world's deepest lake?
3. Why are so many of the Soviet Union's forests still untouched?
4. **Thinking Critically** Write one sentence that best summarizes the land in the Soviet Union.

97

Living In the Soviet Union

What is life like in the Soviet Union?

VOCABULARY

ruling class   Communist

peasant   communism

A Divided Country   About 70 years ago the people in Russia were divided into two classes — the **ruling class** and the **peasants.** The people in the ruling class ran the country. They were educated and lived in the cities or in large country homes. The peasants lived in the villages and worked on the farms. These people had no education. The ruling class lived well, but the peasants were usually very poor.

In 1917 a new government was formed in Russia by a group of people known today as **Communists**. The Communists wanted common ownership of land and industry by all the people. It was the Communists who changed Russia's name to the Union of Soviet Socialist Republics. The ideas of the Communists became known as **communism**. Today the Communists still control the Soviet government. Although they have not succeeded in making all people equal, they did put an end to the country's severe problem with poverty.

Life in the Soviet Union   In the Soviet Union an individual's needs are not as important as the needs of the country as a whole. Factories in the Soviet Union do not produce enough goods for the people. Items like refrigerators, stoves, and television sets are expensive and hard to find. Few

There are not enough refrigerators and televisions to meet the needs of the Soviet people.
■ About how many televisions were in the Soviet Union in 1980?

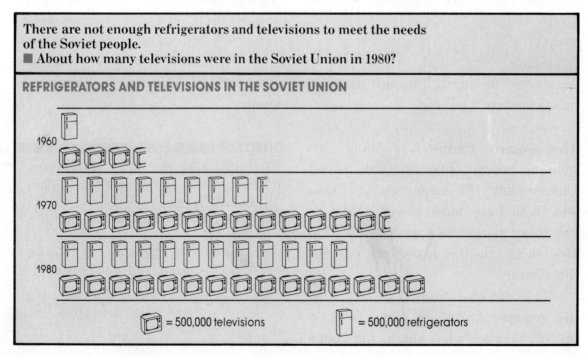

REFRIGERATORS AND TELEVISIONS IN THE SOVIET UNION

1960

1970

1980

= 500,000 televisions   = 500,000 refrigerators

Living in Moscow

Viktor Korenko and his sister Natasha are 10-year-old twins who live in Moscow. Moscow is the capital and the largest city of the Soviet Union. The twins' father is a mechanic. The mother of the twins is a postal worker who delivers mail in one of the city's neighborhoods.

Like other Russian children, Viktor and Natasha began school at the age of 7. They are now in the fourth grade. They go to school every day of the week except Sunday.

Like their classmates, Viktor and Natasha are expected to wear uniforms. Viktor wears grey pants, a grey jacket, and a white shirt. Natasha wears a brown dress with long sleeves, white cuffs, and a white collar. Over her dress, she wears a black apron with pockets. Both Viktor and Natasha wear a red scarf around the neck. The red scarf shows that they are members of the Young Pioneers. This group teaches young people in the Soviet Union about communism.

This year, as fourth graders, Viktor and Natasha have two new subjects to study—Soviet history and nature. Their other subjects include arithmetic, language, music, and art. Next year, in the fifth grade, they will start learning a foreign language, very likely, English. Viktor and Natasha are graded every day in their classwork. The top grade is 5, which is equal to A in American schools.

What does the future hold for Viktor and Natasha? Viktor says he wants to be a railroad engineer. Natasha would like to be a policewoman. If they are to succeed, they know they must work hard in school. At the end of the eighth grade, all Soviet pupils must take a test that covers all that they have learned. For most students, this test will determine the type of job they will prepare for. If Viktor and Natasha do well on the test, they may be on the way to meeting their goals.

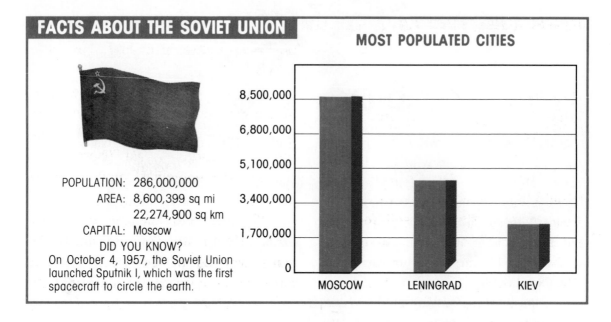

FACTS ABOUT THE SOVIET UNION

MOST POPULATED CITIES

POPULATION: 286,000,000
AREA: 8,600,399 sq mi
22,274,900 sq km
CAPITAL: Moscow
DID YOU KNOW?
On October 4, 1957, the Soviet Union launched Sputnik I, which was the first spacecraft to circle the earth.

people can afford private cars. Sometimes it is even difficult to find enough clothes, shoes, and food.

Government Controls Soviet people are expected to act in a certain way. Government leaders feel they know what is best for the people of their country. There are many ways in which the government lets the people know what is expected of them. A person from the government is always at every place of work. Another government official is at the apartment buildings in which people live. Quite regularly, people meet together at work and in their apartment buildings to hear about the government's plans and wishes. The people who do not agree with the government are watched very closely. They cannot get good jobs, and their children might never be allowed to get a good education.

A person living in the Soviet Union cannot leave the country without the government's permission. Soviet people even need permission to go from one city to another inside their own country.

For a long time the Soviet government did not allow the people to practice any religion. All places of worship were closed. Many Soviet people did not like this and continued, often secretly, to worship. Religion is now allowed, but it is still discouraged by the government.

CHECKUP

1. What is *communism*?
2. Have the Communists succeeded in making all the Soviet people equal?
3. Make a list of the ways in which the government in the Soviet Union controls the lives of its people.
4. **Thinking Critically** How would your life be different if you lived in the Soviet Union?

Farms and Factories In the Soviet Union

How are farms and factories run in the Soviet Union?

Soviet Farms   Most of the Soviet Union's farmlands lie south of the forest regions. The best soil for raising crops is in the European part of the country. Here are the grassy plains called the **steppes** (steps). Just north of the Black Sea is the Ukraine (yü krān'). In the black soil of the Ukraine, crops grow well. In late summer, fields of ripening wheat stretch as far as the eye can see. Other crops include sugar beets and potatoes. Cattle and hogs are also raised.

In most places east of the Ural Mountains, crops do not grow very well. Because of the cold weather, the growing season is too short. Also, there is not enough rainfall for most crops.

Planting and harvesting in the Soviet Union are done in much the same way as in the United States. Farmers in both countries use tractors and other farm machinery.

Working on a Soviet Farm   In other ways, Soviet farms are much different from those in the United States. American farmers usually own the land they work on and the buildings and machinery they use. They decide what crops to plant and how many fields they will use for each crop. They can keep what they harvest or sell it to whomever they wish. The money they earn is theirs to spend as they see fit.

Things are different for farmers in the Soviet Union. There the government owns all of the farms. It owns all the trucks and tractors and other farm machinery. The large farms, known as state farms, are run by the government. State farms usually produce only one product, such as grain, vegetables, or milk. Workers are paid in money by the government. All of the crops are turned over to the government.

A sorting machine on a state farm helps to sort and store cotton.
■ **What is covering the cotton?**

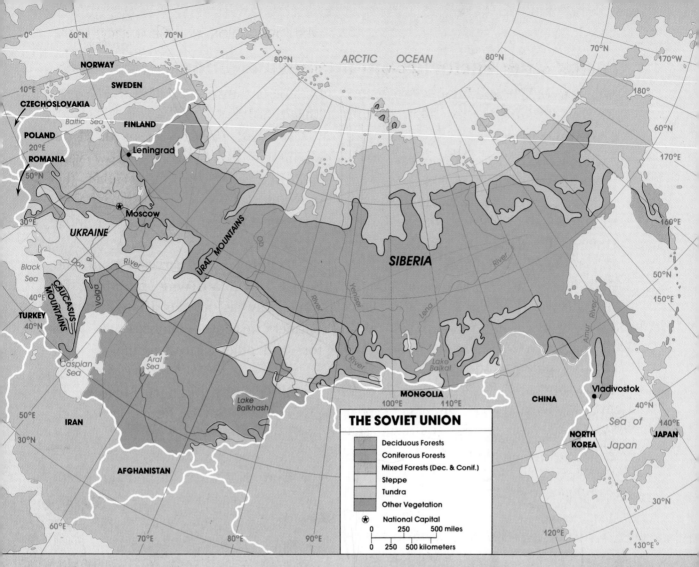

The Soviet Union, spreading over the continents of Asia and Europe, is the world's largest country in area.

■ Which countries share a border with the Soviet Union?

The smaller farms are called **collective farms**. Collective farms raise a variety of crops and livestock. The workers are paid partially in money and partially with a share of what they produce. Most of the crops and livestock raised on all Soviet farms belong to the government.

Every farm family can use a small piece of their land for their own purposes. Soviet farmers like to work on this land because whatever they produce is theirs to use or sell.

Very few Soviet farms grow as much as American farms grow on the same amount of land. Remember that in the Soviet Union the government gets most of the crops produced. Who gets the crops grown on farms in the United States? Does this help explain why Soviet farms do not produce as much as American farms do?

The amount of crops grown on Soviet farms is often not enough to feed the people of the country. Even with its big wheat fields, the Soviet Union often has to buy wheat from other countries.

Soviet Factories The Soviet Union has many factories that make use of the country's **minerals.** Minerals are valuable things obtained from the earth by mining. The Soviet Union has great supplies of coal and iron. Almost all the metals needed in manufacturing are mined in the Soviet Union. Among them are iron, lead, and zinc. There are many oil wells in the Ural Mountains, in the southern part of the Soviet Union, and in Siberia. The Soviet Union is the world's leading country in oil production.

Most large factory regions are near supplies of minerals. For example, there are about ten big industrial cities in the Ural Mountains. These industrial cities have steel mills and factories that make glass, chemicals, and machinery.

Close to Moscow there is another factory region. Moscow is the capital and largest city of the Soviet Union. The factory region around Moscow has the advantages of being able to use the city's railroad lines and of having a large number of people nearby to buy the products.

For many years, most Soviet factories turned out such products as steel, cement, and machinery. Few factories made everyday goods such as shoes, clothes, radios, and toasters. Now, more factories have started making these things.

The factories, like the farms, are owned and managed by the Soviet government. The government decides what goods a factory will make. The workers do not produce enough, and the quality of the products is poor. Also, the goods are hard to buy because they are only sold in stores run by the government.

Improving Transportation Getting from one point to another in the Soviet Union has never been easy. For one thing, the country is so big. For another, so much of it is covered with thick forests.

Radios are being tested in this electronics factory in Lithuania.
■ **Why are radios useful goods?**

Cargo is lined up on the dock of this Volga River port.
■ **What kinds of vehicles can you see?**

Rivers have always served as highways for traffic. Canals connect some of the major rivers, such as the Volga and the Don. But during the winter, most rivers and canals are frozen.

Soviet railway lines center on Moscow. There are many more lines to the west of the Ural Mountains than to the east. However, the longest railway line runs from Moscow to the Pacific coast. It takes about a week to make this trip of 5,600 miles (8,960 km) on the Trans-Siberian Railway.

The Soviet Union does not have nearly so many miles of first-class roads as the United States does. The fastest way to travel between Soviet cities is by air. The airline owned by the government flies to about 60 cities.

The Soviet government is now pushing new roads and railway lines into Siberia to build up that region. The government is encouraging young people to settle there. Despite its very cold climate, Siberia, with its great forests and mineral resources, is looked upon as the Soviet land of the future.

Almost all goods exchanged between the Soviet Union and other countries are transported by sea. In the warmer summer months, ships can use the ports along the coast of the Arctic Ocean. But these ports are frozen nearly 9 months of the year. In the Black and Baltic seas, there are some Soviet ports that remain ice-free almost all year round. These sea routes are an important part of the transportation system of the Soviet Union.

CHECKUP

1. What are the differences between state farms and collective farms?
2. How are farms in the Soviet Union run differently from those in the United States?
3. Why are factories in the Soviet Union found only in certain regions?
4. **Thinking Critically** Make a list of the changes that you would make to improve production on Soviet farms and in Soviet factories.

The Forest of the Amazon River Basin

What are the physical features and the resources of the forest in the Amazon Basin?

VOCABULARY

basin	cacao
jungle	ore
tributary	manganese
river mouth	bauxite

The Largest Tropical Forest   How would you like to go for a walk and come upon a snake 30 feet (9 m) long? Or, what would you do if, while sitting on your back porch, an insect 6 inches (15 cm) long came buzzing around you? These things could not happen anywhere in the United States. But they could happen if you lived in the tropical forest along the Amazon (am′ ə zon) River. Find the Amazon River on the map on page 106.

In Chapter 4 we learned about the forests of Hawaii and Puerto Rico. But no tropical forest can match the one in the **basin** of the Amazon River in South America. A basin is all the lands drained by a river. The land drained by the Amazon River is the largest tropical forest in the world.

You have probably heard about **jungles.** They are places where trees and plants grow in thick tangles in the tropics. Alligators, snakes, insects, and other animals live there. The great broadleaf evergreen forest along the Amazon River is a jungle.

The anaconda snake (inset) is the largest in South America. It lives in the tropical forest of the Amazon River basin.
■ Why does the water appear brown in color?

A Long and Mighty River   Look at the map of the Amazon Basin. You will see that the Amazon Basin stretches from the Atlantic Ocean in the east to the Andes (an′ dēz) Mountains in the west. Most of the Amazon Basin is in the country of Brazil. But as you can see on the map, the Amazon Basin reaches into other countries in South America. What are the names of these countries in South America?

The Amazon River starts high in the Andes Mountains. It flows almost 4,000 miles (6,400 km) to the Atlantic Ocean. This makes the Amazon River the world's second longest river. On the way it is joined by many **tributaries** — smaller rivers that run into a larger river. As it nears the ocean, the Amazon gets bigger and bigger. At the **river mouth** — the place where the river reaches the ocean — the Amazon is 60 miles (96 km) wide and 175 feet (52 m) deep. It carries more water than any other river in the world.

A Hot, Rainy Climate   Look again at the map on this page. As you can see, the Equator runs straight through the Amazon Basin. This means that

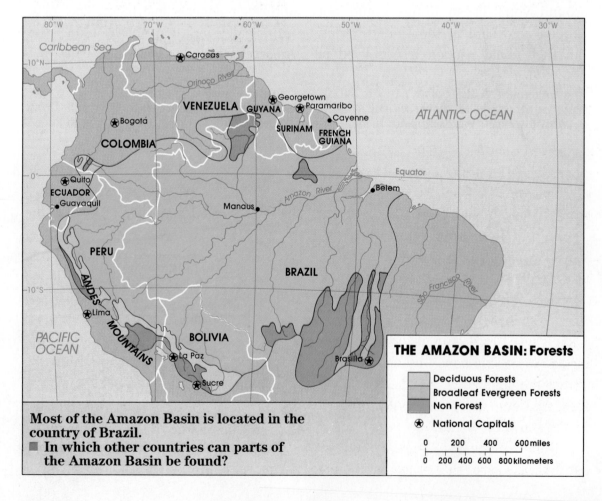

Most of the Amazon Basin is located in the country of Brazil.
■ In which other countries can parts of the Amazon Basin be found?

THE AMAZON BASIN: Forests

Deciduous Forests
Broadleaf Evergreen Forests
Non Forest
⊛ National Capitals

0   200   400   600 miles
0   200 400 600 800 kilometers

the sun at noon is almost straight overhead all year round. When the sun is straight above, the temperature is usually hot. This is the case along the Amazon River. The temperature changes very little from one month to another.

The Amazon Basin also has plenty of rain. Heat and rain make a humid climate. As we learned earlier, a hot and humid climate is perfect for trees and other plants. In fact there are more kinds of trees here than in any other forest in the world.

A Variety of Wildlife   The Amazon Basin has many kinds of wildlife, in the water and on land. Big alligators, electric eels, and piranhas (pə ran′ yəz) live in the rivers. The eels can stun a person with the force of their electric shock. The piranhas are fierce little fish with teeth as sharp as razor blades. These fish attack anyone who is so unwise as to bathe in or so unlucky as to fall into the water where the piranhas live.

In the forest there are such animals as deer, jaguars (jag′ wärz), anteaters, and wild hogs. Some are harmless, but others can be dangerous. For example there are vampire bats. These little animals feed on the blood of cattle and other animals. There are also many kinds of butterflies, spiders, ants, and other insects in the Amazon forest.

Some of the most interesting forest animals are the monkeys. Many

The jaguar is the largest wildcat of the Western Hemisphere.
■ **What is this jaguar's color?**

explorers of the Amazon forest have been awakened at dawn by the ear-splitting yell of the howler monkey. Another Amazon animal is the spider monkey. This skinny animal likes to hang by its tail from a limb while picking fruit or nuts. Have you ever seen howler or spider monkeys in a zoo?

Dangers of the Forest   Why has the Amazon forest never been fully explored? For one thing, it is hard to travel through this forest. Not only do trees and tangled vines block the way, but there are also many swamps near the rivers. Also, the damp heat of the forest is very uncomfortable.

The two cacao pods, about a foot long, are filled with seeds like those shown. ■ How are the seeds, or beans, used?

The forest can be dangerous, too, as you know from reading about some of the wildlife. More dangerous than the alligator or the jaguar, though, is the mosquito. This little insect is a carrier of disease in the tropics. Over the years, various diseases have killed many more people in the Amazon Basin than have snakes or other wild animals.

Natural Resources of the Amazon More and more people are going to the Amazon Basin, even with its dangers. They are drawn there by the promise of its wealth.

First on the list of natural resources is the huge forest. Up to now, lumbering has been carried out only in a small way, close to the rivers. Millions of acres of forest have hardly been touched.

Lumber is not the only thing of value in the forest. From the **cacao** (kə kā′ ō) tree come the seeds from which cocoa and chocolate are made. On another tree, Brazil nuts grow. Have you ever eaten Brazil nuts? The next time you go to a grocery store, look for these large nuts with dark brown shells. Still another tree gives forth sap that is made into rubber.

The Amazon Basin also has many mineral resources. Several **ores** — materials containing one or more minerals — are mined. Steel is made from iron ore. **Manganese** (mang′ gə nēz) and **bauxite** (bôk′ sīt) are found. Manganese is mixed with other metals to make them stronger. Bauxite is the ore from which aluminum is made. Aluminum is the light but strong metal used in making pots and pans, airplanes, boats, soda cans, and many other things. Oil, too, has been found in the Amazon Basin.

CHECKUP
1. Where is the Amazon Basin?
2. Why are many parts of the Amazon Basin still unexplored?
3. What are the natural resources of the Amazon forest?
4. **Thinking Critically** Write a brief description of what it would be like to live in the Amazon Basin.

The People of the Amazon Basin

What kinds of jobs do people have in the Amazon Basin?

Early Settlers   About 135 million people live in Brazil. The Amazon Basin covers almost half of this country. Yet only 4 out of every 100 of Brazil's people live in the Amazon Basin. More and more people are starting to go there, but it is still very thinly settled.

Indians were the first people to live in the Amazon Basin. The first European settlers came from the country of Portugal. People from other European countries followed. Today the population of the Amazon Basin is mixed. Near the mouth of the Amazon River are many black people and some Japanese people. Some Indians continue to live in the forest.

Manaus   A few cities have grown up in the Amazon Basin. One is Manaus, about 900 miles (1,440 km) from the Atlantic Ocean. This river city was started as a fort in a clearing in the jungle. The story of the growth of Manaus is also the story of rubber.

The Indians of the Amazon Basin were the first people to use the sap of the rubber tree. They spread it on their feet and let it dry to make a waterproof covering. But not until about 125 years ago did rubber come into wide use.

At that time the Amazon forest was the only place where rubber trees grew. Workers were brought to Manaus to collect the sap from the trees. The milky white sap was dried over a smoky fire. Then the rubber was

Workers on rubber plantations cut the bark of the rubber trees to remove the sap.
■ What color is the sap that has collected in the pail?

carried by ship to factories in other countries.

Factories called for more and more rubber, and the city of Manaus grew. Homes were built for workers, and offices and storehouses were built for traders. Stores, schools, and churches were also built in Manaus. At the river's edge, bundles of rubber were loaded onto ships from great floating docks.

The price of rubber soon jumped from three cents a pound to three dollars a pound. Many traders became rich. But then the good times for the rubber traders came to an end.

An Englishman took seeds of the rubber tree and planted them in hothouses in England. The new little plants were carried to southern Asia. There the climate is much like that of the Amazon Basin. In only a few years, rubber plantations in Asia were turning out more rubber than Brazil. The Asian rubber was also lower in price. Rubber was no longer a big money-making crop in the Amazon forest. Many traders and workers left. Manaus stopped growing.

A New Way to Make Rubber
Something happened later that further hurt the Amazon rubber business. As you know, rubber in Brazil is made from the sap of the rubber tree. This is called **natural rubber.** Some years ago, a way was found to make rubber from oil and chemicals. This is called **synthetic** (sin thet′ ik)

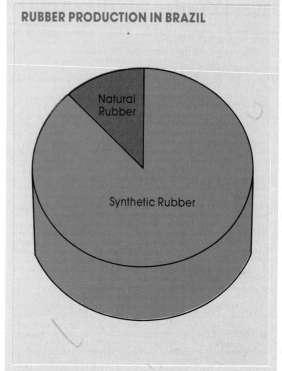

RUBBER PRODUCTION IN BRAZIL

Natural Rubber

Synthetic Rubber

About 87% of the rubber made in Brazil is synthetic rubber.
■ About what percentage is natural rubber?

rubber. Today about two thirds of the rubber produced in the world is synthetic rubber.

Some rubber still comes from the Amazon Basin. But it is not enough to fill Brazil's needs. Manaus is still a trading center. But it has had to turn to other things. Besides rubber, the main articles of trade are lumber, dried fish, Brazil nuts, animal skins, and cacao. A few people make a living catching wild animals and birds to sell to zoos.

Life in a Village   Here and there along the rivers of the Amazon Basin are small villages. The soil there is not very good for crops, but the villagers

110

This floating market in Brazil has fruit for sale.
■ What kinds of fruit can you find?

The Indians today live in the same way that their people have lived for years. Those who are related to each other live together. They form a group known as a **clan.** Each clan lives in a separate village, in huts made of wood and other forest materials. Since it is warm in the forest, the Indians wear little clothing.

Each morning the men leave their village to hunt for food, usually game or fruit. If they do not need food, they may look for colorful feathers. The Indians use these to decorate themselves.

The women stay at home and care for the family. They cook and

raise a few vegetables. They also fish in the rivers. In the forest they collect nuts and hunt animals. The skins of the animals are valuable.

Every few days, village people load their small boats with vegetables, nuts, skins, and other things. They go to a nearby city, such as Manaus, to sell what they have. All boats gather in one place by the riverbank to make a floating market.

Indians of the Amazon Basin   No one knows how many Indians live in the forest. One guess is that there are about 100,000 Indians there. But they are so scattered that no one can really tell.

Some Indians of the Amazon River basin fish much like their ancestors did.
■ What kind of boat is this?

The new Trans-Amazon Highway cuts through the Amazon rain forest.
■ **How will this highway change Brazil?**

work in their small gardens. There they grow beans, corn, and a tropical plant called **cassava** (kə säv′ ə). The roots of this plant are used to make pudding and flour for bread. Have you ever eaten tapioca pudding? It is made from cassava roots.

After two or three seasons, the Indians leave their gardens and start new ones. They do this because the heavy rains wash away the topsoil. Plants do not grow well without topsoil.

From time to time the Indians move their villages. They move to get away from insects, rats, and other animals that live off waste. Whenever people live in groups, there is a lot of waste. The insects and animals that feed on it sometimes carry diseases. The Indians do not have sprays or other means to get rid of these harmful animals. So the Indians pick up their things, burn their houses, and go somewhere else in the forest to start a new village.

Preparing for the Future Great changes are taking place in the Amazon Basin. Today, it is much easier to go into the forest than it used to be. Airlines now fly into Manaus and other cities. Helicopters fly over the forest, exploring it from the air.

The forest still cannot be explored by car. But this will change, too. The government of Brazil is now building a highway that will cut across the jungle. This highway is called the Trans-Amazon Highway. Starting near Peru, it will go all the way to the Atlantic coast. The government hopes that this highway will bring tourists and new industries to the Amazon Basin. Can you guess what the Amazon forest might be like 50 or 100 years from now?

CHECKUP
1. What people live in the Amazon Basin?
2. How did Manaus become a big city?
3. What are some of the things that will bring changes to the Amazon Basin?
4. **Thinking Critically** How is life different in the cities and villages of the Amazon Basin?

Making a Retrieval Chart

WHAT IS A RETRIEVAL CHART?

In this chapter you read about the Soviet Union and the Amazon Basin. It may be hard for you to remember all the facts you read about in this chapter, but there are things you can do to help yourself remember.

1. You can organize facts.
2. You can compare the facts. A retrieval chart is a good way to organize facts. The chart helps you to retrieve, or recall, important information.

SKILLS PRACTICE

Copy one of these charts on a piece of paper. Fill in the boxes on the chart with facts. You might wish to add facts from other books, too.

FORESTS OF THE SOVIET UNION AND THE AMAZON BASIN		
	Soviet Union	Amazon Basin
Type of forest		
Location		
Products		

Now compare the facts on your chart to answer these questions:

1. What kind of forest is found in the Amazon Basin?
2. Where are most of the forests in the Soviet Union?
3. List the forest products for the Soviet Union and the Amazon Basin.
4. The forests of which area supply more products?

FARMING IN THE UNITED STATES AND THE SOVIET UNION		
	Land ownership	Selling the crops
United States		
Soviet Union		

Answer these questions by comparing the facts on the chart:

1. How do farms in the United States differ from farms in the Soviet Union?
2. In which country do the farmers have more freedom?
3. What happens to the crops harvested on American farms?
4. What happens to the crops harvested on Soviet farms?

MORE PRACTICE

Now you are ready to make your own chart. You may wish to make a retrieval chart before you read the next chapter. Look at the headings in the chapter to help you make your chart. Write questions and answers for your chart.

CHAPTER 5 REVIEW

MAIN IDEAS

1. The land of the Soviet Union is mostly flat, although there are some mountain ranges.
2. The Soviet Union's forests provide it with lumber, furs from animals, and other useful products.
3. In the Soviet Union the country's needs are more important than the needs of any one person.
4. The Soviet government has a great amount of control over the lives of the Soviet people.
5. The government owns and controls all farms and factories in the Soviet Union.
6. The forest of the Amazon Basin is the world's largest tropical forest.
7. The forest of the Amazon Basin is a thick jungle through which the Amazon River, the world's second longest river, flows.
8. The natural resources of the Amazon Basin include a variety of wildlife, forests, minerals, and oil.

VOCABULARY REVIEW

Match these terms with the definition. Use a separate sheet of paper.

    a. clan   **c.** jungle
    b. collective   **d.** communism
        farms   **e.** ethnic group

1. Common ownership of land and industry by all the people
2. Indians that are related to each other and live together
3. Place where trees and plants grow in thick tangles in the tropics
4. Farms in the Soviet Union that raise a variety of produce and livestock

5. A group of people who share the same language and customs

CHAPTER CHECKUP

1. Where is the forest belt in the Soviet Union located?
2. Besides timber, what else do the forests of the Soviet Union supply?
3. Where is the Soviet Union's best farmland?
4. In which South American country is most of the Amazon Basin found?
5. **Thinking Critically** Compare and contrast the forests of the Soviet Union with the forests of the Amazon Basin.
6. **Thinking Critically** Write a summary of what life is like in the Soviet Union, as if you were living there and writing a letter to a pen pal in the United States.

APPLYING KNOWLEDGE

Below are four important dates and events in the history of the Soviet Union. Using another resource on the history of the Soviet Union, match the correct date to the event. Then put all the information on a time line.

    1941   1917   1985   1957

United States President Ronald Reagan meets with Soviet leader to discuss world peace

German troops invade the Soviet Union during World War II

Soviets send into space the first spaceship to circle the earth

Communists take control of Russia

SUMMARIZING UNIT 2

REVIEWING VOCABULARY

1. natural resource Forests supply us with many natural resources. Can you name five natural resources that we get from forests?

2. lumber Trees that have been sawed into different forms of wood are called lumber. Which is the leading country in the world in lumber production?

3. rain forest Another name for a tropical forest is *rain forest* because so much rain falls there. Where is the world's largest rain forest?

4. mineral Minerals are valuable things obtained from the earth by mining. Why are minerals important to the factories in the Soviet Union?

5. jungle Jungles are places where trees and plants grow in thick tangles in the tropics. Which two places that you studied in this unit could not have jungles?

EXPRESSING YOURSELF

1. In your opinion In your opinion, is it right for the government of the Soviet Union to have so much control over the people of that country?

2. What would you recommend? Suppose that building the Trans-Alaska Pipeline was impossible. How else would you recommend getting oil from Prudhoe Bay to Valdez?

3. What if . . .? What if you were a native of Puerto Rico and you were given the choice of remaining on the island or moving to the United States. What would you decide to do?

4. In what ways . . .? In what ways do you think life will be different for the people of the Amazon Basin after the completion of the Trans-Amazon Highway?

5. You make the decision If you had lived in Hawaii in 1900, would you have wanted the islands to become part of the United States or to remain independent?

Desert Regions

What do you think of when you hear the word *desert*? Most of you will probably think of things like hot temperatures, little rainfall, sand, and bare earth. All of the above correctly describe some hot deserts. But did you know that there are some deserts that are very rocky and there are other deserts that have interesting animals and valuable minerals? This is because a desert is simply defined as a place with little rainfall and few plants.

Shown here are desert wildflowers growing in the Antelope Valley area of the Mojave Desert in southern California. ■ Why, do you think, is this land called the "Goldfields?"

This desert resort in Tucson, Arizona, provides fun and relaxation.
■ **Why would this be a good place to relax?**

Years ago very few people lived in deserts. Deserts were thought of as worthless pieces of land. But people have come to realize that this is not true. Many people now spend their vacations in resorts built in deserts. One such popular desert resort city in the United States is the city of Tucson, Arizona.

The city of Cairo is in the Sahara, a desert.
■ **Can you tell by looking at this photograph that the city is located in a desert?**

Large cities and towns have even been built in deserts. Look at the photograph to the left. It shows the city of Cairo. Cairo is found in a desert. It is also one of the largest cities in the world.

This desert land in Saudi Arabia receives very little rainfall.
■ What is being used to bring water to the fields?

Although many people live in cities found in deserts, life in a desert is not easy. Because of the lack of rainfall, it is very difficult to farm in a desert. Farmers in deserts have to dig long ditches or build pipelines to bring water from rivers and streams onto their farms. Often these rivers and streams are many miles away. Other people who live in deserts raise sheep, goats, and donkeys. These people move from place to place to find water and food for their animals. There are even some people living in deserts whose life-style is the same as that of people who lived many, many years ago. These people are called Bushmen. The Bushmen are found in the Kalahari Desert in Africa. Bushmen survive by hunting animals and gathering wild plants.

These Bushmen in the Kalahari Desert are hunting animals.
■ What kind of weapon are they using in the hunt?

Opals are mined in the Great Victorian Desert of Western Australia. The inset shows an opal gem.
■ Do you see the various colors in the stone?

Many deserts contain valuable natural resources. Large amounts of oil have been found in some deserts. Other valuable natural resources found in deserts include natural gas, copper, salt, limestone, uranium, and helium.

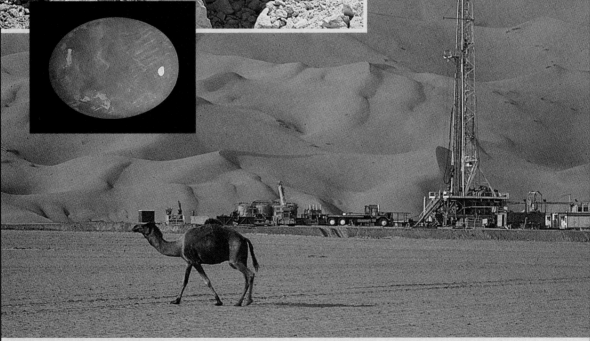

Oil, found beneath the Saudi Arabian deserts, provides most of Saudi Arabia's income.
■ What contrasts do the camel and the oil rig bring to your mind?

119

There are many deserts in the world. Look at the photograph to the right. It shows the Gobi Desert. The Gobi is a flat, dry desert located in northern China and southern Mongolia. Most of the people who live in the Gobi raise animals. The largest desert in the world is found in Africa. Its name is the Sahara. Deserts can also be found on the continent of Australia. Look on the map to find the names of the deserts found in Australia.

Raising animals is one of the main activities in the Gobi Desert. A long pole called an urga is being used to round up these horses.
■ About how long would you guess this pole to be?

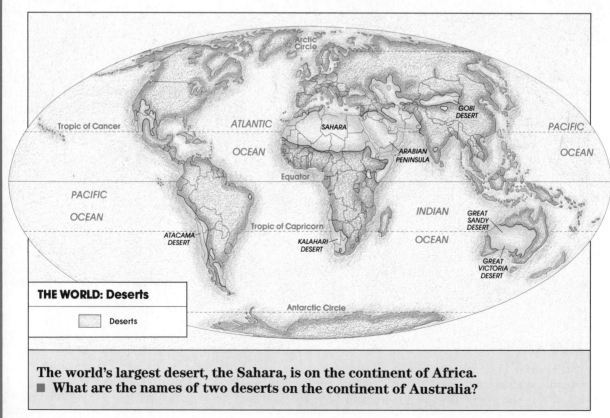

Arctic Circle

Tropic of Cancer

ATLANTIC

OCEAN

SAHARA

GOBI DESERT

PACIFIC

OCEAN

ARABIAN PENINSULA

Equator

PACIFIC

OCEAN

INDIAN

OCEAN

GREAT SANDY DESERT

ATACAMA DESERT

Tropic of Capricorn

KALAHARI DESERT

GREAT VICTORIA DESERT

THE WORLD: Deserts

Deserts

Antarctic Circle

The world's largest desert, the Sahara, is on the continent of Africa.
■ What are the names of two deserts on the continent of Australia?

Houses in villages of the Sahara usually have thick walls made of concrete or dried mud.
■ **Do you see in the foreground the remains of a house?**

The photograph above shows how some people live in the Sahara. Small settlements in the Sahara are found near water. Most have less than 2,000 people living in them. But other people move from place to place in the Sahara, in search of water and food. You will be learning more about the Sahara in Chapter 8.

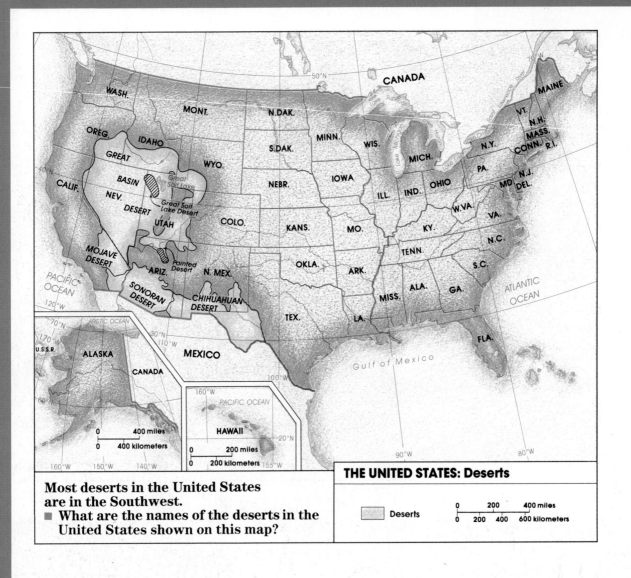

THE UNITED STATES: Deserts

Deserts

| 0 | 200 | 400 miles |
| 0 | 200 400 | 600 kilometers |

Most deserts in the United States are in the Southwest.
■ What are the names of the deserts in the United States shown on this map?

Deserts can even be found in the United States. The Mojave Desert in California contains the lowest point in the United States. It is called Death Valley. Two other North American deserts are found in both the United States and Mexico. These deserts are named the Sonoran (sə nōr′ ən) Desert and the Chihuahuan (chə wä′ wän) Desert.

Another desert region found in the United States is the Great Basin Desert. As with desert regions all over the world, deserts in the United States are both useful and interesting places.

One place that many people think of when United States deserts are mentioned is Monument Valley, shown to the right. Monument Valley is located in Arizona and Utah. It gets its name from the tall rocks that look like big monuments. The cactus plant, shown below, is found in many deserts in the United States. You will be learning more about Monument Valley and cactus plants in Chapter 6.

This view of Monument Valley is in northeastern Arizona. The red sandstone formations rise from the desert floor.
■ Which part of the rocks looks like a monument?

These catcus plants are growing in the Organ Pipe Cactus National Monument in southern Arizona.
■ How would you describe these plants?

6 Deserts of the United States

The Great Basin Desert

What physical features and resources are found in the Great Basin Desert?

VOCABULARY

desert	alfalfa
evaporate	Mormon
ranch	

Dry Land   Can you remember the last time that you had to change your plans because of rain? Maybe you were planning to have a picnic in the park, play baseball after school, or go on a Saturday afternoon bicycle ride. Having to change your plans probably upset you. Although we sometimes wish that it would not rain, we also understand how important rain is. Rain helps plants to grow and supplies us with drinking water. Some places get a lot of rain, whereas other areas get almost no rain at all. A place that gets very little rain is called a **desert**.

Canyonlands National Park is located in southwestern Utah.
■ Why, do you think, could this land be called a desert?

The air is dry over a desert. There are very few clouds. The sun shines almost all day. It is hot during the day but it cools off at night.

Rain does not often fall in the desert. When rain does fall, it comes down hard. The water flows in many directions. It forms small streams that run into larger streams. Every time it rains, the water cuts a deeper streambed. After thousands of years the beds of the larger streams become wide and deep with steep sides. They become canyons. In some deserts there are large canyons.

Not much water sinks beneath the ground when it rains. The heat of the desert makes the water **evaporate**. You know how water heated in a pan on a stove evaporates. It changes from a liquid to a gas that goes into the air. In the same way, much of the rain that falls in a desert evaporates in the heat of the sun.

On page 122 you learned the names of the deserts in the United States. Can you remember all their names? In this chapter you will be studying about four of these deserts. They are the Great Basin Desert, the Painted Desert, the Chihuahuan Desert, and the Sonoran Desert. We will begin by studying about the Great Basin Desert.

Our Country's Largest Desert
As you can see on the map on page 126, the Great Basin Desert is in parts

of the states of California, Nevada, Utah, Arizona, Colorado, Wyoming, New Mexico, Idaho, and Oregon. It is the largest desert in the United States. The Great Basin Desert lies between the Rocky Mountains to the east and the Cascade Range and the Sierra Nevada Mountains to the west. The desert is broken by many hills and mountain ridges. These hills and mountains run from north to south. Between these ridges are long stretches of rock and sand.

Much of the Great Basin Desert is very dry. The amount of rain and melted snow in the desert varies from 4 to 9 inches (10 to 22.5 cm) each year. The climate is cold in the winter and hot in the summer. Most of the rivers in the Great Basin Desert are small. The water in some of these small rivers slowly evaporates. Quite often the rivers disappear in the desert sands.

Open Spaces and Salt The most important natural resource in the area around and in the Great Basin Desert is the open spaces. People raise cattle and sheep on large **ranches** in this area. A ranch is a large farm with grazing land for raising cattle, sheep, or horses. On some of the land, vegetables, fruit, and **alfalfa** (al fal′ fə) are grown. Have you ever seen alfalfa growing? It is a green plant that often grows 2 to 3 feet (60 to 90 cm) high. Alfalfa makes good feed for the livestock.

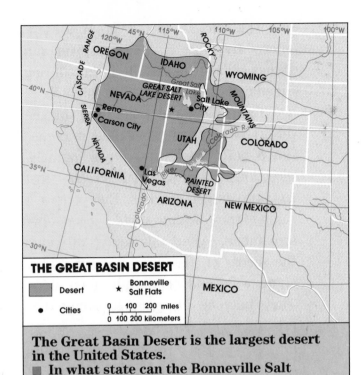

THE GREAT BASIN DESERT

Desert
Cities
Bonneville Salt Flats
0 100 200 miles
0 100 200 kilometers

The Great Basin Desert is the largest desert in the United States.
■ **In what state can the Bonneville Salt Flats be found?**

The Great Basin Desert is also an important mining area. Copper, lead, gold, silver, and zinc are some of the most important minerals found in this area. Large amounts of salt are mined in the Great Basin area. The salt is left behind by water that runs down off the mountains and then evaporates. The Bonneville Salt Flats, located in Utah, is a 100 mile strip of level salt beds. Because the salt beds are very flat and very hard, the area is often used as a racetrack. The Bonneville Speedway is a race car track found on the Bonneville Salt Flats. Many automobile racing records have been set on the Bonneville Salt Flats.

The Great Salt Lake Desert Within the Great Basin Desert is a small area called the Great Salt Lake Desert. It is located in the northwestern part of Utah. The Great Salt Lake is near this desert area. The Great Salt Lake is a large lake with very salty water. As a matter of fact, the water in the Great Salt Lake is about six times as salty as ocean water.

You may be wondering why the Great Salt Lake is so salty. The reason is that a number of small mountain rivers that flow into the Great Salt Lake carry large amounts of salt. These rivers start high in the mountains. As they run down the mountains, they collect salt. The water from these rivers empties into the Great Salt Lake. Once the water gets into

the Great Salt Lake it has no way of getting out. This means that the amount of salt added to the lake is always increasing.

City of the Mormons   An important city is found near the Great Salt Lake. Its name is Salt Lake City. This city is the capital of Utah.

Salt Lake City was started in 1847 by a man named Brigham Young. Brigham Young was a leader of the religious group known as the **Mormons**. Salt Lake City is still the center of the Mormon religion. The city contains many large buildings that are used for religious services. One building, called the Tabernacle, seats over 8,000 people.

Mining is an important industry in the Great Basin Desert. The front end loader (inset) is loaded with raw salt.
■ **Why is this kind of mining often called surface mining?**

Salt Lake City is an important industrial and banking center. The well-known Mormon Temple is also located here.
■ **Do you see the six steeples of the temple?**

Salt Lake City is also an important industrial and transportation center. There are about 700 manufacturing plants in the city because of the many natural resources in the area. Some of the things made by these plants are chemicals, food products, and steel. Railroad tracks and airports connect Salt Lake City with other cities in the United States and around the world.

A few other cities can be found in the Great Basin Desert. Carson City, Reno, and Las Vegas are located in Nevada. These cities were started to serve the people who came into the area to mine the resources found there. Today, people are attracted to these cities because of the open spaces and climate. Las Vegas is one of the most popular vacation spots in the United States.

CHECKUP

1. What is a desert?
2. In which states can parts of the Great Basin Desert be found?
3. What religious group started Salt Lake City?
4. **Thinking Critically** Make a list of reasons why people would want to live in the Great Basin Desert.

The Painted Desert

What is life like for the Navajo living in the Painted Desert?

VOCABULARY

pueblo	loom
dry farming	poverty
reservation	uranium
hogan	helium

The Desert of the Navajo Look at the map on this page and find the place where the borders of New Mexico, Arizona, Colorado, and Utah come together. This place is called Four Corners. Can you guess why it has this name? This is the only place in our country where the borders of four states join at one point.

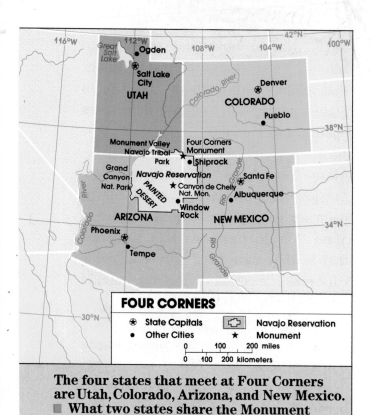

FOUR CORNERS

⊛ State Capitals   🔲 Navajo Reservation
● Other Cities   ★ Monument

0   100   200 miles
0   100   200 kilometers

The four states that meet at Four Corners are Utah, Colorado, Arizona, and New Mexico.
■ What two states share the Monument Valley Navajo Tribal Park?

The land surrounding Four Corners is part of the Great Basin Desert. Part of this desert area has its own name. It is called the Painted Desert because the soil and rocks look as if they had been painted in beautiful colors. At sunrise and sunset the whole area seems to glow in pink and purple. This desert is the home of the Navajo Indians.

The Navajo have made their home in the Painted Desert for many years. In this lesson we shall learn how they have been able to live in such a dry region.

People of the Painted Desert People who have studied the history of American Indians say that the Navajo came from the north about 500 years ago. They found other Indians already living in the Painted Desert. These other Indians lived in villages in homes built of stone or dried clay. Sometimes the buildings were several stories high, like apartment houses.

The first Europeans to see these Indian villages were from Spain. The Spanish word for village is **pueblo** (pweb′ lō). So the Spanish called the Indian villages pueblos. The people in the villages were called the Pueblo Indians.

From the Pueblo the Navajo learned about **dry farming**—growing crops on land where there is little water. They learned the best ways to raise corn, beans, and squash. They

129

also learned how to make blankets and jewelry.

Navajo Families   Today about 100,000 Navajo live on land that the United States government has set aside for them. Such land is called a **reservation**. The Navajo reservation is large. It is bigger than several of our states. The Painted Desert is located in the southern part of the Navajo reservation.

Many Navajo families live in one-room round houses called **hogans** (hō′ gônz). A hogan is made of logs laid on top of one another. The cracks between the logs are filled with clay. Sheepskins make the floor warm. In the middle of the floor is a place to make a fire. The smoke goes straight up through a hole in the middle of the roof. A fire is needed in winter to keep the hogan warm. The desert can be cold then, especially at night.

Most Navajo homes have a **loom**, or a frame used for weaving yarn. Women sit at the loom, making beautiful blankets. These blankets are sold all over the reservation.

While the women weave blankets, the men make beautiful jewelry. They use silver and valuable stones to make necklaces, rings, and other items. The stones come from underneath the ground in the desert.

Things are changing for Navajo children. They never used to go to school. They were taught at home by their parents and grandparents. But

Navajo children return to their hogan from their school.
■ What is the hogan made of?

today, Navajo boys and girls go to school. They study the same things that children throughout the United States study, as well as their own history and customs.

Many New Jobs   The Navajo people love the desert, but it has never been an easy place to make a living. Many Navajo have lived in **poverty**, that is, they have been very poor. Few can make a good living by making blankets and jewelry.

There never used to be many places in the desert where people could get jobs. But things are changing. The future of the Navajo is much brighter. What brought about this change?

The History of the Navajo Indians

The early Navajo lived by gathering wild seeds, berries, and plants. They also hunted animals for meat and skins. They used the animal skins to make dresses. The early Navajo would also get food by raiding other Indian villages in the area.

The most important neighbors of the Navajo were the Pueblo Indians. From them the Navajo learned how to plant seeds and grow food. They also learned from the Pueblos how to make blankets, pottery, and jewelry.

In 1583 the Spanish were the first Europeans to reach the land of the Navajo. The Spanish brought with them sheep and horses. These two animals changed the Navajo way of life. Instead of hunting animals for food and clothing, the Navajo raised sheep. The horses helped them to travel farther than they did before.

By 1848 the land that the Navajo lived on became part of the United States. Fighting broke out between the Navajo and the United States Army. In 1864 the United States government finally forced the Navajo to move to another location, hundreds of miles away. But the Navajo always wanted to return to their own land. In 1868 they were allowed to do so.

Life has changed for the Navajo during the 1900s. Many Navajo have found jobs in factories. Most important to the future of the Navajo has been the discovery of natural resources on their land. The government of the Navajo, called the Tribal Council, has acted wisely on what to do with the natural resources. Many new jobs have been created for the Navajo. As a result the future of the Navajo looks bright.

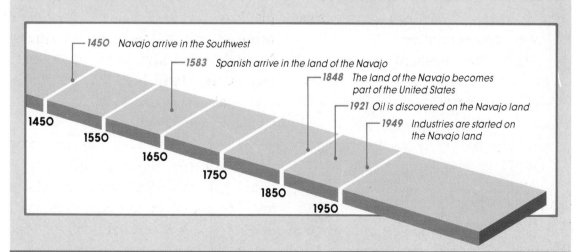

1450 Navajo arrive in the Southwest
1583 Spanish arrive in the land of the Navajo
1848 The land of the Navajo becomes part of the United States
1921 Oil is discovered on the Navajo land
1949 Industries are started on the Navajo land

1450 1550 1650 1750 1850 1950

Valuable resources were discovered in the desert. Among them were oil and gas. These are much needed today for making gasoline and for heating homes. Big supplies of coal have been found, too, as well as **uranium** and **helium**. Uranium is a metal that is used in many plants that make electric power. Helium is a gas that is lighter than air. One of its uses is to lift balloons.

Big companies are today paying the Navajo for the right to mine these resources. Many Navajo work for companies that are getting coal and other resources out of the ground. Our country needs a lot of coal.

Animals of the Desert   People are not the only living thing in the Painted Desert. Ants, beetles, and other insects live in the desert. There are also lizards, snakes, and toads. Owls and bats fly around at night. Larger animals such as foxes, bobcats, and coyotes (kī ō′ tēz) can also be found.

One interesting animal found in the Painted Desert and other deserts in the southwestern United States is the Gila (hē′ la) monster. This lizard, about 20 inches (50 cm) long, may not look like a monster to you. But imagine what it looks like to the mice and baby birds on which the Gila monster likes to feed.

Two other animals found in American deserts are the kangaroo rat and the roadrunner. The kangaroo rat is a lively little animal. It has to move very fast to stay alive. The kangaroo rat is a favorite food of foxes and

The roadrunner, a desert bird of the Southwest, is a fast runner.
■ Why, do you think, did this bird get the name *roadrunner*?

Monument-like mountains of red sandstone rise high in Monument Valley in northeastern Arizona.
■ **Why do you think this place was named Monument Valley?**

coyotes. The roadrunner moves faster on foot than any other American bird does. It can run so fast that it seldom uses its wings to fly.

Visiting the Painted Desert Many tourists now visit the Painted Desert. There are many things for tourists to see. One is Monument Valley. Here, on the border of Arizona and Utah, great rocks rise straight up from the desert floor. Look at the picture above.

Another place visited by tourists is Canyon de Chelly (shā). This canyon is 35 miles (56 km) long. In the steep sandstone walls of the canyon are cliff houses built hundreds of years ago. The Navajo welcome the tourists. Some tourists hire the Navajo as guides. Many other Navajo work in the motels and restaurants that the tourists use.

CHECKUP

1. What four states come together at Four Corners?
2. What is a pueblo?
3. Name three animals that can be found in the Painted Desert and other deserts in the southwestern United States.
4. **Thinking Critically** Explain why and how life is changing for the Navajo Indians.

133

The Chihuahuan and Sonoran Deserts

How are the Chihuahuan and Sonoran deserts the same and different?

VOCABULARY

yucca	resort
cactus	metropolitan area

Deserts in Two Countries   The Chihuahuan and Sonoran deserts are both partly in the United States and partly in the country of Mexico. The largest part of each of these deserts can be found in Mexico. Look at the map below. Find both of these deserts. In the United States, the Chihuahuan Desert stretches from western Texas to southeastern Arizona. The Sonoran Desert is located in southwestern Arizona and southern California. Both deserts extend many miles into Mexico.

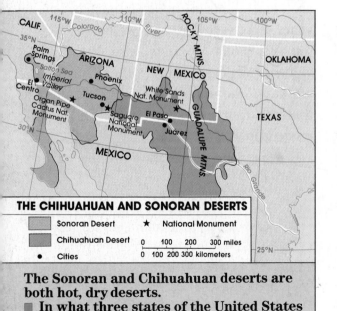

THE CHIHUAHUAN AND SONORAN DESERTS

▨ Sonoran Desert	★ National Monument
▨ Chihuahuan Desert	0 100 200 300 miles
• Cities	0 100 200 300 kilometers

The Sonoran and Chihuahuan deserts are both hot, dry deserts.
■ In what three states of the United States is the Chihuahuan Desert located?

Mountains and Plains   The Chihuahuan Desert is made up of mountain ranges and flat plains. The entire area is about 4,000 to 6,000 feet (about 1,200 to 1,800 m) above sea level. The river called the Rio Grande flows right through the middle of the Chihuahuan Desert. This river forms part of the boundary between the United States and Mexico.

Between the Rio Grande and the Guadalupe (gwäd′ əl üp) Mountains is the Tularosa Valley. The Guadalupe Mountains are located in western Texas. The Tularosa Valley is covered with white sand. The White Sands National Monument in southern New Mexico is located in this valley. The monument contains large amounts of windblown sand. The white sand looks like high mounds of white snow.

Hot Days and Cool Nights   The temperature in the Chihuahuan Desert is hot during the day and cool at night. It is not unusual for the temperature to dip from 90°F (32°C) during the day to below 50°F (10°C) at night.

Mostly low shrubs grow in this desert area. There are very few trees. However, a desert plant called the **yucca** (yuk′ ə) does grow here. The yucca has swordlike leaves and beautiful flowers. The Indians who once lived in the desert ate the fruit of the yucca and made soap from its root. Today the yucca plant is used mainly to decorate homes and buildings.

There are a few farms in the Chihuahuan Desert. Mostly cattle and sheep are raised on these farms. The main crop grown on these desert farms is cotton.

El Paso, Texas   A large city found in the Chihuahuan Desert is El Paso, Texas. El Paso is located on the northern bank of the Rio Grande. Today over 490,000 people live in this city. Many of them have a Mexican background. El Paso serves as a main gateway for people traveling between the United States and Mexico.

Manufacturing is very important in El Paso. Making cotton clothing is the leading industry in the city. Other industries include oil refining and the making of leather goods, especially leather boots. Leather boots made in Texas are famous all over the United States.

El Paso is connected to other cities by railroad tracks, airports, highways, and bridges. Three bridges across the Rio Grande connect El Paso to the city of Juárez (wär' ez), Mexico. A highway in Juárez connects it with Mexico City, the capital of the country.

The Sonoran Desert   The Sonoran Desert is not a flat, sandy, dry piece of land. Mountains and ridges cut across the Sonoran Desert. Some

of the mountains are about 3,000 feet (914 m) high. Several plains and valleys are also located in the Sonoran Desert. The southwestern corner of Arizona is a dry plain. Another plain, located in the Sonoran Desert, is one of the richest farmlands in the world. This plain is called the Imperial Valley. The Imperial Valley is part of California.

The Imperial Valley   Look at the map on page 134. Find the Imperial Valley. In 1900 a man named George Chaffey built a canal that brought water from the Colorado River to the Imperial Valley. Water from the canal

Water from the Colorado River makes Imperial Valley a rich farming region.
■ **How would you describe this land?**

was used to irrigate the land. Soon many farmers moved to the valley.

By 1905 there were 14,000 people living in Imperial Valley. Over 100,000 acres (40 ha) of land were farmed. But a terrible thing happened. The Colorado River broke through the banks of the canal and flooded the valley. The flooding lasted almost 2 years. There was so much water that it filled in a very low part of the land. That body of water is now called the Salton Sea. The farmers did not want to give up their land. Everyone worked hard to repair the break in the canal. Finally the break in the canal was sealed and the Imperial Valley was saved. Today, farmers in the Imperial Valley grow many different kinds of fruits and vegetables.

Desert Cactus   Rainfall in the Sonoran Desert varies. In the low areas it rains only about 3 inches (7.5 cm) or less a year. In the higher areas it rains up to 20 inches (50 cm) a year. Sometimes after a rainfall, especially in the springtime, bright patches of flowers appear. But then it becomes dry again and the flowers die. However, their seeds fall on the earth and new flowers bloom the next spring.

Other plants in the desert have a special way of living. These plants have leaves as thick as leather. Water does not evaporate fast through these leaves. The water is stored by the plants. The **cactus** is such a plant.

Organ-pipe cactuses, such as these, are found in southern Arizona.
■ Does the name *organ pipe* fit?

Have you ever seen a cactus? If you have, you know that it is usually prickly to the fingers. There are many kinds of cactus plants and many sizes. The giant cactus sometimes grows 50 feet (15 m) high. It is able to live and grow because it stores water in its system. Cactus plants can be seen in the lower parts of the Sonoran Desert.

One kind of cactus plant, the saguaro (sə gwä′ rō) cactus, is the state flower of Arizona. There are two national monuments in Arizona that protect and save the cactus. They are the Saguaro National Monument and the Organ Pipe Cactus National Monument. Have you ever visited either of these monuments?

A Growing Population The Sonoran Desert has become a popular place to live in the United States. Many people enjoy living in the desert's dry and warm climate. Many other people retire to this desert area because they enjoy the warm days and cool nights.

Palm Springs, located in southern California, is one of the most popular **resorts** in the country. A resort is a place where people go for recreation and entertainment. Almost 2 million people visit Palm Springs each year. Also, more than 33,000 people make their homes in Palm Springs.

Palm Springs is a very pretty city. Beautiful palm trees line many of the streets. These palm trees are tall and are bushy at the top. The leaves are long and narrow like the blade of a sword. Dates are a fruit that comes from a date palm tree. Coconuts grow on another kind of palm tree, called a coconut palm tree.

Another important city in the Sonoran Desert is Phoenix, Arizona. Phoenix is a **metropolitan area**. A metropolitan area is a large city and surrounding towns, smaller cities, and other communities. Over 1,500,000 people live in the Phoenix metropolitan area. Phoenix is the tenth most populated city in the United States. Along with being a major resort, the city is known for making computers.

In this chapter you have studied about four deserts found in the United States. One other desert is also found in the United States. This desert is located just north of the Sonoran Desert. As a matter of fact, these two deserts border each other. The name of this desert is the Mojave Desert. We will learn more about the Mojave Desert in Chapter 7.

CHECKUP

1. In which country besides the United States are both the Chihuahuan and Sonoran deserts located?
2. Why is the cactus able to survive in the desert?
3. What is a *metropolitan area*?
4. **Thinking Critically** How is the land in the Chihuahuan and Sonoran deserts the same?

Using a Road Map

FINDING YOUR WAY

Imagine that you are taking a trip with your family to the Phoenix metropolitan area. Find the airport on the map. Use the road map below to answer the following questions.

1. What are the numbers of the two interstate highways you would take to go from the airport to where you are staying on Dunlap Avenue?

2. In what directions would you go?

3. Which two colleges would you pass along the way?

LOCATING PLACES

While in the Phoenix area, you and your family want to visit these places: Squaw Peak Park, the state fairgrounds, Big Surf, Heard Museum, and the Phoenix Zoo.

1. Use the letter and number coordinates given in the list of places of interest to locate each place on the map. What are the coordinates for each place?

2. What park is located in box D-2?

3. What are the coordinates of the box where the state capitol is found?

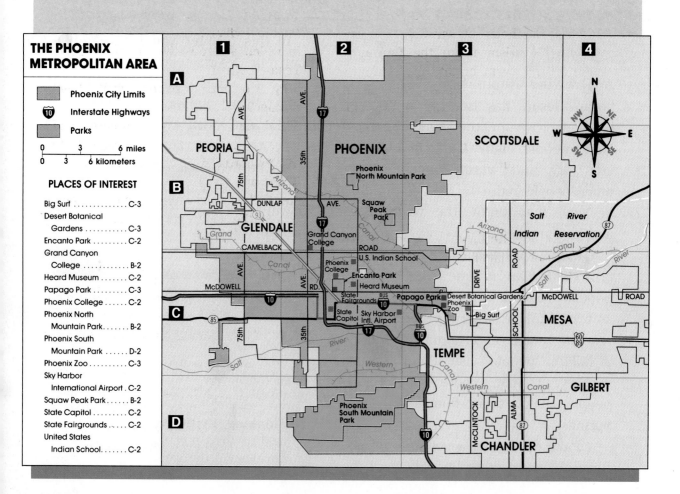

THE PHOENIX METROPOLITAN AREA

Phoenix City Limits

Interstate Highways

Parks

0   3   6 miles
0   3   6 kilometers

PLACES OF INTEREST

Big Surf	C-3
Desert Botanical Gardens	C-3
Encanto Park	C-2
Grand Canyon College	B-2
Heard Museum	C-2
Papago Park	C-3
Phoenix College	C-2
Phoenix North Mountain Park	B-2
Phoenix South Mountain Park	D-2
Phoenix Zoo	C-3
Sky Harbor International Airport	C-2
Squaw Peak Park	B-2
State Capitol	C-2
State Fairgrounds	C-2
United States Indian School	C-2

CHAPTER 6 REVIEW

MAIN IDEAS

1. The Great Basin Desert is the largest desert in the United States.
2. The Great Basin Desert is broken by many hills and ridges. Between the ridges are many flat and long stretches of rock and sand.
3. Important natural resources of the Great Basin Desert are open spaces, copper, lead, gold, silver, zinc, and salt.
4. The Navajo Indians live in and near the Painted Desert.
5. Today many Navajo live in small towns. The men and women sell hand made crafts, such as blankets and jewelry.
6. New industries with more jobs, improved methods of farming, and increased tourism make the future of the Navajo seem bright.
7. Both the Sonoran and Chihuahuan deserts are hot and dry regions located in both the United States and Mexico. The temperature in both deserts is hot during the day and cool at night. Some mountains and large, growing cities can be found in both deserts.
8. The major difference between the Sonoran and Chihuahuan deserts is that there is much more farming in the Sonoran Desert than in the Chihuahuan Desert.

VOCABULARY REVIEW

Choose the correct ending for each sentence. Write your answers on a separate sheet of paper.

1. A place that gets very little rain is a (a) ranch, (b) desert, (c) pueblo.
2. Today most Navajo live on a (a) reservation, (b) ranch, (c) resort.
3. A large metropolitan area in the Sonoran Desert is (a) El Paso, (b) Phoenix, (c) Palm Springs.
4. The Imperial Valley is located in the (a) Painted Desert, (b) Chihuahuan Desert, (c) Sonoran Desert.
5. A desert plant that has thick and sometimes prickly leaves is a (a) yucca, (b) cactus, (c) palm tree.

CHAPTER CHECKUP

1. What happens to most of the rain that falls in the desert?
2. What did the Navajo learn from the Pueblo Indians?
3. In which desert is the city of El Paso, Texas located?
4. Why do many people visit Palm Springs?
5. **Thinking Critically** Compare and contrast life in a desert region and life in the northern forests of Alaska.
6. **Thinking Critically** Make a list of some plants and animals found in deserts in the southwestern United States.

APPLYING KNOWLEDGE

1. Go through magazines and find pictures showing scenes from deserts. Show these pictures in a bulletin-board display.
2. Experiment by growing cactus plants in pots in your classroom. See how long a cactus plant will live without water. Give a lot of water to another cactus and observe what happens.

7 The Mojave Desert

The Land of the Mojave Desert

What are some important physical features of the Mojave Desert?

VOCABULARY

arroyo	Joshua tree
dry wash	creosote bush
dry lake	

A Hot, Dry Desert   In the last chapter you learned about four deserts in the United States. In this chapter we shall look at another desert in the United States. It is called the Mojave (mō hä′ vē) Desert. The Mojave is located in California, about 300 miles (480 km) west of the Painted Desert. Turn to the map on page 149 and find the Mojave Desert. As you can see, the Mojave Desert stretches from the Sierra Nevada Mountains to the Colorado River.

Today, the Mojave Desert is a very popular place. The warm weather has attracted people from all over the country. The Mojave Desert has been a favorite vacation spot for movie

stars for many years. Now, more and more people have decided to move into the area. Cities have started to grow in the Mojave Desert.

Like the other deserts in the United States, the Mojave is hot and dry. But deserts are different in some ways. As you read this chapter, look for ways in which the Mojave Desert is different from other deserts in the United States.

Looking for Water   Parts of the Mojave Desert are low, but the land is not flat. Small mountains cut across the desert. Their sides are rounded. When it rains, water runs down them and forms streams. The water quickly dries up, but the streambeds are left.

A dry streambed is called an **arroyo** (ə roi′ ō). It is also called a **dry wash**.

Coyotes, rabbits, and other desert animals use arroyos as paths. Though the arroyos are dry, water can often be found a foot or so underground. Coyotes seem to know where the water is. When they get thirsty they dig a hole to the water. These holes are sometimes called coyote wells. They attract other wildlife seeking water.

Desert Shrimp   It does not rain often in the Mojave Desert. When it does, though, many low places fill with water. The water is not very deep and soon evaporates. These low

The land of the Mojave Desert is not flat.
■ **What do you see in the background?**

141

spots are called **dry lakes**. Because the sunbaked mud is usually salty, few plants grow in dry lakes.

Some of these dry lakes do not have any water for 15 or 20 years. But when it finally rains, an interesting thing sometimes happens. Several days after the rain falls, the lake is filled with wiggling little shrimp. Do you know what shrimp are? They are small water animals. You can see a picture of them below.

You are probably wondering where the shrimp come from, way out in the dry Mojave Desert. They hatched from shrimp eggs that were

Lakes dry up in the desert because there is so little rain.
■ Is there water in this lake?

Desert shrimp hatch in the lakes that form after a heavy rainfall.
■ What color are these animals?

in the hardened mud of the dry lake. The eggs have been there since the last time it rained. The shrimp that have hatched will now lay eggs. These shrimp will be covered with mud and will die. The eggs will also be covered with mud. When another big rain comes, perhaps years later, the eggs will hatch. The lake will again become alive with shrimp.

Desert Plants The **Joshua tree** is the plant that most people think of when they think of the Mojave Desert. This is an odd-looking evergreen tree. It does not often grow much

Large numbers of Joshua trees are found in the Mojave Desert. The branches of Joshua trees grow up, down, and sideways.
■ **Do you see any branches growing sideways?**

higher than 30 feet (9 m). Its branches grow in different directions—up, down, and sideways. The leaves are long and sharp. Can you guess why they have a thick skin?

There are forests of Joshua trees in some parts of the Mojave Desert. These trees have beautiful white flowers and produce large seeds. Squirrels like to eat the seeds of the Joshua trees.

Another plant that is found in many parts of the Mojave Desert is the **creosote** (krē′ ə sōt) **bush.** These small bushes grow well apart from each other. They often look as if someone had planted them in rows.

There is a mystery about the creosote bush. No other plants grow around it. Is it because the roots of the creosote bush take all the moisture from the ground? Is it because the roots give off a poison that kills seedlings? No one knows for sure.

CHECKUP

1. Where is the Mojave Desert?
2. How is a dry wash similar to a dry lake?
3. How are arroyos created?
4. How do Joshua trees and creosote bushes differ?
5. **Thinking Critically** What is one thing that is different about the Mojave and Painted deserts?

Death Valley

What makes Death Valley different from other parts of the United States?

VOCABULARY

gold rush	sandstorm
sand dune	national monument

A Dry, Hot Valley At the northern edge of the Mojave Desert is a long, narrow valley sunk down between high mountains. It is called Death Valley. Death Valley is the lowest place in the United States. At one point it is 282 feet (85 m) below the level of the sea.

Death Valley is not just the lowest place in the United States. It is also the driest and hottest place. It has about 2 inches (5 cm) of rain a year. In the middle of the summer the temperature rises to more than 115°F (46°C) almost every day. How hot is it in the summer where you live?

A Costly Short Cut The first people ever to go into this hot, dry valley were Indians. They gave the place an Indian name that means "ground on fire."

No one else visited this valley until gold was discovered in California in 1848. A **gold rush** followed as

You can drive through Death Valley. The floor is flat.
■ What scenery are these people enjoying?

The History of the Crossing of Death Valley

In 1848, John Sutter, a landowner in California, made plans to build a sawmill on the American River. The American River is located in northern California. Sutter hired a carpenter named James Marshall. One day, Marshall saw something shining in the stream beside the mill. He picked it up and looked at it closely. It was gold!

The word spread quickly that gold had been found in California. The gold rush began. In 1849, thousands of people set out for California looking for gold. Because the gold rush began in the year 1849, these people were called the "forty-niners."

Many gold seekers traveled in wagon trains to California. The trip was long and dangerous. The trails were rough and often poorly marked. The wagon trains could travel about 10 miles (16 km) a day.

Some of the gold seekers tried to find a shortcut to California through the western mountains and deserts. One such group of travelers found themselves in a hot, dry valley surrounded by mountains. They had used up most of their food and water. The oxen pulling the wagons were so weak they were ready to drop.

Two of the families got out of the valley by following a steep trail. As they reached the top of the high cliffs, the group stopped and looked down into the valley that they had thought they would never leave alive. One of them said, "Good-bye, Death Valley!" Ever since that time, the valley has carried that name.

By 1850, California's population was 10 times what it had been 4 years earlier. In 1850, California became the thirty-first state in the United States.

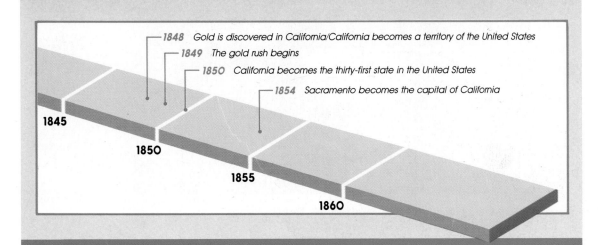

1848 Gold is discovered in California/California becomes a territory of the United States

1849 The gold rush begins

1850 California becomes the thirty-first state in the United States

1854 Sacramento becomes the capital of California

1845   1850   1855   1860

thousands of people hurried to California to hunt for gold. One group of gold seekers tried to take a shortcut. Soon they found themselves in a hot desert valley without food to eat or water to drink.

Visiting Death Valley　It is not as hard to go through Death Valley today as it was in earlier times. But anyone who goes into Death Valley must still be careful. Drivers should have plenty of gasoline, since gas stations are few. Drivers must also carry enough water for the trip through Death Valley.

Going down into the valley, one drives through bare mountains and dry hills. Arroyos and canyons have cut deep into these rocky hills and mountains. The sides of the dry washes are straight and high. They look as if they were cut with a knife.

The floor of the valley is flat. Some areas are covered with dried mud. The mud forms when it rains. Since it does not rain often, the water soon evaporates. The mud dries out and cracks. There are hardly any plants on mud flats. Some of the mud flats are white because the mud has salt in it.

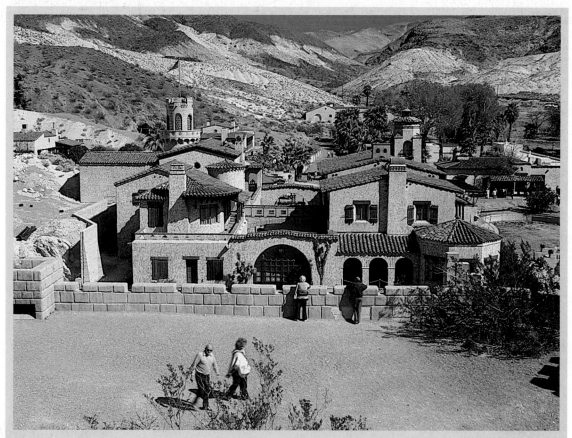

Scottie's Castle is a tourist attraction in Death Valley.
■ **What materials are the buildings made of?**

The afternoon sun makes desert sand dunes look like hills of gold.
■ **How might these sand dunes look different in another year?**

Sand dunes are another sight as one crosses Death Valley. Sand dunes are hills made of fine sand. Quite often the wind blows the sand and changes the shape of the hills. One has to be careful driving through sand dunes. When the wind is blowing, a **sandstorm** can take place. Sand fills the air and blocks the driver's view.

As hot and dry as Death Valley is, life exists there. There are creosote bushes and other small shrubs that come up after a rain. But these shrubs soon dry up. There are animals, too, who live in this hot valley. Among them are lizards, kangaroo rats, ground squirrels, and snakes.

Though Death Valley is harsh, it is a place that tourists like to visit. People go there to see what the desert is like. The government has taken over the land and has made Death Valley a **national monument**. As in a national park, special care is taken to keep the land the way it is.

CHECKUP

1. What do we mean when we say that Death Valley is below sea level?
2. How did Death Valley get its name?
3. How does the land change as one travels into and through Death Valley?
4. **Thinking Critically** Compare crossing Death Valley today to crossing Death Valley during the gold rush.

Farming and Mining in the Mojave Desert

What kinds of farming and mining are done in the Mojave Desert?

VOCABULARY

limestone	open-pit mining
borax	pollution

Importance of Water   Water is one of our most important natural resources. We all need water to live. Also, plants and crops need water to grow. Without water, much of our farmland would be a desert. This is especially true in the state of California. But irrigation has solved many of California's water problems. You learned that irrigation is a way of bringing water from rivers and streams to crops through ditches and canals. Irrigation is also a way of bringing water to people through a set of pipes.

Desert Farming   Today more and more people are moving to the desert. People have discovered that irrigation makes it possible to raise crops in some parts of the Mojave Desert. One of these places is along the Mojave River. To see where the Mojave River runs, look at the map on page 149. The river starts in the San Bernardino (san bər nə dē′ nō) Mountains. From there it flows into the desert toward the city of Barstow.

When the Mojave River first flows into the desert, one can see plenty of water in it. But before long, the water in the river disappears!

You may be wondering how a river can disappear. What happens is that the water sinks into the sands of the desert. But the water is still there, under the ground. All the way to the desert city of Barstow and beyond,

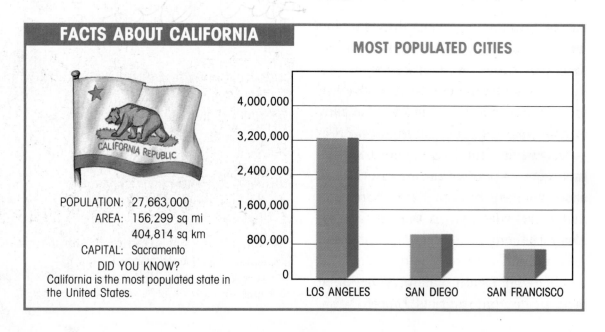

FACTS ABOUT CALIFORNIA

CALIFORNIA REPUBLIC

POPULATION: 27,663,000
AREA: 156,299 sq mi
404,814 sq km
CAPITAL: Sacramento
DID YOU KNOW?
California is the most populated state in the United States.

MOST POPULATED CITIES

4,000,000
3,200,000
2,400,000
1,600,000
800,000
0

LOS ANGELES   SAN DIEGO   SAN FRANCISCO

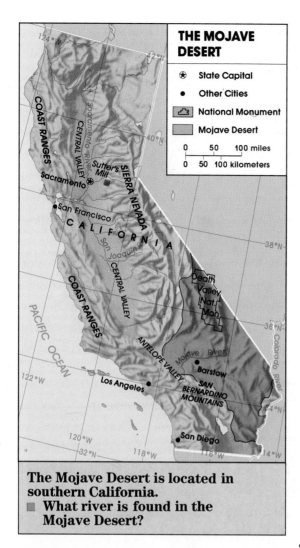

THE MOJAVE DESERT

⊛ State Capital
• Other Cities
National Monument
Mojave Desert

0   50   100 miles
0   50   100 kilometers

The Mojave Desert is located in southern California.
■ **What river is found in the Mojave Desert?**

is located west of the Mojave River. The area is called Antelope Valley. Find it on the map on this page. Antelope Valley has no rivers. Yet it is a good farming region. Farmers grow alfalfa, carrots, melons, and grains. How is it possible to raise crops like these in a place without a river?

The fact is that Antelope Valley is not as dry as it looks. Rain falling in the San Bernardino Mountains runs down into the valley. When it reaches the floor of the valley, it sinks into the ground. People have dug wells to reach this underground water. From the wells they get water to irrigate their fields.

Water is carried to fields in the Mojave Desert through pipes.
■ **Why are wheels attached to the pipes?**

farmers have dug wells in the dry wash of the river. From these wells they get water for their crops.

This water makes a green belt in the desert. Farmers grow potatoes, onions, melons, and alfalfa. Alfalfa is good cattle food and makes the ground rich for other crops. Alfalfa roots go deep into the soil. Why does this make alfalfa a good crop to raise along the Mojave River?

Using Rainwater Another good farming region in the Mojave Desert

149

Mining Resources Some people have come to the Mojave Desert because of its mineral resources. Iron ore is found in several places. There are large amounts of salt and **limestone**. Limestone is used to make cement. In recent years many new homes and factories have been built in California. Can you imagine how much cement is needed for all those buildings? This makes limestone a very important resource.

The Mojave Desert also has large amounts of **borax** (bōr′ aks). This soft white mineral has many uses in factories. It is also used in making washing powder. The next time you go to a supermarket, see if you can find borax. Look on the shelf where there are laundry detergents.

Death Valley is one of the places where borax is found. Years ago, people had to dig for it with picks and shovels in the terrible heat. It was carried out of Death Valley in big, heavy carts. Teams of 20 mules pulled the carts.

Though it is just as hot as ever in the desert, mining is easier today. The deposits of borax are just below the surface. Today, big machines strip the soil away. The borax is then

This borax mine located in the Mojave Desert is near Borno, California.
■ Where is borax mined—above the ground or below the ground?

scooped up by other machines and loaded into trucks. This kind of mining, done on top of the ground, is called **open-pit mining**. Iron ore is also often mined this way. Small supplies of other ores such as gold, silver, lead, and copper are also mined in the hills around Death Valley.

Concerns for the Future   Is the Mojave Desert getting crowded? Not yet, most people would say, but it could be crowded in the future. It is hard to tell just what the movement of more people into the area would do to the desert.

This is the city of Barstow, California.
■ What helps to keep this area
from becoming overcrowded?

Some people fear that more roads will bring more cars. More roads could also bring more industry. Cars and factories could bring **pollution**. That is, they could make the air and land and water dirty. Would all these changes harm the plants and the animals of the Mojave Desert? Many people think they would.

Some fear that the desert is already being harmed by the added numbers of people going there. Do you know what a dune buggy is? It is a kind of car for driving in the desert. People with such cars or with motorcycles sometimes have races in the desert. Those who take part in this sport say it is fun. The land in the desert, they add, is not good for anything else. Others believe that the spinning wheels tear up the desert. This kills plant and animal life, they say, and causes erosion.

Should we encourage more use of the desert? Or should we protect the desert and keep it the way it is? What do you think?

CHECKUP

1. What makes it possible to grow crops in some parts of the Mojave Desert?
2. What natural resources are found in the Mojave Desert?
3. What are some of the problems that the Mojave Desert may face in the future?
4. **Thinking Critically** How do farmers in the Mojave Desert get water to irrigate their fields?

Writing Description

WHAT IS DESCRIPTIVE WRITING?

A description paints a picture of something with words. When you write a description, you want the reader to see the picture.

How do you paint a picture with words? Read the example of descriptive writing below and look for words that help you make a picture. This example describes the travels of some forty-niners to the California goldfields. It is taken from the book *California Gold Days* by Helen Bauer.

For two weeks out of New York the trip was pleasant. Then the ship unloaded on the Isthmus at the mouth of the Chagres River. Here there were only a few bamboo huts with palm-leaf roofs. To the travelers it was a beautiful place. But it was here that their troubles began.

The gold hunters had to hire natives to take them up the Chagres River. No price was too high for them to ask. Sometimes money was taken and the guides ran away. Sometimes they disappeared with the baggage. Many had to wait here because there were no boats. They had a terrible time.

The lucky men were taken up the river in little boats. Their long, polelike paddles sent the boats gliding up the stream. Their trip up the jungle river was one the men never forgot! Tree branches dipped down into the muddy river. Bright flowers, yellow and purple, hung from the trees. Monkeys chattered and swung from the long, thick vines. Parrots and other birds screeched in the treetops. Once in a while there were wild cries from the jungle. Sometimes alligators pushed their noses against the sides of the little boats. It was enough to frighten anyone! The jungle seemed thicker as they went along. Very little sun came through. "We'll never forget the trip up the Chagres!" the men said. They would never forget the hot, steamy days, either. Nor the miserable nights spent in the native villages. But they were on their way to Panama!

At last they came to the end of the river trip. But this was not the end of their travels. They had to travel twenty more miles overland to the coast to get to a ship.

SKILLS PRACTICE

Complete the following. Use a separate sheet of paper.

1. What words did you find that helped you see what the author was describing? "Bright flowers, yellow and purple" and "long, thick vines" are examples that help you "see" the jungle. List at least six other words that helped you see the scene the author was describing.

2. Imagine you were one of the forty-niners traveling to the goldfields. Perhaps you traveled by sea. Maybe you went by wagon. Use your imagination and write a letter home. Describe what you saw along the way. Describe your feelings as you made the long trip. Paint a picture with your words. Your letter should be one page in length.

CHAPTER 7 REVIEW

MAIN IDEAS

1. Not all deserts are alike.
2. The Mojave Desert, located in Southern California, is hot and dry.
3. Small mountains cut across the Mojave Desert.
4. Joshua trees and creosote bushes are two of the most common plants in the Mojave Desert.
5. Death Valley is the lowest, hottest, and driest place in the United States.
6. Irrigation and underground wells have made farming possible in the Mojave Desert.
7. Farmers in the Mojave Desert grow such crops as potatoes, onions, melons, alfalfa, carrots, and grains.
8. Minerals mined in the Mojave Desert include iron ore, salt, limestone, and borax. Small amounts of gold, silver, lead, and copper are also mined.

VOCABULARY REVIEW

Match these terms with the definitions. Use a separate sheet of paper.

a. arroyo   f. limestone
b. creosote bush   g. sand dune
c. borax   h. gold rush
d. dry lake   i. pollution
e. open-pit mining j. sandstorm

1. A windstorm that fills the air with sand
2. A mineral used in laundry powder
3. A wild plant of the Mojave Desert
4. A dry streambed
5. The dirtying of air, land, and water
6. Used in making cement
7. A hill of sand
8. Low places in a desert where water has evaporated
9. Getting minerals out of the ground by scooping up soil on the surface of the ground
10. Thousands of people hurrying to California to hunt for gold

CHAPTER CHECKUP

1. What are the most common plants of the Mojave Desert?
2. In what ways is Death Valley different from other places in the United States?
3. What minerals are found in the Mojave Desert?
4. Why is mining in the desert easier today than it was years ago?
5. **Thinking Critically** Where would you rather live, in the Great Basin Desert or in the Mojave Desert?
6. **Thinking Critically** If you were asked to give Death Valley a different name, what would it be?
7. **Thinking Critically** List the physical features of the Mojave Desert.
8. **Thinking Critically** Do you think it is a good idea to allow dune buggy and motorcycle races in the desert?

APPLYING KNOWLEDGE

You have studied about five deserts in the United States. Develop a chart comparing information about each of the deserts. Your chart should contain information on each of the following topics: *location, type of land, farming, mining,* and *cities.* To make your chart, write the name of each of the deserts down the left-hand side of a piece of paper. Along the top of the paper write the name of each topic.

8 The Sahara and Atacama Deserts

The Largest Desert in the World

What are the main physical features of the Sahara?

VOCABULARY

oasis   camel

Two Large Deserts   In Chapters 6 and 7 we learned that most of the deserts in the United States are in the southwestern part of our country. Can you imagine if our entire country was covered by deserts? What do you think life would be like? There would be hardly any forests or farms. Water would be hard to find. Do you think as many people would live in the United States if it were all desert?

There is one desert in the world that would cover all of the United States except for the states of Alaska and Hawaii. This desert is the Sahara. It is located in northern Africa.

Camel caravans are often used when crossing the Sahara, the world's largest desert.
■ Why, do you think, is the camel an important desert animal?

The Sahara stretches all the way from the Atlantic Ocean in western Africa to the Red Sea in eastern Africa. Locate the Sahara on the map on page 156.

On the continent of South America, there is another large desert. It is called the Atacama (ät ə käm′ ə) Desert. In this chapter we will learn about these two deserts. We will begin by looking at life in the Sahara.

Very Little Rain   As you already know, deserts are not all flat. Look at the map on page 156. You will see a range of mountains along the northern edge of the Sahara. These are the Atlas Mountains. Winds from the Mediterranean Sea and the Atlantic

Ocean bring rain to the northern side of the mountains. There the land is green with trees and other plants. Many people live on the northern side of the mountains.

On the southern slopes of the Atlas Mountains, the land is dry and brown. Why is this so? Look back at the diagram on page 79. It explains what happens to moisture in the air when it is forced to rise over mountains. By the time the air travels over the Atlas Mountains and reaches the Sahara, it is very dry. The Sahara has very little rain.

Rocks and Sand Dunes   In the middle of the Sahara are other mountains. Here are great piles of

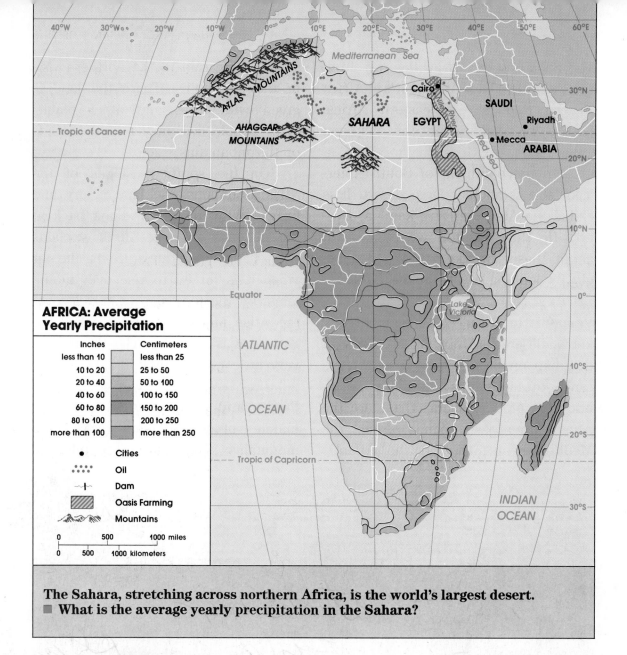

AFRICA: Average Yearly Precipitation

Inches		Centimeters
less than 10		less than 25
10 to 20		25 to 50
20 to 40		50 to 100
40 to 60		100 to 150
60 to 80		150 to 200
80 to 100		200 to 250
more than 100		more than 250

- Cities
- Oil
- Dam
- Oasis Farming
- Mountains

0   500   1000 miles
0   500   1000 kilometers

The Sahara, stretching across northern Africa, is the world's largest desert.
■ **What is the average yearly precipitation in the Sahara?**

huge black rocks. In some places the land looks something like Monument Valley in the Painted Desert. If you do not remember what that was like, look again at the picture on page 133.

Where there are no big rocks, the Sahara is covered with sand and little stones. This kind of desert surface is called gravel. The wind piles the sand in dunes. The sand dunes change as the wind keeps blowing.

Looking For Water The rainfall in the Sahara is less than 4 inches (10 cm) a year. During daylight hours the temperature often reaches 120°F (49°C).

The heat and lack of water make it hard for people to live in the Sahara. Most of those who live there are near an **oasis** (ō ā′ sis). This is a place in the desert where there is enough water for some plants to

156

grow. The water is often under the ground. People dig wells to reach it.

Not all oases get water from wells. The largest oasis in the Sahara is on the banks of the Nile River. Locate the Nile River on the map on page 156. Whereas most of the area around the Nile is desert, a belt of land along the river is green. This land is very good for farming. Water from the Nile lets plants grow along both banks.

Plants and Animals   In almost every oasis in the Sahara, one sees palm trees just like the ones in Palm Springs. As you remember, dates come from date palm trees. This golden-brown fruit grows in bunches of 200

or more. Palm trees have many uses in Africa. People eat the buds and the fruit. From the trunks of the tree, they make sandals for their feet and bowls to eat from. With the tree leaves they cover the roofs of their houses and build fences.

Most of the desert is bare, but here and there are small shrubs and clumps of grass. These few green plants supply food for the antelope. So many of these animals have been killed by hunters that there are not many left.

The animal that most people think of when the Sahara is mentioned is the **camel**. Have you ever seen a camel in the zoo? Camels are not wild animals like antelope. They

An oasis is a welcome sight to desert travelers.
■ **How are the people at the oasis in the photograph below using the water?**

THE USES OF THE CAMEL

For their milk to drink
and for making cheese

For their hides to make
leather bags and buckets

For carrying
people and
goods.

The camel provides many things for people who live in a desert.
■ **What kinds of things do camels provide for desert people?**

are tame animals like cows and horses. In fact, camels have some of the same uses. Like cows, camels supply milk that people drink or make into cheese. The camel's hide is made into leather. Like horses, camels carry people and loads of goods and pull plows. Camels are especially suited to the desert. They can travel great distances without water.

CHECKUP

1. On which continent is the Sahara located?
2. What is an oasis?
3. Describe the tree and the animal that the word *Sahara* brings to mind.

4. **Thinking Critically** How would the Sahara change if it started raining on a regular basis for one whole year?

The People of the Sahara

What are the differences between life in the desert and life in a large desert city?

VOCABULARY

nomad	shrine
Bedouin	Kaaba
mosque	Arab
Moslem	pyramid
Islam	

Moving From One Place to Another Most of the people of the Sahara live along the edges of the desert or in oases. But some live in the midst of the desert. They roam from one place to another and are called **nomads**. Some nomads are also called **Bedouins** (bed′ ù inz).

Nomads live in family groups. Such a group includes children, parents, grandparents, aunts, uncles, and cousins. The nomads raise sheep, goats, camels, and donkeys. These animals must have water to drink and plants to graze on. The plants and sometimes the water are found in different places at different times of the year. They last for only a short time. So the nomads must keep moving.

Nomads live in tents made from the skins of goats and other animals. These desert people wear loose cotton robes. Such clothing protects them from the hot sun and blowing sand. One of the main foods of the nomads is milk from camels and goats.

Sometimes the nomads have to kill one of their animals to get meat.

When the nomads move, they load their belongings onto their camels and donkeys. Nomads often travel many miles to get to new grazing grounds. They stop for water at oases. To get money for the few things they must buy, the nomads sell animal skins, milk, and cheese.

The children of the nomads do not go to school. They help tend the herds of sheep and goats.

Nomads rest near a desert stream.
■ Why are the nomads wearing so much clothing in the hot desert?

159

Living On an Oasis   The busiest place in a small desert oasis is usually its one or more wells. Around the water supply is a little village. The houses are close to each other. They are often built of concrete or dried mud and have thick walls. Each room has a door and a small window. Houses are built like this to keep out the heat and the sand. Sometimes the wind blows so hard that flying sand fills the streets.

In most oases there are date palm trees. There may be enough water so that crops can also be raised. But the area for crops is small. There is not enough water for large farms.

In the middle of the oasis village, there is usually a **mosque** (mosk). This is a place of worship for the **Moslems**. Moslems are people who practice a religion called **Islam** (is′ ləm).

The founder of the Moslem religion was a man named Mohammed. He was born in the city of Mecca. Mecca is located in the country of Saudi Arabia, which is about 300 miles (480 km) east of the Sahara. Find Saudi Arabia on the map on page 156. Most of Saudi Arabia is part of another large desert located on the Arabian Peninsula.

It is the dream of all Moslems to visit Mecca during their lifetime. Moslems from all over the world come to Mecca. When they get there, they go to a **shrine**, or holy place. This shrine is a grey stone building called the **Kaaba** (kä′ bə). At the

Thousands of Moslems visit the Kaaba each year. This holy shrine is located in Mecca, Saudi Arabia.
■ **Why, do you think, do Moslems visit the Kaaba?**

Living in Saudi Arabia

Lailah Khali is a 9-year-old girl who lives in Riyadh (rē äd′), the capital of Saudi Arabia. Her brother is 13-year-old Ibraham. Their father is the manager of a cement factory. Their mother keeps the household running smoothly and raises the children.

Riyadh is an old city far out in the desert. However, it has become the headquarters of Saudi Arabia's oil industry and has seen great changes in recent years. Many old buildings have been torn down. In their place have risen tall office and apartment buildings. Dusty, narrow roads have given way to wide, paved streets lined with palm trees.

The home of the Khali family is in one of the newer parts of the growing city. It is a low, box-shaped building with walls of cement blocks. In the center is a small courtyard open to the sky. A cement wall 6 feet (2 m) high runs all the way around the house. The home is simply but nicely furnished. There are few chairs, since the Khalis, like most Saudi families, prefer to sit on rugs or floor cushions.

Boys and girls must go to separate schools in Saudi Arabia, so Lailah's fourth-grade classmates are girls. Lailah studies arithmetic, geography, history, Arabic, and the religion of Islam. In a later grade she will start learning English.

Each week, Lailah goes to school from Saturday through Wednesday. The "weekend" is Thursday and Friday. Friday is a special day of worship for the Moslems. After each period of 3 months of school, there is a vacation of 1 month.

Girls do not have the same freedom that boys have in choosing the kind of work they will do. Girls are trained in their home to be wives and mothers. Outside the home, only a few kinds of work, such as teaching and nursing, are open to women.

However, changes have been taking place in Saudi Arabia. When Mrs. Khali was a girl, she did not have the opportunity to go to school at all. But today most girls do attend school. The day may come when Lailah and her classmates will have more freedom in choosing their future work.

Most farming in Egypt is done along the banks of the Nile River.
■ Why would the banks of the Nile be a good place for farming?

The World's Longest River The best farming land of the Sahara is along the banks of the Nile River. The Nile is the longest river in the world. After the Nile enters Egypt, it flows for almost 1,000 miles (1,609 km) to the Mediterranean Sea.

Until about 20 years ago, the Nile overflowed its banks every summer. The water was muddy from the soil it carried. When the floodwaters went down, they left a covering of wet soil on the fields beside the river. The soil made the fields good for growing crops.

In 1968 a big dam on the Nile was finished. The dam catches and

Kaaba, Moslems kneel and pray. All streets in Mecca lead to the Kaaba, in the center of the city. Thousands of Moslems come each year to Mecca.

A Hard Life For people going through the desert, oases are pleasant places. After hours in the hot sun, they are happy to get into the shade of the palm trees. But for those living in a small oasis, life is not easy.

The wells often have muddy water and may even dry up. Sometimes, sandstorms sweep the villages. People living there seem almost out of touch with the rest of the world. Only a rough road may connect a desert village with other places. A bus or truck may come to a desert village only once or twice a week.

The Nile River is over 4,000 miles long.
■ What is the name of the world's second longest river?

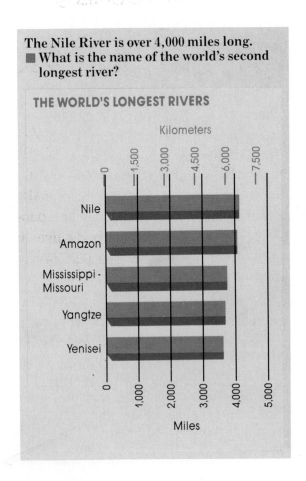

THE WORLD'S LONGEST RIVERS

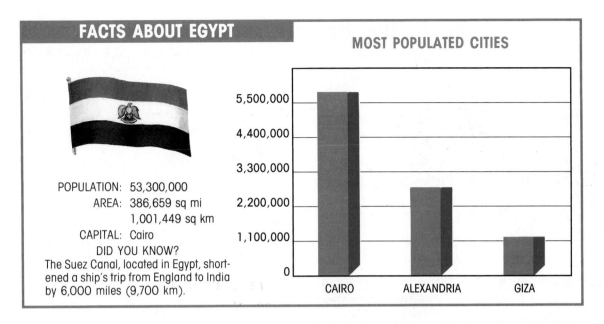

FACTS ABOUT EGYPT

POPULATION: 53,300,000
AREA: 386,659 sq mi
1,001,449 sq km
CAPITAL: Cairo
DID YOU KNOW?
The Suez Canal, located in Egypt, short-ened a ship's trip from England to India by 6,000 miles (9,700 km).

MOST POPULATED CITIES

holds back the floodwaters. When water is needed to irrigate the fields, it is let go from behind the dam. It goes into canals and ditches to water the crops. In their fields the Egyptian farmers raise cotton, corn, rice, wheat, sugarcane, and other crops.

The City of Cairo The largest city of the Sahara is Cairo (kī′ rō). It is the capital of Egypt. Over 5.8 million people live in this old city on the banks of the Nile. Most of the people of Egypt are **Arabs**. Arabs live in other countries, too, in this part of the world.

Cairo is one of the world's oldest cities. Near the city are some **pyramids** that were built more than 4,000 years ago. These huge piles of stone, carefully shaped, hold the bodies of Egyptian kings of long ago.

Some parts of Cairo look just as they have looked for many years.

Narrow, winding streets are lined with little shops. But much of Cairo looks like any modern city. People drive cars along wide avenues. Comfortable hotels welcome thousands of tourists each year. There are modern shopping areas, and there are places with factories.

Cairo is a very crowded city. Many people have moved there from small desert villages. They wanted to get away from the hard life far out in the desert. Some have found a better life, but many still are poor.

CHECKUP

1. Why do the nomads keep moving from place to place in the desert?
2. What are some of the hardships of desert life?
3. Why do most of the people of Egypt live along the Nile River?
4. **Thinking Critically** Would you rather live in a small oasis or in a large city like Cairo?

163

Changing Life in the Desert

How is life changing for people living in the Sahara and in Arab countries?

Changes in Desert Life Many changes are taking place in desert life. For example, people used to travel from one place to another by camel **caravan**. A caravan is a group of people traveling together and carrying loads of goods. Camel caravans used to be the only means of getting food and other supplies to a desert oasis. Camel caravans are still used in some places. But for the most part, trucks now carry goods to oases. Some places in the desert can be reached today only by airplane.

Another change is in the way that the desert people earn a living. There used to be many more nomads living in the desert than there are now. Some still move about the desert with their herds. But many people no longer follow the nomads' way of life. They have moved to large towns and cities. There they work in factories, in stores, and at other jobs.

The nomads still live in tents, but many desert people now live in houses. They buy their food and clothing in stores. They use electricity. They listen to radios. In some oases they plow the fields with tractors. They use pumps to draw water from wells.

Discovering Oil Why have all these changes taken place? The most important reason is the discovery of oil in the Sahara and on the Arabian Peninsula. There is more oil beneath these deserts than anywhere else in the world.

Oil is often trapped deep in the ground under layers of rock. To get the oil, workers must bore into the earth with a sharp drill. The drill is held in place by a tall tower called a **derrick**. After a hole is drilled to reach the oil, it can flow out of the **oil well**. The oil then goes into storage tanks. At this stage it is called **crude oil**.

Oil has been found in the Sahara and on the Arabian Peninsula.
■ Why is oil so important?

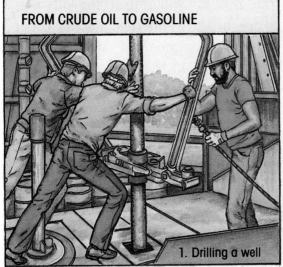

FROM CRUDE OIL TO GASOLINE

1. Drilling a well

2. Pumping the oil from the ground

3. Sending the oil to the refinery by tanker

4. Refining the oil

5. Shipping the refined oil by truck

6. Using gasoline

Unleaded

Regular

A great deal of crude oil from Saudi Arabia and nearby lands is brought to the United States. It is pumped from storage tanks onto oil tankers. These ships take the oil across the ocean to an **oil refinery**. This is a big industrial plant that makes crude oil into such products as gasoline, fuel oil, and **kerosene**. Jet planes use kerosene as fuel.

New Jobs   The oil business has created new jobs for many people of the desert. Some drill for oil. Some work in the refineries that have been built in a number of Arab countries. Some work in the stations where the oil is pumped. Still others work in the ports, loading oil onto tankers.

These jobs have changed the way of life for many people. The money that the governments get for their oil has also brought changes. In some Arab lands, part of this money has been used to build homes, hospitals, and schools. In some countries, plants have been built to change seawater into drinking water.

During the mid-1980s something interesting happened to many of the oil-producing Arab countries. Too much oil was being drilled from the ground. This caused the price of oil to go down. The Arab governments could not get as much money for their oil as they had been getting a couple of years before. But the oil business is still very important to these countries. Because of the large supplies of oil, most governments in this area have plenty of money. They can use this money, if they wish, to improve life for their people.

Many Arab countries have used the money from selling oil to start new industries.
■ What industry is shown above?

CHECKUP
1. What is a caravan?
2. Name some uses for oil.
3. What are some of the ways that Arab governments are using the money they receive for oil?

4. **Thinking Critically** What steps must be taken to make gasoline out of crude oil?

The World's Driest Desert

Why is the Atacama Desert an important place, even though not many people live there?

VOCABULARY

Chilean	sodium nitrate
copper	llama

The Atacama Desert Earlier in this chapter, you studied about the Sahara. The Sahara is a hot and dry desert located on the continent of Africa. On the continent of South America, there is a desert that is drier than the Sahara. It is so dry that there is almost no plant life. Only low, bushlike plants grow along the desert's west coast, where there are always fog and clouds. As a matter of fact, it is the driest desert in the world. It is called the Atacama Desert. The average yearly rainfall in the Atacama is about 1/2 inch (1.3 cm) a year. The desert stretches for about 600 miles (970 km) in the northern part of the country of Chile.

A Strangely Shaped Country Chile is located along the western border of South America. It is more than ten times as long as it is wide. Find Chile on the map of South America on page 359. The western boundary of Chile is the Pacific Ocean. To the east, Chile is bordered by the Andes Mountains. The Andes stretch for nearly 5,000 miles (8,045 km) all along the western edge of South America. The Andes are the world's longest mountain range.

Living in Chile Over 12,000,000 people live in Chile. The people of Chile are called **Chileans**. Most of them live in cities. They work on

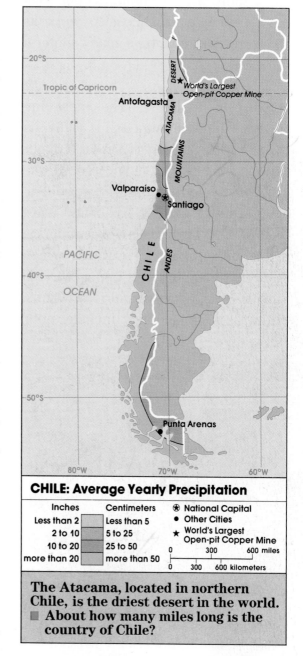

CHILE: Average Yearly Precipitation

Inches	Centimeters	
Less than 2	Less than 5	⊛ National Capital
2 to 10	5 to 25	● Other Cities
10 to 20	25 to 50	★ World's Largest Open-pit Copper Mine
more than 20	more than 50	

0   300   600 miles
0   300   600 kilometers

The Atacama, located in northern Chile, is the driest desert in the world.
■ About how many miles long is the country of Chile?

167

farms, in factories, or in mines. Chile's farmers raise livestock, including cattle, hogs, and sheep. Wheat is the most important crop grown in Chile, but beans, peas, and potatoes are also grown. Factories in Chile make clothing, food products, radios, and televisions. Most Chileans have radios and many more are beginning to get televisions. People in Chile also work as miners of the country's many mineral resources.

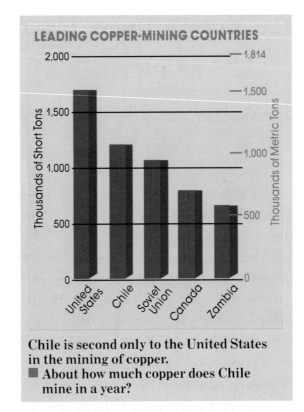

Chile is second only to the United States in the mining of copper.
■ About how much copper does Chile mine in a year?

Mining in Chile The most important mineral mined in Chile is **copper**. The largest open-pit copper mine in the world is located in the Atacama Desert. Copper is a reddish-orange metal. Copper has many uses. One of the main uses for copper is to be made into wire through which electricity can travel. Copper wire is used in telephones and televisions. Other uses for copper include pots, pans, lamps, and jewelry. Chile is the world's second leading country in copper mining. Look at the bar graph above. Which country does more copper mining than Chile?

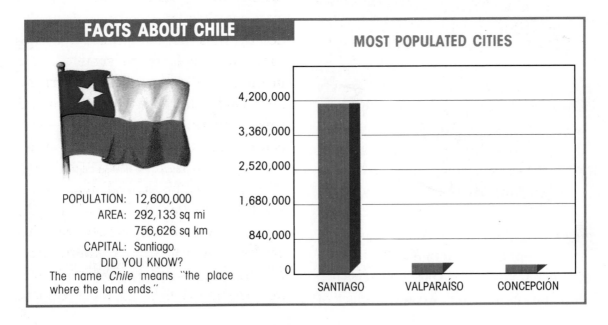

FACTS ABOUT CHILE

POPULATION: 12,600,000
AREA: 292,133 sq mi
756,626 sq km
CAPITAL: Santiago
DID YOU KNOW?
The name *Chile* means "the place where the land ends."

MOST POPULATED CITIES

Another mineral mined in Chile's Atacama Desert is **sodium nitrate**. This mineral is used to make fertilizers and explosives. Mining sodium nitrate was an important industry in Chile until about the year 1928. At that time, synthetic nitrate started to be produced and there was no longer a need for so much sodium nitrate. Today there are only a few sodium nitrate mines still operating in the Atacama Desert. But the towns from which the sodium nitrate was shipped are still found along Chile's western coast. Railroad lines connected the ports in these towns to the mines in the Atacama Desert.

The llama is an animal that is found only in South America.
■ Can you describe what a llama looks like?

A blast is set off at the world's largest open-pit copper mine, in Chile.
■ **Why is there so much dust?**

The Atacama Desert Today   The first people to live in the Atacama Desert were Indians. Their villages were widely scattered throughout the desert. These Indians, called the Atacama, were able to do some farming in the desert. They learned to irrigate their land with water from rivers and small streams. The Indians grew corn, beans, and squash. The Atacama Indians also herded **llamas** (yä′ mä). The llama is an animal that is related to another desert animal that you learned about earlier in this chapter, the camel. But unlike camels, llamas do not have humps. Llamas are found only on the continent

Some of Chile's little fishing villages that are visited today by tourists were once port cities for shipping sodium nitrate.
■ How can you tell this village is visited by tourists?

of South America. Have you ever seen a llama in a zoo?

As Europeans started to settle in South America, the number of Atacama Indians began to dwindle. Today very few ancestors of these Indians are left in the Atacama Desert.

Not many people live in the Atacama Desert today. Most of the people that are there work as miners in the copper mines. Very few of these people stay in the Atacama Desert their entire lives. All supplies that are needed to live, including water, have to be brought into the desert for the miners.

A few small settlements do exist on oases near rivers or streams. Here, limited farming can be done because there is water to irrigate the fields. Potatoes and alfalfa are the crops usually grown on these farms. The port cities that once shipped out sodium nitrate to the rest of the world are now quiet little fishing villages visited by tourists. But the future of the Atacama Desert still rests with the minerals, especially copper, that are found below the ground of this dry land.

CHECKUP

1. Where is the Atacama Desert located?
2. What is the name of the mountains that form Chile's eastern boundary?
3. What is the most important mineral mined in the Atacama Desert?

4. **Thinking Critically** If you were given the chance to change one thing about the Atacama Desert, what would it be?

Understanding Plurals

RULES FOR PLURALS

Nouns that name one person, place, or thing are in the singular form. Nouns that name more than one person, place, or thing are in the plural.

These four main rules will help you change many nouns from singular to plural.

1. Add -s to form most plurals.

    law   laws

2. Add -es to a word that ends in s, ss, sh, ch, x, or zz.

    box   boxes

    church   churches

3. If a word ends in a vowel followed by y, add -s.

    boy   boys

4. If a word ends in a consonant followed by y, change the y to i and add -es.

    army   armies

    A few words change their spelling to form plurals. Some of these words are:

    person to people

    woman to women

A DICTIONARY CAN HELP

Sometimes you may need to use a dictionary for the words that change their spelling in the plural form. Look up the singular form of the word ox. The dictionary will show you the plural form of ox next to the singular form. What is the plural form of ox?

Some words have singular and plural forms that are spelled the same way. Deer is an example.

The deer is drinking water.

Several deer ran across the field.

When you are not sure what the plural form of a noun is, look up the noun in a dictionary.

SOME SINGULAR NOUNS

A list of nouns follows. All of them were used in the chapters that you have just studied. Each word on the list is in the singular form. All these words appear between pages 120 and 166.

a. cactus   **f.** refinery

b. oasis   **g.** tourist

c. sheep   **h.** derrick

d. pueblo   **i.** bush

e. Navajo   **j.** valley

SKILLS PRACTICE

1. Copy this list of nouns on a sheet of paper. Beside each word, write the plural form. You may find the plural of some of these words in the chapters about deserts. If you cannot find the plural form in these chapters, look up the word in a dictionary. If the plural is formed in a special way, the dictionary will show it. If the dictionary does not show the plural, then you will know that the plural is formed by adding s.

2. After you have finished writing the plurals, use the plural form of each word in a sentence. Write sentences about things that you have learned in your study of deserts and the people that live in deserts.

CHAPTER 8 REVIEW

MAIN IDEAS

1. The world's largest desert is the Sahara in northern Africa.
2. The Sahara gets very little rain.
3. There are mountain ranges along the northern edge and in the middle of the Sahara.
4. The palm tree and the camel are the plant and animal most people think of when the Sahara is mentioned.
5. Nomads are small family groups that live in the desert, roaming from one place to another in search of food and water.
6. Cairo, Egypt, is one of the world's largest cities. Today it looks like many other modern cities with comfortable hotels, modern shopping centers, and wide streets crowded with cars.
7. The discovery of oil has brought many changes and improvements to the people of the Sahara and many Arab nations.
8. The Atacama Desert is the driest desert in the world.
9. The Atacama Desert contains large amounts of important minerals, including copper.

VOCABULARY REVIEW

Choose the correct ending for each sentence. Write your answers on a separate sheet of paper.

1. An oasis is (a) a mountain in the desert, (b) a place in the desert where there are plants and water, (c) a dry stream, (d) an area of sand dunes.
2. Caravans are (a) groups of desert travelers, (b) oil-drilling equipment, (c) houses in an oasis, (d) roots of desert plants.

3. Almost every oasis in the Sahara has (a) an oil well, (b) date palm trees, (c) pyramids, (d) a river.
4. The dream of all Moslems is to visit the city of (a) Cairo, (b) Mecca, (c) Jidda, (d) Palm Springs.
5. An important animal to the Atacama Indians was the (a) camel, (b) sheep, (c) llama, (d) horse.

CHAPTER CHECKUP

1. Where is the Arabian Peninsula in relation to the Sahara?
2. Why is the Nile River important to Egypt?
3. How is life in the Sahara changing?
4. What animal is most important to the people of the Sahara?
5. How would you describe the land of the Sahara?
6. What is copper used for?
7. **Thinking Critically** Compare the Atacama Desert with the Sahara.
8. **Thinking Critically** What effects would the discovery of oil in the Atacama Desert have on Chile?
9. **Thinking Critically** How would our lives be different without gasoline?
10. **Thinking Critically** Explain the importance of oases in a desert.

APPLYING KNOWLEDGE

Imagine that you are going to travel by car with your parents into the Sahara. You will drive from the northern coast of Africa to an oasis about 300 miles (480 km) to the south. The road is rough. It will take you about 4 days to get to the oasis. What difficulties might you have? What things will you need to take with you?

SUMMARIZING UNIT 3

REVIEWING VOCABULARY

1. desert   A desert is a place that gets little rain. Few things grow in a desert because of the lack of water. There are deserts in the United States and around the world. Name two deserts in the United States. What is the name of the world's largest desert?

2. cactus   The cactus is a plant that can survive the hot temperatures of the desert. What is special about cactus plants that let them live in the desert?

3. sand dunes   Crossing Death Valley, one can see sand dunes. How are sand dunes formed?

4. oasis   Most of the people who live in the Sahara are near an oasis. Why is an oasis the best place in a desert to live?

5. nomad   People that roam from one place to another in a desert are called nomads. Why do nomads roam from place to place?

EXPRESSING YOURSELF

1. What do you think?   During the 1930s, the United States government felt that the Navajo had too many sheep and other animals grazing on the land. The government decided to ask the Navajo to destroy some of their animals. The Navajo did what the government asked, but they did not like it. What would you have done if you were the Navajo?

2. What if . . .?   What if you and your family were forced to move to a desert and you could only take ten items with you. What would those ten items be?

3. You make the decision   Imagine that you were one of the thousands of gold seekers rushing to California in 1849. Would you decide to take the shortcut through Death Valley or the longer, safer route. Explain your answer as though you were speaking with the group of people traveling to California with you.

4. In your opinion   The governments of the Arab countries get a lot of money from oil and other minerals discovered in the deserts. In what ways could this money be used to best help the people of those countries?

5. Who would you rather be?   In Chapter 8, you studied about the Sahara and Atacama deserts. If you had the choice, would you rather live as a nomad in the Sahara or a copper miner in the Atacama desert?

UNIT

4

Plains Regions

In this unit you will be learning about plains. If you look on pages 34–37, your Picture Dictionary defines a plain as an almost level, often treeless piece of grassy land that stretches for miles and miles. Plains regions are some of the most important places on the earth. Almost half of the earth's land is covered with plains.

Plains are level lands that stretch for many miles. One big area of plains in the United States is in the central part of our country. Wheat is grown on some of these plains.
■ How many combines do you see in this picture?

174

Not all plains are alike. Some plains have good farmland. This farmland can be used for growing crops or raising livestock. Other plains are found along the coasts of countries. These plains are called coastal plains. Although some coastal plains have farmland, there are many large cities located on coastal plains. Millions of people live in cities located on coastal plains.

Some farmland in plains regions is used for grazing. This wild pony grazes in Virginia.
■ Do you think this land is flat?

Many cities are located on our country's coastal plains. Charleston, South Carolina, is on the Atlantic Coastal Plain.
■ Are there many tall buildings in this picture?

Plains regions can be found on every continent except Antarctica. The map below shows where these plains are located. The largest plain in the world is on the continent of Asia, in the northern Soviet Union. It is called the West Siberian Plain. It covers more than 1 million square miles (2.6 million km). The North European Plain, on the continent of Europe, contains some of the world's best farmland.

Farmers are shown stacking dried flax in a field. The fiber of the flax plant is used to make linen.
■ About how tall are the cone-shaped stacks?

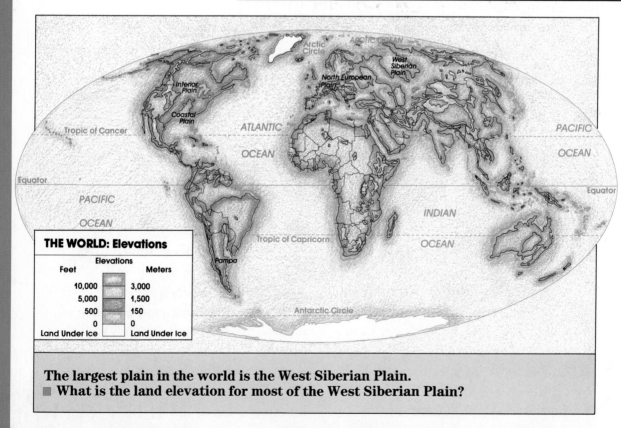

THE WORLD: Elevations

Elevations	
Feet	Meters
10,000	3,000
5,000	1,500
500	150
0	0
Land Under Ice	Land Under Ice

The largest plain in the world is the West Siberian Plain.
■ What is the land elevation for most of the West Siberian Plain?

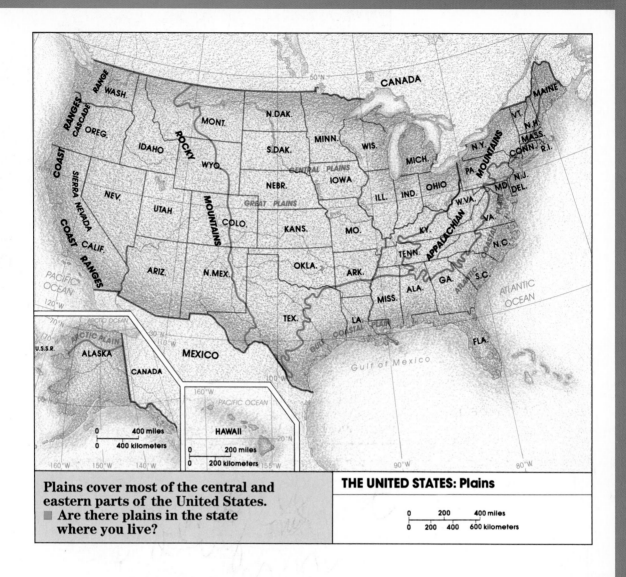

Plains cover most of the central and eastern parts of the United States.
■ Are there plains in the state where you live?

THE UNITED STATES: Plains

0   200   400 miles
0   200   400   600 kilometers

In South America, the large plain in the country of Argentina is called the Pampa. *Pampa* is the Spanish word for "plain." This region is used for raising sheep and cattle and for farming. Can you find the West Siberian Plain, the North European Plain, and the Pampa on the map on page 176? Also, locate on the map the plains regions on the continents of North America, Africa, and Australia.

In the United States there are two big areas of plains. These plains are shown on the map on this page. One is in the middle of our country between the Appalachian and Rocky mountains. These plains are divided into two parts. The first part is called the Central Plains. The Central Plains begin in Ohio and stretch westward into the middle of the state of Kansas.

The Indians were the first people to live on the Central Plains. About 200 years ago settlers from the East started moving onto the Central Plains. These settlers called the Central Plains *prairies* because of the big open meadows of tall, thick grass.

Plains Indians sometimes used animals to pull loads. A load was placed on a platform that rested on two poles.
■ What kinds of animals are pulling these loads?

Corn is Iowa's most important crop. Much of the corn being harvested here will be used to feed hogs and pigs, such as those shown at the right.
■ Iowa is part of what plains region in our country?

The Great Plains are west of the Central Plains, where the land gradually rises to a higher elevation. The Great Plains reach from Kansas, Nebraska, North Dakota, and South Dakota to the Rocky Mountains.

Both the Central Plains and the Great Plains run through Kansas. Kansas City is on the eastern border of the Central Plains region.
■ Can you tell by looking at the flag if there is a strong breeze?

For years the Great Plains were called the Great American Desert because settlers thought that the region was too dry to grow crops in. In time, people realized that the soil in the Great Plains was good and that there was enough moisture for some crops. Quickly, the Great Plains began to be settled just as the Central Plains were.

The rich soil of the Central Plains and the Great Plains is the region's most important natural resource. Most wheat from which our bread and cereals are made is grown on the plains in the central part of the United States. More wheat is grown there than anywhere else on earth. For this reason, the plains in the center of our country are sometimes called the Breadbasket of the World.

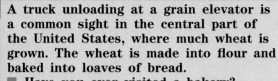

A truck unloading at a grain elevator is a common sight in the central part of the United States, where much wheat is grown. The wheat is made into flour and baked into loaves of bread.
■ Have you ever visited a bakery?

Christopher and Elizabeth often enjoy a snack of whole wheat bread when they come home from school.
■ Do you sometimes have milk, bread, and peanut butter for a snack?

The other area of plains in the United States is along the Atlantic Ocean and the Gulf of Mexico. There are two parts of this coastal plain. They are called the Atlantic Coastal Plain and the Gulf Coastal Plain. Many big cities, including New York City, Boston, New Orleans, and Houston, are located on the coastal plain. These cities developed close to water for transportation purposes. Can you name any other big cities in the United States located on the coastal plain?

New York, the largest city in our country, is on the Atlantic Coastal Plain. New York is an important seaport.
■ Have you ever had the opportunity to visit New York City?

9 Illinois: A State in the Great Lakes Region

The Great Lakes Region

What makes the Great Lakes Region an important part of our country?

VOCABULARY

barge	blizzard
continental climate	tornado

The Great Lakes States Located in the middle of our country is a large plain. As you already know, this plain is divided into two parts, the Central Plains and the Great Plains. Both the Central Plains and the Great Plains are divided into smaller regions. One of the regions in the Central Plains is called the Great Lakes Region. Five large lakes are located in this area. These five lakes are quite close to each other. Their names are Lake Michigan, Lake Huron, Lake Superior, Lake Erie, and Lake Ontario.

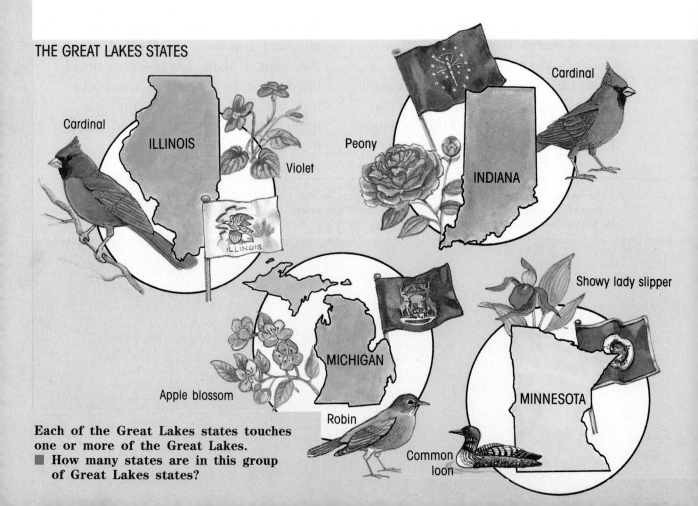

THE GREAT LAKES STATES

Cardinal

ILLINOIS

Violet

ILLINOIS

Cardinal

Peony

INDIANA

Apple blossom

MICHIGAN

Robin

Showy lady slipper

MINNESOTA

Common loon

Each of the Great Lakes states touches one or more of the Great Lakes.
■ How many states are in this group of Great Lakes states?

Together these five lakes are known as the Great Lakes. Locate these five lakes on the map on page 184.

In the Central Plains there are six states that touch one or more of the Great Lakes. They are Minnesota, Wisconsin, Michigan, Illinois, Indiana, and Ohio. These six states along with the states of New York and Pennsylvania make up the Great Lakes Region. New York and Pennsylvania also touch the Great Lakes, but these two states are not part of the Central Plains.

Important Cities   There are some very important cities in the Great Lakes Region. Chicago, Illinois, is the largest of these cities. It is a famous center of industry and transportation. You will learn more about Chicago later in this chapter. Other major cities in the region are Detroit, Michigan; Cleveland, Ohio; Gary, Indiana; Milwaukee, Wisconsin; Duluth, Minnesota; Erie, Pennsylvania; and Buffalo, New York.

Each of these cities is located on or near the shore of one of the Great Lakes. Boats and **barges** can travel from city to city. A barge is a flat-bottomed boat used to transport goods. Products can be shipped from the Great Lakes Region to other parts of the world by using the St. Lawrence Seaway. This seaway connects

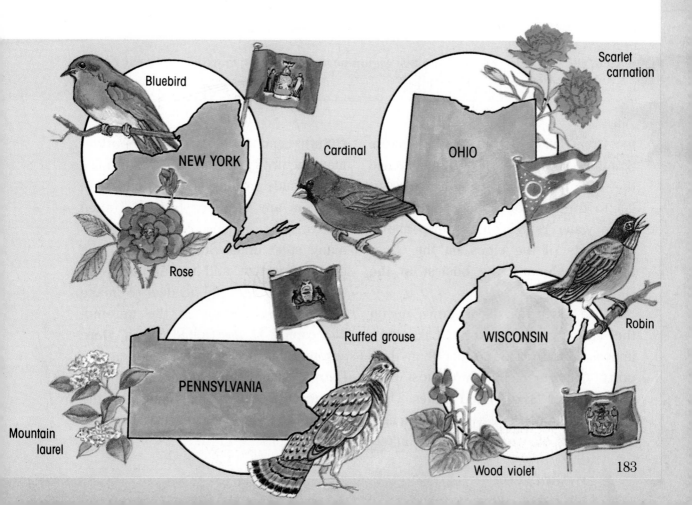

Bluebird

NEW YORK

Rose

Scarlet carnation

Cardinal

OHIO

Robin

Ruffed grouse

WISCONSIN

PENNSYLVANIA

Mountain laurel

Wood violet

183

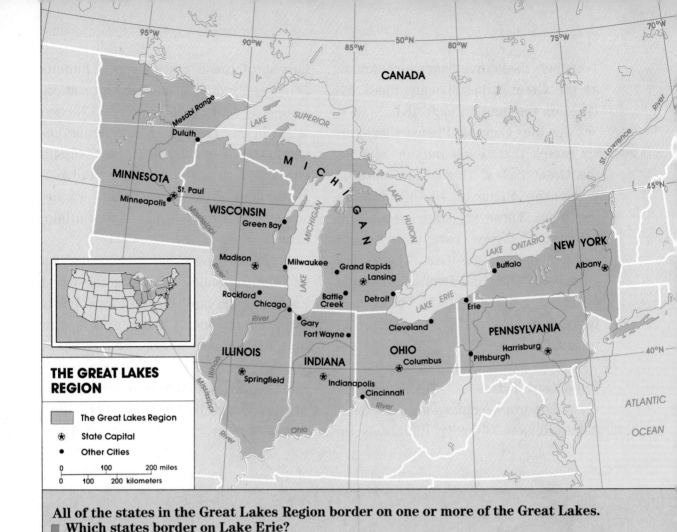

THE GREAT LAKES REGION

	The Great Lakes Region
✵	State Capital
•	Other Cities

0 — 100 — 200 miles
0 — 100 — 200 kilometers

All of the states in the Great Lakes Region border on one or more of the Great Lakes.
■ Which states border on Lake Erie?

the Great Lakes to the Atlantic Ocean. Small boats and barges can also use the Illinois and Mississippi rivers to get to the Gulf of Mexico. Find all of these water routes on the map above. The ports of the cities on the Great Lakes are among the busiest in the United States.

The cities that have grown up on the shores of the Great Lakes are important for reasons other than their ports. Chicago is the third most populated city in the United States. Over 3 million people live in Chicago. The cities of Cleveland, Milwaukee,

Duluth, and Erie are all important manufacturing centers. The flour mills in Buffalo produce more flour than those in any other city in the United States. Gary, Indiana, is known for its many steel mills. Steel is one of the most important and useful metals in the world. Steel is needed to make automobiles. Detroit is the automobile capital of the United States. More automobiles are made in the city of Detroit than in any other city in the country. Detroit's nickname is the Motor City. Have you ever visited any of these cities?

184

Seasonal Changes   In general, the Great Lakes Region has a **continental climate**. This means the summers are hot and humid, and the winters are cold and snowy. People living in the Great Lakes Region are used to harsh winter storms called **blizzards**. Blizzards are snowstorms with high winds. Traveling is very difficult during a blizzard.

Even more dangerous than blizzards are storms called **tornadoes**. Tornadoes are very strong winds that sweep across the land in a narrow path. The winds whirl down from a funnel-shaped, black cloud. The winds are so powerful that they can blow buildings apart and toss automobiles around like tiny toys. Tornadoes are more common in the southern part of the Great Lakes Region than in the northern part.

Many Natural Resources   The natural resources of the Great Lakes Region include many lakes and rivers. The lakes and rivers serve as important waterways for transportation. They are also valuable for fishing and other recreational activities.

The rich soil of the Great Lakes Region is another important natural resource. This soil is good for growing many different kinds of crops. The region's combination of rich soil and the right amount of sunshine and rain makes it one of the best farming areas in the United States.

The Great Lakes states are also rich in mineral resources. Large deposits of coal are found beneath the soil in Illinois, Indiana, and Ohio. At one time, the Mesabi (mə säb′ ē) Range in northern Minnesota had the largest deposits of iron ore in the

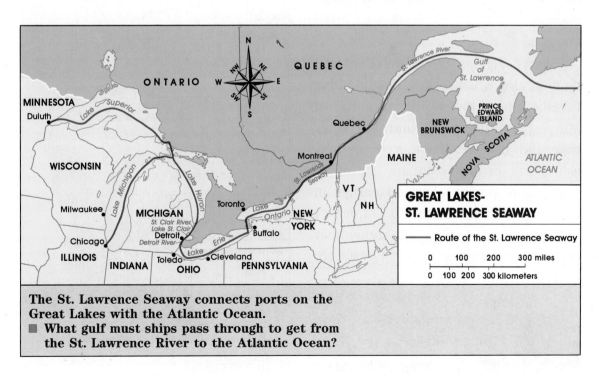

The St. Lawrence Seaway connects ports on the Great Lakes with the Atlantic Ocean.
■ What gulf must ships pass through to get from the St. Lawrence River to the Atlantic Ocean?

At this Minnesota factory each piece of cheese is covered with plastic.
■ What is the purpose of the cover?

products. Corn is grown throughout the region. Illinois ranks second only to Iowa in the production of corn. As you will learn later in this chapter, corn is a crop that has many uses.

The states of Minnesota, Michigan, and Wisconsin have many dairy farms. The next time you see a car with a Wisconsin license plate on it, you will read: AMERICA'S DAIRYLAND. Large amounts of butter and cheese come from Wisconsin.

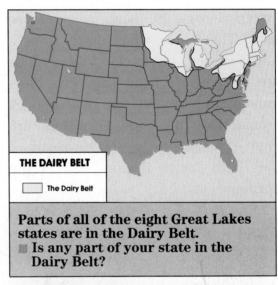

THE DAIRY BELT

☐ The Dairy Belt

Parts of all of the eight Great Lakes states are in the Dairy Belt.
■ Is any part of your state in the Dairy Belt?

United States. However, the United States uses great amounts of this resource. Today most of the very best ore has been used up. Now much of our ore comes to us from other countries. Iron ore is needed to make steel.

Large forests cover much of the land in the Great Lakes Region. Pine forests cover the northern parts of Minnesota, Wisconsin, and Michigan. Oak and hickory trees grow in several parts of the southern states of the region. As you learned earlier in this book, forests are an important natural resource. Can you remember some of the ways in which forests are useful?

Corn and Dairy Products   Two important farm products of the Great Lakes Region are corn and dairy

UNITED STATES: Corn

☐ Corn

States in the Great Lakes Region grow a lot of corn.
■ Is corn grown in your state?

Other crops grown in the Great Lakes Region are soybeans, oats, barley, and alfalfa. Most of the crops are used to feed animals. Among the most important animals raised in the region are cattle and pigs.

Industry in the Great Lakes Region

Some of our country's largest industries are located in the Great Lakes Region. Most of the farm machinery used in our country is manufactured in the Great Lakes Region. Some large meat-packing plants are located in the city of Chicago and in other parts of the region. These plants need refrigerators to keep the meat cold. Making these refrigerators is an important industry in the Great Lakes Region.

The northern states, especially Wisconsin, have plants which process milk into cheese and other dairy products. Battle Creek, Michigan, is

Many large meat-packing plants are located in the Great Lakes Region. These plants prepare and package meat. The United States has about 5,000 meat-packing plants.
■ What kind of meat, do you think, is being prepared here?

**The Great Lakes waterways help industry in the Great Lakes Region.
A huge boat nears one of the Soo Locks at Sault Ste. Marie, Michigan.**
■ **How would you describe this boat?**

famous for producing different kinds of cereals, especially cornflakes. Industries in Buffalo, New York, produce transportation equipment, machinery, and paper products.

There are two main reasons why the Great Lakes Region is a successful industrial center. The first is the large amounts of natural resources that are available. The second reason is good transportation. Waterways, railroad tracks, and airports all connect the Great Lakes Region to other parts of the United States and the world.

As you can see, the Great Lakes Region is an important part of the United States. It has important cities, large farms, and many industries. Almost in the middle of this region is the state of Illinois. Illinois also has large cities, farms, and industries. Studying about Illinois will help you better understand what the entire Great Lakes Region is like.

CHECKUP

1. What are the eight states in the Great Lakes Region?
2. Name the five Great Lakes.
3. What are two important farm products of the Great Lakes Region?
4. **Thinking Critically** Why did the Great Lakes Region become an important industrial center?

Farming in Illinois

What two products are most important to farmers in Illinois?

VOCABULARY

barbed wire	reaper
steel plow	insulin

Early Settlers in Illinois Indian tribes once lived in the area that is now Illinois. Forests and tall grass covered the land. The first European settlers came to Illinois to hunt animals for their fur. But soon, farmers started to move into Illinois. They cleared the land and started to grow crops. It did not take long for the farmers to realize how rich the soil in Illinois was.

These farmers had problems with animals wandering onto their fields and eating or destroying their crops. In 1873 a farmer by the name of J. F. Glidden, from De Kalb, Illinois,

This McCormick Harvesting Machine Company advertisement dates back to about 1875. Before the McCormick reaper came into use, farmers had to cut grain by hand at harvesttime.
■ In what year was the company established?

"OUR FIELD IS THE WORLD."

LIGHT DRAFT. SUPERIOR DESIGN.

CLEAN AND RAPID CUTTER.

McCormick No. 2 IRON MOWER.

McCormick Harvesting Machine Co., Chicago.

ESTABLISHED 1831.

Barbed wire was invented by J. F. Glidden in 1873. Its purpose was to protect crops and animals.
■ Why, do you think, was barbed wire very useful for this land?

solved the problem. Glidden invented something that would protect his farmland. His invention was called **barbed wire**. Barbed wire is two or three steel wires twisted together with sharp points called barbs about every 12 inches (30 cm). Farmers used barbed wire to fence in their land. It was a good way to protect both their crops and their animals.

Two other inventions also helped the early farmers in Illinois. These inventions were the **steel plow** and the **reaper**. The steel plow made it easier for the farmer to turn over the soil and prepare it for planting. Before the steel plow, most plows were made of wood. The reaper also made farming easier. It is a machine that is used to harvest crops. Railroads and waterways also helped farmers get their products to market places near and far.

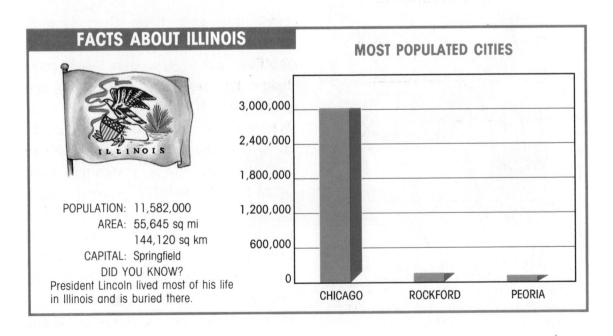

FACTS ABOUT ILLINOIS

ILLINOIS

POPULATION: 11,582,000
AREA: 55,645 sq mi
144,120 sq km
CAPITAL: Springfield
DID YOU KNOW?
President Lincoln lived most of his life in Illinois and is buried there.

MOST POPULATED CITIES

	3,000,000
	2,400,000
	1,800,000
	1,200,000
	600,000
	0
CHICAGO	ROCKFORD	PEORIA

Corn and Beef You already know that corn is an important crop in Illinois. But did you know that if you were to load all the corn grown in Illinois in one year onto train cars, you would have a train that stretches for 7,600 miles (12,228 km)? That is more than twice the distance between New York and California. That is a lot of corn! Look at the bar graph on this page to find the names of the five leading corn-producing states. About how much corn does Illinois produce in one year?

What do farmers do with all that corn? Most of us have eaten corn on the cob at a picnic. At some time you may have also eaten canned or frozen kernels of corn. Some corn is

This farmer in Plainfield, Illinois, is harvesting corn.
■ **What products are made from corn?**

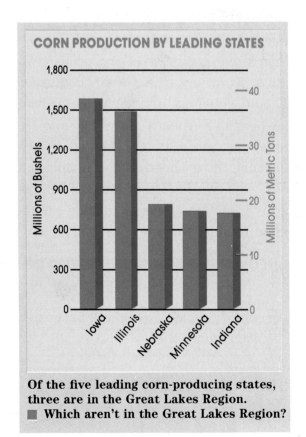

CORN PRODUCTION BY LEADING STATES

Of the five leading corn-producing states, three are in the Great Lakes Region.
■ **Which aren't in the Great Lakes Region?**

made into corn flour. Corn flour is used to make corn bread and corn muffins. Have you ever had cornflakes for breakfast? Cornflakes and other cereals are made from corn. When was the last time you went to a movie theater? While you were watching the movie, you might have eaten a large bucket of popcorn. Some people also enjoy making popcorn at home. Can you think of any other products that are made from corn?

Most of the corn grown in Illinois is used to feed animals. Illinois is one of the leading states in raising

191

Illinois raises more soybeans than any other state in the United States. Soybeans grow well throughout Illinois.
■ How many rows of plants is this farmer cultivating?

hogs and cattle. Have you ever heard the expression *"corn on the hoof?"* It means that the corn is not sold as a grain but is used to feed animals from which we get meat.

Cattle and hogs give us more than just meat. Of course, milk comes from cows. Skins from these animals are also used to make some types of clothing. Doctors even use a liquid taken from cattle and hogs as a medicine to help control a disease called diabetes. This medicine is called **insulin**.

Other Farm Products   Another important product grown on farms in Illinois is soybeans. Soybeans are a good source of protein, which we need to stay healthy. In the United States, we get most of the protein we need from meat. In other countries, people get most of their protein from soybeans. Soybeans have become an important crop in the United States because it is needed by people all over the world. Other farm products grown on Illinois farms include pumpkins, onions, tomatoes, and melons.

CHECKUP

1. What are some of the uses of corn?

2. What does the expression *"corn on the hoof"* mean?

3. What is insulin used for?

4. **Thinking Critically** In what ways have the steel plow and the reaper helped farmers?

Industry in Illinois

VOCABULARY

food processing	peat
bituminous	hardware

Industry Develops   You learned earlier in this chapter that the Great Lakes Region is an important industrial center. Illinois is one of the most industrial states in the region. As in most other places, industry in Illinois developed to help meet the needs of the people.

Two of the earliest industries in Illinois were started in the cities of Moline and Chicago. In 1847, John Deere opened a factory that made steel plows in the city of Moline. In that same year, in Chicago, a man named Cyrus McCormick started a business that made reapers. Do you remember what a reaper does? Today, Illinois is still a center for manufacturing farm equipment. Farmers from all over the country buy their farming machinery from companies in Illinois.

Second to the production of farm machinery in Illinois is the **food-processing** industry. In food-processing plants, farm products are prepared for sale in stores. Meat packing is an important food-processing industry in Illinois. Meat packing must be done quickly to make sure that the meat stays fresh. Other food-processing plants process dairy products, fruits, vegetables, corn, and soybeans and other grains. Products such as cereal, butter, and cheese are all made in food-processing plants.

Mineral Resources and Industry
Illinois is one of the leading states in the mining of **bituminous** (bə tü′ mə nəs), or soft coal. Bituminous coal is used in making steel. Another mineral

Illinois is an important state located in the middle of the Great Lakes Region.
■ About how many miles (km) is it from Chicago to the state capital of Springfield?

193

resource found in Illinois is oil. Large deposits of oil are found beneath the ground in the southeastern part of the state.

Clay, limestone, sand, stone, and **peat** are also found in the state. Peat is decayed moss and plants used to make fuel and fertilizers. Using waterways, Illinois ships its mineral resources to other industrial centers in the United States.

Transportation Industry 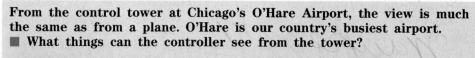 Waterways connect Illinois with the other states in the Great Lakes Region, the Atlantic Ocean, and the Gulf of Mexico. The city of Chicago is the transportation center of the state. O'Hare Airport is our country's busiest airport. Miles and miles of railroad tracks and highways connect Chicago with other parts of the state and country. Also, Chicago's location on Lake Michigan makes the city an important port.

Other kinds of industries are needed to help support the transportation industry. Trains and airplanes need to be maintained and repaired. Boats and barges need to be loaded

From the control tower at Chicago's O'Hare Airport, the view is much the same as from a plane. O'Hare is our country's busiest airport.
■ What things can the controller see from the tower?

Illinois is one of the leading states in the making of electrical equipment. This includes such things as radios and television sets. The television assembly plant above is in Chicago.
■ What is the purpose of the signs hanging in the work area?

and unloaded. Travelers need places to eat and sleep. Thousands of people in Illinois work in industries related to transportation.

Meeting People's Needs Many people live in the Great Lakes Region. About 11 1/2 million people live in Illinois alone. Industries have developed to meet the needs of these people. Industries in Illinois produce radios, television sets, and telephone equipment. Many **hardware** products are also made in Illinois. Hardware products are things made of metal, like tools, locks, nails, and screws. Other products made in Illinois and used by people are athletic equipment, clothing, shoes, and medicines. Many of these products are also sold in other parts of the country.

CHECKUP

1. What is John Deere famous for?
2. What types of food-processing plants are found in Illinois?
3. Name two important mineral resources found in Illinois.
4. **Thinking Critically** How is industry in Illinois meeting the needs of the people of the state?

195

Cities Then and Now: Galena and Chicago

Why are the cities of Galena and Chicago important to Illinois?

Changing Times   About 150 years ago, there were not many large cities in Illinois. Today there are many large cities, like Springfield, Champaign, Peoria, and Chicago. But not every city in Illinois has a large population. Some cities have fewer people today than they did years ago. One such city is Galena.

Galena is located in the northwest corner of the state. Although Galena is no longer the growing city it once was, it is still important. Galena has been able to **preserve**, or protect from change, life as it was in Illinois many years ago. Studying about the history of a city like Galena can be both fun and interesting.

The Early Days   Galena is a city with a lot of history. It was founded in the 1820s, and by 1845 it was one of the largest cities in Illinois.

Many people moved to Galena to work in lead mines. Lead is a soft, heavy metal that is used to make pipes and other things. Others moved to Galena to start businesses and

detail, Chicago Historical Society

In 1856, Galena was one of the most prosperous cities in Illinois.
■ What do the big river boats tell you about Galena?

The History of Illinois

Indians were the first people to live in the area that is now called Illinois. The first Europeans in Illinois were French explorers, Jacques Marquette (mär ket′) and Louis Jolliet (zhôl yā′), who arrived in 1673. They were followed by French traders who came to hunt animals for their furs and to trade with the Indians. By 1717, Illinois was part of a French colony.

When English traders started to move into Illinois, the French became angry. A war between the two countries started. This war was known as the French and Indian War. It was fought between the years 1754 and 1763. In the war the English defeated the French and Indians. The English took control of Illinois and other French colonies in North America. More English settlers started to move into Illinois.

The United States became an independent country in 1783. Illinois was made a state in 1818. Illinois developed as a transportation center for the entire country.

Throughout the 1800s, Illinois continued to grow. New industries started to appear. People from other countries started to move into Illinois. These people are known as immigrants. They worked on farms and in factories. By the beginning of the 1900s, Illinois was a leader in farming and industry.

In 1860, Abraham Lincoln was elected President of the United States. At the time he was elected President, Lincoln lived in Springfield, Illinois. President Lincoln is most famous for ending slavery in the United States. Today, Illinois is so proud of Abraham Lincoln that the state license plates have the saying *Land of Lincoln.*

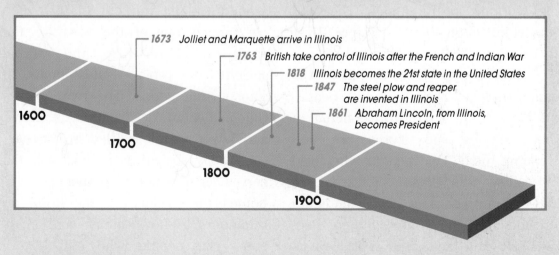

1673 Jolliet and Marquette arrive in Illinois
1763 British take control of Illinois after the French and Indian War
1818 Illinois becomes the 21st state in the United States
1847 The steel plow and reaper are invented in Illinois
1861 Abraham Lincoln, from Illinois, becomes President

1600 1700 1800 1900

Galena, Illinois, still has many homes that date from the 1800s. The Bedford House, above, was built in 1850.
■ Do you think this home would be a pleasant house to live in?

stores to meet the needs of the people working in the mines. The lead was shipped on the Mississippi River to other parts of the country.

Many people living in Galena became wealthy. They built big, beautiful homes and large stores. Some of these homes and stores are still standing today. One person who lived in Galena was Ulysses S. Grant. In 1869, Grant became the eighteenth President of the United States. People can still see and visit Grant's home in Galena.

Galena Today   As the mines around Galena ran out of lead, people moved out of the town to find work elsewhere. Also, the railroad started to replace steamboats in transporting goods. The river port in Galena became less important. Fewer and fewer people settled in Galena.

Today, Galena is a small city that serves as a window to the past. The homes, the streets, and the stores are reminders of how things were in the past. The people who still live in Galena try to preserve the buildings.

Some of the buildings and homes have been **restored**, or rebuilt to the way they used to be.

A City That's Still Growing   In some ways, Chicago is today what Galena was more than 100 years ago. Chicago is an active and busy city. It is a business and transportation center. People move to Chicago to start businesses and to find jobs, just as people once did in Galena.

Chicago is also much different from Galena. For one thing, Chicago is much larger. As you know, the city now has a population of over 3 million people. But the whole metropolitan area of Chicago has a population of about 7 million people. As you learned in Chapter 6, a metropolitan area is made up of a large city and surrounding smaller cities, towns, and other communities. Another difference between Chicago and Galena is that Chicago has many more connections with other places. Airplanes, railroads, automobiles, and ships can easily reach Chicago. Chicago has continued to grow, whereas Galena has stopped growing.

Chicago's History   The first people to live in the area that later became Chicago were Indians. Then in 1772 a black man named Jean Baptiste Pointe Du Sable (jôn bap′ tist pwĕt du sah′ bul) built a home and a trading post in this area. Du Sable was a hardworking trader and farmer. He grew corn and raised cattle to eat

In 1779, Chicago looked much different than it does today. Jean Baptiste Pointe Du Sable (inset) was its first permanent settler.
■ Can you find Du Sable's cabin in both the photograph and the stamp?

detail, Chicago Historical Society

Jean Baptiste
Pointe Du Sable
22

Black Heritage USA

In this 1869 view from a bridge, the Chicago River was crowded with ships.
■ What kind of ships are shown?

Chicago Historical Society. ICHi-03731

(4,800 km) of railroad track. The population of Chicago had grown to over 100,000 people, making it the largest city in Illinois.

In October 1871 a large fire destroyed most of downtown Chicago. Many people were left homeless. Rebuilding Chicago was a difficult job. But the new buildings brought new industries and more people to Chicago. By 1890, Chicago's population had grown to over 1 million people. Throughout most of the 1900s, Chicago's population has continued to grow.

Chicago Today   Chicago is still a leader in industry and transportation. But there are some problems that the

In 1871 the great fire at Chicago destroyed 17,000 buildings.
■ What kept these boats safe from the flames of the fire?

and trade. His trading post grew larger every year. Many people came to the Chicago area to visit Du Sable's trading post. As a result, the population started to grow.

In March of 1837, Chicago was made a city. The major industry of the city was transportation. A canal connected Chicago to the Mississippi River. But it was the coming of the railroad that made Chicago the transportation center for the whole country. By the year 1856, Chicago had ten railroad lines and over 3,000 miles

Chicago, one of the world's great cities, is a leader in industry and transportation. Harold Washington (inset) was the city's first black mayor. ■ Would you like to be mayor of a large city someday?

city must deal with. There are not enough jobs for all the people who want to work. Some people are forced to live in overcrowded conditions. The number of crimes has increased.

But just as in the past, the people of Chicago are not giving up on their city. In 1983, Harold Washington was elected mayor. He was the first black mayor in the history of the city. Before he died, Mayor Washington worked hard to rebuild Chicago's neighborhoods, to make the city safe, and to provide help for the needy. All

of Chicago's problems have not yet been solved. But the city's people are continuing to work as hard as ever to keep Chicago a great city.

CHECKUP

1. Name some major cities in Illinois.
2. What natural resource made Galena an important city?
3. Who was the first black mayor of Chicago?
4. **Thinking Critically** Compare the growth of Galena with the growth of Chicago.

201

Understanding Cause and Effect

EVENTS HAVE RELATIONSHIPS

When one thing happens, it sometimes causes something else to happen. For example, a car was driven too fast. It went off the road and hit a tree. We call this a cause-and-effect relationship. The cause of what happened was the speed of the car. The effect was the car's leaving the road and hitting a tree.

It is important in social studies to be able to tell if one event causes another. Picking out cause-and-effect relationships is a part of the skill of thinking clearly. In the reading that follows, look for cause-and-effect relationships.

A STORY

The first settlers on the Great Plains used plows drawn by horses and oxen. The plows cut into the soil only 5 or 6 inches (12 or 15 cm). The roots of grasses and other plants were deeper. These roots kept the topsoil tied to the soil below.

Then new farm machines came into use. The new plows, drawn by tractors, cut deep into the soil. They destroyed the plant roots. With their new machines, farmers could plant and harvest more crops. The farmers tore down fences and cut trees and bushes to make bigger fields.

During the 1930s there was a long drought. Crops died from lack of moisture. When the wind blew, dry topsoil filled the air because there were no roots to hold the soil in place. Without trees, bushes, or fences to separate the fields, there was nothing to break the force of the wind. The sky often became dark with "black blizzards."

When rain finally did fall, there were no roots or dead leaves to soak up the water. It washed away more topsoil. The water cut deep channels in the fields and ran into the streams and rivers. When it rained hard, the rivers overflowed their banks, causing floods.

The dust storms destroyed thousands of acres of farmland. Many families left the Great Plains and sought work in other parts of the United States.

SKILLS PRACTICE

Copy the following list on a separate sheet of paper. Mark a *C* beside each item that was a cause of the dust storms. Mark an *E* beside each item that was an effect.

1. A drought
2. Floods
3. Windy weather
4. Deep plowing of the soil
5. People leaving their farms
6. "Black blizzards"
7. Making larger fields

Below are three things that can cause other things to happen. For each of these causes, write a sentence that tells what might be one or more effects.

8. The pollution of a lake
9. The discovery of oil
10. The building of a large factory

CHAPTER 9 REVIEW

MAIN IDEAS

1. The Great Lakes Region includes the states of Minnesota, Wisconsin, Michigan, Illinois, Indiana, Ohio, Pennsylvania, and New York.
2. Rich soil and the right amount of sunshine and rainfall makes the Great Lakes Region one of the best farming regions in the United States.
3. Many of our country's largest industries are in the Great Lakes Region.
4. Corn and beef are the two most important farm products in Illinois.
5. Other farm products from Illinois are soybeans, pumpkins, onions, tomatoes, and melons.
6. Two important mineral resources found in Illinois are bituminous coal and oil.
7. Illinois' major industries are the production of farm machinery, food processing, and transportation.
8. Other things made by Illinois industries include hardware products, athletic equipment, clothing, shoes, and medicines.
9. Galena is a small city that gives us a good idea of how people in Illinois lived many years ago.
10. Chicago, the third most populated city in the United States, is an important center of industry and transportation.

VOCABULARY REVIEW

Choose the correct ending for each sentence. Write your answers on a separate sheet of paper.

1. The total number of states in the Great Lakes Region is (a) eight, (b) six, (c) five.
2. A tornado is (a) a very strong wind, (b) a snowstorm, (c) an ice storm.
3. If you wanted to see a reaper, you would go to a (a) meat-packing plant, (b) mine, (c) farm.
4. Decayed moss used to make fuel is (a) clay, (b) peat, (c) stone.
5. Lead was important to the growth of the city of (a) Chicago, (b) Galena, (c) Moline.

CHAPTER CHECKUP

1. What are the names of the five Great Lakes?
2. What is a continental climate?
3. **Thinking Critically** How did waterways help in the development of the Great Lakes Region?
4. **Thinking Critically** Why is studying about Illinois a good way to learn about the Great Lakes Region?
5. **Thinking Critically** Suggest some ways that you could help to preserve the history of your community.

APPLYING KNOWLEDGE

1. On an outline map of the United States, color each of the Great Lakes blue and each of the states in the Great Lakes Region red. Then label each lake and each state.
2. Collect pictures that show the different uses for corn. If you are having a hard time finding pictures, create your own drawings that show different uses for corn. Arrange your pictures and drawings into a collage. At the top of your collage, write the title *The Many Uses of Corn*.

10 Maryland and Louisiana

The Coastal Plain of the United States

What is the coastal plain of the United States like?

VOCABULARY

coastal plain   tideland
swamp

Land Along the Coast The Central Plains is not the only plains area in the United States. There is another plain that stretches along the coast of the Atlantic Ocean and the Gulf of Mexico. This plain is called a **coastal plain**. A coastal plain is flat land that lies along a coast. The part of the coastal plain in the United States that stretches from the Atlantic Ocean to the Appalachian Mountains is called the Atlantic Coastal Plain. The part that extends several hundred miles inland from the Gulf of Mexico is called the Gulf Coastal Plain. Many states are located on the coastal plain. Maryland is one of the states found on the Atlantic Coastal Plain. Louisiana is on the Gulf Coastal Plain. In

this chapter you will be studying about these two coastal plain states.

Plains Are Different All plains are alike in that they are made up of land that is quite level. But in other ways plains are different. For example, the Central Plains can get very hot in the summer and very cold in the winter. On coastal plains there is not as big a difference between summer and winter temperatures. The reason is the closeness of coastal plains to a large body of water. Water warms up more slowly than land, and it also cools off more slowly. Therefore the breezes from the water keep the coastal plains from getting as hot or as cold as the Central Plains.

There is also a difference between the soil of the Central Plains and that of coastal plains. The soil of the Central Plains is very good for farming. But the soil of coastal plains is often mixed with sand. Although some plants, like tomatoes, grow very well in sandy soil, most plants do not grow well in this kind of soil.

Visiting a Coastal Plain There are even differences within coastal plains. In some areas, coastal plains are covered with **swamps** (swomps). A swamp is low ground that is often covered with water. One such area on the Atlantic Coastal Plain is the Blackwater Refuge in Maryland. Do you remember what a refuge is? It is

In this picture, ocean tides are shown washing up against the Atlantic Coastal Plain.
■ How would you describe this land?

An oil rig almost fills this Louisiana marshland.
■ What supports the oil derrick?

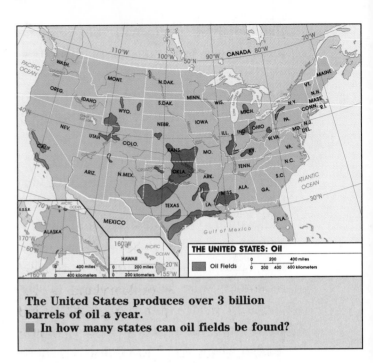

THE UNITED STATES: Oil

The United States produces over 3 billion barrels of oil a year.
■ In how many states can oil fields be found?

a place that protects people or animals. The land of the Blackwater Refuge is flat and wet. In the Blackwater Refuge you can find many different kinds of geese, ducks, and other birds. Sometimes visitors will even see a bald eagle flying away from a tall tree. The bald eagle is a symbol of our country.

In other coastal plains areas there is mining going on. One of the resources mined is oil. South of the city of New Orleans, Louisiana, you can see hundreds of oil wells all around. Many of the wells are in the **tidelands**. These are the underwater lands just off the coast. The oil is pumped out of these underwater lands by large derricks standing on platforms floating on top of the water.

There are also differences in how the land of a coastal plain is used. In some places the land can be used for farmland. Some parts of coastal plains are covered with large cities. For example, the largest city in the United States, New York City, is located on the Atlantic Coastal Plain. In this chapter you will be studying about two other large cities located on coastal plains. These cities are Baltimore, Maryland, and New Orleans, Louisiana. Let's begin our study of coastal plains by taking a look at the state of Maryland.

CHECKUP

1. What is a coastal plain?
2. Where is the coastal plain in the United States located?
3. What are the two parts, or sections, of the coastal plain in the United States called?
4. **Thinking Critically** Why, do you think, are there many large cities in the United States on the coastal plain?

Maryland

What are Maryland's most important farm products and industries?

VOCABULARY

Fall Line	broiler
fossil	colony
growing season	independence

The Fall Line   The state of Maryland is located on the Atlantic Coastal Plain. But not all of Maryland is flat. Look on the map on page 208. Find the line that separates the Atlantic Coastal Plain from other regions. This is a line of small waterfalls and rapids. It is called the **Fall Line**. East of the Fall Line the land is flat. But west of the Fall Line the land features include plateaus, valleys, ridges, and mountains.

All together there are five regions in Maryland. They are called the Atlantic Coastal Plain, the Piedmont, the Blue Ridge, the Appalachian Ridge and Valley, and the Appalachian Plateau. Although Maryland is small in size, it is a state that has many different landforms. That is why Maryland is sometimes called America in Miniature.

The Coastal Plain in Maryland Find the Chesapeake (ches′ ə pēk)

At the Great Falls in Maryland, just outside of Washington, D. C., the Potomac River enters the Atlantic Coastal Plain.
■ Can you tell if the water in the falls is moving swiftly?

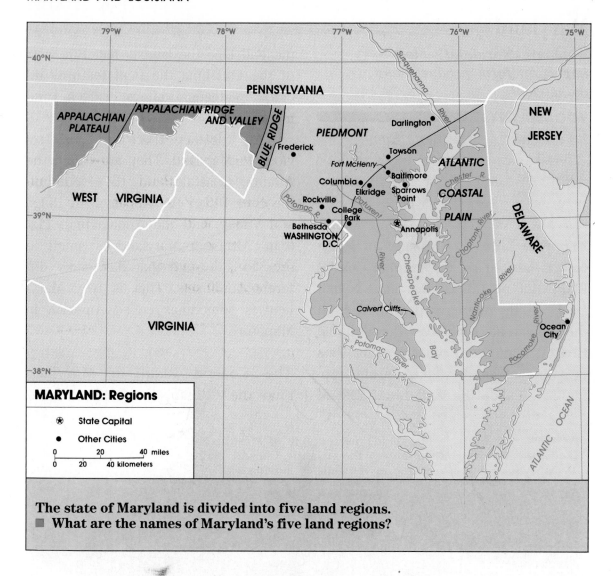

MARYLAND: Regions

⊛ State Capital

• Other Cities

0   20   40 miles
0   20   40 kilometers

The state of Maryland is divided into five land regions.
■ **What are the names of Maryland's five land regions?**

Bay on the map of Maryland on this page. This bay divides the coastal plain in Maryland into two parts, the Eastern Shore and the Western Shore. The land on the Eastern Shore is very flat. It is on the Eastern Shore that the Blackwater Refuge is located. Do you remember reading about this refuge at the beginning of the chapter? The land of the Western Shore is a little higher and has some hills. In 1952 a bridge was built over the Chesapeake Bay to connect the Eastern Shore and the Western Shore.

On the western shores of the Chesapeake Bay is a very interesting place. It is called Calvert Cliffs. These cliffs are made of sand and clay and rise 50 to 100 feet (15 to 30 m) above the Chesapeake Bay. Within these cliffs, **fossils** have been found. A fossil is the hardened remains of plants or animals that lived many years ago. Some of the fossils found at Calvert

Cliffs are 15 to 20 million years old. Scientists from all over the world have visited Calvert Cliffs to study these fossils.

Maryland's Climate   There is a difference in climate between eastern Maryland and the western part of the state. In the eastern lowlands and the coastal plain, the summers are hot and humid. The average temperature during the winter in this part of the state is about 35°F (2°C). In western Maryland, summers are cooler. This is especially true in the mountainous areas. Winter temperatures in the western part of Maryland average about 28°F (−2°C).

Maryland's precipitation is fairly even throughout the state. The southern plains and the western highlands receive a bit more precipitation than the lowlands get. The **growing season** along the Atlantic Coastal Plain is about 210 days a year. A growing season is the time of the year when crops can be grown. In other parts of the state, the average growing season is about 120 days a year.

A Lot of Farmland   About 50 percent of the land in Maryland is

Calvert Cliffs rise above the water on the western shores of the Chesapeake Bay. The fossil in the inset was found on the beach at Calvert Cliffs. It might be millions of years old.
■ Does this fossil look like a plant or an animal?

Newly hatched chicks are carefully inspected in this Maryland hatchery.
■ What would the inspectors be looking for?

wheat, cucumbers, apples, and tobacco are among some of the crops grown in Maryland. Most of the vegetables and fruits grown in Maryland are sold fresh in the nearby cities or are sent to food-processing plants.

Many Industries   Many of the people who live in Maryland work in industry. Maryland has plenty of resources to support all of the state's industries. Coal is Maryland's most important mineral resource. Coal is needed to make steel. A large steel

used for farming. Many farmers in Maryland raise chickens. Have you ever had a **broiler** for dinner? Broilers are young chickens that are good for cooking. Broilers are Maryland's leading farm product. Chickens are also raised for their eggs. Many farmers also raise dairy cattle. Milk is Maryland's second leading farm product.

Farmers in Maryland raise many other products. Corn, soybeans, hay,

At Sparrows Point, melted iron is poured into a furnace to make steel.
■ Do you think the furnace is big?

mill is located in Sparrows Point, Maryland. There are a number of steel, aluminum, and other metal industries in Baltimore and other cities throughout the state of Maryland. The products of these industries can easily be shipped from Maryland to other parts of the United States and the world. Large ships can travel from ports in Maryland through the Chesapeake Bay into the Atlantic Ocean.

Maryland's leading industry is the making of electrical machinery and equipment. Most of the state's industries are centered around the city of Baltimore. One of the most important products made by these industries is computers. Today, computers are important to all of us. Have you ever used a computer at school or at home?

There are other industries that provide jobs for people in Maryland. Some people work in Maryland's fishing industry. The Chesapeake Bay, the Atlantic Ocean, and the many inland rivers and lakes offer a variety of tasty freshwater and saltwater fish. Maryland produces more oysters than any other state in the United States. Other industries in Maryland include food processing and the making of chemicals.

People and Cities   Indians were the first people to live in the area that would become Maryland. But by the early 1600s, people from England started to move into Maryland. Maryland became an English **colony**. A colony is a place that is settled by people who leave their own country but remain citizens of that country. Great Britain had 13 colonies in what became the United States. In 1776 these 13 colonies won their **independence** from Great Britain, and formed

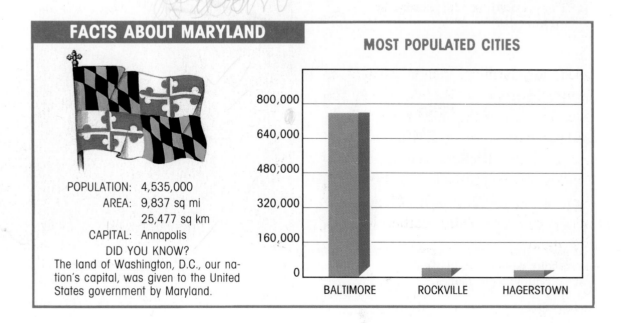

FACTS ABOUT MARYLAND

POPULATION: 4,535,000
AREA: 9,837 sq mi
25,477 sq km
CAPITAL: Annapolis
DID YOU KNOW?
The land of Washington, D.C., our nation's capital, was given to the United States government by Maryland.

MOST POPULATED CITIES

800,000 / 640,000 / 480,000 / 320,000 / 160,000 / 0

BALTIMORE   ROCKVILLE   HAGERSTOWN

their own country. Independence for a people means being free to rule their own country.

Today over 4 million people live in Maryland. Most of these people live in or around cities. Baltimore, Bethesda, Columbia, and Towson are some of Maryland's most populated cities. The city of Annapolis is the capital of Maryland.

Annapolis is also the home of the United States Naval Academy. The Naval Academy, which was started in 1845, is a four-year college that trains men and women to become officers in the United States Navy. Students at the United States Naval Academy are called midshipmen. After they finish college, midshipmen serve in the United States Navy.

At the United States Naval Academy in Annapolis, Maryland, men and women train to become officers in the United States Navy and Marine Corps.
■ How many flags are there in the picture?

The History of Maryland

The land that we now know as Maryland was once part of a large region that England claimed in North America. In 1632 the king of England gave a piece of land around the Chesapeake Bay to his friend Lord Baltimore. In honor of Queen Henrietta Maria of England, the land was named Maryland.

In March 1634 two ships, the *Ark* and the *Dove*, sailed up the Chesapeake Bay with the first settlers to arrive in Maryland from England. Lord Baltimore made Maryland a place where people could practice their own religion as they wished. Maryland remained a part of Great Britain until 1776.

In 1776, Maryland joined with the 12 other British colonies in North America to fight a war for their independence. This war is called the Revolutionary War. In the year 1783 the Revolutionary War ended. The 13 British colonies became an independent country called the United States of America.

During the Civil War, 1861 to 1865, Maryland fought on the side of the North. One of the worst battles of the war was fought in Maryland. It was the battle of Antietam. More than 22,000 soldiers were killed or wounded during this battle.

Since the Civil War, Maryland has continued to develop. During World War I and World War II factories and shipyards in Maryland turned out products needed to fight the war. After World War II, bridges, tunnels, and airports were built to improve transportation in the state. Maryland is also a leader in the field of education. The University of Maryland and Johns Hopkins University are two of the state's best colleges.

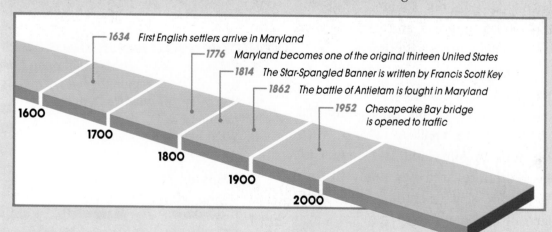

1634 First English settlers arrive in Maryland
1776 Maryland becomes one of the original thirteen United States
1814 The Star-Spangled Banner is written by Francis Scott Key
1862 The battle of Antietam is fought in Maryland
1952 Chesapeake Bay bridge is opened to traffic

1600 1700 1800 1900 2000

Baltimore's inner harbor attracts many visitors. The harbor has shops, restaurants, museums, and national landmarks.
■ Does this harbor look modern?

Baltimore is the state's most populated city, with about 760,000 people. One of the world's largest natural harbors is located in Baltimore. Many imports and exports pass through the port at Baltimore.

Many people visit Maryland for their vacation. Maryland has sandy beaches to relax on and many historic places to visit. A favorite vacation spot in Maryland is Ocean City. The Baltimore area has many historic places to visit including the birthplace of baseball's most famous player Babe Ruth. Fort McHenry is also in Baltimore. It was during a British attack on Fort McHenry in 1814 that our national anthem was written by Francis Scott Key.

CHECKUP

1. What are the names of Maryland's five physical regions?
2. What is Maryland's leading farm product?
3. What special college is located in Annapolis?
4. **Thinking Critically** How, do you think, would life be different for the people of Maryland if the Chesapeake Bay did not exist?

214

Louisiana

Why is Louisiana an important farming and industrial state?

VOCABULARY

silt	Creole
hurricane	Cajun
slave	jazz

Where a Great River Ends Turn to the map of the United States on pages 354–355. Locate the state of Louisiana on the map. If you look at the southern coast of Louisiana you will see there a river that empties into the Gulf of Mexico. Can you find the name of this river? It is the Mississippi River. With your finger trace the path of the Mississippi River from where it ends in the Gulf of Mexico all the way to its beginning. You should end up in northwestern Minnesota. The Mississippi River flows for 2,348 miles (3,779 km). It is the most important inland waterway in the United States. Many of our country's farm products and industrial products are shipped on the Mississippi River to the Gulf of Mexico.

The Mississippi River is very important to Louisiana. The waters of the Mississippi carry a lot of soil with them. As the river reaches the Gulf of Mexico it deposits most of this soil, along with sand and some ground stone, onto the shallow shores along the coast of Louisiana. This mixture of soil, sand, and ground stone is called **silt**. Over a period of time, this silt continues to build up and forms a delta. Do you remember what a delta is? If not, look back to your Picture Dictionary on pages 34–37. Throughout the years, many miles of land have been added to the southern coast of Louisiana.

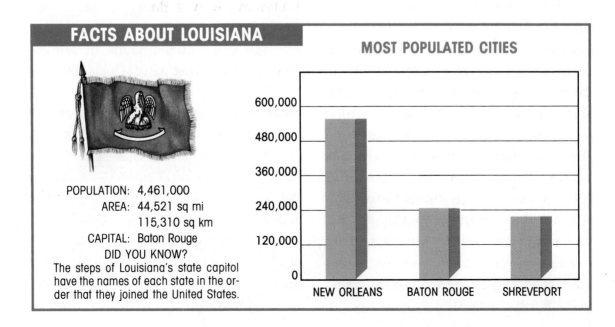

FACTS ABOUT LOUISIANA

POPULATION: 4,461,000
AREA: 44,521 sq mi
115,310 sq km
CAPITAL: Baton Rouge
DID YOU KNOW?
The steps of Louisiana's state capitol have the names of each state in the order that they joined the United States.

MOST POPULATED CITIES

Bar chart with vertical axis labeled 0, 120,000, 240,000, 360,000, 480,000, 600,000 and horizontal axis labeled NEW ORLEANS, BATON ROUGE, SHREVEPORT.

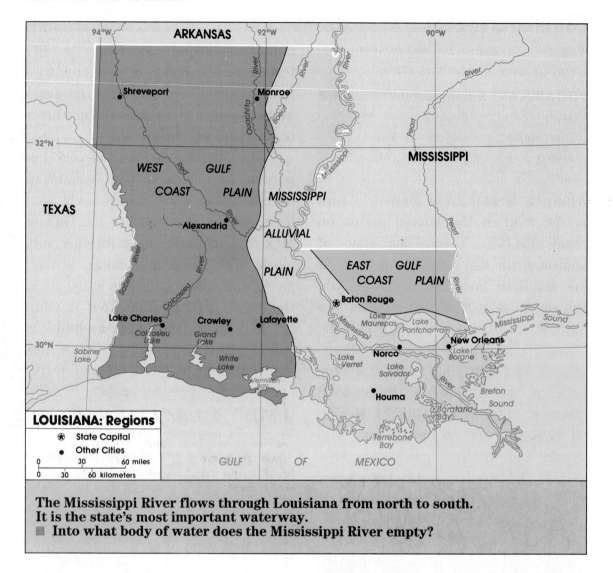

The Mississippi River flows through Louisiana from north to south. It is the state's most important waterway.

■ **Into what body of water does the Mississippi River empty?**

Regions of Louisiana The state of Louisiana is divided into three regions. The Mississippi Alluvial (ə lü′ vē əl) Plain is the land that is found along the path of the Mississippi River. This plain runs from the Arkansas state border to the Gulf of Mexico. Part of this region is a delta which is located at the mouth, or end, of the Mississippi River. This delta covers about 13,000 square miles (33,700 sq km) and is the richest farm–land in Louisiana.

The other two regions of Louisiana are the West Gulf Coastal Plain and the East Gulf Coastal Plain. The West Gulf Coastal Plain includes all the land in Louisiana west of the Mississippi Alluvial Plain. This plain has many swamps. Under the swamps deposits of salt, natural gas, oil, and sulfur are found. The East Gulf Coastal Plain is the land found east of the Mississippi Alluvial Plain. This region has swamps in the south and west, and rolling hills in the north.

A Hot and Humid Climate The temperature in Louisiana changes very little from one part of the state to another. In southern Louisiana the average temperature during the winter is about 55°F (13°C). During the summer the average temperature is about 82°F (28°C). In northern Louisiana the average winter temperature is about 6 degrees cooler than in the southern part of the state. Summer temperatures stay about the same in the northern and southern parts of Louisiana. Overall, the climate of Louisiana can be described as hot and humid.

Louisiana receives a lot of rain. The average rainfall for the state is almost 60 inches (152 cm) a year. The combination of a lot of rain and a

Hurricanes often cause floods that damage homes.
■ Can you find signs of damage caused by the strong winds?

Cypress trees grow in this Louisiana swamp.
■ Are these trees growing in water?

hot, humid climate gives Louisiana a long growing season. Throughout the state the growing season is between 220 and 350 days a year. In the southern parts of the state, crops can be grown all year round.

Now and then, violent storms hit the coast of Louisiana from the Gulf of Mexico. These storms carry winds of 75 to 150 miles per hour (120 to 241 km per hour) and heavy rain. This kind of violent storm is called a **hurricane**. When a hurricane strikes, it can cause flooding and can destroy homes and buildings.

Louisiana's Resources   As you have read earlier, the swamps of the West Gulf Coastal Plain contain many minerals, including oil, natural gas, salt, and sulfur. Louisiana ranks third, behind Texas and Alaska, of all the states in the United States in the production of oil. Most of the natural gas mined in Louisiana is found in the southern part of the state near the oil fields. Louisiana leads the country in the production of salt and is second in the production of sulfur. Sulfur is used to make fertilizers, chemicals, and many other products.

Another important resource found in Louisiana is forests. Because Louisiana gets a lot of rain, many different trees, flowers, and shrubs grow there. Forests cover about half the land in Louisiana.

The brown pelican, Louisiana's state bird, has a very long beak, called a bill.
■ How does the pelican use his bill?

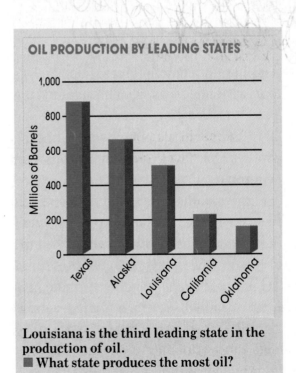

OIL PRODUCTION BY LEADING STATES

(Bar graph showing Millions of Barrels on y-axis from 0 to 1,000. States on x-axis: Texas, Alaska, Louisiana, California, Oklahoma.)

Louisiana is the third leading state in the production of oil.
■ What state produces the most oil?

Many different animals live in the forests of Louisiana. These animals include minks, raccoons, foxes, skunks, snakes, and wild hogs. Deer and wildcats roam the wooded swamp areas, and alligators and nutrias live in the coastal marshes. A nutria is an animal that looks like a beaver. Many different kinds of birds also make their home in Louisiana, including the brown pelican. The brown pelican is Louisiana's state bird.

Sugarcane, a plant from which we get sugar, is grown on farms and plantations in parts of Louisiana. Here the cane is cut by a machine. Sometimes it is harvested by hand.
■ Is the sugarcane a tall plant?

Farming in Louisiana With rich soil, a mild climate, and a long growing season, Louisiana is a leading farming state. The most important farm product in Louisiana is soybeans. Do you remember what soybeans are used for? If not, look back to Chapter 9. Louisiana farms also produce sugarcane, cotton, rice, and sweet potatoes. Cattle, chickens, and hogs are raised on farms in the southwestern part of the state.

Farms in Louisiana supply northern and eastern states with fruits and vegetables during the winter and spring months. Products such as beans, cabbage, peppers, tomatoes, strawberries, and other vegetables are shipped from farms in Louisiana. Louisiana is a leading state in strawberry production. These products are sold in stores and markets in states where the weather gets too cold during the winter to grow these crops.

Industry   Louisiana is a center for many industries. One reason for this is the supply of oil and natural gas that is found in the state. Another reason is that the state has a good transportation system. Ports along the Mississippi River, highways, and airports make shipping manufactured goods to other parts of the country easy.

The largest industry in Louisiana is the production of chemicals. Turn to the map of Louisiana and locate the cities of Baton Rouge, Lake Charles, New Orleans, and Shreveport. There are large chemical plants in each of these cities. These plants produce drugs, fertilizers, plastics, soap, and paint.

Another important industry in Louisiana is the refining of oil. Once oil is taken from the ground it must be made, or refined, into other products, like gasoline. There are many refining plants in Louisiana. Norco, Baton Rouge, and Lake Charles have the largest refineries in the state.

Food processing is also an important industry in Louisiana. New Orleans is a center for refining sugarcane into sugar. The city of Crowley has many rice mills. Farmers sell rice grain to these mills. The mills then refine this grain into the rice that we eat.

Because of its location on the Gulf of Mexico, Louisiana is a leading state in the fishing industry. The state is known for the shrimp and oysters that are caught off its coast. Crayfish, catfish, and other kinds of fish are also caught in the state's inland waters. The city of New Orleans is known for having some of the best fish restaurants in the United States.

The People of Louisiana   Around 1682 the French became the first Europeans to settle in the land that would later be called Louisiana. The French were followed by the Spanish. Both groups settled in the southern part of the state. By 1700, French

Fishing is an important industry in the state of Louisiana.
■ **Would you like a job sorting fish?**

settlers from Canada started to move into southern Louisiana. In the early 1800s the English, the Irish, and the Scottish started settling in northern Louisiana. Many blacks were also brought into the state at this time as **slaves**. A slave is a person who is owned by another person.

Today about 4,461,000 people live in Louisiana. Many of the people living in southern Louisiana are relatives of the first early settlers. Those who are related to the French or Spanish settlers are called **Creoles** (krē′ ōlz). The people who are related to the French Canadians are known as **Cajuns** (kā′ jənz). Northern Louisiana still has a large number of people with English, Irish, or Scottish backgrounds living there. About one third of the state's population today is black. People from the countries of Yugoslavia, Italy, China, the Philippines, and Vietnam are now also settling in Louisiana.

New Orleans　About two thirds of the people of Louisiana live in urban

The History of Louisiana

In 1541 a Spanish explorer named Hernando de Soto became the first European to explore the region that later became Louisiana. He was looking for gold. When no gold was found, the Spanish did not stay in the region. But in 1682, a Frenchman from Canada named Robert de La Salle led a group of people in canoes down the Mississippi River. He went ashore a few miles north of the Gulf of Mexico. La Salle claimed all the lands along the river for France. He named the region Louisiana, after King Louis XIV of France.

In 1803, France sold the entire Louisiana territory to the United States. At the time the Louisiana Purchase, as it is called, doubled the size of the United States. In 1812, the southernmost part of the Louisiana territory became the state of Louisiana.

In that same year of 1812, the United States went to war against Great Britain. This war was called the War of 1812. The last major battle of the war was fought in New Orleans. A famous American, Andrew Jackson, led the Americans to victory at the battle of New Orleans. In 1829, Jackson became the seventh President of the United States.

In 1861 a war started between the northern and the southern states of the United States. One of the reasons for the war was that the southern states wanted slavery and the northern states did not. This war, which lasted until 1865, was called the Civil War. During the Civil War, Louisiana fought on the side of the South. The state and its people suffered greatly during the Civil War. In the end the North won the Civil War and slavery came to an end in the United States. After the war, Louisiana slowly built itself back up. Railroads were built and industry grew.

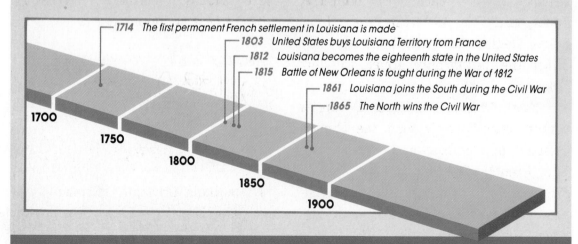

1714 The first permanent French settlement in Louisiana is made
1803 United States buys Louisiana Territory from France
1812 Louisiana becomes the eighteenth state in the United States
1815 Battle of New Orleans is fought during the War of 1812
1861 Louisiana joins the South during the Civil War
1865 The North wins the Civil War

1700   1750   1800   1850   1900

On one side of Jackson Square is the St. Louis Cathedral.
■ How do some visitors travel around the square?

areas. The four most populated cities in the state are New Orleans, Baton Rouge, Shreveport, and Houma. Baton Rouge is the state capital.

The city of New Orleans is an important port on the Mississippi River. The port of New Orleans is the busiest port in the United States. Ships from the Gulf of Mexico unload their products at the port in New Orleans. As you learned in Chapter 9, boats and barges from the Great Lakes Region can travel all the way down the Mississippi River to New Orleans.

New Orleans is also a tourist center. Many people visit the French Quarter in downtown New Orleans. The French Quarter has many old French and Spanish buildings. Visitors to the French Quarter can see what New Orleans looked like in the late 1700s and early 1800s. Thousands of tourists visit the French Quarter each year during the Mardi Gras (mär′ dē grä′) festival. New Orleans is also the birthplace of a kind of music known as **jazz**. Today, jazz music can still be heard in many places in New Orleans. Meetings and sporting events are held in the Louisiana Superdome, located just outside New Orleans. The Superdome is the world's largest indoor arena.

CHECKUP

1. Into what body of water does the Mississippi River empty?
2. What type of climate does Louisiana have?
3. What is Louisiana's most important farm product?
4. **Thinking Critically** Explain why the Mississippi River is so important to Louisiana.

Reading a Mileage Chart

In this chapter you studied about some of the major cities in the states of Louisiana and Maryland. If you were asked how many miles it is from Baltimore, Maryland, to New Orleans, Louisiana, how would you find out that information? The best way to find out how many miles it is between two places is to use a mileage chart.

The mileage chart below shows the distances between some major cities in the United States. Use it to find out the distance between Baltimore and New Orleans. Put a finger on *Baltimore* in the left column. Put a finger of your other hand on *New Orleans* in the top row. Now move both fingers, one down and one across, until they meet. They should meet at 1,145. It is 1,145 miles (1,842 km) between the two cities.

SKILLS PRACTICE

It takes a little practice to read a mileage chart. Soon it will be very easy for you. Practice your chart-reading skills by answering the questions below.

1. How many miles is it from Miami to San Francisco?
2. Which two cities are closest together? Look for the smallest number on the chart, and then move one finger up to the name of the city and one across to the name of the second city.
3. Which city is closest to Seattle?

MILEAGE CHART	Atlanta	Baltimore	Boston	Chicago	Denver	Houston	Los Angeles	Miami	New Orleans	New York City	Salt Lake City	San Francisco	Seattle
Atlanta		670	1065	675	1385	810	2205	665	480	850	1900	2525	2725
Baltimore	670		395	690	1650	1465	2660	1125	1145	175	2100	2870	2735
Boston	1065	395		965	1960	1845	2985	1515	1535	215	2365	3115	3000
Chicago	675	690	965		1015	1080	2050	1335	925	790	1405	2155	2090
Denver	1385	1650	1960	1015		1020	1045	2045	1290	1785	505	1275	1315
Houston	810	1465	1845	1080	1020		1540	1205	355	1630	1440	1920	2275
Los Angeles	2205	2660	2985	2050	1045	1540		2745	1890	2875	705	390	1155
Miami	665	1125	1515	1335	2045	1205	2745		860	1300	2555	3140	3400
New Orleans	480	1145	1535	925	1290	355	1890	860		1320	1760	2280	2615
New York City	850	175	215	790	1785	1630	2875	1300	1320		2190	2940	2825
Salt Lake City	1900	2100	2365	1405	505	1440	705	2555	1760	2190		750	835
San Francisco	2525	2870	3115	2155	1275	1920	390	3140	2280	2940	750		825
Seattle	2725	2735	3000	2090	1315	2275	1155	3400	2615	2825	835	825	

CHAPTER 10 REVIEW

MAIN IDEAS

1. A coastal plain is flat land that lies along the coast.
2. The coastal plain in the United States is divided into two sections, the Atlantic Coastal Plain which borders the Atlantic Ocean, and the Gulf Coastal Plain which borders the Gulf of Mexico.
3. In some parts of the coastal plain in the United States, there are swamps; in other parts the land is used for farming or for mining minerals. There are also large cities found on the coastal plain.
4. Products from Maryland's farms include broilers, eggs, dairy cattle, corn, soybeans, hay, wheat, cucumbers, apples, and tobacco.
5. Maryland's major industries include fishing; food processing; and the making of electrical machinery and equipment, steel and other metal products, and chemicals.
6. Louisiana is an important farming state because the soil is very rich. Many crops, including soybeans, sugarcane, cotton, rice, and sweet potatoes are grown in Louisiana. Cattle, chickens, and hogs are also raised on farms in Louisiana.
7. Because of the large supplies of oil and natural gas, and a good transportation system, Louisiana is an important industrial state.

VOCABULARY REVIEW

Match these terms with their definitions. Use a separate sheet of paper.

   a. tidelands
   b. silt
   c. hurricane
   d. coastal plain
   e. fossil

1. Underwater lands just off the coast
2. Hardened remains of plants or animals that lived many years ago
3. A mixture of soil, sand, and ground stone
4. A violent storm with high winds and heavy rain
5. Level land along the coast

CHAPTER CHECKUP

1. Which of Louisiana's regions is found along the path of the Mississippi River?
2. What resources are mined on the coastal plain in Louisiana?
3. Name Maryland's five physical regions.
4. **Thinking Critically** In what ways are coastal plains different from the Central Plains?
5. **Thinking Critically** List some reasons why you think the state of Maryland is sometimes called America in Miniature.

APPLYING KNOWLEDGE

On a road map of the United States trace a route along the coastal plain from Baltimore, Maryland, to New Orleans, Louisiana. Make a list of the cities and states that your route passes through. Choose one of the cities on your list for a report. Include in your report any information you find especially interesting about the city. Share your report with your classmates.

11 China, Kenya, and Australia

China

Why is the North China Plain an important part of the country of China?

VOCABULARY

dike	high
famine	technology

People and Land   Do you know how many people live in the United States? Today, about 243 million people live in our country. The United States is the fourth most populated country in the world. The most populated country in the world is China.

Over 1 billion people live in China. That is almost 5 times as many people as live in the United States. In fact, about one fifth of all the people on the earth live in China.

Turn to the map of the world on pages 350 and 351. You will notice that China is on the continent of Asia. China is a very large country. Only the countries of the Soviet Union and Canada have more land than China. Within China the land is very different from place to place. In southwestern China there are large moun-

tains called the Himalayas (him ə lā′ əz). Mt. Everest, the world's highest mountain, is found in the Himalayas. Mt. Everest is 29,028 feet (8,848 m) high. That is about 5 1/2 miles (9 km) high. In northwestern China there are large areas of deserts. China also has some broad plains. In the northeastern part of the country is one of those plains. It is called the North China Plain. Find the North China Plain on the map on pages 362–363.

The North China Plain runs along the Pacific Ocean for about 600 miles (960 km). Flat farmlands stretch to the horizon. Most farm people live in villages on the plain. At the northern end of the plain is China's capital, Peking [Beijing]. (The word Beijing is in brackets to show how the people of China pronounce the name of their capital. When other Chinese place-names first appear in this chapter, the Chinese pronunciation will follow in brackets.)

The Yellow River   The North China Plain has good farmland because of a river that runs through the plain. The river is called the Hwang Ho [Hwang He]. It starts in the mountains and runs through highlands made up of soft yellow soil. As the Hwang Ho flows through this region it picks up large amounts of this soil. Because of this the Hwang Ho is also called the Yellow River.

On foot, on bicycles, in trolleybuses, and in cars, people crowd this busy street in Shanghai, China's leading port city.
■ What powers the trolleybuses in this photograph?

When there has been a big rain, the Hwang Ho may rise over its banks and flood the plain. After a while the flood ends and the water on the plain dries up or drains away. But the soil that was in the water settles on the fields. It makes the land more fertile. The Hwang Ho has risen over its banks many times in the past. In fact, floodwaters over hundreds of years have built the North China Plain.

Dangers of the River   The flooding has made good land for crops. But it has had bad effects, too. Sometimes the floodwaters have destroyed villages. During one flood in 1887, floodwaters from the Yellow River created a lake the size of Lake Erie. This flood destroyed 1,500 towns and villages. For this reason the Yellow River is sometimes called China's Sorrow.

The Chinese have built dams to hold back the floodwaters. They have also built **dikes** all along the river. A dike is a bank of earth built to keep water from flowing onto the fields.

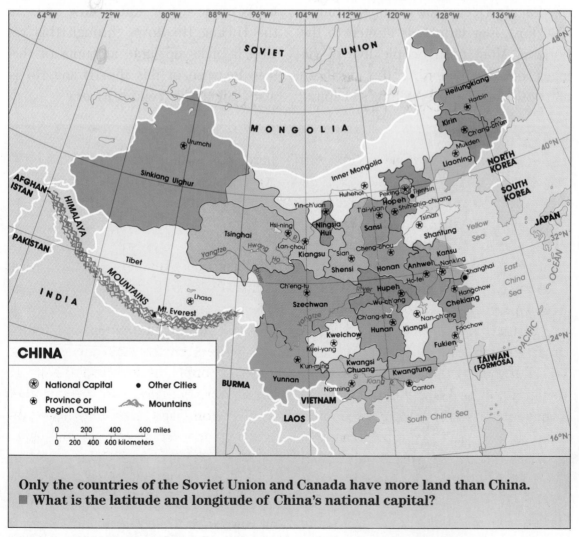

Only the countries of the Soviet Union and Canada have more land than China.
■ **What is the latitude and longitude of China's national capital?**

Besides the Hwang Ho, China has another great river, the Yangtze, which empties into the East China Sea near Shanghai.
■ **What does this barge traffic tell you about China's rivers?**

The dikes have had to be built higher and higher. This is because so much soil settles to the bottom of the river. As it fills the riverbed, the water is raised higher. Today the river is higher than the plain in many places. If a dike gives way, a great deal of farmland and many villages are flooded.

Building the dikes and keeping them higher than the river is hard work. It takes thousands of workers to carry the soil and build the dikes. Today machinery is being used more than in the past to move the soil. However, work of this kind is still done largely by hand in China. All of this hard work has not totally controlled the flooding. Long periods of hard rain will often result in floodwaters surging through weak spots in the dams and dikes.

A Changing Climate   During the summer the weather on the North China Plain is hot and damp. There is also much rain. The weather is pleasant during the spring and fall.

Winters on the plain are cold, and there is often snow. People have to dress warmly. They pad their clothes with cotton. They also keep warm by wearing one set of clothes on top of another. If you ask a Chinese person how cold it is, he or she may say "One layer of clothes," or "Two layers of clothes."

Members of a Chinese commune, or farming community, begin harvesting a wheat field on the North China Plain.
■ **Are these workers using machines?**

Wheat and Cotton The rich soil and the climate make the North China Plain a good place for farming. About 60 percent of China's wheat is grown here. Only the United States and the Soviet Union grow more wheat than China. The North China Plain produces about half of China's cotton. Other important crops are soybeans, vegetables, and tobacco. China leads the world in the production of rice, but most of this crop is grown in southern China.

Life on a Farm Do you remember learning about farming in the Soviet Union? In Chapter 5, you learned that the government in the Soviet Union owns most of the land and operates the farms. Well, farms in China are run much the same way. About 35 years ago farmers had to give up their land to the government. Since that time China's government has been run by Communists.

The little farms of old China have been combined into big farms. Farm people are put into groups. One group may be told to grow wheat, another to grow vegetables. Still another group may raise hogs or take care of farm machinery. Machines are now coming into use on the farms, but much work is still done in the old way.

Many farm fields are still plowed by animals. They are planted, weeded, and harvested by hand. Government leaders say how much of a crop will be grown and where it will be used. Most of the crops are used to feed people in the cities.

China's big task has always been to get enough food for all of its people. Even with its large population, China's farmers have almost always been able to provide enough food. China imports only a small part of the total amount of food it needs to feed the people of the country. Much depends on the weather. Floods or droughts can cause **famine** (fam′ ən). A famine takes place when there is not enough food. In the past, thousands of people in China have died in times of famine.

Changing Times During the early 1980s a new Communist leader took over in China. In order to continue to meet the needs of the country's growing population, the Chinese government has decided to make some big changes in farming. The most important change has been to give to each farmer a small piece of land to grow their own vegetables and other crops.

Today the government of China still takes a portion of what the farmers grow. Nothing is taken from what farmers grow on their small plots. The farmers are allowed to sell the products from this piece of land at public markets that are found in nearby cities and towns. These changes have made farmers work harder. The harder they work, the more food they will produce. This helps both the government and the farmers. At the same time, all of the people in the country are better off because there is more food available.

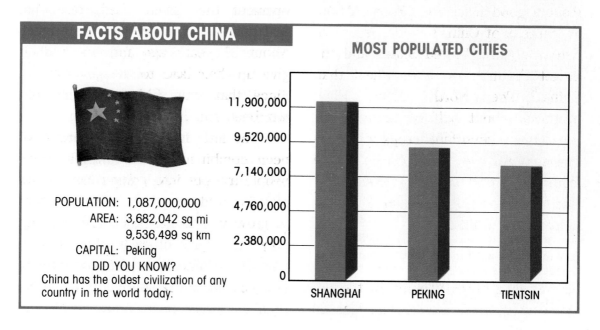

FACTS ABOUT CHINA

POPULATION: 1,087,000,000
AREA: 3,682,042 sq mi
9,536,499 sq km
CAPITAL: Peking
DID YOU KNOW?
China has the oldest civilization of any country in the world today.

MOST POPULATED CITIES

SHANGHAI — PEKING — TIENTSIN

Growing Industries For many years, China had few large factories. Most manufacturing was carried on in small workshops or in homes. When the Communists came to power in 1949, it was decided to build up China's industry. Since that time, industry in the country has grown steadily.

The biggest industrial areas on the North China Plain are in Peking and Tientsin [Tianjing]. Tientsin is a river port and a trading center.

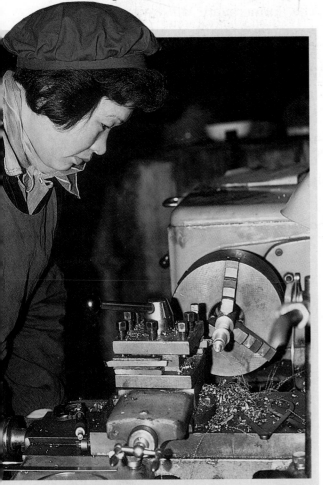

A worker in a Chinese factory runs a metal-cutting machine.
■ Does this worker wear any protective clothing?

Both Peking and the Tientsin have big iron and steel mills. Chemicals, cloth, bricks, machinery, and glass are some of the things that are manufactured in these two cities.

The growth of industry depends largely on minerals. China has much underground wealth. It ranks high among the countries of the world in coal, tin, and iron ore. However, many of China's mineral resources have not yet been developed. These resources include oil and natural gas. It is believed that China has the resources to become a great industrial country.

China's industries are controlled by the government. During the 1950s, every business, large and small, was run by the government. In recent years, however, the Chinese government has loosened its control over some small businesses. But the country's larger businesses are still under government control. The Chinese government tells these industries what and how much to produce, how much to pay the workers, and where their products can be sold.

Because of these tight controls, workers have not been happy. For many years they have not produced as much as they could have. To solve this problem the government has started a plan that rewards hard workers with bonuses, or extra money.

There are other problems with China's industry that the government is trying to solve. Many of the country's factories have been using old

Many young people in China's schools are now being trained in the use of computers.

■ **Do the computers in the photograph look like the ones you might see in your school or classroom?**

machinery. Now the government is buying new, modern machines from other countries. They have also invited people from other countries into China to teach the Chinese workers how to use the new machines. The Chinese are also trying to teach their children about **high technology.** High technology is the use of up-to-date tools and machines that do jobs that were once done by people. The government of China has set up a program that sends Chinese students to school in other countries. These students are learning how to make and use these modern tools and machines.

CHECKUP

1. About how many people live in China?
2. Why is the Hwang Ho sometimes called China's Sorrow?
3. What farm products are grown on China's North China Plain?
4. **Thinking Critically** How have China's farms and factories changed during the 1980s?

Kenya

How do Kenya's physical features affect where its people live?

VOCABULARY

cash crop	game reserve

An African Plain   The plain that you have just learned about is on the continent of Asia. Now you will learn about a plain on the continent of Africa. It is in the country called Kenya (Ken' yə).

Turn to the map on page 235. You will see that part of Kenya's eastern boundary is along the Indian Ocean. Also notice that the Equator runs almost right through the middle of Kenya.

Since Kenya is right on the Equator, one would expect it to be hot there. Much of Kenya is hot. But it may surprise you to find out that there is snow the year round in one part of this tropical country.

The place where snow can always be found is on the top of a very high mountain named Mount Kenya. For every thousand feet that land rises in elevation, the temperature drops about 3.5°F (1.9°C). Mount Kenya is more than 17,000 feet (5,100 m) high. So the temperature at the peak is about 60°F (32°C) colder than it is at sea level.

Mombasa   If you were to go to Kenya on a ship, you would probably land on the coastal plain at Mombasa (mäm bäs' ə). This city has one of the best harbors in Africa. Kenya's coastal

Zebras graze near Kenya's southern border. In the rear, in neighboring Tanzania rises Kilimanjaro, Africa's highest mountain.
■ What does the baobab tree in the picture remind you of?

plain is mostly hot and humid. But it is pleasant along the sandy beaches. You would be cooled by breezes off the Indian Ocean. Coconut palm trees would shelter you from the hot sun.

The coastal plain is but one of several plains in the country of Kenya. Plains cover about two thirds of the country. Most of these plains are on top of plateaus.

Kenya's Plains   The plains in Kenya rise in elevation from near sea level at the coast to around 4,000 feet (1,200 m) further inland. In some parts of the plains the climate is almost desertlike. Rainfall in these areas is usually less than 10 inches (25 cm) a year. The temperature changes with the elevation of the land. In lowland areas the average temperature is about 80°F (27°C). At the higher elevations, the temperature averages about 60°F (16°C).

Because of the climate, very little farming takes place on Kenya's plains. Some farming is carried out along the coast. Inland only small bushes, shrubs, and grass grow on the hot, dry plains.

Not many people live on the Kenya plains, except along the country's coast. The inland plains of Kenya have no large cities or towns. Only small groups of nomads live on Kenya's dry inland plains. These people travel from place to place in search of grazing land and water for their animals.

Where People Live   About one third of Kenya is made up of hills and mountains. This region in the southwestern part of the country is known as the highlands.

The weather is pleasant in the highlands. The temperature does not usually go above 80°F (27°C) or below 40°F (4°C). There is a good amount of rainfall at this elevation.

The highlands have some beautiful scenery. You already know about snow-covered Mount Kenya. It is on the eastern edge of the highlands. At the western edge is Lake Victoria. It is the second largest freshwater lake in the world. Only Lake Superior, one

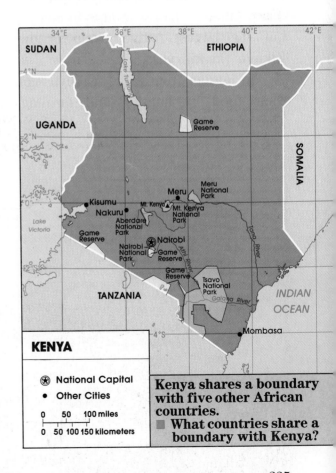

Kenya shares a boundary with five other African countries.
■ What countries share a boundary with Kenya?

of the five Great Lakes, is larger. Do you remember learning about the Nile River in Chapter 8? Look at the map of Africa on page 360. You will see that Lake Victoria is one of the starting points of the Nile River.

Most of the people in Kenya live in the highlands. The most fertile soil in the country can be found in this region. Nairobi (nī rō′ bē), Kenya's capital and largest city, is located in the highlands.

The People of Kenya   Over 20 million people live in the country of Kenya. Most Kenyans are people whose relatives have lived in the region for hundreds of years. There are many different native groups in Kenya, but the largest native group is the Kikuyu (ki kü′ yü).

In earlier times the Kikuyu got their food by hunting and farming. The men did the hunting. The women did the farming. People produced just enough food for their own use.

About 100 years ago the British came to Kenya. They took control of the region. The British were not much interested in the hot coastal plain or the dry north. But they liked the pleasant highlands. They settled there and started farming. They built a railroad to connect the coastal region with the highlands. This railroad runs from Lake Victoria to Mombasa.

As the railroad line moved west from Mombasa, new towns grew up. One of them was Nairobi. Settlers came to Kenya from Great Britain, India, and other countries. Life started to change for the Kikuyu and other native groups. The newcomers took over much of the best farmland. Many of the natives went to work on the farms of the settlers.

Kenya's native groups, especially the Kikuyu, were not happy with their

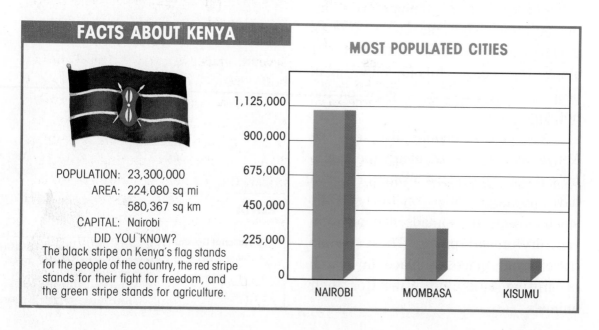

FACTS ABOUT KENYA

POPULATION: 23,300,000
AREA: 224,080 sq mi
580,367 sq km
CAPITAL: Nairobi
DID YOU KNOW?
The black stripe on Kenya's flag stands for the people of the country, the red stripe stands for their fight for freedom, and the green stripe stands for agriculture.

MOST POPULATED CITIES

NAIROBI	~1,075,000
MOMBASA	~300,000
KISUMU	~150,000

Living in Kenya

When Jomo Muta walks out the door of his home in the morning, he looks across the green fields and sees, far in the distance, a snow-capped mountain. It is Mount Kenya. Some day, Jomo tells himself, he will climb that mountain to the very top.

Jomo is a 9-year-old Kikuyu boy who lives in a small farming village in the highlands of Kenya. The youngest of three children, Jomo has a 17-year-old brother, Elimo, and an 11-year-old sister, Grace.

The Mutas' farm is about 5 acres (2 ha) in size. Jomo's father raises corn, beans, potatoes, and a few other vegetables. Mrs. Muta grinds some of the corn to make corn meal.

The Muta family uses almost all the crops for food, but in some years the garden produces more than the family needs. The government may then buy some of the extra crops. Sometimes Mrs. Muta takes vegetables to sell at an open-air market in a large town a few miles away.

Children in Kenya are not required to go to school. However, most children attend school for at least 7 years. Jomo is in the fourth grade. He learns to read and write and use numbers. He also learns English, which is widely spoken in Kenya. The official language in Kenya is Swahili.

The government of Kenya supplies free schooling to pupils only through the seventh grade. Beyond that, a pupil's family must pay a fee. The Muta family could not afford to have Elimo continue school. After finishing the seventh grade, he went to work on a coffee plantation.

A year ago, Jomo's uncle moved to the city of Nairobi. He got a job in a factory that makes cloth. He tells Jomo that it is very exciting to live in a city. But Jomo is not sure he would like it. He knows he would miss the green fields and the sight of snow-capped Mount Kenya. Jomo thinks he might prefer to become a farmer like his father.

new way of life. They wanted their land back. They wanted their own government. A long struggle for independence began. Finally, in 1963, the Kenyans got their independence. Nairobi became the capital of the new country.

Farming and Industry After Kenya got its freedom, much land was returned to the Africans. Most people still make a living by farming. The Kikuyu and other groups no longer raise crops just for their own use. They raise more than they need. They sell the rest.

Kenya is known for its many coffee and tea plantations in the highlands. You have seen coffee and tea in your home or in grocery stores. Do you know what coffee and tea come from?

Coffee comes from red berries that grow on a small tree. Each berry contains two small seeds called beans. After workers have picked the berries, machines remove the beans, wash them, and take off the outer skins. The beans are then roasted in ovens. Finally they are ground and put into cans or bags for sale at stores. Sometimes stores grind the beans.

Tea comes from a plant about 3 to 4 feet (90 to 120 cm) high. When the plant reaches a certain age, new leaves and buds appear. Workers pick the new leaves and buds. They are then crushed, dried, sorted, and put into packages.

Red berries from the coffee plant (inset) are sorted for the market.
■ How are the beans being sorted?

Much of the coffee and tea that Kenya produces is sold to other countries. Tea and coffee are **cash crops** for the Kenyans. Cash crops are crops grown mainly for sale and not for use by the people who grow them.

The people of the highlands and the coastal plain grow other crops for their own use. Among them are corn, wheat, potatoes, and beans. Farmers also raise cows for milk and cattle for meat.

Industry in Kenya is growing. Factories prepare food products, building materials, and cloth. Kenya does not have the mineral wealth that large industries need. There is an oil

MAKING TEA

1. Picking tea from tea plants

2. Spreading leaves on large racks

3. Drying the leaves in drying machines.

4. Separating the leaves by size

5. Packing the tea into chests

6. Shipping the tea to other countries

Nairobi, the capital of Kenya, is a modern city with many tall buildings.
■ Do you recognize the plant in the foreground of the picture?

refinery at Mombasa, but the oil is brought there from other countries. Most of the country's industries are found in the cities of Mombasa and Nairobi.

Visiting Kenya   Entertaining tourists is a big business in Kenya. More than 400,000 people visit this country each year. Some go to enjoy the sandy beaches and the tropical climate of the coastal plain. But many of Kenya's tourists go to see the wild animals that live in Kenya. Many of the animals that are found only in zoos in the United States roam over the grasslands of Kenya. Among these animals are lions, elephants, giraffes, rhinoceroses, and zebras.

Once there were great herds of these animals in Kenya. But hunters killed many of them. Finally Kenya's government set aside lands where the animals are protected. Some of these lands are called **game reserves.** Others are national parks. Most of these lands are in or close to the highlands. However, there is one large game reserve on the northern plains. Today it is against the law for hunters to shoot these animals even outside the places where they are specially protected.

More than 40,000 Kenyans have jobs in the tourist business. They guide visitors on trips to the parks and game reserves. They provide food and shelter for the visitors.

Kenya's wild animals are a valuable natural resource. Visitors used to go to Kenya to shoot these animals and bring back their horns or mounted heads. Today the visitors shoot the animals not with guns but with their cameras. Kenya's elephants, giraffes, zebras, and other wild animals will continue to be there in the future for people to enjoy.

CHECKUP

1. How does Kenya's coastal plain differ from the plains found farther inland?
2. Where do most of Kenya's people live?
3. Why do many tourists visit Kenya each year?
4. **Thinking Critically** Do you think that British control of Kenya was good or bad for the country?

Australia

What makes Australia an interesting and different country?

VOCABULARY

aborigines   **station**
territory

A Country That Is a Continent
Look at the map on page 7 and find the names of the seven continents. On this map you will notice that Australia is one of the seven continents. But Australia is also a country. How can this be? You know that continents are very large pieces of land. Most continents have many countries. These countries all have their own, separate government. But all of the continent of Australia is ruled by the same government.

Different Animals   You will also notice on the map on page 7 that Australia is an island. This has made Australia different. Animals could not come in from other continents. Animals in Australia developed in their own way. Some of these animals are different from animals anywhere else in the world.

For example, there is the platypus (plat′ ə pəs). This is a furry animal about the size of a woodchuck. But it has a flat bill, feet like a duck, and it lays eggs!

Then there is the koala (kō ä′ lə). This little animal looks like a teddy bear. It lives in trees, eats the leaves, and hangs by its toes from the branches.

Still another animal found in Australia is the kangaroo (kang gə rü′). These tall animals can hop along at 40 miles (64 km) an hour on their strong hind legs. The mother kangaroo has a pouch in which she carries her baby until the little one is 8 to 10 months old.

Australia is also the home of about 700 different kinds of birds. The world's only black swans live in Australia. About 140 different kinds of snakes also live in Australia, including the tarpan and the tiger snake. They are among the most poisonous snakes in the world.

Larger members of the kangaroo family stand about 6 feet (1.8 m) tall.
■ What color is this kangaroo?

South of the Equator Look at a globe. Find the United States of America and then find Australia. As you can see, Australia is south of the Equator. The United States is, of course, north of the Equator. So in the United States we sometimes speak of Australia as being the country "down under."

Remember looking at the two photographs on page 39? One showed a winter storm in New York City. The other showed people in summer clothes standing on a sandy beach in Sydney, Australia. Both photographs were taken in December. The reason for the different weather in the two cities is that the seasons in Australia are the opposite of those in the United States. When it is winter in the United States, it is summer in Australia. If you do not remember why this is, look again at the diagram on page 38.

Settling Australia The first people to live in a country are called **aborigines** (ab ə rij′ ə nēz). Australia's aborigines probably came from southwestern Asia. For hundreds of years these people lived by hunting, fishing, and gathering roots and other plant food. Relatives of Australia's aborigines still live in the country. However, they make up only a very small part of Australia's people today.

People from Great Britain made the first settlements in Australia in the late 1700s. They were people who had been in British prisons. In those days jails in Great Britain were very crowded. The British government decided to send some of those who had broken laws to Australia.

The first settlers arrived in 1787. They landed on the eastern shore and started the settlement of Sydney. They had a hard time at first. However, the soil along the coast was good for crops. Soon other settlers came. They, too, made their homes along the eastern coast.

The first settlers from Great Britain knew little about Australia before

they landed. But they could not have come ashore at a better place. Let us see why.

Rain, Trees, and Good Soil   The settlers landed on a narrow plain. It runs along most of Australia's eastern coast. This plain is green with grass and trees.

At the northern end of the coastal plain are tropical forests. The rainfall here is sometimes more than 100 inches (250 cm) a year. The weather is not as rainy farther south. But there is enough rain for plants all along the coast, and the soil is rich.

The explorer Captain Cook claimed Australia for Great Britain in 1770.
■ **Do you know the name of the flag?**

A Variety of Land   Behind the narrow coastal plain are highlands made up of plateaus, hills, and low mountain ranges. The highlands are called the Great Dividing Range because the mountain slopes divide the flow of the region's rivers.

Australia's highest mountains lie at the southern end of the Great Dividing Range. In the winter these mountains are snow covered. At lower elevations, Australia seldom has snow. West of the Great Dividing Range are the central lowlands. In the north the lowlands are dry and few people live there. In the south, though, there is more moisture and good farmland can be found.

From the central lowlands all the way to the shores of the Indian Ocean is a huge dry region. The center of this big area is a desert. Bordering the desert are flatlands where enough grass grows for cattle and sheep to graze. But only in the southwestern corner of this vast dry region is there enough rain for crops.

Australia's People   Australia is nearly the same size as the United States, but it has far fewer people. As you know our population is about 243 million. Australia's population is more than 16 million. The states of New York and California in the United States each have more people than the country of Australia has.

Australia is divided into six states and a number of **territories.** Most

243

territories are regions that have not been developed enough to become states. Some of Australia's territories are small Pacific islands with very few people.

About two thirds of the Australian people live in the southeastern part of the country. Here there is enough water for farms and factories and for people's personal needs. Australia has 11 cities with more than 100,000 people in each. All but one of these cities is in the southeast. The exception is Perth, which is located in southwestern Australia.

Australia's largest cities are Sydney, Melbourne, Brisbane, and Adelaide. Each is on the coast and each is a state capital. The one large city that is not on the coast is Canberra. This is Australia's national capital, just as the city of Washington, D.C., is our national capital. Find all of these cities on the maps on page 245.

A Lot of Farmland   Farmland covers most of the land in Australia. Most of this land is used for raising sheep and cattle. The most important farm product in Australia is wool from sheep. Sheep are also raised for meat. Sheep and cattle are raised on big ranches that Australians call **stations.** Many of these stations are in the central lowlands.

Only about 5 percent of Australia's farmland is used for raising crops. Even so, farmers grow enough food to meet most of the needs of the country's people. Wheat is Australia's second most important farm product. A variety of other crops are grown in Australia, including sugarcane, oats, rice, and cotton. Fruits such as bananas, pineapples, and coconuts are also grown.

Minerals and Industry   Australia has many industries. The eastern

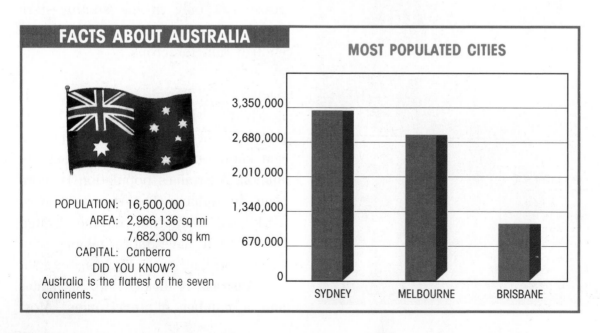

FACTS ABOUT AUSTRALIA

POPULATION: 16,500,000
AREA: 2,966,136 sq mi
7,682,300 sq km
CAPITAL: Canberra
DID YOU KNOW?
Australia is the flattest of the seven continents.

MOST POPULATED CITIES

3,350,000
2,680,000
2,010,000
1,340,000
670,000
0

SYDNEY   MELBOURNE   BRISBANE

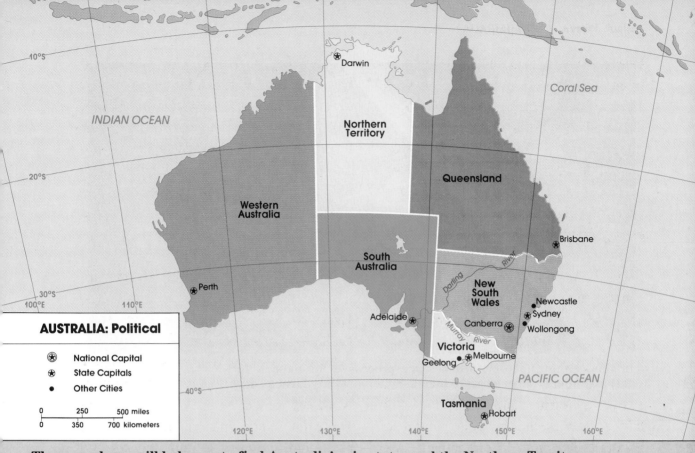

AUSTRALIA: Political

National Capital
State Capitals
Other Cities

0   250   500 miles
0   350   700 kilometers

The map above will help you to find Australia's six states and the Northern Territory.
The map below shows the country's land elevations.

■ Which state does not share a border with any other state or territory?
■ What is the land elevation around the city of Canberra?

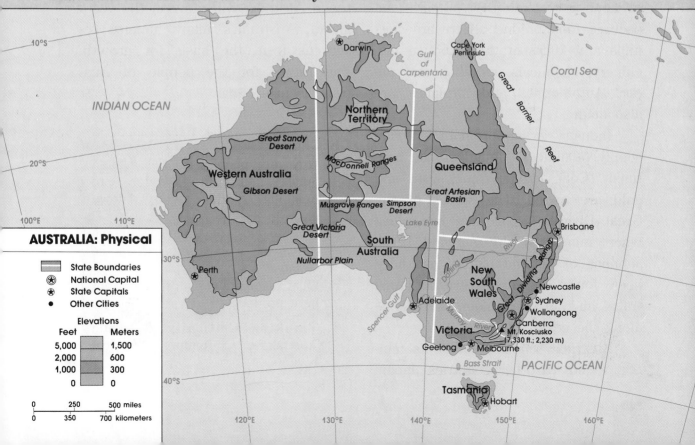

AUSTRALIA: Physical

State Boundaries
National Capital
State Capitals
Other Cities

Elevations
Feet   Meters
5,000   1,500
2,000   600
1,000   300
0   0

0   250   500 miles
0   350   700 kilometers

In this canning factory, peaches are processed for export. Irrigation projects have greatly increased Australia's farm production.
■ How are the peaches moving to the work stations?

coastal plain from Newcastle to Melbourne could be called the industrial zone of Australia. All along this strip of land are plants that prepare and package food products. Here are steel mills and factories that produce machinery, chemicals, clothing, and paper. Automobiles and airplanes are also made.

Industry is supported by the rich supply of minerals found on the continent. Coal, copper, zinc, iron, and gold are mined. The slopes of the Great Dividing Range are one place where mineral wealth is found. Large supplies of oil and natural gas have been found in some parts of Australia and in the underwater lands along the coast.

Australia sends much of its mineral wealth to other countries. Japan, European countries, and the United States are its best customers.

It is likely that trade and industry in Australia will grow in the years ahead. Australia's many mineral resources form the basis for growth. The future for the people of Australia is promising.

CHECKUP

1. Why do people in the United States sometimes refer to Australia as the country "down under"?
2. Why do most of Australia's people live in the southeastern part of the country?
3. What is Australia's most important farm product?
4. **Thinking Critically** Describe Australia's different physical regions.

246

Using a Table

TABLES PRESENT FACTS

A table is a way of presenting facts. The facts are in columns that run down the page and in rows that go from left to right across the page. The facts put forth in a table are often in the form of numbers. A table is very useful in answering such questions as How big? How many?

A TABLE ABOUT COUNTRIES

Below is a table of facts about the three countries you have studied in this chapter. Beneath the title at the head of each column is a label. It shows the kind of information found in that column.

1. Column 1 has each country's name.
2. Column 2 has each country's area.
3. Column 3 shows the population.
4. Column 4 shows the population density for each country.
5. Column 5 shows the percentage of urban population, that is, people living in cities.
6. Column 6 shows life expectancy, in years. Life expectancy is the *average age* to which people live.

7. Column 7 shows adult literacy. This means the percentage of grown-ups who can read and write.

To find a fact—for example, the population of Kenya—go to the line on which the name *Kenya* appears. Then follow to the right on that line until you come to the column that is labeled "Population."

SKILLS PRACTICE

Use the table to find the answers to the questions that follow. Write the answers on a separate sheet of paper.

1. Which country has the lowest percentage of urban population?
2. Which country has the most people?
3. Which column best shows how these countries compare in the health of their people?
4. Which country has the most land area?
5. Which column shows which countries have had better school systems?
6. Which country has the lowest population density?

A TABLE OF FACTS ABOUT AUSTRALIA, CHINA, AND KENYA						
1. Country	2. Area	3. Population	4. Population Density	5. Urban Population	6. Life Expectancy	7. Adult Literacy
Australia	2,966,136 sq mi (7,682,300 sq km)	16,500,000	6 per sq mi (2 per sq km)	86%	75	100%
China	3,682,042 sq mi (9,536,499 sq km)	1,087,000,000	295 per sq mi (114 per sq km)	32%	64	82%
Kenya	224,080 sq mi (580,367 sq km)	23,300,000	104 per sq mi (40 per sq km)	16%	53	40%

CHAPTER 11 REVIEW

MAIN IDEAS

1. The North China Plain has good farmland because the Hwang Ho runs through the plain. At times, the river overflows its banks, depositing fertile soil onto the North China Plain.
2. Peking, the capital of China, is located on the North China Plain.
3. Most of Kenya's people live either in the cities located on the coastal plains or in the highlands where the weather is more pleasant than on the hot, humid inland plains.
4. Australia is the only country that is also a continent.
5. Many of the animals found in Australia can be found nowhere else in the world.
6. Australia has many physical regions including mountains, tropical forests, deserts, and lowlands.

VOCABULARY REVIEW

Fill in each blank with the word or phrase that best completes the sentence.

1. A part of Australia that is not a state is called a _____.
2. In China a flood or drought has sometimes caused a food shortage called a _____.
3. The first people to live in a country are called _____.
4. In Kenya, tea and coffee are considered to be _____ because they are grown mainly for sale.
5. _____ is the use of up-to-date tools and machines that do jobs that were once done by people.

CHAPTER CHECKUP

1. What makes the North China Plain such fertile farmland?
2. From which country did the people of Kenya gain their independence in 1963?
3. Why was it necessary for Kenya's government to set up game reserves?
4. What is the name of the animal found in Australia that hops at 40 miles (64 km) an hour?
5. Where are many of Australia's industries located?
6. **Thinking Critically** How does "China's Sorrow" both help and hurt the people of the North China Plain?
7. **Thinking Critically** How are Kenya's plains different from the North China Plain?
8. **Thinking Critically** Why, do you think, is it important for Australia's farmers to grow enough food to meet the needs of all the country's people?

APPLYING KNOWLEDGE

1. In this chapter, you learned about many different animals. Some are found in Kenya, and others are found in Australia. Choose one of the animals to do a report on. Draw a picture of your animal. Make an oral report to your classmates about your animal.
2. In this chapter you have learned something about life in China, Kenya, and Australia. If you were to live in one of these countries, which would you prefer? On a sheet of paper write the reasons why.

SUMMARIZING UNIT 4

REVIEWING VOCABULARY

1. preserve People preserve, or protect from change, many things from the past. How are the people in Galena, Illinois, preserving their city's past?

2. coastal plain Flat lands found along a coast are called coastal plains. What are the names of the two parts of the coastal plain in the United States?

3. colony A place that is settled by people who leave their own country but remain citizens of that country is called a colony. Name one state in the United States that was once a colony of Great Britain.

4. high technology Using up-to-date tools and machines that do the jobs once done by people is called high technology. How is the Chinese government helping its people learn how to use these modern tools and machines?

5. cash crop Tea and coffee are cash crops in Kenya. Why are these two crops called cash crops?

EXPRESSING YOURSELF

1. What if . . .? What if the St. Lawrence Seaway dried up and ships could not reach the Atlantic Ocean from the Great Lakes Region. What effects would this have on people living in the region and in other parts of the United States?

2. Thinking like a historian How, do you think, would history have changed if Maryland and the other 12 British colonies had not broken away and formed their own country?

3. You make the decision Imagine that you are a farmer living in China. You are given a chance to move to the United States to work as a farmer in Maryland or Louisiana. Would you decide to leave China? If so, in which state would you choose to live?

4. What do you think? For many years Chinese factories were using old machines and tools. Now the Chinese government is trying to teach factory workers about high technology. How do you think the factory workers feel about this change?

5. Who would you rather be? Would you rather be the owner of a large sheep farm in Australia or a large coffee plantation in Kenya?

Mountain Regions

Have you ever seen a mountain? Some people live near mountains and see them every day. Others go to the mountains for fun. Mountain climbing, fishing in a mountain stream, and camping on a mountain slope are all activities that people do in the mountains.

A climber gazes at Mount Everest, the world's highest mountain, which rises 5½ miles (8.8 km) above sea level in the Asian Himalayas.
■ In what year did this expedition take place?

1983 EVEREST WEST EXPEDITION
SAN FRANCISCO, CALIFORNIA

Four cars and a bus are shown rounding a hairpin curve in the Swiss Alps.
■ Is the bus going up the mountain or down the mountain?

Mountains reach high into the air. They rise above the land around them. Mountains also affect people's travel. Travel from one side to the other is not easy. Thus mountains have much to do with where towns and cities grow, especially before the development of modern transportation. But there are cities that have developed in mountain regions.

The city of Innsbruck in the Austrian Alps draws many tourists all year round.
■ What might be a winter attraction in Innsbruck?

Today, thousands of people live in cities in mountain regions. Many more people spend their vacations in these cities. What kind of recreational activity do you think is very popular in cities located in mountain regions?

251

Mountains also have many natural resources. Trees, lakes, rivers, and streams are some of the natural resources that we get from mountain regions. Coal is another important natural resource that we get from many mountain regions.

Deep under the earth a drill mines for coal and dumps it into a shuttle car to be taken to the surface.
■ How many miners do you see in this photograph?

This senate office building in Washington, D.C., is made out of granite, a strong and long-lasting rock. Inset: A granite quarry in Vermont.
■ Does this building look like it was built to last?

There are also many different kinds of rocks found in mountain regions. Some of these rocks, like granite, are used to make buildings. There may be some buildings in your community made from granite. Can you name any?

High mountain peaks and long mountain ranges can be found all over the world. In Europe, the largest mountain range is called the Alps. The Alps make up most of the land in the countries of Switzerland, Austria, and Liechtenstein. Parts of the Alps can also be found in the countries of France, Italy, Germany, and Yugoslavia.

Some coastal mountains have deep water-filled inlets.
■ **Can you find the two people in the photograph?**

The Ural Mountains make up part of the border between the continents of Europe and Asia. They are located in the country of the Soviet Union. Can you locate the Ural Mountains on the map below?

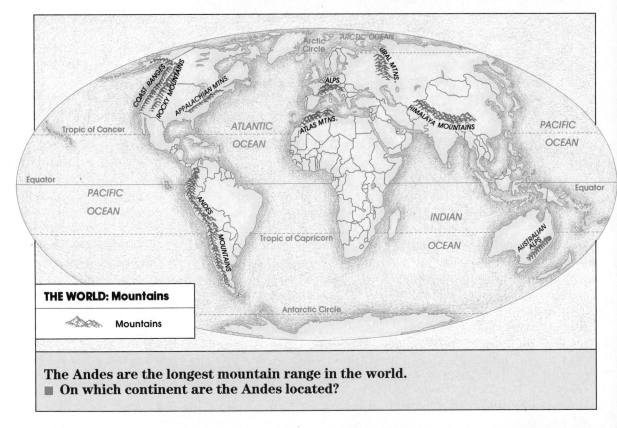

THE WORLD: Mountains

Mountains

The Andes are the longest mountain range in the world.
■ **On which continent are the Andes located?**

A small group of llamas trots along a country road high in the Andes Mountains of Peru.
■ **What do the llamas have on their backs?**

There are mountain ranges in South America, Africa, and Australia. A mountain range is a line of mountains. The Andes mountain range, located on the west coast of South America, is the longest in the world. The longest mountain range in Africa is the Atlas Mountains. These mountains are located in northern Africa, between the countries of Tunisia and Morocco. The highest mountains on the continent of Australia are the Australian Alps. They are found in the southeastern part of Australia. In the winter these mountains are covered with snow and attract many skiers.

In Africa's Atlas Mountains a man walks along a valley stream with his sheep.
■ How would you describe this valley?

Fishing for rainbow trout is one of the joys of a mountain vacation.
■ What is this fisherman wearing?

A small Greek town crowns the top of a mountain cliff above the sea.
■ Do you see many tall buildings in the town?

255

In the United States there are three main mountain ranges. Sometimes the line stretches for hundreds of miles. These mountain ranges are called the Appalachian Mountains, the Rocky Mountains, and the Coast Ranges. Locate these three mountain ranges on the map of the United States below.

The Rocky Mountains are the largest mountain range in North America. They extend for more than 3,000 miles (4,800 km). The Rocky Mountains extend from the state of Alaska through the country of Canada and across the United States and into Mexico.

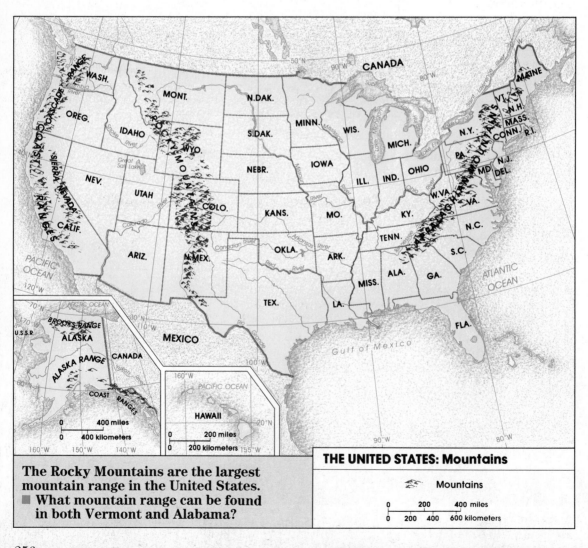

The Rocky Mountains are the largest mountain range in the United States.
■ What mountain range can be found in both Vermont and Alabama?

THE UNITED STATES: Mountains

Mountains

0   200   400 miles
0   200   400   600 kilometers

The Appalachian Mountains are the oldest mountains in North America. They were formed about 230 million years ago. The name *Appalachian* comes from the Apalachee Indians. The Appalachian Trail is a 2,000-mile hiking trail that runs from Mt. Katahdin in Maine to Springer Mountain in Georgia. The trail passes through 14 states, two national parks, and eight national forests.

In the distance is Mount Mitchell in North Carolina's Black Mountains. It is the highest point east of the Mississippi.
■ In what season of the year was this picture taken?

The third major mountain range found in the United States is called the Coast Ranges. The Coast Ranges extend from Alaska through Canada into southern California. Twelve separate mountain ranges make up the Coast Ranges.

Mount Whitney, part of the Sierra Nevada range of California, rises almost 3 miles (4.8 km) above sea level.
■ Why, do you think, are these mountains snow-covered?

12 Colorado

How Mountains Are Formed

In what ways are mountains formed?

VOCABULARY

crust   core
mantle

The Make-up of the Earth Have you ever held an apple in your hand? An apple has three layers. The earth, like an apple, also has three layers. The outer layer of the earth is called the **crust**. It is thin like the skin of an apple. The earth's crust is a layer of rock that covers the whole earth. The crust is even found under the oceans. The earth's crust is from 3 to 19 miles (5 to 31 km) thick. We live on the earth's crust.

Under the crust is the **mantle**. This is the thickest layer of the earth. The mantle is like the white part of the apple. In some places the mantle is about 1,800 miles (2,900 km) thick. Most scientists think that the mantle is very hot.

Below the mantle is the inner layer of the earth, called the **core**. The core of the earth is like the core of an apple. The core of the earth is believed to be made up of very hot liquid.

Volcanoes Form Mountains

Sometimes a great amount of pressure builds up below the earth's crust. When the pressure becomes too great, the crust finally breaks. This is called a volcano. Do you remember learning about volcanoes in Chapter 4? The lava that is forced out of the holes in the crust of the earth sometimes takes the form of a cone. When the lava hardens, it forms what we call a mountain.

Sometimes the pressure that builds up below the earth's surface is not great enough to break through the crust. When this happens the earth arches or folds, forming a mountain or chain of mountains. The Appalachian Mountains in the eastern part of the United States were formed this way.

Have you ever seen mountains with very steep cliffs on one side? These are formed when the earth's crust just slightly cracks and one side of the crack rises higher than the other side. Some of the mountains in the states of Wyoming, Utah, and California were formed in this way.

Another way in which some mountains are formed is by erosion.

Cattle graze in a grassy area below the Sangre de Cristo Mountains, a part of the Rocky Mountains, in Colorado.
■ **Have you seen the mountains in Colorado?**

Remember that *erosion* means "the wearing away of the earth's surface by wind, ice, running water, or waves." Rainwater and flowing rivers wash away the soil and sand, and leave huge rocks exposed. After millions of years, enough rocks are exposed to form a mountain.

Mountains and People   For many years, mountains made traveling difficult and sometimes impossible. When people from Europe came to North America to make colonies, they settled along the coast of the Atlantic Ocean. It took these people almost 150 years to cross the Appalachian Mountains. Today, the automobile and the airplane make traveling over mountains much easier.

Over the years, people have found that mountains are a valuable source of natural resources. Some people hunt animals found in mountains for their meat, and some make clothing out of animal skins. Other people use the grassy slopes of some mountains to raise animals. Many minerals can be mined from mountains. Forests are another valuable resource found on mountains. Today, people also use mountains as recreation areas. Skiing, hiking, camping, and mountain climbing are a few of the recreational activities that people enjoy doing in the mountains.

In 1775, Daniel Boone and a party of pioneers blazed a trail westward through the Cumberland Gap in the Appalachian Mountains.
■ Was each of the pioneers riding horseback?

Cross-country skiing is one of the many recreational activities people enjoy doing in the mountains.
■ **Have you ever been snow skiing?**

Learning About Mountains High and beautiful mountains can be found all over the world. You have already learned about the names of some of the world's mountain ranges on pages 250–257. In this chapter you will learn about the mountains in the state of Colorado. Do you know the name of the mountains that are found in Colorado? If not, look back at the map that is on page 256. These mountains are called the Rocky Mountains, or Rockies. They are the highest mountains in the United States.

CHECKUP

1. What is the name of the very hard outer layer of the earth?
2. Why is traveling over mountains easier today?
3. What kind of natural resources are found in mountains?

4. **Thinking Critically** Summarize the four ways that mountains can be formed.

The Rooftop State

How does the land of Colorado change as you travel through the state?

VOCABULARY

timberline   Continental
solar energy   Divide

The Rocky Mountains   Do you remember studying about mountain ranges in Alaska in Chapter 3? Mountain ranges, as you know, are groups of connected mountains. On pages 250–257 you studied about three long mountain ranges in the United States. Of these three mountain ranges, the Rocky Mountains are the longest. The Rocky Mountains start in the Canadian Yukon Territory and go through Canada into the United States. They run southward from Montana down through Wyoming and Colorado into New Mexico.

In this chapter we are going to look at the state that has the highest peaks in the Rockies—Colorado. In eastern Colorado you will find that the land is flat for about 300 miles (480 km). But then, as you near the center of the state, you can see high mountains rising from the land. There are over 50 mountain peaks in the Colorado Rockies that are higher than 14,000 feet (4,270 m).

Traveling Through Colorado   The city of Denver, Colorado, is near the

Here we see an autumn view of the San Juan Mountains, one of the main mountain ranges of the Rocky Mountains in Colorado.
■ What do you see in the picture that indicates it is autumn?

262

Rocky Mountains. It is the capital of Colorado and is the state's largest city. From Denver you can go on through the Rockies by way of the Eisenhower Memorial Tunnel. After you leave the tunnel, you see high peaks all around you. A few miles to the north of the tunnel is Rocky Mountain National Park. In this park alone there are about 65 mountain peaks that are over 10,000 feet (3,050 m) high. Because of the many high mountain peaks found in Colorado, the state has been nicknamed the Rooftop State.

Traveling west from the Eisenhower Memorial Tunnel, you see many mountain valleys and sparkling lakes. Evergreen forests cover the lower slopes of the Rockies. However, on the tops of the higher mountains it is too cold and windy for trees to grow. The point at which trees no longer grow on the slope of a mountain is called the **timberline**.

The part of the state lying west of the Rockies is the Colorado Plateau. The land is hilly with deep valleys. It is lower than the Rocky Mountains but higher than the Great Plains.

Warm Summers and Cold Winters

The climate in Colorado is quite different in the summer and winter. Summers can be quite hot, while winters are usually very cold. It is always cooler in the mountains than on the plains.

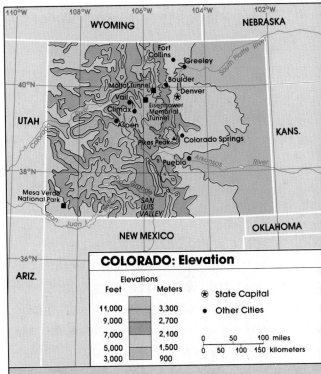

COLORADO: Elevation

Elevations		
Feet	Meters	
11,000	3,300	✷ State Capital
9,000	2,700	● Other Cities
7,000	2,100	
5,000	1,500	
3,000	900	

Land elevations in Colorado range from 3,000 feet to over 11,000 feet.
■ **What part of Colorado has the lowest elevation?**

The amount of precipitation varies. The western slope of the Rockies gets the most rain and snow. There is less precipitation on the eastern slope.

Because Colorado receives lots of sunshine, it is one of the best states for the use of **solar energy**. This is energy that comes from the sun. Engineers are trying to find the best ways to use the sun's rays to heat houses. They know that using solar energy will help us to save our supplies of natural gas and oil.

Where Rivers Begin   A number of large rivers begin in the Rocky

These people are rafting through the rapids on the Arkansas River in the central part of Colorado.
■ **Why, do you think, is this called white water rafting?**

Mountains in Colorado. One is the Colorado River, which flows between the Painted Desert and the Mojave Desert. Another is the Rio Grande. Do you remember studying about the Rio Grande in Chapter 6?

These two rivers flow in different directions. The Colorado River flows to the west and eventually empties, or drains, into the Gulf of California. The Rio Grande flows to the east and drains into the Gulf of Mexico.

The line of mountain ridges that separates these two drainage areas is the **Continental Divide**. In Colorado the Continental Divide runs along the highest land of the Rocky Moun-

tains. Rain and melting snow on the western side of the Rockies run into rivers that drain into the Pacific Ocean or into a body of water such as the Gulf of California. Water draining from the eastern side of the mountains goes into rivers that empty into the Gulf of Mexico or the Atlantic Ocean.

CHECKUP
1. Why is Colorado sometimes called the Rooftop State?
2. Why is learning how to use solar energy important?
3. What is the Continental Divide?
4. **Thinking Critically** Describe how the land of Colorado is different in the eastern, central, and western parts of the state.

Colorado Yesterday and Today

How has life in Colorado changed over the years?

Millions of Years Ago   Before any people lived in the area that we now know as Colorado, large animals roamed the area. These animals are called **dinosaurs** (dī′ nə sôrz). There are no dinosaurs living today. They lived on the earth many millions of years ago. Some of these dinosaurs were 20 feet (6 m) high and 90 feet (27 m) long.

If dinosaurs lived so long ago, how do we know so much about them? We know about them because scientists have found bones from these animals in Colorado and in other parts of the world. One can see the skeleton of a huge dinosaur in a Denver museum.

Many years after the last of the dinosaurs died, Indians started to settle in the area that is now Colorado. These Indians used stone and **adobe** (ə dō′ bē) to build their houses. Adobe is a mixture of clay and straw. Today, people can visit some of the houses in which these Indians lived. An old Indian village is inside the Mesa Verde (mā sə verd ē) National Park in southwestern Colorado. Find this national park on the map of Colorado on page 263.

No one knows what happened to the first Indian groups that lived in this region. They left the area, but we are not sure why. They might have left because of a shortage of water or because they were forced to leave by other Indians.

When the first Spanish explorers came to what is now Colorado, they found two different groups of Indians. One group lived on the flatlands east of the Rocky Mountains. These Indians are called Plains Indians. The other Indians, called the Ute (yüt) Indians, lived in the Rocky Mountains. There are still Utes living on reservations in Colorado today.

Prehistoric fossil remains are viewed at the Dinosaur National Monument.
■ Do you see the scientist?

"Pikes Peak or Bust"   Few people settled in Colorado until the late 1850s. Then in 1858, gold was discovered in a small stream outside of Denver. Just as people rushed to California in 1849, thousands of people came to Colorado looking for gold and also silver. The cry of these new settlers who had to travel over long and hard trails to reach the goldfields became "Pikes Peak or Bust." Pikes Peak is a mountain peak in the Colorado Rockies.

Mines were started, and towns grew up near them. As time went on, some of the mines ran out of minerals. When this happened, most of the people left the mining towns. Yet the buildings are still standing in some of these old towns. These towns, where few, if any, people live today, are called **ghost towns**.

Mountain Travelers   Do you remember reading about the problems early settlers in the eastern United States had with crossing the Appalachian Mountains? Well, settlers bound for the Pacific coast had many of the same problems. The only difference was that the Rocky Mountains were much higher and much more difficult to cross than the Appalachian Mountains were.

Some of the once-bustling western mining towns of the 1800s are today ghost towns, as this one is.
■ Have you ever visited a ghost town?

The History of Colorado

Indians were the first people to live in the area that we now know as Colorado. In the 1700s, Spanish and French explorers to the region found a number of Indian tribes scattered all over the area.

Eastern and central Colorado were made part of the United States in 1803, as part of the Louisiana Purchase. The rest of Colorado became part of the United States in 1848, after a war with the country of Mexico.

In 1876, Colorado became the thirty-eighth state in the United States. In the years that followed, the mining industry grew. Other industries also started to develop. In 1899 the first sugar beet plant opened.

As Colorado's population continued to grow, the need for better transportation increased. The Moffat Tunnel was completed in 1927. In 1973 the Eisenhower Memorial Tunnel opened. More people also meant a need for more water storage. In 1959 the Colorado-Big Thompson Project was completed. This project is a series of dams, reservoirs, and tunnels that bring water from western Colorado through the Rockies to the farms of eastern Colorado.

Today, Colorado is one of the ten fastest-growing states in the United States. It is a leader in a number of different fields. New companies have recently moved into the state. These companies are working on the development of different forms of energy, such as solar energy, which we can use in the future. Also, the United States Air Force Academy is located near Colorado Springs. This is a college that trains men and women to become officers in the United States Air Force.

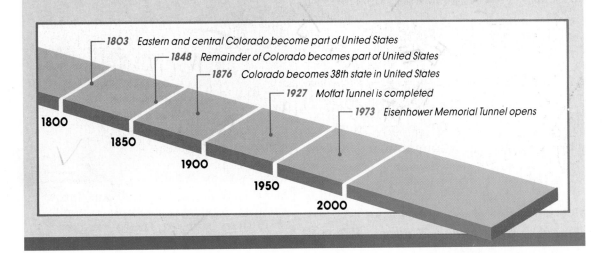

1803 Eastern and central Colorado become part of United States
1848 Remainder of Colorado becomes part of United States
1876 Colorado becomes 38th state in United States
1927 Moffat Tunnel is completed
1973 Eisenhower Memorial Tunnel opens

1800
1850
1900
1950
2000

Tunnels through the mountains make travel easier. Colorado's Eisenhower Memorial Tunnel is the world's highest.
■ Can you find the air vents on top?

Animals were used to carry food and other things that settlers needed. Burros (bur' ōz) were valuable animals for carrying goods. These animals look like small horses. They can carry large loads on their back. Burros are very surefooted on steep mountain trails.

Travelers had to look for valleys in the mountains where they could pass through. One of the early routes went along the Arkansas River into the Rockies. In later years, tunnels were dug in the mountains to make travel easier. A railroad line goes through the Moffat Tunnel, west of Denver. The Eisenhower Memorial Tunnel, which you read about earlier,

is the highest automobile tunnel in the world. But even with these tunnels, getting through the mountains is often hard, especially in the winter. When heavy snows fall, highways have to be closed until snowplows have cleared them.

Living in Colorado Today   Over 3 million people live in Colorado. Most live on the plains east of the Rocky Mountains. The greatest number of people live in and around Denver.

Though Denver is not in the mountains, it is located on the high plains. Its high elevation above sea level has given it the nickname the Mile-High City. Other cities in Colorado include Fort Collins, Boulder,

Denver, Colorado's capital and largest city, is a transportation center.
■ Is there much traffic at this time?

Greeley, Colorado Springs, and Pueblo. All these cities are on the plains, but all of them are close to the Rocky Mountains.

As you already know, Denver is Colorado's largest city and the capital of the state. Over 500,000 people live in the city. But Denver's metropolitan area has a population of over 1 million people. Denver is the transportation center for the states in the Rocky Mountain region. Denver also is an important tourist city.

A Variety of Industry   Colorado has many different kinds of industry. It is the leading manufacturing state in the Rocky Mountain region. Food processing is one of the industries found in Colorado. Some of the food-processing plants process sugar beets into white crystals of sugar. Other plants pack meat. Still other food-processing plants freeze or can fruits and vegetables.

Mining is another important industry in Colorado. People no longer rush to Colorado to look for gold and silver. But oil and natural gas are found in the state. Colorado has a great deal of shale, a kind of rock. Sometimes shale has oil in it. Another mineral mined in Colorado is called molybdenum (mə lib′ də nəm). This is a metal that is added to iron and steel to make them hard. Other minerals mined in Colorado are coal, lead, and copper.

Tourism is a very important industry in Colorado. Every year the state welcomes millions of tourists. Most of them enjoy going to the Rocky Mountains. Some mountain towns, such as Aspen and Vail, have become popular resorts. During the winter they attract thousands of people who go there to ski on the hillsides. People go to mountain resorts at other seasons, too, to enjoy the sunshine and fresh air and scenery.

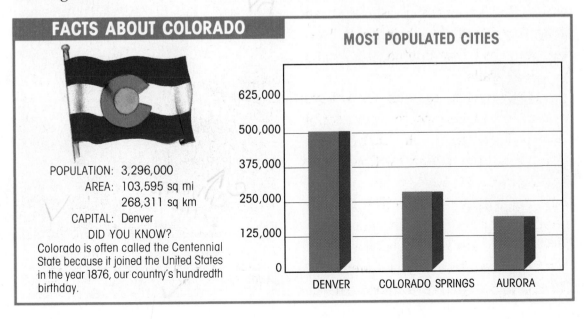

FACTS ABOUT COLORADO

POPULATION: 3,296,000
AREA: 103,595 sq mi
268,311 sq km
CAPITAL: Denver
DID YOU KNOW?
Colorado is often called the Centennial State because it joined the United States in the year 1876, our country's hundredth birthday.

MOST POPULATED CITIES

	625,000	500,000	375,000	250,000	125,000	0
DENVER	COLORADO SPRINGS	AURORA

Animals and Crops Even during the early mining days, some people who came to Colorado chose to raise cattle and sheep. They sold milk and meat to the miners. Farming and ranching are still carried on.

There are good grazing lands on both sides of the Rocky Mountains. Colorado is a leading state in both cattle and sheep raising.

As you know, Colorado has many food-processing plants. One of the reasons for this is that Colorado's farmers grow many different kinds of crops. Sugar beets are grown on farms near Greeley. Wheat farming is important on the plains of eastern Colorado. Corn is also raised there. Potatoes, lettuce, cabbage, carrots, and spinach are grown on the heavily irrigated land of the San Luis (san loo' is) Valley.

Solving the Water Problem Getting enough water for crops has been a problem for the farmers who settled on the plains in Colorado. This is because rain falls mostly on the western side of the Rockies. There is plenty of water there. But most of the

Colorado is a leading state in sheep raising. Here, sheep graze on ranchland high in the Rocky Mountains.
■ Why, do you think, does this ranchland need fencing?

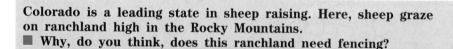

Dams help to solve Colorado's water problems by controlling, collecting, and directing the water of the major rivers.
■ Is this dam made of rock, dirt, or concrete?

people of Colorado live on the drier eastern plains.

To solve the water problem, tunnels have been dug through the mountains. Water flows through these tunnels from the western side of the mountains to the eastern side. The water is collected in **reservoirs** (rez′ ər vwärz). These are storage places where water can be collected and used when needed. Reservoirs look like little lakes.

Completing the tunnels for water took years and cost a great deal of money. One tunnel through the Rocky Mountains is more than 13 miles (21 km) long. But the water brought from the western side of the Rockies has made the dry plains of eastern Colorado into good farmland.

CHECKUP

1. What kind of animals lived millions of years ago in the area that we now call Colorado?
2. What brought many settlers to Colorado in the late 1850s?
3. What kinds of industry are found in Colorado today?
4. **Thinking Critically** Describe Colorado as if you were talking to an early Indian who lived in the region.

271

Reading a Diagram

WHAT IS A CROSS SECTION?

A cross section is a diagram that shows how elevation changes from one place on the earth to another. As you learned in Chapter 1, elevation is the height of the land above sea level. A cross section has two scales. The scale at the bottom is the horizontal scale. It measures distance in miles or kilometers. The vertical scale at the side of the cross section measures elevation in feet or meters.

The diagram on this page shows different elevations across the state of Colorado. It shows what the earth would look like if it were sliced from top to bottom. By reading the diagram, you can learn about the differences in elevation of the plains, the plateaus, and the mountains of Colorado.

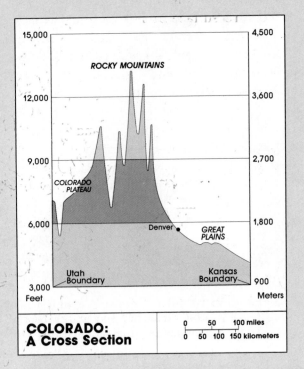

COLORADO:
A Cross Section

SKILLS PRACTICE

Study the diagram and answer the questions below. Write your answers on a separate sheet of paper.

1. What is the title of this diagram?
2. What range of elevation does the color orange represent on the diagram?
3. What is the name of the mountain range shown on the diagram?
4. How many feet high is the highest point of the mountains shown on the diagram? How many meters?
5. What is the elevation of Denver?
6. Is Denver or the Colorado Plateau at the higher elevation?
7. About how many feet higher is Denver than the Great Plains at the Kansas boundary?
8. How many miles is it from the Kansas boundary to the Utah boundary?
9. How many miles closer is Denver to the Kansas boundary than to the Utah boundary?
10. After studying the diagram, would you say that Colorado is a flat state or a mountainous state?

CHAPTER 12 REVIEW

MAIN IDEAS

1. Mountains are formed by hardened lava left from a volcano; when the earth's surface arches or folds due to pressure below the earth's surface; when the earth's crust is just slightly cracked and one side of the crack rises higher than the other; and by erosion.
2. In eastern Colorado the land is made up of flat plains. The central part of the state consists of the high Rocky Mountains. Western Colorado is a plateau with hills and deep valleys.
3. The Rocky Mountains are the highest mountains in the United States.
4. Millions of years ago large animals, called dinosaurs, lived in the area we now know as Colorado.
5. In 1858, gold was discovered outside of Denver. Thousands of people rushed to Colorado looking for gold. Because of this, towns started to develop in Colorado.
6. Today, Colorado has many kinds of industries including food processing, mining, and tourism.

VOCABULARY REVIEW

On a separate sheet of paper, write the letter of the word or phrase that correctly completes each sentence.

1. The hard outer layer of the earth is called the (**a**) mantle, (**b**) crust, (**c**) core.
2. Energy that comes from the sun is called (**a**) precipitation, (**b**) drainage, (**c**) solar energy.
3. The Continental Divide in the United States runs along (**a**) the Appalachian Mountains, (**b**) the Mississippi River, (**c**) the Rocky Mountains.
4. A reservoir is a storage place for (**a**) sugar beets, (**b**) water, (**c**) wheat.
5. Animals that roamed the earth millions of years ago are called (**a**) dinosaurs, (**b**) burros, (**c**) sheep.

CHAPTER CHECKUP

1. Why are mountains considered a valuable source of natural resources?
2. Which state has the highest peaks in the Rocky Mountains?
3. What is so important about the Eisenhower Memorial Tunnel?
4. What is the timberline?
5. What did the early Indians who lived in Colorado use to build their houses?
6. What is a ghost town?
7. How was the problem of getting water to eastern Colorado solved?
8. **Thinking Critically** Explain the four ways that mountains are formed.
9. **Thinking Critically** What kind of tools, do you think, did the miners need to get the gold and silver out of the ground?
10. **Thinking Critically** What is your favorite activity in the mountains?

APPLYING KNOWLEDGE

1. Find a picture of a dinosaur in a book in your library. Then draw your own picture of a dinosaur.
2. Choose one of the resorts in Colorado and find out all you can about it. Make an oral report about the resort to your class.

13 Tennessee

Three States in One

What are the three regions of Tennessee?

VOCABULARY

Appalachian Trail

Changing Elevations Do you remember studying about the country of Chile in Chapter 8? Chile is more than ten times as long as it is wide. The state of Tennessee is almost the opposite of Chile. Tennessee stretches for about 432 miles (695 km) from the Great Smoky Mountains in the east to the Mississippi River in the west. The state is almost four times as wide as it is long. Find Tennessee on your Atlas map of the United States on pages 356–357.

If you were to walk from the western border to the eastern border of Tennessee, it would be a steady climb upward. The lowest spot in the state is by the Mississippi River. The highest point of the state is on the border between Tennessee and North Carolina.

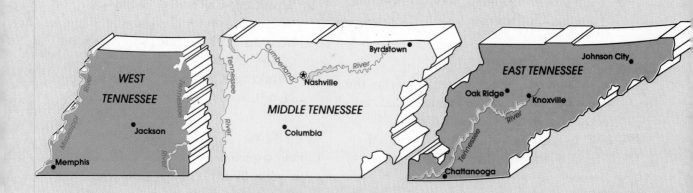

TENNESSEE: Regions

⊛ State Capital
• Other Cities

Tennessee's three regions are shown on this map. Look at the map at the right to find the land elevations in each part of the state.
■ What are the names of Tennessee's regions?
■ Which region has the highest land elevation?

Tennessee is made up of three very different regions. The regions are named East Tennessee, Middle Tennessee, and West Tennessee. Because these three regions are so different, Tennessee is sometimes referred to as being three states in one. Let's begin our study of Tennessee by looking at these three regions.

East Tennessee

East Tennessee is very mountainous. Mountains can be found all along the eastern border of Tennessee. The highest mountain peak in the state is located in East Tennessee. Its name is Clingman's Dome. This mountain is 6,642 feet (2,025 m) high. There are also a number of mountain ranges found in this region. These mountain ranges include the Appalachian Mountains and the Great Smoky Mountains.

Within the Great Smoky Mountains is one of the most beautiful national parks in all of the United States. Its name is Great Smoky Mountains National Park. This is also one of the most popular national parks in the country. Each year about 9 million people visit this national park. The park stretches for over 500,000 acres (202,500 ha), between Tennessee and North Carolina.

Clingman's Dome is found in Great Smoky Mountains National Park. The **Appalachian Trail** crosses through this national park. The Appalachian Trail is a 2,000 mile (3,200

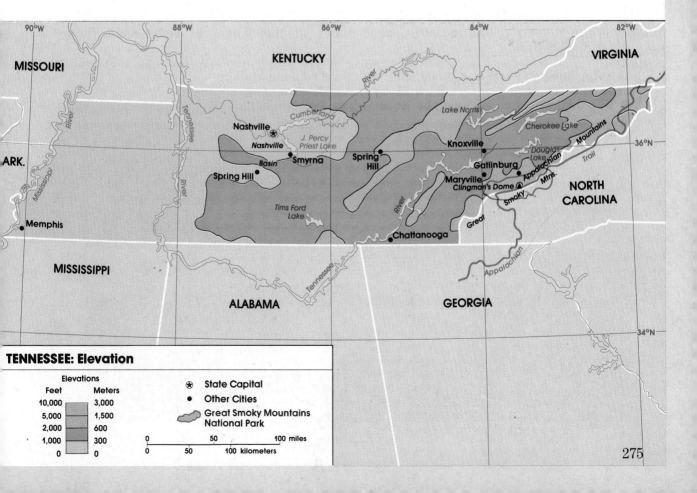

TENNESSEE: Elevation

Elevations		
Feet	Meters	
10,000	3,000	
5,000	1,500	
2,000	600	
1,000	300	
0	0	

⊛ State Capital
● Other Cities
Great Smoky Mountains National Park

0   50   100 miles
0   50   100 kilometers

km) hiking trail that runs from the state of Georgia all the way to the state of Maine. There are also hundreds of smaller hiking trails in the park. Hikers along the trails can see deer, bears, and many kinds of birds. Thousands of people enjoy hiking along these trails each year.

No hotels or restaurants are allowed in the Great Smoky Mountains National Park. If you plan to stay longer than a day, you must sleep at a campsite. To do this you will need to have a sleeping bag or a tent. If you need food, you must walk or drive to one of the towns just outside the park. One such town in Tennessee is Gatlinburg. Most of the people who live in Gatlinburg make their living by serving tourists. The town has hotels, restaurants, grocery stores, and amusement parks. There are several towns like Gatlinburg in both Tennessee and North Carolina.

Between the mountains are valleys and ridges. These areas have fertile farmland. East Tennessee also has a large plateau that is found west of the Appalachian Mountains. The land in this part of the state rises from 1,500 to 1,800 feet (457 to 549 m) above sea level. Most of the coal mined in Tennessee comes from this part of the state. You will be learning more about coal mining in Tennessee later in this chapter.

Middle Tennessee   In this part of Tennessee you will find mostly low, rolling hills. The Nashville Basin can be found in Middle Tennessee. The land in this basin is very good for

The Appalachian Trail is a 2,000-mile (3,200-km) hiking trail. Thousands of people enjoy hiking along the trail each year.
■ **How will these hikers find the Appalachian Trail?**

Farmers in many parts of Tennessee raise cattle. Green pastures in the Nashville Basin provide good grazing ground for cattle.
■ Do farmers raise cattle near where you live?

raising animals. Cattle and other animals graze in the green pastures found on the Nashville Basin. Farmers also grow some crops in this part of the state.

Two of the state's most important rivers run through this region. Find the Cumberland and Tennessee rivers on the map on page 275. The Tennessee River borders both Middle Tennessee and West Tennessee. Later in this chapter, you will be learning more about why these two rivers are so important to Tennessee.

West Tennessee The part of Tennessee called West Tennessee is a part of the Gulf Coastal Plain. The Gulf Coastal Plain begins at the Gulf of Mexico and reaches as far north as Illinois. Do you remember studying about the Gulf Coastal Plain in Chapter 10? The Mississippi River, the western border of Tennessee, is

also part of the region of West Tennessee.

The coastal plain in West Tennessee can be divided into two parts. One part is hilly land that runs for about 10 miles (16 km) along the western banks of the Tennessee River. The other part is very flat land that ends at the Mississippi River. This is the lowest part of the state. The average elevation in this area is around 300 feet (91 m). Sometimes this part of West Tennessee is called the Mississippi Bottoms.

CHECKUP

1. What are the names of Tennessee's three regions?
2. What is the name of the highest mountain peak in Tennessee?
3. What is the Appalachian Trail?
4. **Thinking Critically** Explain the differences between the types of land in each region of Tennessee.

277

Tennessee's Natural Resources

What important natural resources can be found in Tennessee?

VOCABULARY

shaft mine   dam
Tennessee Valley Authority

Tennessee's Mountains   Some of Tennessee's natural resources can be found in the state's mountains. As you already know, people from all over the country come to enjoy the beauty of the outdoors in the Great Smoky Mountains. But Tennessee's mountains also provide us with forest products and natural resources.

Natural resources, such as marble, are mined in Tennessee's mountains. Marble is a hard, shiny stone. Marble is used to make buildings, statues, and tabletops.

Coal   Another important resource mined in Tennessee is coal. As you read earlier, most of the state's coal is mined in East Tennessee. Most of the coal mined in Tennessee is bituminous, or soft, coal.

There are different ways of mining coal. When coal is close to the surface, big machines strip away the soil and rocks that lie over the coal. Then other machines dig out the coal and load it onto trucks.

Most of the time, though, the coal is too far under the ground to be reached from the surface. Sometimes it is hundreds of feet below the surface. Then tunnels have to be dug to the coal. Let us see how coal is mined when it is far below the surface of the earth.

Digging for Coal   One kind of mine is called the **shaft mine**. Passages called shafts are dug straight down to the level of the coal deposits. The miners enter and leave by one shaft, while another shaft is used for bringing out the coal. Each shaft has an elevator called a hoist.

Tunnels are dug from the lower part of the shaft to the coal deposits. Miners used to dig the tunnels and the coal with picks and shovels. They shoveled the coal into small cars that ran on tracks. The cars were then

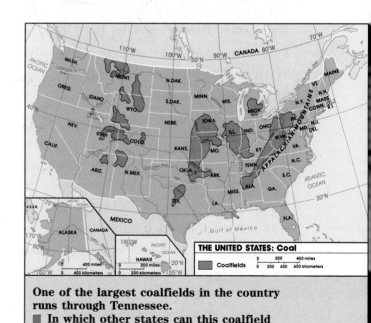

THE UNITED STATES: Coal

One of the largest coalfields in the country runs through Tennessee.
■ In which other states can this coalfield be found?

One way that coal is mined in Tennessee is through shaft mines.
■ What are the two shafts in the diagram above used for?

After the coal is taken to the surface, it is washed. Wet coal cannot supply much heat, so it is dried. At this point the pieces of coal are sometimes sorted by size.

The coal is then carried away to be sold. Most coal is hauled in railroad cars, but some is carried in trucks and barges. Coal is also sometimes moved by pipeline. When this is done, the coal is crushed and mixed with water so that it can be pumped through the pipeline. This coal must then be dried before it can be used to burn as a fuel.

Over the years, many coal miners have been killed or badly hurt in accidents in the underground tunnels. There is always the danger that tunnel roofs or tunnel walls may fall. Deadly gases sometimes gather in the tunnels, so air has to be blown into the mine from the surface. Sometimes water must be pumped from the tunnels. Coal dust can sometimes cause an explosion. When miners breathe in the dust, it can harm their lungs. Today mines are safer than they used to be, but getting coal from the earth is still hard and dangerous work.

Other Minerals   Besides marble and coal, there are other resources that are mined in Tennessee. For example, Tennessee leads all states in the production of zinc. Zinc is often used in electric batteries and as a coating to stop things from rusting.

drawn by mules to the shaft where the coal was lifted to the surface.

Today mining coal is different from what it used to be. Most of the work is done by machines. Machines remove the coal from the walls, load it in cars or on conveyor belts, and do other steps that were once done by hand. Today one miner operating a machine can get the same amount of coal in the same amount of time that it took many miners of the past, working with picks and shovels.

Most of the state's zinc is also mined in East Tennessee.

Another important resource found in East and Middle Tennessee is limestone. Do you remember learning about limestone in Chapter 7? Limestone is used in making cement. Other natural resources mined in Tennessee include iron, oil, natural gas, and phosphate (fos′ fāt) rocks. Phosphate rocks are used to make fertilizers. Clay, sand, and gravel are also mined in the state.

Water Resources   You have already learned about some of Tennessee's important rivers—the Mississippi, Cumberland, and Tennessee. The Tennessee River begins in Knoxville, Tennessee and flows southwest into the state of Alabama. Then the river curves northward and back into Tennessee. It eventually empties into the Ohio River in the state of Kentucky. The Cumberland River flows mostly from the east to the west. It too joins the Ohio River in Kentucky.

Tennessee's rivers used to cause the state's farmers big problems. At times the rivers would overflow their banks. These floods would wash away some of the state's most fertile soil. Time after time farmers lost their crops. This made it very hard for Tennessee's farmers to earn a living. In 1933, the federal government in Washington, D.C., set up the **Tennessee Valley Authority**, more commonly known as the TVA, to help the farmers with their problems.

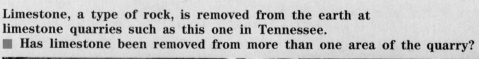

Limestone, a type of rock, is removed from the earth at limestone quarries such as this one in Tennessee.
■ Has limestone been removed from more than one area of the quarry?

Norris Dam near Norris, Tennessee, controls the waters of the Clinch and Powell rivers.
■ **Do you see the boats on the reservoir created by the dam?**

The TVA, as it is most commonly called, built **dams** to help control the river floods. A dam is a wall built across a river or stream that stops the flow of water. Lakes or reservoirs of water are created by the dam. The water can then be released from behind the dam when it is needed. The TVA built over 30 dams in Tennessee.

The dams built by the TVA helped Tennessee in three ways. First, the floods were controlled. Second, the TVA made it possible to build hydroelectric power plants. Do you remember studying about hydroelectric power in Chapter 3? It is used to make electricity. These plants have provided electricity for many of the people of Tennessee. The third way the TVA helped Tennessee was that the lakes that were made behind the dams could be used for recreational purposes.

CHECKUP

1. What important natural resources can be found in Tennessee's mountains?
2. What are shaft mines used for?
3. In what three ways did the TVA help Tennessee?
4. **Thinking Critically** Summarize how coal is mined when it is found far beneath the earth.

Farming and Industry

Why is Tennessee an important farming and industrial state?

VOCABULARY

service industry	Parthenon

Tennessee's Climate The climate varies from one end of Tennessee to the other. The temperatures in the mountains of East Tennessee range from about 35°F (2°C) in the winter to about 75°F (24°C) in the summer. The temperatures in West Tennessee are somewhat warmer.

Most of Tennessee's precipitation falls in the form of rain, although the state does get some snow. Overall the state averages about 50 inches (130 cm) of precipitation a year. The mixture of precipitation and mild temperatures throughout most of the year means that Tennessee farmers can grow many different kinds of crops.

Tennessee Farming Tennessee has a lot of farmland. The best farmland is in the western part of the state. Soybeans are the state's most important crop.

Another important crop in Tennessee is tobacco. Most of the tobacco is grown in East and Middle Tennessee. Tennessee is the fourth leading state in the United States in the production of tobacco.

Other crops grown in Tennessee include corn, cotton, and hay. Corn is one of the few crops that is grown throughout the state. Cotton is grown mainly in West Tennessee. Tennessee is a leading state in growing cotton. Most of the hay, grown in Middle Tennessee, and the corn is used to feed livestock. Livestock, such as beef and dairy cattle, hogs, and broiler chickens, brings in more money to Tennessee farmers than any other

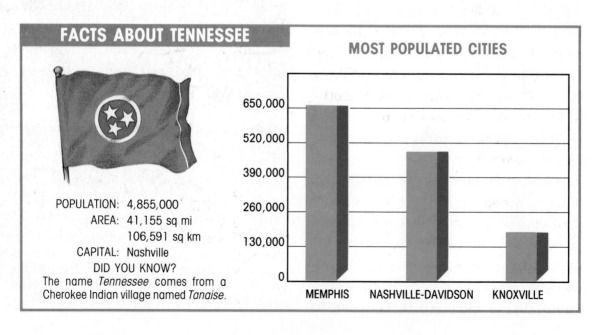

FACTS ABOUT TENNESSEE

POPULATION: 4,855,000
AREA: 41,155 sq mi
106,591 sq km
CAPITAL: Nashville
DID YOU KNOW?
The name *Tennessee* comes from a Cherokee Indian village named *Tanaise*.

MOST POPULATED CITIES

(bar graph with y-axis values: 0, 130,000, 260,000, 390,000, 520,000, 650,000; x-axis: MEMPHIS, NASHVILLE-DAVIDSON, KNOXVILLE)

farm products. Sheep and mules are also raised in Tennessee.

Tennessee is well known for raising horses. Many people like to ride horses for recreation. One of the most popular horses for recreational riding is the Tennessee walking horse. Have you ever had a chance to ride a horse?

Growing Industries Tennessee has many different kinds of industry. There are a number of reasons why there is so much industry in the state. One reason is that the people of the state take pride in what they do and work hard at their jobs. Another reason is that there are good schools in the state that train people to do the kinds of jobs that are needed in industry. Also, Tennessee has a variety of natural resources to use. Natural resources are important to industries.

The largest industry in Tennessee is the making of chemicals. The most important product made by the chemical industry is medicine. Other chemicals are used to make things such as yarn for carpets and clothing, paint, plastics, and soap.

Food processing is another important industry in the state. This kind of industry is needed because of the many different crops grown in the state. Some of the food processing plants freeze or can fruits and vegetables. There are also large meatpacking plants in the cities of Chattanooga, Knoxville, and Memphis.

The Tennessee walking horse is a popular show horse. Pictured here is the 1986 World Grand Champion.
■ **Would you like to ride this horse?**

Tennessee has many forests. One of Tennessee's leading industries is making wood products, such as guitars.
■ **Does anyone you know play a guitar?**

The making of cars and trucks is another industry in Tennessee.
■ **Do you see the robots being used?**

centered around the state's largest cities. Selling manufactured products to people is one type of service industry. The cities of Memphis, Nashville, and Knoxville are centers of this type of industry. Memphis is also one of the country's most important medical research centers. These centers try to find out how to cure certain kinds of illnesses.

Other industries in the state include the making of automobiles and aluminum. Large automobile plants are located in the cities of Spring Hill and Smyrna. The plant in Smyrna uses robots to do some of the work. The Aluminum Company of America, better known as Alcoa, has a large aluminum plant in Alcoa, Tennessee. Alcoa is the largest producer of aluminum in the United States.

Visiting Tennessee As you learned earlier in this chapter, many people visit the Great Smoky Mountains National Park in Tennessee each year. Tourists also visit Tennessee to boat and fish in the lakes that were made by the TVA.

Making forest products is also a leading industry in Tennessee. There are over 13 million acres (over 5 million ha) of forests in the state. Some of these forests are used to make products such as lumber, hardwood floors, and furniture. Tennessee is one of the leading states in the country in the production of lumber. The state ranks third of all the states in making furniture.

Tennessee has many **service industries** throughout the state. Service industries offer services to people rather than manufacture goods. Most of the service industries are

Music lovers from all over the world visit Tennessee to hear music performed by many different musicians. Near Nashville is the Grand Ole Opry House. This is a famous music hall where musicians perform country music. This is a kind of music that was first played by people who lived around the Appalachian Mountains in the early 1800s.

The Parthenon in Nashville is a replica, or copy, of the ancient Greek temple in Athens, Greece (inset).
■ What likenesses do you notice between the two buildings?

Record albums of all different kinds of music are recorded in Nashville and Memphis. Elvis Presley, one of America's most famous musicians, lived in Memphis. Elvis Presley is noted for making rock and roll music popular in this country.

Many people also visit Tennessee's historic sites. The homes of three past Presidents of the United States are found in Tennessee. In Columbia, tourists can visit President James K. Polk's home. President Andrew Johnson's home is in Greeneville. President Andrew Jackson's home is just outside the city of Nashville. This house is called the Hermitage. Many tourists to Tennes-

see also visit the **Parthenon**, a full-size copy of the original temple built in Greece thousands of years ago. Parts of the original Parthenon are still found standing in Greece today. The Parthenon in Nashville, Tennessee, is the only full-size copy in the world of the original Greek temple.

CHECKUP

1. What is Tennessee's most important farm crop?
2. Name three reasons why there is so much industry in Tennessee.
3. Why do so many tourists visit Tennessee?
4. **Thinking Critically** Would you rather work as a Tennessee farmer or in one of the state's industries?

The People of Tennessee

How have the people of Tennessee helped both their state and our country?

VOCABULARY

tribe	Congress
Trail of Tears	volunteer

Early Settlers Many years ago, Indians were the only people who lived in the area that would later become Tennessee. These Indians were divided into three main **tribes**. A tribe is a group of people that form a community under a leader or leaders. The names of these tribes were the Cherokee (cher′ ə kē), Chicksaw, and Creek. But by the 1830s other settlers to the area forced all the Indians onto reservations in what is now Oklahoma. None of the Indians wanted to leave their homeland. The Cherokee Indians called their journey to their new home the **Trail of Tears**.

Settling Tennessee As a result of exploration of the area between 1541 and 1682, the countries of Spain, England, and France all claimed the land of Tennessee. After the end of the French and Indian War in 1763, Britain claimed all of the lands in North America east of the Mississippi River. This included Tennessee.

In the 1770s, new settlers from North Carolina and Virginia traveled over the Appalachian Mountains into Tennessee. Some of these settlers were led by a man named Daniel Boone. The trail that Daniel Boone took to Tennessee became known as Wilderness Road. This was the main route for new settlers traveling over the Appalachian Mountains. In 1796,

The Cherokee were forced to leave their homes. They traveled what was called the Trail of Tears to reach Oklahoma.
■ How does this painting show the sadness felt by the Cherokee?

Tennessean Andrew Jackson (inset) was the seventh President of the United States. His home in Nashville, the Hermitage, is well known.
■ Do you know anyone who has visited the Hermitage?

Tennessee was made the sixteenth state in the United States.

Helping Our Country Grow During the 1800s, Tennessee helped the United States grow in many ways. Three men who became President of the United States were from Tennessee. Andrew Jackson, James K. Polk, and Andrew Johnson were all President of the United States at different times in the 1800s. All three men also represented Tennessee in the United States **Congress** before becoming President. Congress is the group of

people, who meet in Washington, D.C., to make the laws for our country. Another famous person from Tennessee to serve in Congress was Davy Crockett. Before serving in Congress, Crockett became famous as a hunter and a good storyteller.

In 1846, the United States went to war with the country of Mexico. Tennessee sent over 2,000 **volunteers** to help win the war. A volunteer is a person who does something of his or her own free will. Ever since that time Tennessee has been known as the Volunteer State.

The History of Tennessee

In 1541, a Spaniard named Hernando de Soto was the first European to see the land that would later become Tennessee. Years later, French and English explorers would also explore the region. It was not until 1763, after the end of the French and Indian War, that the British gained total control of the area. Tennessee was made part of the colony of North Carolina.

In 1789, the state of North Carolina gave the Tennessee region to the United States government. Tennessee became an official territory of the United States. By 1796, Tennessee was made the sixteenth state.

For the next 60 years, Tennessee continued to grow. Then in 1861, the Civil War started in the United States. Tennessee fought with the Confederate army during the war. One of the biggest battles of the Civil War was fought at Shiloh, Tennessee. The North won the battle of Shiloh. In 1865 the North won the Civil War.

It took many years for Tennessee to recover from the Civil War. Many homes and buildings were ruined and thousands of people were without homes. Most of the large farms of Tennessee, called plantations, were divided into smaller farms after the war. However, at the same time, industry in the state started to develop. This new industry helped Tennessee's recovery from the war by making many new jobs.

The 1900s have been a time of growth for Tennessee. New industries have started. Highways, railroads, and airports have been built. The Tennessee Valley Authority built dams to control river flooding and to supply hydroelectric power. Nashville and Memphis have become centers for different kinds of music in the United States. In 1982 a world's fair was held in Knoxville. This world's fair helped to attract people from all over the world to Tennessee.

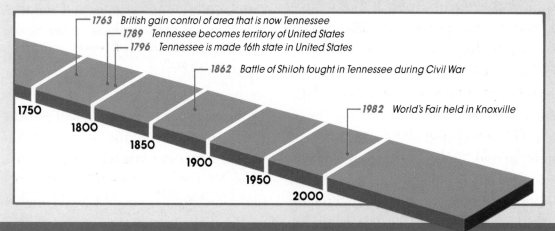

1763 British gain control of area that is now Tennessee
1789 Tennessee becomes territory of United States
1796 Tennessee is made 16th state in United States
1862 Battle of Shiloh fought in Tennessee during Civil War
1982 World's Fair held in Knoxville

1750   1800   1850   1900   1950   2000

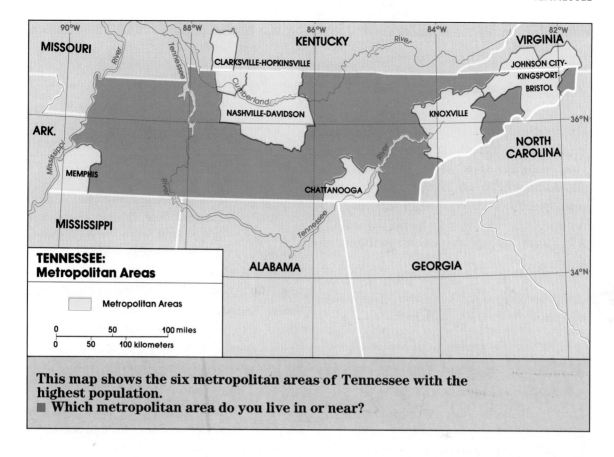

TENNESSEE:
Metropolitan Areas

☐ Metropolitan Areas

0   50   100 miles
0   50   100 kilometers

This map shows the six metropolitan areas of Tennessee with the highest population.
■ **Which metropolitan area do you live in or near?**

Living in Cities Throughout the 1700s and 1800s most of the people that lived in Tennessee were farmers. Then in the early 1900s, the state started to change from a farming state to an industrial state. People began to move off of the farms and into or around the cities. Today, about three fifths of Tennessee's 4,855,000 people live in metropolitan areas. The largest of these metropolitan areas are around the cities of Nashville, Memphis, and Knoxville.

The most populated city in the state is Memphis. Memphis has a population of over 650,000 people. Memphis is the industrial center of western Tennessee. The capital of the state is Nashville. Nashville is also the second most populated city in Tennessee. Other large cities in Tennessee are Knoxville and Chattanooga. Find all these cities on the map on page 275.

CHECKUP

1. What were the names of the three Indian tribes that once lived in Tennessee?
2. How did Tennessee get the nickname of the Volunteer State?
3. What is the name of Tennessee's capital city?
4. **Thinking Critically** Why, do you think, did the Cherokee call their journey from Tennessee to Oklahoma a Trail of Tears?

Making an Outline for a Report

ORGANIZING IDEAS

In making a report, it is important that your organize your ideas. To do so, you should make an outline. An outline is a plan made before you begin writing your report. One easy way to make an outline is to write questions you have about the topic.

Below is an outline for a report about a famous person from Tennessee. His name was Davy Crockett.

OUTLINE

The topic is Davy Crockett.
I.   When did Davy Crockett live?
II. How did he become popular?
III. How did Davy Crockett serve the people of Tennessee?

A REPORT ABOUT DAVY CROCKETT

Davy Crockett was born in Tennessee in 1786. Crockett's family moved around Tennessee quite often. The family finally settled in Jefferson County.

While growing up, Davy became a skillful hunter. In 1813, he joined the army. His ability as a hunter helped him to become a good soldier.

Crockett was also a storyteller. He became famous throughout Tennessee for telling funny stories. Most of his stories were about himself.

His ability as a good soldier and a storyteller made Davy Crockett very popular. In 1827, he was chosen to serve the people of Tennessee in Congress. He served in Congress until 1835.

In 1836, Crockett joined 185 men to defend a Texas fort, called the Alamo, against an attack by Mexican troops. Crockett and the other men fought bravely. But they were greatly overmatched by the Mexicans. Davy Crockett and all of the men who fought with him were killed during the battle.

SKILLS PRACTICE

Notice that each question in the outline is answered in the report. Now you can try to write an outline on one of these topics.

Hiking on the Appalachian Trail
Taking a Vacation in Tennessee

Follow these steps.

1. Take notes on the topic you choose from your textbook or books in the library.
2. Ask yourself what questions your notes answer about your topic.
3. Write down your topic and list the questions with Roman numerals.
4. Under each numeral, write information that will help to answer your questions.

You now have an outline. From your outline you will be able to write a report on your topic.

CHAPTER 13 REVIEW

MAIN IDEAS

1. West Tennessee is part of the Gulf Coastal Plain, Middle Tennessee has rolling hills and the Nashville Basin, and East Tennessee is very mountainous.
2. Important natural resources found in Tennessee include forests of oak and hickory trees, marble, coal, zinc, limestone, iron, oil, natural gas, phosphate rocks, and water.
3. Farms in Tennessee grow soybeans, tobacco, corn, cotton, and hay. Some farms also raise cattle, hogs, chickens, and riding horses.
4. Making chemicals is Tennessee's most important industry. Other industries include food processing, service industries, making automobiles, making aluminum products, and tourism.
5. The first people to live in the area that is now Tennessee were Indians.
6. Andrew Jackson, James K. Polk, and Andrew Johnson were three famous people from Tennessee. All three men served as a member of Congress and also as President of the United States.
7. Tennessee sent many volunteers to help our country win a war against Mexico. Because of this the state was nicknamed the Volunteer State.

VOCABULARY REVIEW

On a separate sheet of paper write the word or phrase that correctly completes each sentence.

1. The Appalachian Trail runs from Georgia to the state of (**a**) Tennessee, (**b**) Maine, (**c**) Pennsylvania.
2. One way that coal is mined is through (**a**) dams, (**b**) shaft mines, (**c**) Congress.
3. A wall built across a river or stream that stops the flow of water is called a (**a**) shaft mine, (**b**) dam, (**c**) Trail of Tears.
4. In Nashville, many tourists visit a full-size copy of the (**a**) Parthenon, (**b**) Grand Ole Opry House, (**c**) Hermitage.
5. A group of people that form a community under a leader or leaders is called a (**a**) Congress, (**b**) service industry, (**c**) tribe.

CHAPTER CHECKUP

1. Why is Tennessee sometimes referred to as being three states in one?
2. What is the name of the popular national park that is found in Tennessee?
3. Why was the Tennessee Valley Authority set up?
4. What is the name of the popular riding horse that is raised in Tennessee?
5. What are service industries?
6. **Thinking Critically** Suggest ways that you think would make coal mining safer.
7. **Thinking Critically** If you had a chance to visit Tennessee what would you most like to see?

APPLYING KNOWLEDGE

Choose one of the people mentioned in this chapter to research. After your research is completed, give an oral report to your class on the person you chose. Include a drawing of what your person looked like.

14 Yugoslavia and Switzerland

Yugoslavia

What are the physical features of Yugoslavia?

VOCABULARY

Mediterranean climate

The Balkan Peninsula   Look at the Atlas map of Europe on page 366. Find the Adriatic (ā drē at' ik) Sea and the Black Sea. Between these two bodies of water is a mountainous piece of land on which a number of countries are located. This land is called the Balkan Peninsula because of the Balkan Mountains that are found on the peninsula.

The countries on the Balkan Peninsula are called Balkan countries. These countries include Albania, Bulgaria, Romania, Greece, most of Yugoslavia, and a part of Turkey. Find these countries on the map on page 367.

A Mountainous Country   The country of Yugoslavia has many

The city of Sarajevo, Yugoslavia, was the site of the 1984 Winter Olympic Games.
■ What sign are the athletes forming in the picture?

mountains. Almost three fourths of the land in Yugoslavia is mountains or highlands. The country can be divided into three regions. These regions are the Coastal Region, the Interior Highlands, and the Pannonian (pə nō′ nē ən) Plain.

The Coastal Region is a very narrow strip of land along the Adriatic coast. In some places, steep mountain cliffs rise from the sea. Yugoslavia's jagged coastline, which also includes many small islands, makes many good natural harbors. Many tourists visit this part of Yugoslavia each year.

The largest region in Yugoslavia is the Interior Highlands. Most of this region is mountainous. The highest mountain peak in Yugoslavia, Mount Triglav (trē′ gläv), is found in this region. Mount Triglav is 9,393 feet (2,863 m) high. Many people who enjoy winter sports, such as skiing, visit this part of Yugoslavia. In 1984 the Winter Olympic Games were held in the city of Sarajevo (sär′ ə ye vô). Sarajevo is located in the Interior Highlands.

The Pannonian Plain is a region of mostly flat land. There are some low hills in the region. It is in this region that most of Yugoslavia's farming is done. The country's most important river, the Danube (dan′ yüb), is found in this region. The Danube starts in the country of West Germany and eventually empties into

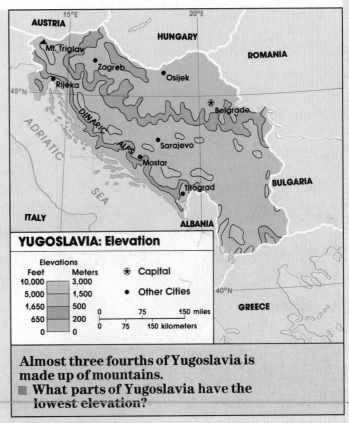

Almost three fourths of Yugoslavia is made up of mountains.
■ What parts of Yugoslavia have the lowest elevation?

293

the Black Sea. The Danube and its tributaries are used as shipping routes.

Different Climates   Yugoslavia has three very different kinds of climates. Along the Adriatic Coast there is a **Mediterranean climate**. This means that it is hot and dry during the summer and mild and rainy during the winter. In the mountainous areas the summers are short and cool, while the winters are long and cold. The country's plains have a continental climate. Do you remember what a con-

tinental climate is? A place that has a continental climate has hot summers and cold winters.

Natural Resources   The most important natural resource in Yugoslavia is forests. Most of the Interior Highlands is covered by forests. About one third of the country is made up of forests of beech, oak, birch, elm, juniper, and pine trees. Yugoslavia's forests are used for recreational purposes and for providing lumber. Animals such as deer, bears, and wild pigs are hunted in the forests.

Rivers are another important natural resource in Yugoslavia. Hundreds of rivers, which start in the mountains and flow through the valleys, are sources for producing hydroelectric power. More than half of Yugoslavia's electricity is made by hydroelectric power plants.

There are also many mineral resources found in Yugoslavia. Iron, aluminum, copper, lead, zinc, and nickel are all mined in the country. More and more of these minerals are being mined each year.

The walled city of Dubrovnik, on Yugoslavia's Adriatic coast, is a popular tourist attraction.
■ What color are the buildings' roofs?

CHECKUP
1. Where is the Balkan Peninsula found?
2. What are the three regions of Yugoslavia?
3. What important event was held in Sarajevo in the winter of 1984?
4. **Thinking Critically** Explain why a continental climate is different from a Mediterranean climate.

Living in Yugoslavia

How has life in Yugoslavia changed since the Communists took control of the country?

VOCABULARY

republic	ally

Where the People Live   About 23,600,000 people live in Yugoslavia. The country is divided into six states called **republics**. Each republic has its own laws and government. Within each republic there is one main ethnic group. An ethnic group is people who share the same language, customs, and often the same religion.

About 40 years ago, most of the people of Yugoslavia lived in small villages. They lived by working on small farms. Today, about half of the people live in urban areas. Some of the major cities in Yugoslavia are Sarajevo, Zagreb (zäg′ reb), and Belgrade, the capital.

Government   In 1945, Communists gained control of the government in Yugoslavia. The government was headed by a man named Tito. Tito made Yugoslavia an **ally** of the Soviet Union. This means that the two countries agreed to help defend each other. The Communists in Yugoslavia took control of all the factories, farms, and other businesses in the country.

Although Yugoslavia and the Soviet Union were allies, Tito would not let his country be totally controlled by the Soviets. This eventually caused the two countries to stop being allies. Communism in Yugoslavia started to develop in its own way. The government in each republic was given more power. Some of the country's smaller industries were given to the workers rather than the government to run.

Tito remained in control of Yugoslavia until his death in 1980. Today, the country's government is still working to make Yugoslavia more industrialized. The new leaders also want to keep Yugoslavia free from control by other countries.

Tito, born Josip Broz, was the ruler of Yugoslavia from 1945 to 1980.
■ What country does the map show?

Working in Yugoslavia For many years, Yugoslavia was thought of as a poor country. Things have changed in the last 40 years, since Tito came to power in the country. Improvements in industry have helped the country grow. In that same time, farming in Yugoslavia has also improved.

Today about 80 percent of Yugoslavia's industries are run by the government. The other 20 percent are owned by private citizens. These are usually small stores and shops. But the government allows the workers to decide what to produce and where to sell the products. The money that is made by the privately owned industry is split three ways. One part goes to the government, another part goes to the workers, and the third part is used to improve the industry. In this way, the workers know that the more they produce, the more money they will earn.

Some of Yugoslavia's industries include the making of automobiles, electrical machinery and equipment, and the production of chemicals. The Yugoslavs are skilled workers in wood, and produce many wood products.

Like industry, farms in Yugoslavia are owned by the government. But in 1974 the government allowed each farmer to own up to about 25 acres (10 ha) of land. On this land they could grow whatever crops they wished and sell the products to whomever they wanted. The money they received from selling their crops was kept by the farmer. There are also larger cooperative farms and state farms in Yugoslavia. On cooperative farms the workers decide what to grow and they divide the money that they make from selling the crops. On state farms the government decides what should be grown, and the workers are paid for their work. The

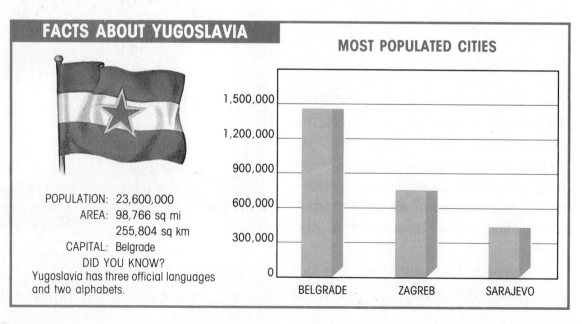

FACTS ABOUT YUGOSLAVIA

POPULATION: 23,600,000
AREA: 98,766 sq mi
255,804 sq km
CAPITAL: Belgrade
DID YOU KNOW?
Yugoslavia has three official languages and two alphabets.

MOST POPULATED CITIES

1,500,000	
1,200,000	
900,000	
600,000	
300,000	
0	
BELGRADE	ZAGREB	SARAJEVO

Living In Yugoslavia

The Vidovich family live in a city near the Adriatic coast in the republic of Croatia. Their home is not large, but it is comfortable. The Vidoviches feel fortunate to have their own home. Most of their friends live in small apartments.

The Vidovich children, 10-year-old Stefan and 12-year-old Vlasta, attend school. In Yugoslavia the law requires children between the ages of 7 and 14 to go to school. Mr. Vidovich works in a factory that makes automobiles. Mrs. Vidovich runs a small souvenir shop for tourists.

The day starts very early for the Vidovich family. Mr. Vidovich usually starts work around 7:00 A.M. But before Mr. and Mrs. Vidovich leave for work and Stefan and Vlasta leave for school, the family enjoys a breakfast together. Their breakfast usually includes bread with butter and jam, and a cup of coffee for the adults. Stefan and Vlasta have a glass of hot milk with their bread. Lunch is usually eaten arcund 2:30 in the afternoon. Dinner is not served until late in the evening. Popular dinner dishes include veal, lamb, mutton, or stuffed tomatoes.

Between lunch and dinner most of the family chores are completed. The children do their homework. Mr. Vidovich usually works around the house or takes care of the family car. Mrs. Vidovich cleans the house and does the cooking.

Weekends are a time of relaxation. The Vidoviches enjoy going to the opera, the theater, the movies, and soccer games. Soccer is a very popular sport in Yugoslavia and throughout Europe. Like most Yugoslavs, the Vidoviches take a summer vacation. Stefan and Vlasta especially enjoy visiting a neighboring country or going to a beach along the coast.

Skiing is a popular sport in Yugoslavia's interior highlands. This resort is in the northwestern republic of Slovenia.
■ **Is skiing a winter sport in your community?**

major crops are wheat, corn, and sugar beets.

Trade and Tourism   Yugoslavia trades with countries all over the world. Yugoslavia's mines produce a number of minerals for export. Some of the other major exports of Yugoslavia are machinery, automobiles, and textiles. Have you ever seen an automobile named the Yugo? This car is exported from Yugoslavia.

Tourism brings in a lot of money to Yugoslavia. As you already know, the 1984 Winter Olympic Games were held in Sarajevo. Many tourists ski in Yugoslavia's mountains or enjoy the beaches along the coast. Servicing the tourists provides many jobs for the people of Yugoslavia.

CHECKUP

1. What are the states in Yugoslavia called?
2. What control does the government have over industry and farming in Yugoslavia?
3. What is the difference between a cooperative farm and a state farm?
4. **Thinking Critically** Would you have supported Tito's decision not to allow the Soviet Union to totally control Yugoslavia?

A Country in the Alps

What are Switzerland's physical features?

VOCABULARY

landlocked   avalanche
glacier

A Small Country   Have you ever heard of a mountain range called the Alps? The Alps are among the most famous mountains in the world. The Alps are found in many countries on the continent of Europe. They are the largest group of mountains in Europe. In the country of Switzerland, the Alps cover almost 60 percent of the land. Turn to the map on page 366 and find the country of Switzerland.

You will notice that Switzerland is a small country. Switzerland is a **landlocked** country. That means it does not border a sea or an ocean. Switzerland is much like Colorado, which you studied in Chapter 13. There are plateaus, narrow valleys, and high, sharp mountains.

The Swiss Alps   The Alps that are found in Switzerland are called the Swiss Alps. The highest peak in the Swiss Alps is Monte Rosa, which is 15,203 feet (4,634 m) above sea level. Among the more than 100 other peaks is the Matterhorn. This peak, well-known to mountain climbers and skiers, is on the border between Switzerland and Italy. This mountain peak is so well-known that there is even a ride at Disneyland in California named after it. **Glaciers** lie on the Matterhorn's upper slopes. A glacier is a large body of ice that very slowly moves downhill.

The valleys among the peaks of the Alps are so narrow that in some cases they do not get much sunshine. They are in the shadow of the mountains almost all day. If a person stands on one side of the valley and shouts, the words will bounce back from the other side. This is called an echo. Have you ever heard an echo of your voice?

The Matterhorn, shaped like a pyramid, rises on the Swiss-Italian border.
■ What is the building made of?

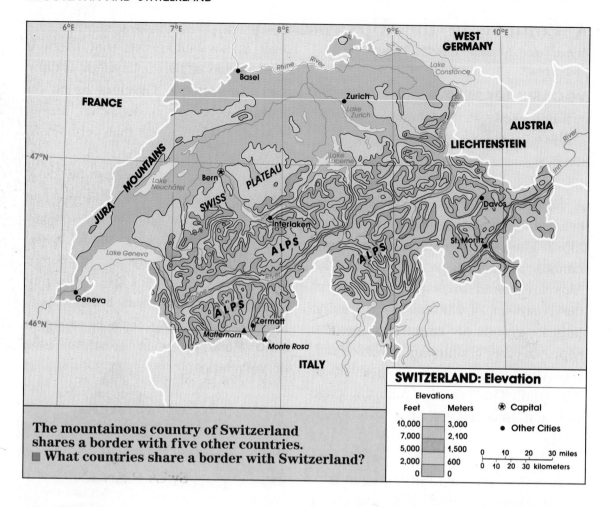

The mountainous country of Switzerland shares a border with five other countries.
■ **What countries share a border with Switzerland?**

The Alps are not the only mountains in Switzerland. Along the northwestern border of the country are the Jura (jùr′ə) Mountains. Between the Alps and the Jura Mountains is the Swiss Plateau. It is a region of hills, lakes, and small plains.

Rivers and Lakes Some of the most important rivers of Europe start in the Swiss Alps. Among them are the Rhine and the Rhône rivers. They start only a few miles apart, but they go in opposite directions.

Do you remember studying about the Continental Divide in Chapter 13?

The Alps are on the continental divide in Europe. The Rhine River flows northward from Switzerland and finally reaches the North Sea. The Rhône River, on the other hand, flows south and empties into the Mediterranean Sea.

Switzerland also has many lakes. At the eastern side of the country is Lake Constance. At the western side of Switzerland are Lakes Geneva (jə nē′ və) and Neuchâtel (nü shə tel′). Other lakes include Lake Lucerne (lü sern′) and Lake Zurich (zùr′ik).

There are few beaches along the lakes. The mountains rise sharply from

300

the shores. Many of the lakes are deep, with clear, cold water.

The Mountains and Temperature As you know, the higher one goes in the mountains, the colder it gets. Thus Switzerland, with its many mountains, has big differences in temperature.

The average summer temperature on the Swiss Plateau is about 70°F (21°C). In the winter the temperature is about 30°F (−1°C).

High in the mountains, temperatures are colder than on the Swiss Plateau. In some little communities high up in the mountains, the average temperature in winter is below 0°F (−18°C). In the summer it may be no more than 40°F (4°C). How do

The Rhine River rises in Switzerland and empties into the North Sea.
■ **How would you get to the island shown in the photograph?**

these temperatures compare to those found on the Swiss Plateau?

Switzerland's Resources One of Switzerland's most important natural resources is its scenery. The high mountains with their snow-capped peaks, the green valleys, and the clean lakes make Switzerland one of the most beautiful countries in the world.

Another important resource of Switzerland is its rivers. Many dams have been built along the fast-moving rivers that come down from the mountains. Great amounts of hydro-electric power are produced.

Switzerland has few minerals. The only such resource that is mined in the Alps is granite (gran′it). This is a

Lucerne, Switzerland, is a beautiful city on the shore of Lake Lucerne.
■ **Are there tall buildings here?**

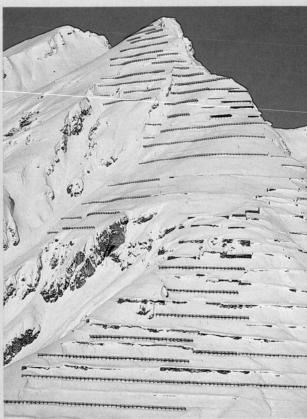

The Swiss build steel barriers to guard against the danger of winter avalanches. At right, such guards are shown in place on a mountainside.
■ Why do such barriers have to be strong?

very hard stone used to make buildings and monuments.

About one fourth of Switzerland is covered with forests. Yet there is not much lumbering carried on. This is because there are laws against cutting most of the forests. Many of the trees are on mountain slopes. The roots keep the soil and snow in place. Without the trees, rains might wash the soil away, and **avalanches** might take place. Do you remember studying about mud slides in Puerto Rico in Chapter 4? Well, an avalanche is like a mud slide, except that large amounts of snow, rather than mud, slide down a steep mountainside. Avalanches can destroy or bury buildings and even whole villages.

CHECKUP

1. How is the land in Switzerland the same as the land in the state of Colorado?
2. What are the Alps in Switzerland called?
3. What are two of Switzerland's most important natural resources?
4. **Thinking Critically** What, do you think, are the disadvantages of being a landlocked country?

Living in Switzerland

What kind of farming is done in Switzerland?

VOCABULARY

meadow

The Swiss People About 6,600,000 people live in Switzerland. Amost two thirds of them live in cities. The largest cities are Zurich, Basel (baz′ əl), Geneva, and Bern. Find these cities on the map on page 300. Which one is the capital of Switzerland?

As you can see from the map, all of these big cities, except Basel, are on the Swiss Plateau. Basel is north of the Jura Mountains. On what river is Basel a port?

Mountains cover about 70 percent of Switzerland. The Swiss Alps offer some of Europe's finest mountain scenery. Tourism is a major business in this small mountain country.

The people of Switzerland speak several different languages. The largest number speak Swiss-German. Near the border with France, most Swiss people speak French. In the part of Switzerland that lies closest to Italy, Italian is the language that is most often used by the people.

Small Towns and Villages About one third of the Swiss people live in small towns and villages. Many of these little communities are in the Swiss Alps.

Some people in the Alps make a living from farming, but life is not easy in this rugged region. There is little good land for crops. The growing season is short. However, the people of the Alps have learned to make the best use of the mountainous area where they live.

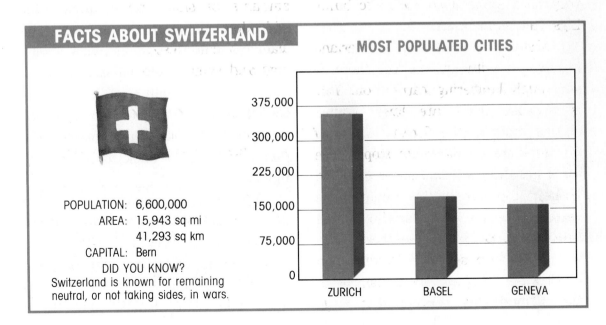

FACTS ABOUT SWITZERLAND

POPULATION: 6,600,000
AREA: 15,943 sq mi
41,293 sq km
CAPITAL: Bern
DID YOU KNOW?
Switzerland is known for remaining neutral, or not taking sides, in wars.

MOST POPULATED CITIES

375,000
300,000
225,000
150,000
75,000
0

ZURICH   BASEL   GENEVA

Life on a Farm   Most farmers in the Alps raise livestock. They own cows, sheep, and goats. During the winter these animals are kept on the farms in the little villages. But during the summer the herds of cows, sheep, and goats are driven high up in the mountain **meadows** of the Alps. A meadow is a piece of grassy land mainly used as a pasture for animals.

It is a big day in the little villages when the herds leave for their summer pastures. Bells of different shapes and sizes hang from the necks of the animals. As they move along the paths, the bells make musical sounds. Nearly all the village people move higher up in the mountains to be near the animals and take care of them during the summer months.

Making cheese from milk is an important Swiss industry.
■ What is the steel rod doing?

Cows graze in this meadow in the canton of Appenzell, in eastern Switzerland.
■ Can you describe this scene?

The high meadows are beautiful during the summer. The sunlight pours down through the clear mountain air from a blue sky. Flowers add color to the green grass of the meadows.

Life is full of chores, though, for those who are with the animals. The cows have to be milked twice a day. There is no place in the mountains to sell milk, and it will turn sour if it is not used. So the farmers make it into cheese. At the end of the summer, the cheese is brought back to the village and is sold.

The Swiss make very good cheese. In fact, one kind of cheese sold all over the world is called Swiss cheese, even though it is today made in other countries besides Switzerland. You can usually tell Swiss

Switzerland is a wine-producing country. Vineyards surround the Swiss castle above. Inset: Grapes are put into a large vat to be crushed.
■ Do you think making wine would be easy work or hard work?

cheese by the holes of different sizes in it.

Other Farming On the Swiss Plateau there is good farmland where crops grow well during the summer months. Along the road from Zurich to Geneva one sees many farms. Wheat, potatoes, sugar beets, and grapes are grown.

The Swiss government encourages the raising of food crops. So the government tries to see that the farmers earn as much money as factory workers do. If the prices of farm products get too low, the government buys the products at fair prices.

The farmers of Switzerland produce a little more than half of the food that the people of the country need. The rest of it has to be bought from other countries.

CHECKUP

1. What are Switzerland's largest cities?
2. Where are many of the small towns and villages in Switzerland found?
3. What do most of Switzerland's farmers raise?
4. **Thinking Critically** Why, do you think, does the Swiss government encourage the country's farmers to raise food crops?

Industry Leads the Way

What are Switzerland's most important industries?

Many Industries   You might think that a country without many natural resources would have very little industry. This is not true of Switzerland. It is highly industrialized.

Two things have helped Switzerland to become a strong industrial country. One is the great amount of hydroelectric power produced by the falling water of its rivers. In Switzerland hydroelectric power runs the machines of the factories.

The other reason that Switzerland has become a big industrial nation is the people themselves. The people are the country's most important natural resource. They are very skillful craftsworkers. The Swiss people take pride in what they do, and they are highly trained. They are among the best watchmakers in the world. Many watches and parts of watches sold in the United States are manufactured in Switzerland. The Swiss make things other than watches. Chemicals, paper, and cloth are among other products made in Switzerland. The Swiss are well-known for such foods as cheese and chocolate.

Transportation and Trade   Getting from one part of a mountainous

This dam, in Switzerland's Valais canton, is the world's highest. Hydroelectric power runs most Swiss industries, including this chocolate factory.
■ Have you tasted Swiss chocolate?

306

Bridges and tunnels help the Swiss overcome the difficulty of getting from one mountainous region of their country to another.
■ **How would you describe this landscape?**

region to another part is not easy. The mountains block the way.

Even with the difficulty of transportation, Switzerland still carries on a good deal of trade with other countries. It has to get most of the raw materials for its factories from other parts of the world. Most of the watches, machinery, and other products of Swiss factories are sent to other countries.

Switzerland's location in the middle of Europe is a good one for trade. West Germany, France, and Italy are among Switzerland's main trading partners. The Swiss also do much trading with the United States.

Swiss Banks Banks, as you probably know, take care of people's money. Banks also make loans available to people and help people in many other ways.

Many people in other countries put their money in Swiss banks. One reason people put their money in those banks is that Switzerland has long been looked on as a very safe country.

A country that keeps out of wars is thought of as a safe country for banking. The country of Switzerland has kept out of wars for many years. Switzerland is a **neutral** (nü′ trəl) country. It does not take sides in disputes between other countries. Some people feel that their money is safer in a bank of a neutral country than in a bank of a country that might get into a war.

Interlaken, a Swiss town of about 5,000 people has long been a popular tourist resort. It is located in the Aare River valley, between the Lake of Thun and the Lake of Brienz.
■ What is the name of the hotel in the picture?

Visiting Switzerland More than 5 million tourists visit Switzerland each year. They go there to ski, to climb mountains, and to enjoy the scenery. In resort towns in the Alps are some of the world's best hotels. Among these resort towns are St. Moritz, Davos, Zermatt, and Interlaken. Many people go to these resorts to learn the skills needed to manage a hotel or restaurant.

The Swiss are very good at teaching these skills because they want to make their hotels and restaurants the best in the world. They have worked at this to attract visitors to their country. They have been very successful.

CHECKUP

1. Why does Switzerland have so many industries?
2. Why is getting from one place to another in Switzerland so difficult?
3. Why do many people in other countries keep their money in Swiss banks?
4. **Thinking Critically** Do you think it is right for Switzerland to remain neutral in wars?

Keeping a Diary

A WRITTEN RECORD

In a diary you keep a written record of what you do and how you feel about things that are important to you. Usually you keep this written record in a little book with blank pages. There is a space on the pages for you to write something for every day in the year.

Here are four entries that Jane wrote in her diary.

TO AUNT MARY'S HOUSE

Dear Diary,   May 1

Tomorrow we are going to drive to Aunt Mary's house in Washington, D.C. Mom says that it will take 2 days to drive there. Aunt Mary's house is not far from the Capitol.

Dear Diary,   May 2

We left home early this morning. Dad drove and I sat in the front with him. Mom and my brother, Jack, were in the back seat.

After driving all day, we stopped for the night in a comfortable motel. The road was very good and we were able to travel fast.

Dear Diary,   May 3

Today we reached Washington, D.C. Aunt Mary was glad to see us. Later in the morning we went into the city by the Metro. This is a new subway. It is comfortable and fast.

Dear Diary,   May 4

Today the White House was open to visitors. We made a tour of this wonderful building. We enjoyed looking at the paintings of the Presidents. We had lunch in a restaurant. Then we took a cab to the Capitol. From the front of the building we looked down the long grassy mall. Far away at the other end is the Lincoln Memorial. In between is the tall, thin Washington Monument. This is a monument to our first President. Dad says that tomorrow we can visit these monuments.

SKILLS PRACTICE

1. Now make believe that you and the rest of your family are taking a trip to Yugoslavia. Write diary entries for your first two days there. Tell what you did, where you traveled, and what you saw.

   In writing your diary entries, begin your diary entries with these sentences.

   First entry What a busy day this has been since our plane landed in Sarajevo.

   Second entry Today we visited the site of the 1984 Winter Olympic Games.

2. You may want to get additional information about Yugoslavia from books in your library.

CHAPTER 14 REVIEW

MAIN IDEAS

1. Yugoslavia is a European country on the Balkan Peninsula.
2. Almost three fourths of the land in Yugoslavia is mountainous.
3. The three physical regions in Yugoslavia are the narrow strip of land along the Adriatic coast called the Coastal Region, the mountainous Interior Highlands, and the mostly flat land of the Pannonian Plain.
4. Yugoslavia is divided into six states called republics.
5. Since the Communists took control of Yugoslavia, most of the country's industries and most of the farmland is owned and run by the government.
6. The Alps are the largest group of mountains in Europe.
7. The land of Switzerland has high sharp mountains, plateaus, and narrow valleys.
8. One of Switzerland's most important resources is its scenery.
9. Most farmers in Switzerland raise livestock. But some farmers on the Swiss Plateau raise crops such as wheat, potatoes, sugar beets, and grapes.
10. Switzerland's important industries include making watches and watch parts, chemicals, paper, cloth, cheese, and chocolate.

VOCABULARY REVIEW

Match the terms with the definitions. Use a separate sheet of paper.

   a. republics   d. neutral
   b. glacier   e. meadow
   c. landlocked

1. Not having a border on a sea or an ocean
2. Not taking sides in a dispute between countries
3. What states in Yugoslavia are called
4. A large body of ice that very slowly moves downhill
5. A piece of grassy land that is mainly used as a pasture for animals

CHAPTER CHECKUP

1. What are the names of the Balkan countries?
2. What is a Mediterranean climate?
3. Why is Tito an important person in the history of Yugoslavia?
4. What is the difference between a glacier and an avalanche?
5. What language do most of the Swiss people speak?
6. **Thinking Critically** Compare how farms and factories are run in Yugoslavia with the way they are run in the Soviet Union.
7. **Thinking Critically** How, do you think, would Switzerland be affected if the country were not landlocked?

APPLYING KNOWLEDGE

1. Write a letter to an imaginary friend in Yugoslavia. Explain to your friend why you would like to visit his or her country.
2. Visit or call a travel agent. Ask for materials about Switzerland to help you plan a vacation there. Include plans of when you will go, how you will travel, where you will stay, what you will do there, and what clothing you will bring. Present your plans in the form of an oral report.

SUMMARIZING UNIT 5

REVIEWING VOCABULARY

1. solar energy   Many companies in Colorado are working on developing solar energy. Can you explain what solar energy is and why it is so important?

2. Appalachian Trail   Many people enjoy hiking along the Appalachian Trail. Where in the United States is this trail located?

3. shaft mine   One way that coal is mined in Tennessee is by using a shaft mine. How are shaft mines used to get coal out from underground?

4. landlocked   The country of Switzerland is a landlocked country. What does it mean when a country is landlocked, and how does being landlocked affect trade with other countries?

5. glacier   Glaciers can be found on some of the high slopes in the Swiss Alps. What are glaciers and why can they be so dangerous?

EXPRESSING YOURSELF

1. What if?   What if gold had never been discovered in Colorado? What effects would this have had on the settlement of this state?

2. Thinking like a geographer   Imagine that East Tennessee had no mountains and the land was very flat. How would this affect the lives of the people who live in that part of the state?

3. What would you do?   Imagine that you were working for the United States government in the early 1800s. You are given the job of telling the Indians living in Tennessee that they would have to move to a reservation. How would you tell these people that they would have to leave their land?

4. Who would you rather be?   Would you rather be a farmer on a collective farm in Yugoslavia or a livestock farmer in Switzerland?

5. How would you feel?   As you know, Switzerland is a neutral country. This means that it does not take sides in disputes between countries. How would you feel if the United States government asked you to help defend Switzerland from an attack by another country?

Regions Working Together

We all depend on other parts of the world for some of the things we need. For example, if you lived in an urban area, you would depend on resources found in other regions. Very little of the food you would eat comes from the land within your city. Instead, it comes from the part of the world where it grows the best. The same is true of many of the natural resources that you would use. Natural resources, such as lumber to build buildings and oil to heat your homes and run your automobiles, are usually not found in big cities. But because regions of the world work together, these products are available to people in large cities and other urban areas.

A shopper in a North Carolina supermarket can buy lemons from California as well as homegrown apples.
■ The pineapple in the picture may have come from what state?

Just as people who live in big cities and towns need goods and resources from other places, people who live in rural places depend on cities, too. Farmers depend on selling their goods to markets in big cities. These markets make the farm products available to the millions of people living in or around the city. Without these large city markets, it would be much harder

Logs for export are loaded aboard a ship at this Washington port.
■ For what purposes might these logs be used?

Using electric shears, a textile worker cuts out seat cushions for chairs.
■ How many different colors can you see?

for farmers to sell their fruits and vegetables. Factories in big cities make clothing, tools, and machinery that people in rural areas need. The machines and tools make the farmer's job easier and more productive. Large clothing factories make a wide variety of clothes available to people all over the world. These clothes come in many different styles and sizes.

313

The pictures on these pages show some of the ways in which people of the world not only meet and help each other, but also play games and have fun together. People everywhere depend on people of other regions for things that they need and want. People from all of the world's countries must work together to make the world a better place in which to live.

People of many different nations met during the opening ceremony at the 1988 Summer Olympics in Seoul, South Korea.
■ Can you find the symbol for the Olympics in the picture?

Every 4 years, Boy Scouts from all over the world hold camp-outs, called World Jamborees. Here they meet in Alberta, Canada.
314 ■ What does the inset photograph tell you about Scouting?

The American Field Service (AFS) gives scholarships to foreign students to study in the U.S.
■ What does the young man's T-shirt say?

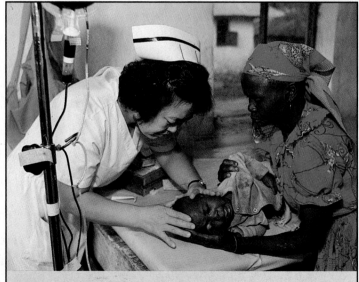

A Korean American nurse, a volunteer for Worker Concern, examines a sick baby in Uganda, Africa.
■ How does this American nurse help others?

Margaret Thatcher, the British prime minister, visits Japan.
■ Why are such visits useful?

15 People Need Each Other

People, Industries, and Transportation

Why do states and regions depend on each other for the things they need?

VOCABULARY

surplus

Getting the Things We Need Have you ever thought about all the different things you use each day? Choose one day of the week, and then make a list of the things you use during that day. Your list will include the clothes you wear, the food you eat, the toys and games you play with, and the paper and other supplies that you use in school. Surely you can think of many more things that you use during one day. The list is practically endless.

Have you ever thought about where the things that you use come from? We make very few of the things that we use. We depend on other people to supply us with these things. Some of the things that we use are made close by. Others come from

faraway places. Some of the things that we use are easy to make. Others are made in large factories that use the most up-to-date machines and tools. In this chapter you will learn how people from different places in our country and from different countries in the world work together to make the things that we need.

Depending on Each Other   Many of the things that all of us need and use come from natural resources. As you know, natural resources are things that people use that are supplied by nature. However, natural resources are not found everywhere in equal amounts.

Oil, natural gas, and coal are valuable natural resources. From these resources come fuels for heating. From oil comes gasoline for cars and trucks. You learned earlier that we get oil from such states as Alaska and Louisiana. Oil is also found in other states, like Texas. Other natural resources include metals found in the earth. Forests, rich soil, and a good climate are also natural resources. You know that much of our food comes from crops that need rich soil and the right climate.

Some states and regions have more of one kind of natural resource than they can use. This is called a **surplus** (sėr′ plus). States sell their surplus natural resources to other

Containers filled with goods for transport by ship are stacked on a dock in the port city of Seattle, Washington.
■ **Why, do you think, have the goods been put in containers?**

states that do not have enough of these particular resources. For example, you know that Alaska has a lot of oil. But because of the cold climate, Alaska cannot grow all the food it needs to feed its people. So Alaska sells oil to other states. At the same time, it must buy food from those states that have a surplus of food. To do this, good forms of transportation are needed.

Better Transportation   States and regions must have a good transportation system if they are to depend on one another for the things they need and use. In the early days of our country, there were few roads. Ships that sailed along the coasts and boats that went up and down the rivers were the best means of transportation. As time went on, new roads, canals, and railroads were built.

Today we have good highways stretching across our country. Trucks carry raw materials and manufactured products from one part of the United States to another. Ships, boats, and railroads are still important means of transportation. Also, some materials are now shipped by airplane. All of these means of transportation make it possible for states and regions to depend on each other.

Trucks, heavily loaded with cut lumber, are parked at the side of this California highway.
■ **What is the first truck pulling?**

318

Industry Develops Transportation has also played an important part in the development of industry in our country. Many years ago, people made most of the things they needed in their homes or in little shops. Today many of the things that people need and use come from factories.

The first factories in the United States were located in the northeastern part of the country. These factories were built beside rivers. The power of running water turned wheels that ran the machinery in the factories. The machines ran by waterpower. Later, industry began to develop around the Great Lakes Region.

Even very heavy goods can be shipped by airplanes.
■ **How is this cargo being moved?**

Using the Waterways Besides using water to run their machines, industries also used water for transportation. Waterways were used to bring factories the raw materials they needed. Waterways were also used for taking the products of the factories to stores.

As transportation improved, other industrial centers developed. The states of California and Texas are now centers of industry. Oil and natural gas have helped industry develop in these states. Both states are also on coasts where raw materials and manufactured goods can be carried by ships. There are smaller industrial centers in other parts of the country. They are usually located close to supplies of the materials they use. Better ways of transportation have made it easier to move goods to markets. But even with the growth of industrial centers, states and regions do not produce everything they need. They still depend on each other for many things.

CHECKUP

1. What do many of the things we need and use come from?
2. What were the best means of transportation in the early days of our country?
3. Where were the first factories in the United States located?
4. **Thinking Critically** What, do you think, would happen if states and regions had no surplus of materials and resources?

How an Airplane Is Made

Why is the airplane industry in the United States a good example of how people and industries depend on each other?

VOCABULARY

headquarters	recession
assembly line	depression
unemployed	

Where Airplanes Are Made   Have you ever flown in an airplane? If so, what kind of airplane was it? Thousands of people fly every day, in all different kinds of airplanes. Some people fly in small airplanes. But most of us fly in larger airplanes. Airplanes can be seen taking off and landing at airports all over the country each day.

Have you ever thought about how all of these airplanes are made? Most of the larger airplanes made in the United States are put together at large plants in the states of California, New York, and Washington. But not all of the parts needed to make the airplanes are made at these plants. Most of the airplane parts are made in factories in other areas of the United States and the world. These parts must then be transported to the plants where the airplanes will be put together. Let's take a look at how an airplane is made.

Making an Airplane   One of the largest airplane manufacturers in the United States is the Boeing Company. Boeing makes both small and large airplanes. The **headquarters**, or business center, of the Boeing Company is located in Seattle, Washington.

Building an airplane calls for careful attention to details. Here workers assemble the rear part of the body of a small plane.
■ How many persons are working on the part in the foreground?

A Boeing engineer uses a computer with a display terminal as he works on the design of an airplane.
■ **Can you think of why this kind of computer would be a useful tool?**

Boeing makes their large airplanes in a large plant just north of Seattle. The main building at this plant has more space from wall to wall and from ceiling to floor than any other building in the world. Visiting this building, you can see workers building several different airplanes at the same time. The large size of the building makes the huge airplanes look like toy models.

Before an airplane can be made, workers known as engineers must decide how the airplane is going to look. This is done with the help of computers. Boeing needs the help of companies that make and sell computers to do this. Once the design of the airplane is finished, certain tools are needed to make sure that all the parts of the airplane fit together perfectly. Once again, Boeing depends on other companies to make some of the tools it needs.

Many different parts are needed to make an airplane. The outside, or the frame, of an airplane is usually made of aluminum, steel, titanium, or some other kind of metal. Titanium is a lightweight metal like aluminum. Boeing can get most of the aluminum that it needs in Washington.

321

Washington makes more aluminum than does any other state. But the other metals must be brought to the Boeing plant from other places. For example, large amounts of steel are made in the cities of Gary, Indiana, and Pittsburgh, Pennsylvania.

The frames for Boeing's airplanes are made at the Seattle plant. But an airplane frame cannot fly without many other parts. Have you ever seen the part of an airplane where the pilot sits? It is called the cockpit. In the cockpit are the controls that the pilot uses to fly the airplane. Most of these instruments are made for Boeing by other companies. All airplanes also have radios on

A pilot is shown in the copilot's seat in a large airplane, a Boeing 747.
■ What do the instrument panels tell you about a pilot's job?

board so that the pilot can talk to people on the ground. These radios are also sold to Boeing. Large airplanes today have computers on board. Like the other instruments found in the cockpit, these computers are made by other companies.

Of course, all airplanes need an engine in order to fly. Airplane manufacturers must buy engines from companies that make the engines for their airplanes. Even the seats, carpets, and the other parts of the inside of an airplane are often made and put into the airplane by other companies.

Sparks fly as steel is made in a Gary, Indiana, steel mill.
■ What kind of protective clothing is the worker wearing?

322

Boeing 747 airplanes are shown being built in Seattle, Washington.
■ How many engines will be put on each wing?

As you can see, most parts of an airplane except for the frame are made by many different companies and brought to Boeing. These different parts are put onto the airplane by using an **assembly line**. An assembly line is a row of workers and machines along which work passes until the product is finished. On an airplane assembly line, the frame of the airplane is rolled on its wheels to stations where a specific kind of work is done. At Boeing the airplane is moved from one station to another about every 4 days. After the finished airplane comes off the assembly line, it is sent to the paint shop to be painted. Boeing has the paint for its airplanes made by a paint company. Once an airplane is painted, it is tested and then delivered to the buyer.

As you can see, it takes the cooperation of many people to make an airplane. Over 50,000 different parts go into making one airplane. It would be nearly impossible to put an airplane together without good forms of transportation. Boeing chose Seattle as the place in which to build its plant because this city can be reached by land, sea, and air. Boeing has even built some special trains to transport extra large pieces of airplanes from other places to Seattle.

This Boeing 747 belongs to Qantas, Australia's international airline.
■ What animal do you think is shown on the tail of this airplane?

323

Affecting People   Large airplane manufacturers like Boeing depend on many companies to help make their airplanes. Most of these companies are found in other states in the United States. But sometimes, parts are made by industries in other countries, like Australia, Canada, England, Japan, and Spain. These industries depend on the business that the airplane manufacturers provide for them. Without this work, many people would be **unemployed**, or without jobs.

Boeing is a good example of an industry that affects many other people and many other industries. In the Seattle area, 10 percent of all workers are employed by Boeing. When Boeing does well, other businesses in the area also do well. There is plenty of work for people to do. They earn enough money to buy what they need.

But when business at Boeing slows down, businesses and stores of all kinds suffer. People may lose their

Seattle is located between Puget Sound, an inlet of the Pacific, on the west, and Lake Washington on the east. The city makes good use of ferries and other waterborne transportation.
■ In what season do you think this picture was taken?

Unfortunately, in a time of recession a store might sometimes be forced to go out of business.
■ **Can you think of reasons why this store might be selling out?**

jobs. With less people working, there is less money for people to spend. When many people are out of work for a number of months and the sale of goods drops, we call it a **recession** (ri sesh′ ən). Such a recession took place in the northwestern United States in the early 1970s. Almost half of the workers at Boeing lost their jobs at that time. Many of those people moved to other parts of the country to find work. When a recession becomes very bad, with many more people losing jobs and with very little buying and selling of goods for a long time, it is called a **depression** (di presh′ ən).

You have seen how this one industry can affect people in many different states and regions. Many other industries also depend on people all over the country. Life would be much harder for all of us if we could not get the many things we need from other states and regions.

CHECKUP
1. Where is the Boeing Company headquarters located?
2. What is an assembly line?
3. What is the difference between a recession and a depression?
4. **Thinking Critically** What industries in your community depend on other states and regions?

Making Steel in South Korea

How does South Korea's steel industry help South Korea and other countries?

Locating South Korea South Korea is on a peninsula to the east of the country of China. Look at the map on this page. Find the country of South Korea. You will notice that the country of North Korea is found on the same peninsula as is South Korea.

For thousands of years these two countries were united. Then in 1948, two separate countries were formed called North Korea and South Korea. In the early 1950s a war was fought between the two countries. This war is known as the Korean War. During the war the United States and some other countries helped South Korea. These countries stopped North Korea from taking over South Korea. Today the United States and South Korea are still allies.

The official name for South Korea is the Republic of South Korea. It is a small country, with an area of only about 38,150 square miles (98,824 sq km). South Korea is smaller in area than the state of Illinois, which you studied in Chapter 9. However, South Korea has a large population. Nearly 43 million people live in South Korea.

South Korea has changed over the past 25 years. Today it is one of the most advanced industrial countries in the world. More and more people are leaving their farms to work in factories and other types of businesses. One reason for this change is the improvements made in South Korea's schools. Laws in South Korea require all students to finish sixth grade. Most students graduate from high school. The best students go on to attend college. Another reason for the growth of industry in South Korea is the availability of **laborers**, or workers.

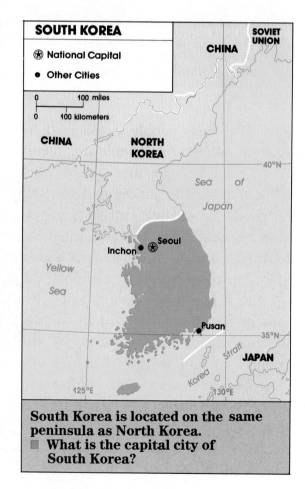

South Korea is located on the same peninsula as North Korea.
■ What is the capital city of South Korea?

South Korea's Steel Industry

Among the most important industries in South Korea is the making of steel. South Korea is one of the world's leading producers of steel. Steel is a very important product. It is used in the construction of buildings, highways, and bridges. Steel is also used to make ships and automobiles. Today, South Korea is one of the world's leading countries in shipbuilding. South Korea is also beginning to export automobiles to other parts of the world. These two industries as well as other industries in the country depend on the steel industry.

To make steel you need iron ore, coal, limestone, and other kinds of metals. South Korea must import iron ore, coal, and the other metals that are needed to make its steel. Some of these materials come from as far away as the United States and Canada.

South Korea has modern plants for making steel. Today most of the machines used in these plants are made right in South Korea. But this was not always the case. For a while South Korean industries depended on other countries to supply them with these machines.

Shipbuilding has become one of South Korea's leading industries. A supertanker is shown under construction in a dry dock.
■ **What might the crane in the picture be used for?**

Living In South Korea

Kim Sang and his sister, Kim Sook, live with their parents and grandparents in a small village about 20 miles (32 km) south of Seoul. Their village is made up of groups of small houses built close together. The roofs of the houses are covered with bright red tiles.

The inside of the Kim house is nicely decorated. But there are no beds or chairs. People sit on cushions and mats during the day. At night they bring out mattresses to sleep on. Meals are served on beautifully decorated low tables. When not in use the tables are hung on the walls, like decorations. Clothes, sheets, and blankets are kept in decorated chests.

During mealtime a bowl of rice is placed in front of each person. The main dish is placed in the middle of the table. Members of the family use a spoon with a long handle to serve themselves. They put the food on top of the rice and eat with chopsticks.

Kim Sang and Kim Sook are expected to behave properly at all times, especially when they are around their grandparents. Showing respect for elders is very important in South Korea. For example, talking loudly or quarreling in front of elders is considered a sign of disrespect.

In school, Kim Sang and Kim Sook study the Korean language, social studies, arithmetic, science, physical education, music, and art. They also study a special subject called moral education. This class teaches them to become good citizens.

The Kim family enjoys doing things together. The children enjoy the park, where they can ride on the seesaw. On windy days, Kim Sang enjoys flying a kite. This is a popular activity in South Korea. The Kims also enjoy visiting the city of Seoul. Life is so different there. The streets are wide and busy. There are tall, modern buildings and stores that sell many beautiful things. Even though the Kims always enjoy a trip to Seoul, they are glad to return to their village.

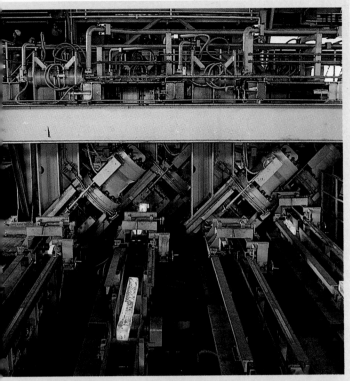

Steel made in South Korean mills was used to make these cars for export.
■ Why are such exports important to the Korean economy?

To run the steel plants, energy is needed. Oil is one kind of natural resource that is used to make energy. South Korea has no oil fields. It must rely on other countries to supply its oil needs.

Selling the Steel It would be impossible for South Korea to make its steel without the help of other countries throughout the world. To make the steel, South Korea must buy the things that it does not have. To have the money to do this, South Korea sells its steel and other products made from steel, such as ships and automobiles, to other countries.

In this way the countries of the world are helping each other. South Korea's steel mills provide jobs for many of that country's people. The steel that South Korea sells also helps to create jobs for the people in other countries. The South Korean people are proud of the way they are helping themselves and other people around the world.

CHECKUP
1. What is South Korea's official name?
2. What has helped South Korea become an advanced industrial country?
3. What is one of South Korea's most important industries?
4. **Thinking Critically** What effects would the closing of South Korea's steel mills have on the people of that country?

Finding Information in a Library

WHAT IS A CARD CATALOG?

A library is a source of much information. You know that a library has many books. Do you know how to find the one that has the information you need?

One way to find a book is by using the card catalog. The card catalog is a listing of all the books in the library. Information about the books is filed on cards that are kept in drawers. Each book is listed alphabetically by the subject, the title, and the author's last name.

In this chapter you learned something about the making of airplanes in the United States. Now you might want to find a book that will tell you more about airplanes. How can you use the card catalog to find such a book?

USING A CARD CATALOG

First, you can look in the card catalog under A for the subject *airplanes*. You will probably find several cards under this heading. These are subject cards. One card lists a book entitled *Airplanes*, by Jeanne Bendick. The card tells you on what shelf in the library this book may be found. If you have trouble using the card catalog or finding the book, the librarian will help you.

It may be that you already know the title of the book you want. Perhaps a friend told you that *Airplanes* is a good book. In that case you will look under the letter A for the title, *Airplanes*. This is a title card.

Your friend who liked the book may have said, "I have forgotten the title, but I remember that the author's name is Bendick." In that case you will look under the letter B to find Bendick. You may find several books by Bendick. These cards are author cards. If you do not know the author's first name, you may have to look through the book titles on the author cards until you find a title that seems to be right.

SKILLS PRACTICE

Now see how well you can use the card catalog. Write down the type of card and the letter under which you will find the following:

a. A book about South Korea
b. A book written by Elaine Fay
c. A book about airplane engines
d. The book *Exploring Space*
e. A book written by Judy Blume
f. A book about the Korean War

In the next chapter you will study about your own state. You will use the library to answer some of the questions in that chapter. Go to the library now to find out in what books you can get information about your state. Under what subject will you look in the card catalog?

Look at all the cards under that subject. Make a list of books you can use for finding information about your state. Beside each title, write the name of the author. Keep your list to use in studying the next chapter.

CHAPTER 15 REVIEW

MAIN IDEAS

1. States and regions depend on other states and regions for many of the things that people need because the things people need are not found everywhere in equal amounts.
2. Many of the things that all of us need and use come from natural resources.
3. Good means of transportation make it possible for states and regions to depend on each other.
4. The airplane industry is a good example of how industries depend on each other. Airplane manufacturers depend on other industries to make many of the parts that are needed to make airplanes. Other industries depend on the work that the airplane manufacturers give them.
5. Airplane manufacturers depend on other businesses that make airplane parts. People who work for industries that make airplane parts depend on getting steady work from the airplane manufacturers.
6. A recession is a time when many people are out of work for a number of months and the sale of goods drops. A depression is when many more people lose their jobs and there is very little buying and selling of goods for a long time.
7. South Korea's steel industry provides many jobs for the people there who work in the steel mills and in other industries that depend on steel.
8. South Korea exports steel to many countries of the world.
9. Today, South Korea is one of the most advanced industrial countries in the world.

VOCABULARY REVIEW

Choose the correct ending for each sentence. Write your answers on a separate piece of paper.

1. Having more than can be used is called a (**a**) depression, (**b**) surplus, (**c**) recession.
2. The first factories in the United States were located in the (**a**) West, (**b**) Southwest, (**c**) Northeast.
3. The business center of a company is called the (**a**) headquarters, (**b**) assembly line, (**c**) capital.
4. A time when many people are without jobs and there is very little buying and selling of goods for a long time is called a (**a**) recession, (**b**) surplus, (**c**) depression.
5. A name for workers is (**a**) natural resources, (**b**) laborers, (**c**) computers.

CHAPTER CHECKUP

1. Why were the first factories in the United States built near water?
2. How did improvements in transportation help the development of industry in our country?
3. South Korea is found on the same peninsula as what other country?
4. What grade in school are all children in South Korea required to finish?
5. **Thinking Critically** In what ways do you depend on other people and regions to get the things that you need?

APPLYING KNOWLEDGE

In your library find a book on the history of the airplane. Read it, and then give a report to your class on the information you found to be most interesting.

16 Your State and You

Studying Your Community

How can you learn about the history of your community?

VOCABULARY

local history	historical source
monument	historical
historical	document
marker	oral history

Finding the Answers This chapter is different from the other chapters in this book. In those chapters you were told about a region or state or country. In this chapter you will be asked many questions. The questions will be about your community and your state. By finding the answers to these questions, you will learn much about the community and the state in which you live.

Some of you may live in one of the states that you studied earlier in this book. If so, reviewing the pages on your state will help you answer some of the questions found in this chapter. But you will not find all the

answers in an earlier chapter. You will need to do some research on your own. Let's start the study of your state by looking at the community in which you live.

Where You Live   The place where you live is called your community. Every community has its own history. Do you remember what history is? It is the study of the past. What is the name of the community in which you live?

Every community is different. Some are large, and others are small. One community may be 200 years old. Another may have been started just 10 years ago. But all communities have some things in common. All communities have places where people live. Communities also have stores, schools, and places of worship. Most communities also have a group of men and women who make laws and see that the laws are carried out. This group of people is known as the community's government.

Communities are started for different reasons. Some are started where there is good farmland for growing crops. Many communities are started near transportation centers. Communities also grow because of the jobs that they offer. Where is your community located? Do you know how your community was started?

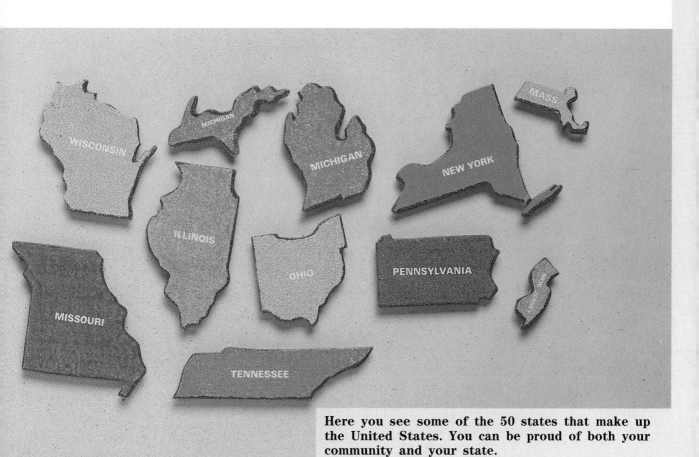

Here you see some of the 50 states that make up the United States. You can be proud of both your community and your state.
■ Is your state or a neighboring state shown here?

Looking Around You The history of your community is called **local history**. The beginnings of a community, the people who have lived there, important events that have happened there, and even old buildings make up local history. To learn about the local history of your community, try to find answers to the following questions.

1. Who were the first people to live here? Why did they come here?
2. Why is this community located where it is?
3. Why did this community grow?

Sometimes, buildings can be your first clues in finding out about local history. Why a building was built and who built it are good questions to start you on your search. You can start with just about any building, from your own house to the grocery store down the street. By studying these buildings you may learn where people in the past lived in your community, where they went for entertainment, what kinds of jobs your community once offered, and how your community has changed over the years.

Monuments and Markers A **monument** is something that is built to honor a person or event. A monument can be a building, a sculpture, or a tower. Are there any monuments in your community? You can learn about local history by studying

This old gristmill at Pigeon Forge, Tennessee, is a national historic site. The mill has been in operation since 1830.
■ For how many years has this mill been in operation?

Monuments honor people or events. This statue in Concord, Massachusetts, honors the Minutemen of the Revolutionary War.
■ **Does your community have a statue that honors someone?**

monuments. Another way to learn about your local history is by reading **historical markers**. Historical markers are signs that show where old and important buildings are located, where a battle was fought, or where some other event took place. Sometimes a historical marker will tell about an important meeting that took place in a building. The marker may tell about a famous person who lived in a certain building.

Using Other Sources Monuments and markers are two kinds of **historical sources**. A historical source is something or someone that tells about the past. But there are also other kinds of historical sources. For example, old newspapers are a kind of historical source. They explain what happened in the past. Advertisements in old newspapers can give you clues about life in the past. They can tell you what kinds of goods people could buy and how much goods cost. Can you think of another kind of advertisement in an old newspaper that would tell you how people lived?

A **historical document** is a written record of the past. Letters are one kind of historical document. By

335

Old toys such as these are artifacts.
■ How do these toys from the past compare with toys that you have?

If you want to learn about the past from others, you must be a good listener.
■ In what ways is a tape recorder a useful tool for oral history?

reading old letters you can find out what people thought about and how they lived. Sometimes, old letters will even tell you about past events in a community.

Old photographs are another way of learning about your community. Photographs can show how people dressed in the past and what houses looked like. Do you remember studying about how to use old photographs in Chapter 2? If not, look back to page 32.

People can be good historical sources, too. Talking with people who remember the past is a good way to learn about your local history. This is called **oral history**. Here are some questions you might ask.

1. How long have you lived in this community?
2. What was it like to live here many years ago?
3. Has this community changed much since you have lived here?

Saving Our History   People who work at finding out about a community's history are called local historians. Local historians do research, or search for facts, about a community. After careful research a local historian might write a book about a community's history. Has a book been written about your community's past?

Historical societies and museums also work to keep a community's history. A historical society is a group of people who are interested in history.

This restored seaport village in Mystic, Connecticut, reminds visitors of the mid-1800s.
■ Does a restoration such as this show pride in local history?

These people gather together and keep historical sources and things that are important to local or state history. A museum is a place that preserves and displays things that were used by people in the past. Is there a historical society or museum in your community?

Libraries also help to save your community's history. A nearby library may have several books about your community. The library may also have old newspapers, photographs, and historical documents. All of these sources make learning about the history of your community exciting.

By learning about the history of your community, you are learning about the history of your state. Studying the history of your state is a lot like studying the history of your community.

CHECKUP

1. How is every community different?
2. What is local history?
3. What is the difference between a historical source and a historical document?

4. **Thinking Critically** Why, do you think, is studying your community's history important?

337

Learning About the Land

How can you learn about the land in your state?

VOCABULARY

| physical map | political map |

Finding Your State Let us begin the study of your state by finding where your state is located in the United States. Turn to the map on pages 354–355. This is both a physical and political map of the United States. As a **physical map**, it shows mountains, plains, and other forms that land and water take. As a **political map**, it shows the names, the boundaries, and some of the cities of the 50 states. Find your state on the map.

In this book you have learned about four kinds of regions: forest regions, desert regions, plains regions, and mountain regions. In which kind of region is your state? Is it, perhaps, in more than one kind of region? As you learned in Unit 5, the Rockies and the Appalachians are two large mountain ranges in the United States. Do the Rockies or the Appalachians pass through any part of your state? Do some other mountains pass through your state? If so, what are they called?

Is your state wholly or partly on plains? If so, are they the Central Plains or a coastal plain? Might your state be on both kinds of plains?

Many states share a border with a body of water. Does your state have one or more river boundaries? Five of our states border on the Pacific Ocean. Do you live in one of these states? Five of our states border on the Gulf of Mexico. Do you live in one of these states? An even larger number of states share a border with Canada. Do you live in one of these states? The Great Lakes border on eight states. Do you live in one of these states? How many states share a border with the Atlantic Ocean? Do you live in one of these states?

The state of Maine and several other states share a border with the Atlantic Ocean.
■ Is this coast rocky or sandy?

YOUR STATE AND YOU

How many states border on your state? What are the names of these neighboring states?

Weather The United States is such a big country that the weather is quite different from one place to another. For example, Memphis, Tennessee, gets more than 65 inches (165 cm) of precipitation a year, but Albuquerque (al′ bə kər kē), New Mexico, gets less than 10 inches (25 cm). The average temperature in Minneapolis, Minnesota, in December is 19°F (−7°C), but in Miami, Florida, it is 68°F (20°C). To find out the kind of weather your state has, you can check in a local newspaper or with a local

---

These newspaper maps tell about the weather on November 6, 1985.
■ **Did any precipitation fall in the state of New Jersey on that day?**

Weather

Local readings and outlook from Ion Weather Inc. at Morristown Airport, for 24 hours ending 5 p.m. yesterday.

Yesterday

High: 54 **Low:** 40 **Humidity:** 72 pct. **Winds:** NW at 12 mph
Degree days: 18 **Month to date:** 84 **Season to date:** 529

The record high temperature for Morristown for this date was 78 in 1938. The record low was 28 set in 1931.

The sun rises today at 6:35 a.m., sets at 4:47 p.m. and will rise tomorrow at 6:36 a.m.

The State

Sparta
50/.00

Hackettstown
52/.00

Morristown
53/.00

Newark
54/.00

NYC
55/.00

Philadelphia
56/.00

Trenton
54/.00

Millville
57/.00

State map shows temperatures and 24-hour precipitation readings taken at 2 p.m. yesterday.

Shore map shows yesterday's high temperatures and today's tides.

The Shore

Monmouth

Ocean

Burlington

Atlantic

Cape May

Sandy Hook
Ocean: 56
Air: 53
Hi: 2:37a, 2:51p
Lo: 8:52a, 9:33p

Pt. Pleasant
Ocean: 56
Air: 52
Hi: 2:07a, 2:21p
Lo: 8:12a, 8:53p

Seaside Hts.
Ocean: 56
Air: 52
Hi: 2:04a, 2:18p
Lo: 8:08a, 8:49p

Atlantic City
Ocean: 57
Air: 56
Hi: 2:11a, 2:25p
Lo: 8:17a, 8:58p

Cape May
Ocean: 57
Air: 58
Hi: 2:35a, 2:49p
Lo: 8:36a, 9:17p

Used by permission of Daily Record, Morristown, NJ

radio station. Every state also has weather stations. Weather stations have equipment that keep daily records of the weather. You can write to a weather station near your home to ask for information on the weather in your area.

Is the weather the same throughout the whole state? If not, how does it differ from one part of the state to another? Why is it different? If there are mountains in your state, how do they affect the weather? If there are large bodies of water in or close to your state, what effect do they have on the weather?

Water is an important natural resource. This is one of Oregon's many lakes.
■ Does your state have a large number of rivers and lakes?

Weather stations provide forecasts and reports of weather for all parts of our country.
■ Which state is shown on the screen in this picture?

Your State's Resources In earlier chapters you learned how important natural resources are to a region or state. You learned, too, that natural resources differ from one state to another.

For example, iron ore is found in only 18 of the 50 states. Is iron ore found in your state? Are there oil fields in your state? In Chapter 3, you learned that Alaska has large forests. Are there forests in your state? If your state has forests, what kinds of trees are found in them?

Does your state have any minerals? If so, what are they? Are they found all over the state or in one

Each state has a state bird. The cardinal is the state bird for seven different states.
■ Do you know which of these birds is a cardinal?

place? Is one mineral more important to your state than others? If so, what is that mineral? What other natural resources does your state have? To find this information you will need to do research in a library. One book that may help you is your state manual. This book has various kinds of information about your state. Have you ever seen or used your state manual?

Our country has many different kinds of birds, animals, and fish. They are important to all of us. Each state has a state bird. Use an encyclopedia to find out the name of your state bird and the names of other kinds of animals that can be found in your state. What kinds of fish can be found in the bodies of water in and around your state?

CHECKUP

1. What is the difference between a physical map and a political map?
2. How many states border the Pacific Ocean?
3. Why is the weather in our country so different from one place to another?
4. **Thinking Critically** How does your state's land and climate affect how the people there live?

341

The People of Your State

How can you learn about the people of your state?

VOCABULARY

senator	unemployment
representative	

Large States and Small States There are great differences in population among the 50 states. Seven states have more than 10 million people each. Is your state one of these seven states? On the other hand, 9 states have less than 1 million people each. Is your state one of these states? What is the population of your state? Where does it rank in population among the 50 states?

Is the population of your state spread out evenly over the whole state? Or does one part of the state have more people than do other parts? Do more people live in cities or in rural areas?

What is the largest city in your state? About how many people live there? What other large cities are there in your state?

What kinds of jobs do the people of your state have? Is there one kind of work that is especially important in your state? If so, what is that kind of work?

Farming the Land You know from what you read earlier in this book that farms differ a great deal. In some states the most important crop is corn. In other states it is soybeans. And in still others it may be fruit, sugarcane, or wheat.

Is your state known for one farm product more than for others? Do the farmers of your state raise large amounts of wheat or corn? Do they raise large amounts of vegetables? If so, what kinds of vegetables are raised? What kinds of fruit are grown?

Are there cattle ranches in your state? If so, what kinds of cattle are raised there? Are there dairy farms? Do farmers in your state raise poultry or horses? The United States Department of Agriculture puts all this information into a book which comes

Cabbage may be one of the vegetables raised in your state.
■ **What is the size of this cabbage?**

out once a year. This book is called *Agricultural Statistics*. You can use this book to learn more about farming in your state and in other states.

Industry in Your State   Some states have much more industry than do others. For example, you learned in earlier chapters that many chemical products are made in Maryland. Are chemical products made in your state? You learned, too, that Louisiana has many oil refineries. Does your state have oil refineries?

Do you know where you can find out the kinds of industries your community and state has? One place you can look is in the Yellow Pages of your telephone book. In the Yellow Pages you will find a listing of most

of your community's industries and other businesses. Another way to get this information is by writing to your local Chamber of Commerce. The Chamber of Commerce is a group of people that help industry and business in your town and state. They will be able to give a list of all the industries found in your community and throughout your state.

Where are the factory products of your state sold? Are most of them sold inside your state? Or are they sold outside?

What kind of power is used to run the factories of your state? Is hydroelectric power important in your state? Are there dams where hydroelectric power is generated? If so, on what rivers are these dams located?

In more recent years the high-tech industries in many states have grown. Shown here are workers in a computer assembly plant in Texas.
■ Would you like the job of putting together computers?

Moving Goods and People It is necessary for a state to have good means of transportation. Farmers must be able to get their crops to market. Manufacturing plants have to bring in materials and natural resources. The products they make go to stores all over the country. People have to be able to go quickly from their homes to where they have jobs. If we could not get from one place to another, our way of life would break down.

Use a road map to find out how people in your state get from one place to another. What are the major highways? What cities do they run between?

Are waterways used for carrying people and goods in your state? What kinds of waterways are there? Are rivers used for transportation in your state? If so, which rivers are they?

What railroad lines come into your state? Where do they come from? Where are the biggest airports in your state?

Government The government of the United States is carried on in Washington, D.C. Each state elects two **senators** and one or more **representatives**. These people go to Washington, D.C. to help make laws and decide on other matters that are important to our country.

The President of the United States is the head of the government in Washington, D.C. Who is the President now? Who are the two senators from your state? States with large populations have more representatives in Washington, D.C. than do states with smaller populations. How many representatives does your state

The United States Capitol in Washington, D.C., is where the senators and representatives from all of the states meet.
■ Have you had an opportunity to visit the Capitol?

344

Yellowstone National Park was the first national park in our nation. The Morning Glory Pool is one of many natural wonders in the park.
■ What is the temperature of the Morning Glory Pool?

send to Washington, D.C.? One of these representatives is chosen by the people of your community. What is the name of your representative?

The government in Washington, D.C. carries out business that is important to the whole country. Each state also has a government that carries out business that is important to the state. The state government is located in the state capital. What is the capital of your state? The head of the state government is the governor. Who is the governor of your state?

Visiting Places in Your State Where in your state do people go to have a good time? Are there resorts in your state? Are they on the seashore, in the mountains, or in some

other place? Most states have colorful brochures and pamphlets that show different places to have fun. Also, some states use television commercials to show different resorts and places of interest that people can visit. Does your state have any commercials about places of interest that are shown on television?

Are there any national parks in your state? If so, what are their names and where are they? What is it that brings people to these parks? You can write to the United States Parks Department for information on all of your country's national parks.

Does your state have any state parks? If so, where are they? What are the names of some of these state parks?

Basketball, a sport invented in the United States, is popular in most communities.
■ **Do you like to play basketball?**

Check the sports section of your local newspaper to find out what sports are played in your state. Does your state have big-league teams in baseball, football, soccer, basketball, or hockey? If so, where do these teams play? Does your state have a center for concerts and other musical events?

Solving Problems All states have problems. Two problems that are found in some states are **unemployment** and pollution. Unemployment means not having enough jobs for all the people who want to work. Pollu-

tion is a big problem in many states today.

What problems does your state have? Is there much unemployment? Is the pollution of air or water a problem?

What is being done in your state to solve its problems? Do you think that more should be done? Can you think of anything else that might be done to make life better in your state?

We Can All Be Proud We are all proud of our country. Just as we have pride in America, we should have pride in the state in which we live.

Perhaps you are proud of your state because of the beauty of its mountains, seashores, lakes, or plains. Perhaps you are proud of the kind of people who live there. Or you may be proud of the things that your state offers to its people. Is it a good state to work in? Are there good places for recreation? Are there good schools, colleges, and places of worship? What other things about your state might you be especially proud of?

CHECKUP

1. How many states have a population of more than 10 million people each?
2. Why is it necessary for a state to have good means of transportation?
3. Who is the head of our government in Washington, D.C.?
4. **Thinking Critically** Why do you think your state is a good place to live?

Studying Your Family's History

YOUR FAMILY TREE

Like every state and every community, every family has a history. A written history of a family is called a genealogy (jē nē äl′ ə jē). It is a record of the births, deaths, and marriages in a family.

Sometimes when people do a genealogy of their family, they put the information onto a family tree. This is a list of all your family members, starting with you and working backwards in time. You can start a family tree by asking the following questions.

1. When and where was I born?
2. What was my mother's last name before she was married?
3. When and where were my parents born?

4. What are the names of my grandparents? When were they born?

SKILLS PRACTICE

Does your family have a written history? If not, maybe you can start one. Look at the chart below. What is the title of the chart? On a separate piece of paper draw a chart that looks like the one below. Then start to fill in each space on your chart with the correct information. Questions 1 through 4 above have given you a head start on filling in your chart. How much more of the chart can you fill in? You may have to interview aunts, uncles, cousins, and anyone else who can help you fill in your family tree. Good luck!

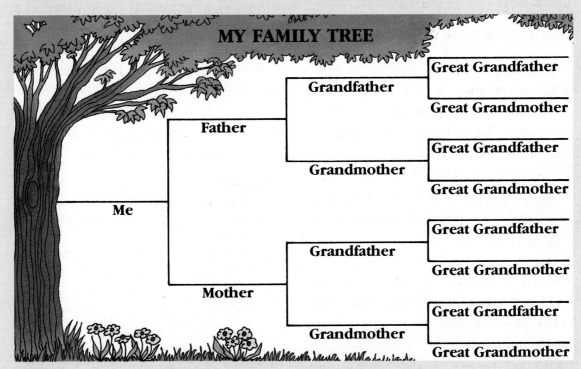

MY FAMILY TREE

- Me
  - Father
    - Grandfather
      - Great Grandfather
      - Great Grandmother
    - Grandmother
      - Great Grandfather
      - Great Grandmother
  - Mother
    - Grandfather
      - Great Grandfather
      - Great Grandmother
    - Grandmother
      - Great Grandfather
      - Great Grandmother

CHAPTER 16 REVIEW

MAIN IDEAS

1. The history of your community is called local history.
2. You can learn about the history of your community by looking at monuments, by reading historical markers, by studying historical sources and documents, and by listening to oral history.
3. Local historians, historical societies, museums, and libraries all help us preserve our local history.
4. You can learn about the land in your state by studying physical and political maps, by finding out the kind of weather your state has, and by learning about your state's resources.
5. You can learn about the people of your state by finding out what kinds of jobs the people in your state have and what things in your state attract people to live in or visit it.
6. It is necessary for states to have good means of transportation.
7. Each state elects senators and representatives to go to Washington, D.C., to help make laws and decide on other matters that are important to our country.
8. Pollution and unemployment are two problems that are found in some states today.
9. You can be proud of your country and your state.

VOCABULARY REVIEW

Match these terms with the definitions. Use a separate sheet of paper.

- **a.** physical map
- **b.** senator
- **c.** unemployment
- **d.** local history
- **e.** oral history

1. A person chosen by a state to help carry out the country's business in Washington, D.C.
2. Not having enough jobs for all the people who want them
3. The history of your community
4. A map that shows mountains, plains, and other natural features
5. Talking with people who remember the past

CHAPTER CHECKUP

1. List two ways in which you can study the history of your community.
2. How do historical societies help to preserve the history of a community?
3. What is your state's most valuable farm product?
4. In what city is the government of your state carried out?
5. **Thinking Critically** What historical sources are available to help you study your local history?
6. **Thinking Critically** Of all the jobs that people in your state have, which one would you most like to have?

APPLYING KNOWLEDGE

1. Every state has problems that the people there are trying to solve. Find out some of the problems that your state is working to solve. Then create a poster that will encourage people to help solve one of these problems.
2. Imagine that you are a local historian for your community. Research how your community was started. Then write a one-page report on what you discovered about the beginnings of your community. Read your report to your classmates.

SUMMARIZING UNIT 6

VOCABULARY REVIEW

1. depression   During a depression, people's lives are affected in many ways. What is a depression, and how is it different from a recession?

2. local history   Many people enjoy studying local history. What is local history, and how can people find out more about their local history?

3. historical document   One way of learning about your local history is by studying historical documents. What are some things that are considered to be historical documents?

4. physical map   Maps help people learn about their state. What is a physical map, and how is it different from a political map?

5. senator   Every state has people representing it in Washington, D.C. These people are called senators and representatives. What is the difference between a senator and a representative?

EXPRESSING YOURSELF

1. What would happen?   States depend on each other to get things that its people use and need. One thing that many people use and need is oil. What, do you think, would happen if all the oil wells dried up? How would our lives change?

2. What if?   What if the airplane had never been invented? How would this affect people and businesses all over the world?

3. You make the decision   Imagine that you are a farmer in South Korea. A new factory opens near the village where you live. You are given a chance to work in this factory. Would you decide to keep your farm or work in the factory?

4. In your opinion   You know that every state has representatives in Washington, D.C. These people work at solving some of our country's most serious problems. If you were a senator or representative from your state, what problem would you try to solve first?

5. Thinking like a historian   Imagine that you had to fill a box with things that would help people living in the year 2050 to learn about the community in which you live. What would you put in the box?

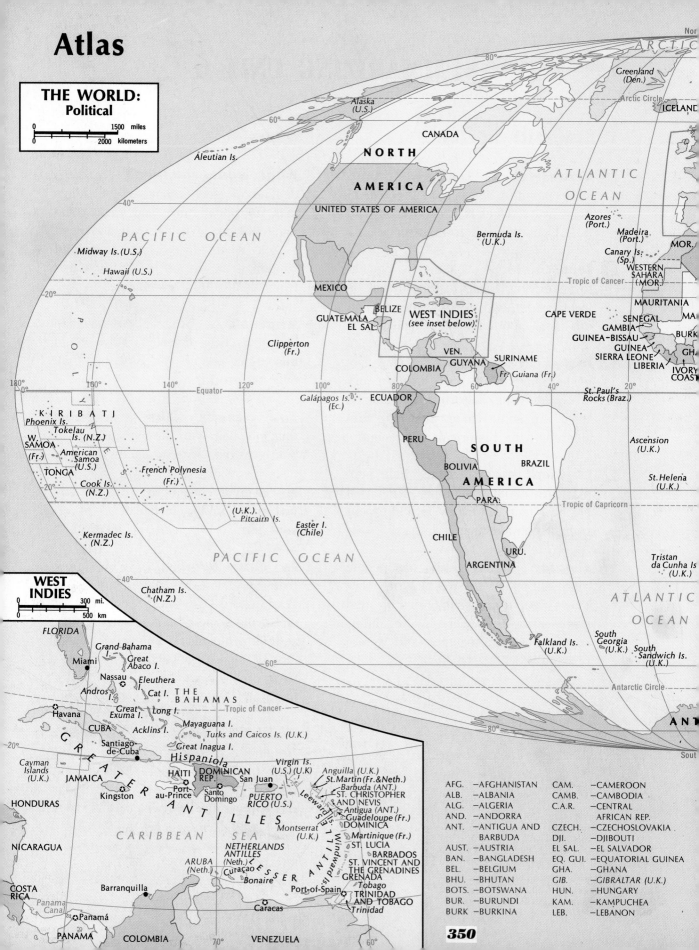

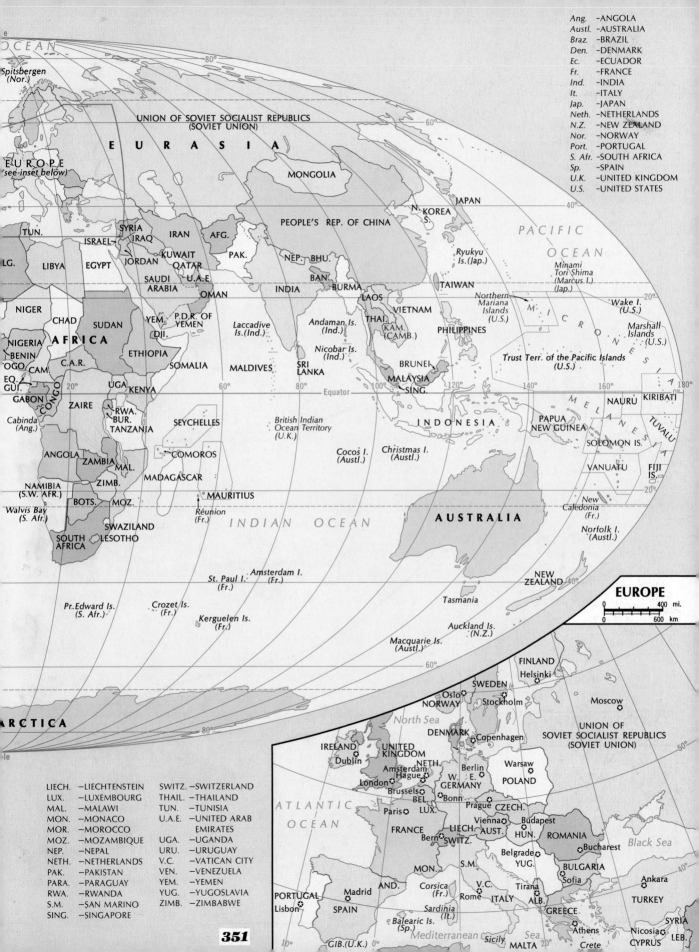

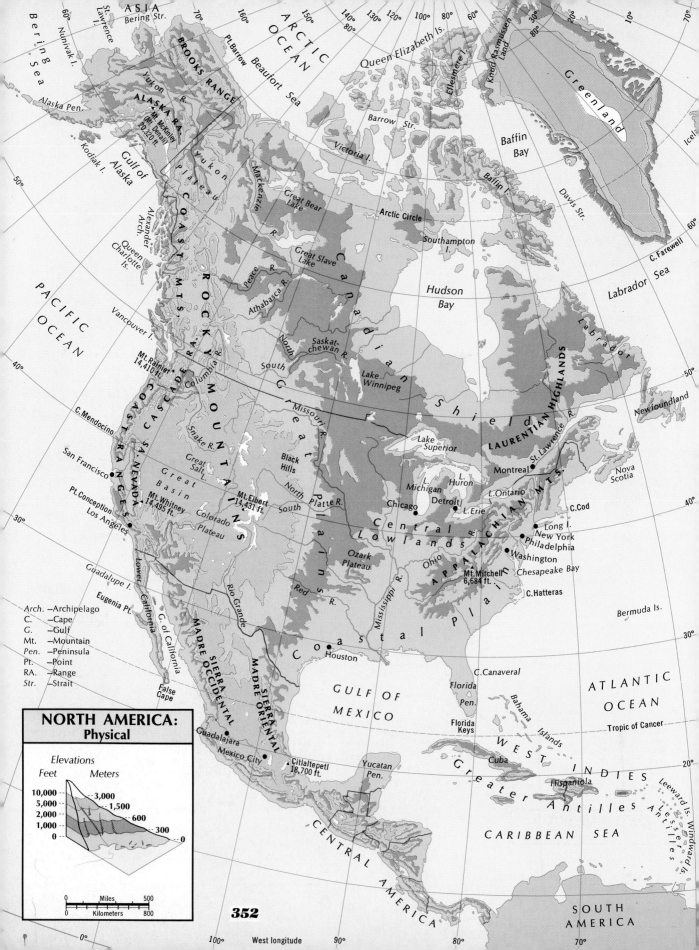

NORTH AMERICA:
Physical

Elevations

Feet	Meters
10,000	3,000
5,000	1,500
2,000	600
1,000	300
0	0

Miles 0 — 500
Kilometers 0 — 800

Arch. —Archipelago
C. —Cape
G. —Gulf
Mt. —Mountain
Pen. —Peninsula
Pt. —Point
RA. —Range
Str. —Strait

ASIA
Bering Str.
St. Lawrence I.
Nunivak I.
Bering Sea
Alaska Pen.
Kodiak I.
Gulf of Alaska
ALASKA RA.
Mt. McKinley (Mt. Denali) 20,320 ft.
BROOKS RANGE
Yukon R.
Yukon Plateau
Pt. Barrow
Beaufort Sea
ARCTIC OCEAN
Queen Elizabeth Is.
Ellesmere I.
Knud Rasmussen Land
Greenland
Iceland
C. Farewell
Davis Str.
Baffin Bay
Baffin I.
Barrow Str.
Victoria I.
Mackenzie R.
Great Bear Lake
Arctic Circle
Southampton I.
Hudson Bay
Labrador Sea
Newfoundland
Labrador
Great Slave Lake
Peace R.
Athabasca R.
COAST MTS.
ROCKY MOUNTAINS
Alexander Arch.
Queen Charlotte Is.
Vancouver I.
North Saskatchewan R.
South
Saskatchewan R.
Lake Winnipeg
Canadian Shield
LAURENTIAN HIGHLANDS
St. Lawrence R.
Nova Scotia
C. Cod
Long I.
PACIFIC OCEAN
C. Mendocino
Mt. Rainier 14,410 ft.
CASCADE RA.
Columbia R.
Snake R.
Great Salt L.
Great Basin
COAST RANGES
SA. NEVADA
Mt. Whitney 14,495 ft.
San Francisco
Pt. Conception
Los Angeles
Colorado Plateau
Mt. Elbert 14,431 ft.
Black Hills
Missouri R.
North Platte R.
South Platte R.
Lake Superior
L. Michigan
L. Huron
Chicago
Detroit
L. Erie
L. Ontario
Montreal
New York
Philadelphia
Washington
Chesapeake Bay
APPALACHIAN MTS.
Central Lowlands
Ozark Plateau
Ohio R.
Mt. Mitchell 6,684 ft.
C. Hatteras
Great Plains
Red R.
Mississippi R.
Rio Grande
Colorado R.
Lower California
Eugenia Pt.
Guadalupe I.
G. of California
SIERRA MADRE OCCIDENTAL
SIERRA MADRE ORIENTAL
False Cape
Guadalajara
Mexico City
Citlaltepetl 18,700 ft.
Houston
Coastal Plain
GULF OF MEXICO
C. Canaveral
Florida Pen.
Florida Keys
Bahama Islands
Yucatan Pen.
CENTRAL AMERICA
CARIBBEAN SEA
Cuba
Hispaniola
WEST INDIES
Greater Antilles
Lesser Antilles
Leeward Is.
Windward Is.
ATLANTIC OCEAN
Tropic of Cancer
Bermuda Is.
SOUTH AMERICA
West longitude

352

NORTH AMERICA: Political

ASIA

ARCTIC OCEAN

Barrow

Beaufort Sea

GREENLAND (Den.)

Thule

ICELAND

Yukon R.

Alaska (U.S.)

Fairbanks

Anchorage

Gulf of Alaska

Dawson

Arctic Circle

Pond Inlet

Baffin Bay

Juneau

Port Radium

Great Bear Lake

Godthaab

PACIFIC OCEAN

Great Slave Lake

Churchill

Hudson Bay

Labrador Sea

Edmonton

C A N A D A

Victoria

Vancouver

Calgary

Goose Bay

Seattle

Regina

Lake Winnipeg

Seven Islands

Gander

Portland

Spokane

Winnipeg

St. John's

Columbia

Quebec

Missouri R.

Great Lakes

Montreal

San Francisco

Great Salt L.

Minneapolis

St. Paul

Ottawa

Halifax

Salt Lake City

UNITED STATES OF AMERICA

Milwaukee

Toronto

Los Angeles

Omaha

Chicago

Detroit

Buffalo

Boston

Cleveland

Denver

Colorado

Kansas City

Cincinnati

Pittsburgh

New York

San Diego

Phoenix

St. Louis

Washington

Philadelphia Baltimore

Arkansas R.

Ohio R.

Norfolk

Guadalupe I. (Mex.)

El Paso

Memphis

Bermuda Is. (U.K.)

Rio Grande

Dallas

Atlanta

Tropic of Cancer

San Antonio

Houston

G. of California

Monterrey

New Orleans

ATLANTIC OCEAN

GULF OF MEXICO

MEXICO

Grand Bahama I.

Great Abaco I.

Miami

Guadalajara

Nassau

Eleuthera I.

THE BAHAMAS

Andros I.

Cat I.

Long I.

Den. —DENMARK
Fr. —FRANCE
Neth. —NETHERLANDS
Mex. —MEXICO
U.K. —UNITED KINGDOM
U.S. —UNITED STATES

Havana

Gr. Exuma I.

Mayaguana I.

CUBA

Acklins I.

PUERTO RICO (U.S.)

Mexico City

Cayman Islands (U.K.)

Gr. Inagua I.

Virgin Is. (U.S.&U.K.)

Orizaba

Santiago-de-Cuba

DOMINICAN REPUBLIC

Belmopan

HAITI

Santo Domingo

ANTIGUA AND BARBUDA

Guadalajara

BELIZE

JAMAICA

Port-au-Prince

ST. CHRISTOPHER-NEVIS

GUATEMALA

Kingston

Guadeloupe (Fr.)

Guatemala

HONDURAS

DOMINICA

San Salvador

Tegucigalpa

CARIBBEAN SEA

Martinique (Fr.)

EL SALVADOR

NICARAGUA

Neth. Antilles (Neth.)

ST. LUCIA

Managua

Aruba (Neth.)

ST. VINCENT AND THE GRENADINES

San José

Panama Canal

GRENADA

COSTA RICA

Panamá

SOUTH AMERICA

PANAMA

TRINIDAD AND TOBAGO

353

West longitude

Legend

✿ National capitals

● Other cities

| 0 | 500 miles |
| 0 | 800 kilometers |

UNITED STATES OF AMERICA: Physical-Political

CONN.	—CONNECTICUT
D.C.	—DISTRICT OF COLUMBIA
MASS.	—MASSACHUSETTS
MD.	—MARYLAND
N.H.	—NEW HAMPSHIRE
R.I.	—RHODE ISLAND
VT.	—VERMONT
W.VA.	—WEST VIRGINIA

C.	—Cape
Mt.	—Mountain
Pen.	—Peninsula
Pk.	—Peak

✪ National capitals
★ State capitals
● Other cities

Elevations

Feet	Meters
12,000	3,658
9,000	2,743
5,000	1,524
2,000	610
1,000	305
500	152
0	0

Miles 300
Kilometers 500

355

CANADA

BRITISH COLUMBIA
Vancouver • Pacific Time Zone
50°
ALBERTA
SASKATCHEWAN
CANADA
MANITOBA

WASHINGTON
Olympia ★ • Seattle
Portland •
Salem ★
Eugene •

OREGON

Spokane •

Columbia R.

Mountain Time Zone

Central Time Zone

Missouri R.

Great Falls •
Helena ★ MONTANA

Billings •

NORTH DAKOTA
★ Bismarck

Grand Forks •

Fargo •

MINN

45°

IDAHO
Boise ★
Idaho Falls •
Pocatello •
Snake R.

WYOMING
Casper •

Laramie •
Cheyenne ★

Rapid City •
SOUTH DAKOTA
★ Pierre

Sioux Falls •

NEBRASKA
N. Platte R.
Grand Island •
S. Platte R.
Platte R.

Omaha •
Lincoln ★

40°

NEVADA
Reno •
Carson City ★
Sacramento ★
San Francisco •

Salt Lake City ★
West Valley •
Provo •

UTAH

Denver ★ Aurora
COLORADO
Colorado Springs •

KANSAS
Topeka ★

Wichita •

35°

CALIFORNIA

Las Vegas •

ARIZONA

Los Angeles •

San Diego •

Phoenix ★
Mesa •

Tucson •

Santa Fe ★
Albuquerque •

NEW MEXICO

Las Cruces •

OKLAHOMA
Oklahoma ★ City

Lawton •

Tulsa •

Dallas •

PACIFIC OCEAN

30°

TEXAS

Austin ★

Houston •

Rio Grande

MEXICO

A S I A
SOVIET UNION
TENTH TIME ZONE IN U.S.S.R.
ELEVENTH TIME ZONE IN U.S.S.R.
Arctic Circle
180°
170°
150°
140°
70°

Alaska Time Zone

ALASKA

Yukon R.
Fairbanks •

Pacific Time Zone

CANADA

Monday
International Date Line
Sunday

BERING SEA

Willow • Anchorage •

Juneau ★

Gulf of Alaska

MEXICO

60°

Hawaii-Aleutian Time Zone

ALEUTIAN ISLANDS

0   200 miles
0   300 kilometers

356

West longitude

CARIBBEAN SEA

Guajira Pen.
Margarita I.
Tobago
Trinidad
Caracas
Maracaibo
Orinoco R. Delta

80° 60° 50° 40°

G. of Panama
Cauca R.
Magdalena R.
Meta R.
Mt. Tolima 19,049 ft.
Bogotá
Malpelo I.
Llanos
Orinoco R.
GUIANA HIGHLANDS
Angel Falls
Devils I.
C. Orange

Caqueta R.
Orinoco R.
Río Negro
Japura
A M A Z O N
Amazon R. Delta
Marajó
Equator 0°

Mt. Chimborazo 20,561 ft.
Gulf of Guayaquil
Marañón R.
B A S I N
Amazon R.
Japurá
Juruá
Purus R.
Tapajós R.
Xingu R.
Tocantins R.
C. São Roque

Aguja Pt.
Ucayali R.
Madeira
Araguaia R.
Tocantins R.
Parnaíba R.
São Francisco R.

Mt. Huascaran 22,205 ft.
A N D E S
Beni R.
Mamoré R.
Mato Grosso Plateau
Brasília
B R A Z I L I A N
10°

Lima
Mt. Ancohuma 21,490 ft.
Lake Titicaca
L. Poopó
H I G H L A N D S

PACIFIC OCEAN
M O U N T A I N S
Pilcomayo R.
Gran Chaco
Paraguay R.
Mt. Bandeira 9,462 ft.
20°

San Felix I. San Ambrosio I.
Salado R.
Paraná R.
São Paulo
C. Frio
Rio de Janeiro
Tropic of Capricorn

Paraná R.
Uruguay R.
ATLANTIC OCEAN

Mt. Aconcagua 22,834 ft.
30°

Juan Fernández Is.
Santiago
P a m p a s
Buenos Aires
Montevideo
Río de la Plata

Colorado R.
Blanca Bay
San Matías Gulf
Valdés Pen.
40°

Chiloé I.
P a t a g o n i a
Chonos Arch.
Gulf of San Jorge

Taitao Pen.
C. Tres Puntas

Grande Bay
Strait of Magellan
Strait of Magellan
Falkland Is. (U.K.) (Malvinas Is.)
50°

Tierra del Fuego
Cape Horn

90° 80° 70° 60° 50° 40° West longitude 30° 20°

Arch. —Archipelago
C. —Cape
G. —Gulf
Mt. —Mountain
Pen. —Peninsula
Pt. —Point

SOUTH AMERICA: Physical

Elevations
Feet   Meters
10,000   3,000
5,000   1,500
2,000   600
1,000   300
0   0

Miles 0   500
Kilometers 0   800

358

SOUTH AMERICA: Political

Barranquilla
Cartagena
Maracaibo
Caracas
Valencia
Port-of-Spain
TRINIDAD AND TOBAGO
Barquisimeto
Cúcuta
San Cristóbal
VENEZUELA
Orinoco R.
Georgetown
Paramaribo
Medellín
Bucaramanga
GUYANA
SURINAM
Cayenne
Bogotá
Fr. Guiana (Fr.)
Malpelo I. (Col.)
COLOMBIA
Cali
Quito
ECUADOR
Guayaquil
Iquitos
Manaus
Amazon R.
Equator
Belém
São Luis
Fortaleza
Trujillo
PERU
Recife
Maceió
BRAZIL
Callao
Lima
Cuzco
Arequipa
Lake Titicaca
La Paz
BOLIVIA
Salvador
Brasília
(Federal District)
PACIFIC OCEAN
Sucre
Belo Horizonte
Chuquicamata
PARAGUAY
Rio de Janeiro
Antofagasta
São Paulo
Niterói
Santos
Asunción
Tropic of Capricorn
Curitiba
San Felix I. (Chile)
San Ambrosio I. (Chile)
Tucumán
Pórto Alegre
Córdoba
Santa Fe
Paraná
URUGUAY
CHILE
Valparaíso
Rosario
Santiago
Buenos Aires
Montevideo
Juan Fernández Is. (Chile)
La Plata
Paraná
Rio de la Plata
ATLANTIC OCEAN
Concepción
ARGENTINA
Mar del Plata
Bahía Blanca
Strait of Magellan
Falkland Is. (U.K.) (Malvinas Is.)
Punta Arenas

Col. —COLOMBIA
Fr. —FRANCE
U.K. —UNITED KINGDOM

National capitals
Other cities

0   500 miles
0   800 kilometers

West longitude

359

ATLANTIC OCEAN

EUROPE

Azores

Madeira Is.

Canary Is.

C. Blanco

C. Verde

Strait of Gibraltar

Casablanca

ATLAS MOUNTAINS

S A H A R A

AHAGGAR PLATEAU

TIBESTI

MTS.

Senegal R.

Niger R.

Lake Chad

Benue R.

Grain Coast
C. Palmas
Ivory Coast
Gold Coast
Slave Coast

Fernando Po

Gulf of Guinea

São Tomé

C. Lopez

Equator

Zaire R.

Kinshasa

Zaire Basin

Ubangi R.

Zaire R.

Kasai R.

SHABA

Mediterranean Sea

Gulf of Sidra

Alexandria

Cairo

Suez Canal

Sinai Pen.

ASIA

Libyan Desert

Nile R.

Tropic of Cancer

Nubian Desert

Red Sea

ERITREA

Blue Nile

ETHIOPIAN HIGHLANDS

Gulf of Aden

Somali Pen.

White Nile

Lake Albert

Lake Turkana

Lake Victoria

Mt. Kenya 17,058 ft.

Mt. Kilimanjaro 19,340 ft.

Massai Steppe

Zanzibar

Lake Tanganyika

ATLANTIC OCEAN

Bihé Plateau

Lake Malawi

C. Delgado

Comoro Is.

MADAGASCAR

Mozambique Channel

Zambezi R.

Victoria Falls

Okavango Swamp

Namib Desert

Kalahari Desert

Johannesburg

Limpopo R.

DRAKENSBERG

Zulu-land

INDIAN OCEAN

Orange R.

Vaal R.

Cape of Good Hope

Cape Agulhas

AFRICA: Physical

C. —Cape
Mt. —Mountain
Pen. —Peninsula

Elevations

Feet	Meters
10,000	3,000
5,000	1,500
2,000	600
1,000	300
0	0

Land below sea level

Miles
0   800

0   1200
Kilometers

360

Tropic of Capricorn

30° West longitude   0°   East longitude

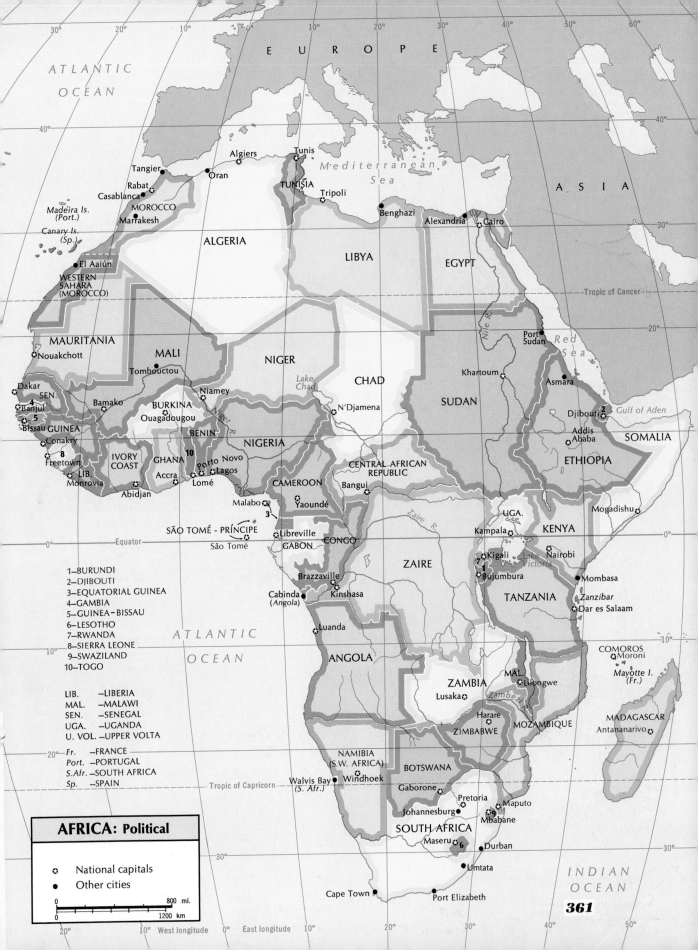

AFRICA: Political

EUROPE

ATLANTIC OCEAN

Mediterranean Sea

ASIA

Tangier
Algiers
Tunis
TUNISIA
Oran
Tripoli
Benghazi
Alexandria
Cairo
Rabat
Casablanca
MOROCCO
Marrakesh
Madeira Is. (Port.)
Canary Is. (Sp.)
El Aaiún
WESTERN SAHARA (MOROCCO)

ALGERIA

LIBYA

EGYPT

Tropic of Cancer

MAURITANIA
Nouakchott

MALI
Tombouctou

NIGER

CHAD

Lake Chad

SUDAN
Khartoum

Port Sudan

Red Sea

Asmara

Gulf of Aden

Nile R.

Dakar
SEN.
4 Banjul
5 Bissau GUINEA
Conakry
8 Freetown
LIB. Monrovia

Bamako
BURKINA
Ouagadougou
Niamey
BENIN
NIGERIA
10
GHANA
Porto Novo
Accra
Lagos
Lomé

N'Djamena

CENTRAL AFRICAN REPUBLIC
Bangui

Djibouti 2
Addis Ababa
ETHIOPIA
SOMALIA

Niger R.

IVORY COAST
Abidjan

CAMEROON
Malabo
Yaoundé
3
SÃO TOMÉ - PRÍNCIPE
São Tomé

Libreville
GABON
CONGO

Zaire R.

UGA.
Kampala

Mogadishu

KENYA
7 Kigali
1 Bujumbura
Lake Victoria
Nairobi
Mombasa

Equator

Brazzaville
Kinshasa

ZAIRE

TANZANIA
Zanzibar
Dar es Salaam

1—BURUNDI
2—DJIBOUTI
3—EQUATORIAL GUINEA
4—GAMBIA
5—GUINEA–BISSAU
6—LESOTHO
7—RWANDA
8—SIERRA LEONE
9—SWAZILAND
10—TOGO

Cabinda (Angola)

Luanda

ATLANTIC OCEAN

COMOROS
Moroni
Mayotte I. (Fr.)

ANGOLA

ZAMBIA
Lusaka

MAL.
Lilongwe

Zambezi R.

LIB. —LIBERIA
MAL. —MALAWI
SEN. —SENEGAL
UGA. —UGANDA
U. VOL.—UPPER VOLTA

Fr. —FRANCE
Port. —PORTUGAL
S.Afr.—SOUTH AFRICA
Sp. —SPAIN

Harare
ZIMBABWE
MOZAMBIQUE
MADAGASCAR
Antananarivo

NAMIBIA (S.W. AFRICA)
BOTSWANA

Tropic of Capricorn

Walvis Bay (S. Afr.)
Windhoek
Gaborone
Pretoria
Maputo
9 Mbabane

Johannesburg

SOUTH AFRICA
Maseru 6
Durban

Umtata

INDIAN OCEAN

Cape Town
Port Elizabeth

361

AFRICA: Political

✦ National capitals

● Other cities

0   800 mi.
0   1200 km

20° 10° West longitude 0° East longitude 10° 20°

ARCTIC OCEAN

Spitsbergen

North Land

Novaya Zemlya

Kara Sea

Taymyr

Barents Sea

Yenisey R.

Kola Pen.

La Plain

SCANDINAVIA

North Sea

Stockholm

Baltic Sea

Hamburg

Berlin

Elbe R.

Rhine R.

Vistula R.

Baltic Plains

Leningrad

Dvina R.

Volga R.

North European Plain

Moscow

Dnieper R.

Don R.

Volga R.

Ural R.

URAL MOUNTAINS

Ob R.

West Siberian Plain

Ishim R.

Irtysh R.

Ob R.

ALTAI

Kirgiz Steppe

Kazakh Uplands

Lake Balkhash

Kama R.

Aral Sea

Turan Lowland

Syr Darya

Amu Darya

TIEN SHAN

Tarim Basin

BRITISH ISLES

London

Paris

Loire R.

PYRENEES

IBERIAN PENINSULA

Madrid

Tagus R.

Str. of Gibraltar

ATLANTIC OCEAN

Madeira

Balearic Is.

ALPS

Po R.

Milan

Corsica

Sardinia

Tyrrhenian Sea

Rome

Adriatic Sea

CARPATHIAN

Danube R.

Bucharest

Black Sea

Sicily

Maltese Is.

Ionian Sea

Aegean Sea

Crete

ANATOLIA (Asia Minor)

Istanbul

Cyprus

Mediterranean Sea

CAUCASUS MTS.

Caspian Sea

Plateau of Iran

Tehran

Plateau of Tib

KUNLUN

HIMALAYA

Mt. Everest 29,028 ft.

HINDU KUSH

Indus R.

Sutlej R.

Delhi

Ganges R.

Ganges Plain

Indian Desert

Euphrates R.

Tigris R.

Baghdad

Mesopotamia

ZAGROS MOUNTAINS

Syrian Desert

Sinai Pen.

HEJAZ

ARABIAN PENINSULA

Persian Gulf

Gulf of Oman

Karachi

ASIR

Red Sea

AFRICA

Hadhramaut

Gulf of Aden

Socotra

Arabian Sea

Bombay

Deccan Plateau

Godavari R.

WESTERN GHATS

EASTERN GHATS

Madras

Laccadive Is.

Sri Lanka

Maldives

INDIAN OCEAN

East longitude

Tropic of Cancer

Equator

Arctic Circle

Pen. Laptev Sea
130° 140° 150° 70° 160° 60° 170°

Central Siberian Plateau

S I B E R I A

Lower Tunguska

CHERSKI RA.

VERKHOYANSK RA.

Lena R.

KOLYMA RANGE

CENTRAL RA.

Bering Sea

Aleutian Is.

International Date Line
Monday

Sunday

40° 170° 30°

170°

Sea of Okhotsk

Kamchatka Peninsula

Tropic of Cancer

180°

20°

SAYAN MTS.
Yenisey R.
Angara R.
Lake Baykal
Shilka R.
Aldan R.
Amur R.
Sakhalin

Kuril Islands

170°

Mt. —Mountain
Pen. —Peninsula
RA. —Range
Str. —Strait

MTS.

Mongolian Plateau

The Gobi

GREAT KHINGAN MTS.

Manchuria Plain
Harbin
Shenyang

Hokkaido

Sea of Japan

Honshu

Tokyo
Fujiyama
12,388 ft.
Kyoto
Shikoku
Kyushu

EURASIA: Physical

Elevations
Feet   Meters
10,000 —— 3,000
5,000 —— 1,500
2,000 —— 600
1,000
0 —— 300
0 —— 0

Land below sea level

Miles 800
0
Kilometers 1200

NAN SHAN

S H A N
of
et

Great Wall
Hwang Ho
Peking (Beijing)
Yellow R.
Tientsin
Dairen

North China Plain

Yellow Sea

Korea Strait

Shanghai

East China Sea

Okinawa

Ryukyu Islands

10°

Y A S

Brahmaputra R.
Calcutta
Irrawaddy R.
Salween R.

Chungking
Yangtze R.

BOHEA HILLS

Canton
Si R.
Hong Kong

Taiwan

Philippine Sea

PACIFIC OCEAN

Hainan

Luzon Strait

Luzon

Manila

Philippine Is.

Samar

Equator 0°

Admiralty Is.

New Ireland

Bay
of
Bengal

Andaman Is.

INDOCHINA
PENINSULA

Mekong R.

Ho Chi Minh City

South China Sea

Mindoro
Palawan
Panay
Negros

Mindanao

New Britain

10°

Andaman Sea
Nicobar Is.

Gulf of Siam

Celebes Sea

Halmahera

SNOW MTS.

New Guinea

Aru Is.

150°

Str. of Malacca

Malay Pen.

Natuna Is.

Kalimantan (Borneo)

Sulawesi (Celebes)

Buru
Ceram

Arafura Sea

Coral Sea

Sumatra

Mentawai Is.

Bangka

SUNDA ISLANDS
Java Sea

Jakarta Java Bali Lombok Sumbawa Sumba Flores Timor

AUSTRALIA

90° 100° 120° 130° 140° 150°

363

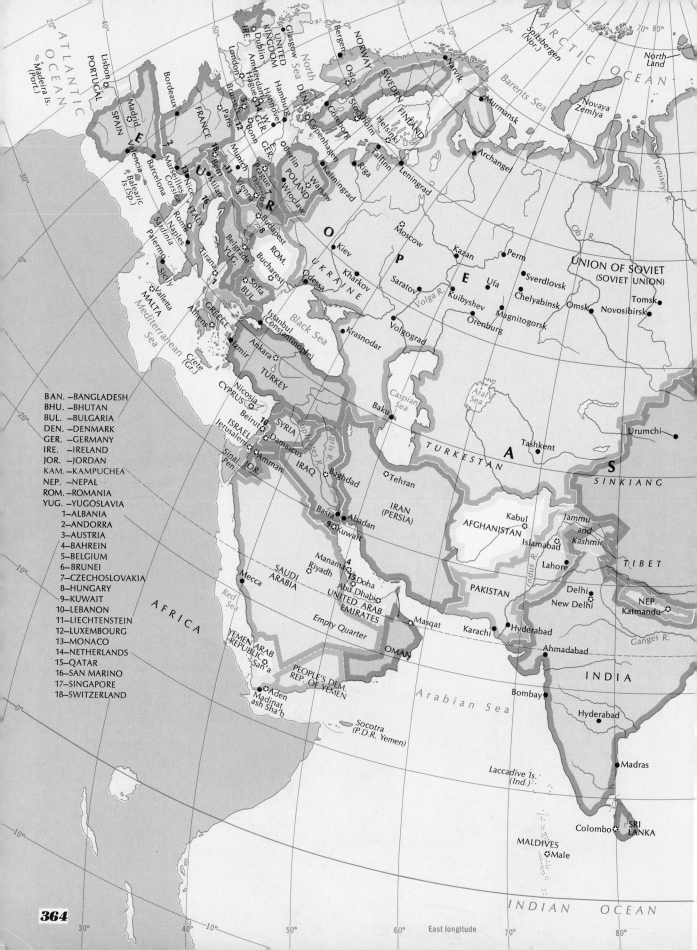

ATLANTIC OCEAN
Madeira Is. (Port.)
PORTUGAL
Lisbon
SPAIN
Madrid
Valencia
Barcelona
Balearic Is. (Sp.)
Bordeaux
FRANCE
Paris
London
UNITED KINGDOM
Dublin
IRE.
Glasgow
Amsterdam
Hague 14
Brussels 5
Hamburg
W. GER.
E. GER.
Bonn
Munich
Berlin
POLAND
Warsaw
Wrocław
Prague 7
Danube
Budapest 8
Vienna 3
Bern 11
Milan
Marseilles
Nice 13
Corsica
ITALY
Rome
Naples
Sicily
Palermo
Sardinia
Valletta
MALTA
Mediterranean Sea
Crete (Gr.)
Athens
GREECE
Tiranal 1
Belgrade
YUG.
Sofia
BUL.
ROM.
Bucharest
Wien
Bergen
Oslo
NORWAY
SWEDEN
Göteborg
Stockholm
Copenhagen
DEN.
North Sea
Helsinki
FINLAND
Tallinn
Riga
Leningrad
Kaliningrad
Narvik
Murmansk
Spitsbergen (Nor.)
ARCTIC OCEAN
North Land
Novaya Zemlya
Barents Sea
Archangel
UNION OF SOVIET (SOVIET UNION)
Moscow
Kiev
UKRAINE
Kharkov
Odessa
Saratov
Krasnodar
Volga R.
Kazan
Perm
Ufa
Sverdlovsk
Kuibyshev
Chelyabinsk
Magnitogorsk
Orenburg
Omsk
Tomsk
Novosibirsk
Yenisey R.
Ob R.
Volgograd
Black Sea
Istanbul (Constantinople)
Izmir
Ankara
TURKEY
Nicosia
CYPRUS
Beirut
ISRAEL
Jerusalem
Damascus 10
SYRIA
Amman
JOR.
Sinai Pen.
IRAQ
Baghdad
Basra
Abadan
Kuwait 9
Tehran
IRAN (PERSIA)
Caspian Sea
Baku
Aral Sea
Tashkent
TURKESTAN
Urumchi
SINKIANG
ASIA
Kabul
AFGHANISTAN
Jammu and Kashmir
Islamabad
Lahore
TIBET
Manama 4
Riyadh
Doha 15
Abu Dhabi
UNITED ARAB EMIRATES
SAUDI ARABIA
Mecca
Red Sea
AFRICA
Empty Quarter
YEMEN ARAB REPUBLIC
San'a
PEOPLE'S DEM. REP. OF YEMEN
Aden
Madinat ash Sha'b
Socotra (P.D.R. Yemen)
Masqat
OMAN
PAKISTAN
Karachi
Hyderabad
Indus R.
Delhi
New Delhi
NEP.
Katmandu
Ganges R.
Ahmadabad
INDIA
Bombay
Hyderabad
Arabian Sea
Laccadive Is. (Ind.)
Madras
Colombo
SRI LANKA
MALDIVES
Male
INDIAN OCEAN
East longitude

BAN. —BANGLADESH
BHU. —BHUTAN
BUL. —BULGARIA
DEN. —DENMARK
GER. —GERMANY
IRE. —IRELAND
JOR. —JORDAN
KAM. —KAMPUCHEA
NEP. —NEPAL
ROM. —ROMANIA
YUG. —YUGOSLAVIA
1—ALBANIA
2—ANDORRA
3—AUSTRIA
4—BAHREIN
5—BELGIUM
6—BRUNEI
7—CZECHOSLOVAKIA
8—HUNGARY
9—KUWAIT
10—LEBANON
11—LIECHTENSTEIN
12—LUXEMBOURG
13—MONACO
14—NETHERLANDS
15—QATAR
16—SAN MARINO
17—SINGAPORE
18—SWITZERLAND

EURASIA: Political

✺	National capitals
●	Other cities

0 — 800 mi.
0 — 1200 km

Gr. — GREECE
Ind. — INDIA
Jap. — JAPAN
Nor. — NORWAY
Port. — PORTUGAL
Sp. — SPAIN
U.K. — UNITED KINGDOM
U.S. — UNITED STATES
U.S.S.R. — SOVIET UNION

New Siberian Is.
Aleutian Is. (U.S.)
Siberia
SOCIALIST REPUBLICS
Yakutsk
Lena R.
Krasnoyarsk
Irkutsk
Amur R.
Magadan
Kamchatka Pen.
Sea of Okhotsk
Kuril Islands (U.S.S.R.)
Bering Sea
Sakhalin
Khabarovsk
Sapporo
MANCHURIA
Harbin
Vladivostok
Sea of Japan
JAPAN
Tokyo
Yokohama
Ulan Bator
MONGOLIA
INNER MONGOLIA
Fushun
Shenyang
N. KOREA
Pyengyang
Seoul
S. KOREA
Pusan
Kyoto
Kobe
Nagoya
Osaka
Great Wall
Peking
Tientsin
Dairen
Tsingtao
Kitakyushu
Taiyuan
Hwang Ho
Lanchow
Sian
Nanking
Shanghai
East China Sea
Wuhan
PEOPLE'S REPUBLIC OF CHINA
Chengtu
Yangtze R.
Chungking
Taipei
Ryukyu Is. (Jap.)
TAIWAN
Lhasa
Thimbu
BHU.
Brahmaputra R.
BAN.
Dacca
Calcutta
Kunming
Canton
Hong Kong (U.K.)
Macao (Port.)
PACIFIC OCEAN
Mandalay
BURMA
Hanoi
Bay of Bengal
Rangoon
Vientiane
LAOS
Hue
Da Nang
VIETNAM
South China Sea
Manila
PHILIPPINES
THAILAND
Bangkok
KAM.
Mekong R.
Ho Chi Minh City
Phnom Penh
Davao
Andaman Is. (Ind.)
Nicobar Is. (Ind.)
Bandar Seri Begawan
Manado
MALAYSIA
Borneo
Djajapura
IRIAN JAYA
New Guinea
PAPUA NEW GUINEA
Lae
Port Moresby
Medan
Kuala Lumpur
Pontianak
Samarinda
Sulawesi (Celebes)
INDONESIA
Sumatra
Bandjermasin
Ujung Pandang
Timor
Arafura Sea
Coral Sea
Palembang
Jakarta
Bandung
Java
Surabaja
AUSTRALIA

365

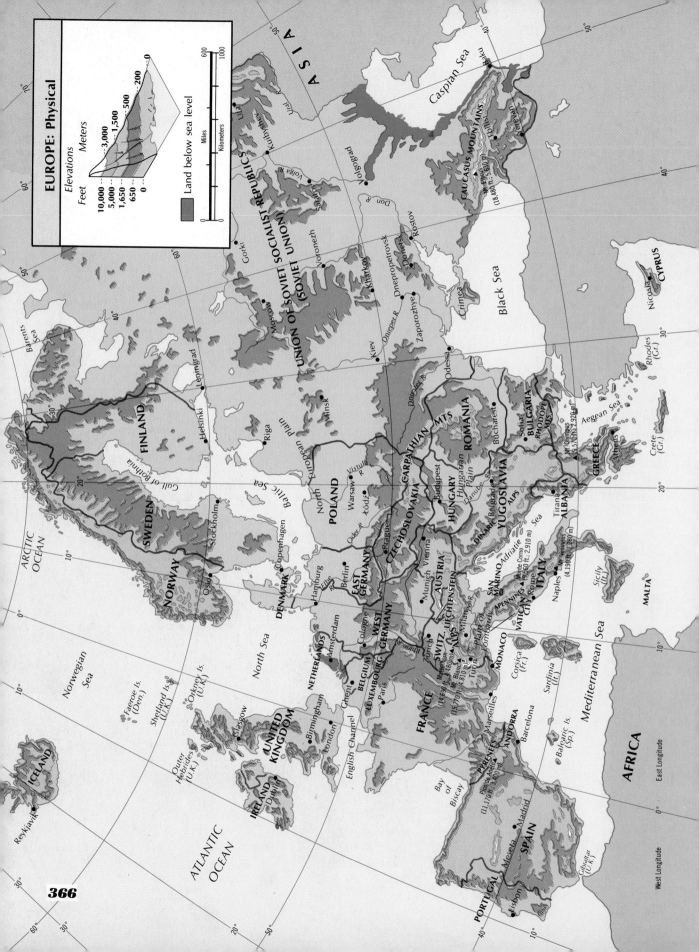

EUROPE: Physical

Elevations

Feet	Meters
10,000	3,000
5,000	1,500
1,650	500
650	200
0	0

Land below sea level

Miles

Kilometers

ASIA

ARCTIC OCEAN

Barents Sea

ICELAND

Reykjavik

Norwegian Sea

NORWAY

SWEDEN

FINLAND

Gulf of Bothnia

Leningrad

Helsinki

Ufa

Kuibyshev

Ural R.

Volga R.

Gorki

Moscow

UNION OF SOVIET SOCIALIST REPUBLICS (SOVIET UNION)

Volgograd

Don R.

Rostov

Caspian Sea

Baku

CAUCASUS MOUNTAINS

Mt. Elbrus (18,480 ft.; 5,630 m)

Tbilisi

Yerevan

Saratov

Voronezh

Kharkov

Dnepropetrovsk

Donetsk

Kiev

Dnieper R.

Dniester R.

Zaporozhye

Minsk

Riga

Baltic Sea

European Plain

North European Plain

Black Sea

Crimea

Odessa

CYPRUS

Nicosia

Rhodes (Gr.)

Faeroe Is. (Den.)

Shetland Is. (U.K.)

Orkney Is. (U.K.)

Outer Hebrides (U.K.)

Glasgow

UNITED KINGDOM

Birmingham

London

IRELAND

Dublin

English Channel

North Sea

NETHERLANDS

Amsterdam

Ghent

BELGIUM

LUXEMBOURG

Cologne

DENMARK

Copenhagen

Hamburg

Elbe R.

Berlin

EAST GERMANY

WEST GERMANY

Oslo

Stockholm

Warsaw

Vistula R.

POLAND

Łódź

Oder R.

Prague

CZECHOSLOVAKIA

CARPATHIAN MTS

Budapest

Vienna

Munich

AUSTRIA

LIECHTENSTEIN

SWITZ.

ALPS

HUNGARY

Hungarian Plain

Danube R.

ROMANIA

Bucharest

YUGOSLAVIA

DINARIC ALPS

Belgrade

Tirana

ALBANIA

BULGARIA

Sofia

RHODOPE MTS.

GREECE

Mt. Olympus (9,570 ft.; 2,911 m)

Athens

Crete (Gr.)

Aegean Sea

Adriatic Sea

Paris

FRANCE

Bay of Biscay

Pico de Aneto (11,170 ft.; 3,400 m)

PYRENEES

ANDORRA

Barcelona

SPAIN

Meseta

Madrid

PORTUGAL

Lisbon

Gibraltar (U.K.)

Balearic Is. (Sp.)

Mediterranean Sea

MALTA

Sardinia (It.)

Corsica (Fr.)

ITALY

Rome

VATICAN CITY

Naples

Mt. Vesuvius (4,190 ft.; 1,280 m)

Sicily (It.)

APENNINES

SAN MARINO

MONACO

Marseilles

Rhône R.

Lyons

Turin

Po R.

Plain of Lombardy

Milan

Monte Como

Monte Rosa (15,200 ft.; 4,634 m)

Matterhorn (14,690 ft.; 4,480 m)

Mt. Blanc (15,770 ft.; 4,810 m)

Zurich

Monte Cenis (9,560 ft.; 2,910 m)

ATLANTIC OCEAN

AFRICA

East Longitude

West Longitude

366

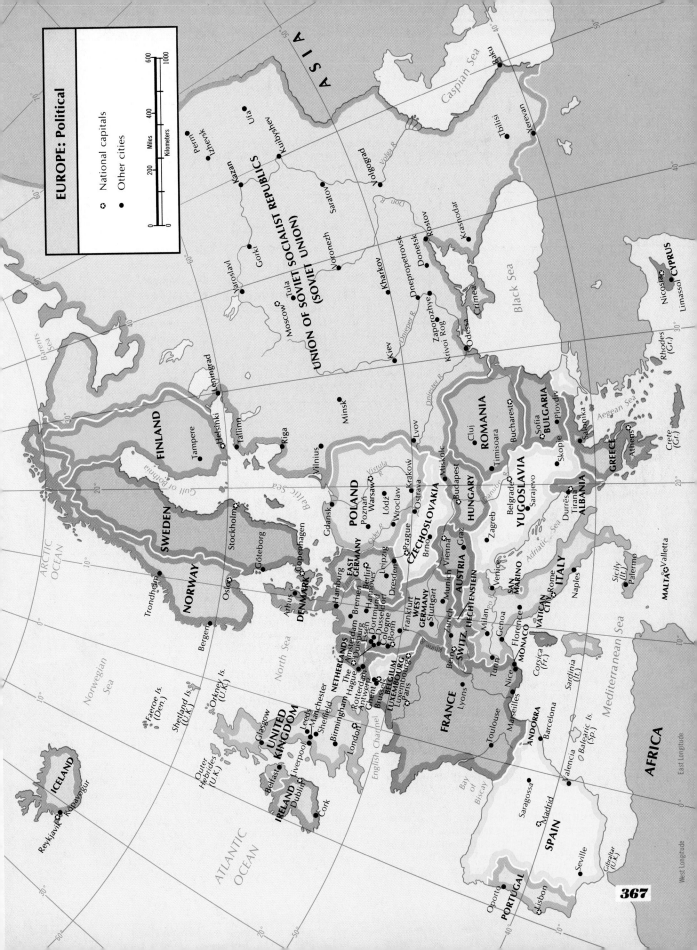

EUROPE: Political

✿ National capitals
• Other cities

Miles
Kilometers
600
400
200
0
1000

ASIA

Caspian Sea

Barents Sea

UNION OF SOVIET SOCIALIST REPUBLICS (SOVIET UNION)

Perm
Izhevsk
Ufa
Kazan
Kuibyshev
Yaroslavl
Gorki
Saratov
Voronezh
Volgograd
Volga R.
Don R.
Moscow
Tula
Rostov
Krasnodar
Donetsk
Dnepropetrovsk
Kharkov
Krivoi Rog
Zaporozhye
Kiev
Odessa
Crimea

CYPRUS
Nicosia
Limassol

Rhodes (Gr.)

Black Sea

Baku
Tbilisi
Yerevan

Leningrad
Helsinki
Tampere
Tallinn
Riga
Minsk
Vilnius
Dnieper R.
Lvov
Dniester R.

FINLAND

Gulf of Bothnia

SWEDEN
Stockholm
Göteborg

NORWAY
Trondheim
Bergen
Oslo

ARCTIC OCEAN

ICELAND
Reykjavík
Kópavogur

Faeroe Is. (Den.)
Shetland Is. (U.K.)
Orkney Is. (U.K.)
Outer Hebrides (U.K.)

Norwegian Sea

ATLANTIC OCEAN

UNITED KINGDOM
Glasgow
Belfast
IRELAND
Dublin
Cork
Liverpool
Manchester
Leeds
Sheffield
Birmingham
London

North Sea

English Channel

DENMARK
Copenhagen
Århus
Gdansk

Baltic Sea

POLAND
Warsaw
Poznań
Łódź
Wrocław
Kraków
Vistula R.
Oder R.

EAST GERMANY
Hamburg
Bremen
Hannover
Berlin
Leipzig
Dresden

NETHERLANDS
The Hague
Amsterdam
Rotterdam
Antwerp
Ghent
BELGIUM
Brussels
LUXEMBOURG
Luxembourg
Dortmund
Essen
Duisburg
Düsseldorf
Cologne
Bonn
Frankfurt
WEST GERMANY
Stuttgart
Munich

Prague
CZECHOSLOVAKIA
Brno
Ostrava

Miskolc
Budapest
HUNGARY
Graz
Vienna
AUSTRIA
LIECHTENSTEIN
SWITZ.
Bern
Zurich

Danube R.

ROMANIA
Cluj
Timisoara
Bucharest
Sofia
BULGARIA
Plovdiv

YUGOSLAVIA
Belgrade
Zagreb
Sarajevo
Skopje

Adriatic Sea

Aegean Sea

GREECE
Salonika
Athens

Crete (Gr.)

Durrës
Tirana
ALBANIA

SAN MARINO
Venice
Milan
Genoa
ITALY
VATICAN CITY
Rome
Naples
MONACO
Florence
Turin
Nice
Marseilles

Corsica (Fr.)

Sardinia (It.)

Sicily (It.)
Palermo

MALTA
Valletta

Mediterranean Sea

FRANCE
Paris
Lyons
Toulouse

Bay of Biscay

ANDORRA
Barcelona

SPAIN
Madrid
Saragossa
Valencia
Seville

Balearic Is. (Sp.)

Gibraltar (U.K.)

PORTUGAL
Oporto
Lisbon

AFRICA

West Longitude
East Longitude

MALTA

Tunis

GAZETTEER

The Gazetteer is a geographical dictionary. It shows latitude and longitude for cities and certain other places. Latitude and longitude are shown in this form: (41°N/74°W). This means "41 degrees north latitude and 74 degrees west longitude." The page reference tells where each entry may be found on a map.

Key to Pronunciation

a	hat, cap	i	it, pin	ou	house, out	zh	measure, seizure
ā	age, face	ī	ice, five	sh	she, rush	ə	represents:
ã	care, air	ng	long, bring	th	thin, both	a	in about
ä	father, far	o	hot, rock	ŦH	then, smooth	e	in taken
ch	child, much	ō	open, go	u	cup, butter	i	in pencil
e	let, best	ô	order, all	u̇	full, put	o	in lemon
ē	equal, see	oi	oil, voice	ü	rule, move	u	in circus
ėr	term, learn						

This Key to Pronunciation is from *Scott, Foresman Intermediate Dictionary*, by E.L. Thorndike and Clarence L. Barnhart. Copyright © 1983 by Scott, Foresman and Company. Reprinted by permission.

Adelaide (ad′ əl ād). Capital of the Australian state of South Australia. Located near a gulf of the Indian Ocean. (35°S/139°E) p. 245.

Adriatic Sea (ā drē at′ ik sē). Part of the Mediterranean Sea located between Italy and the Balkan Peninsula. p. 366.

Africa (af′ ri kə). The earth's second largest continent. p. 7.

Alaska Highway (ə las′ kə hī′ wā). Highway that connects Dawson Creek, British Columbia, Canada, and Fairbanks, Alaska. It is 1,523 miles (2,451 km) long. p. 55.

Alaska Range (ə las′ kə rānj). Mountains in south central Alaska. Mount McKinley, the highest peak in North America, is in this range. Its elevation is 20,320 ft (6,194 m). p. 55.

Albuquerque (al′ bə kėr kē). Most populated city in New Mexico. Located on the Rio Grande. (35°N/107°W) pp. 356–357.

Aleutian Islands (ə lü′ shən ī′ lənds). Chain of islands extending west from the Alaska Peninsula. p. 55.

Alps (alps). Mountains in south central Europe. The highest peak is Mont Blanc, at 15,771 ft (4,807 m). pp. 362–363.

Amazon Basin (am′ ə zän bās′ ən). Area drained by the Amazon River and its tributaries. p. 106.

Amazon River (am′ ə zän riv′ ər). Second longest river in the world. Its tributaries begin in the Andes and the Guiana Highlands. It flows across northern Brazil and into the Atlantic Ocean at the Equator. p. 106.

Anchorage (anq′ kə rij). Most populated city in Alaska. Located on Cook Inlet, an arm of the Pacific Ocean. (61°N/150°W) p. 55.

Andes Mountains (an′ dēz moun′ tənz). High mountains that stretch north to south along the western side of South America. Highest peak, with an elevation of 22,840 ft (6,690 m), is Mount Aconcagua. p. 358.

Annapolis (ə nap′ ə ləs). Capital of Maryland. Located on the Chesapeake Bay. Site of the United States Naval Academy. (39°N/77°W) p. 208.

Antarctica (ant ärk′ ti kə). The earth's third smallest continent. p. 7.

Antelope Valley (ant′ əl ōp val′ ē). Valley located west of the Mojave River. p. 149.

Appalachian Mountains (ap ə lā′ chən moun′ tənz). Chain of mountains stretching from Canada to Alabama. The highest peak is Mount Mitchell, at 6,684 ft (2,037 m). pp. 354–355.

Appalachian Trail (ap ə lā′ chən trāl). Hiking path in the Appalachians. It stretches more than 2,000 miles (3,218 km), from Mount Katahdin, Maine, to Springer Mountain, Georgia. p. 275.

Arabian Peninsula (ə rā′ bē ən pə nin′ sə lə). Large peninsula located east of the Red Sea. pp. 362–363.

Arctic Circle (ärk′ tik sėr′ kəl). Line of latitude located at 66½° north latitude. p. 12.

Arctic Ocean (ärk′ tik   ō′ shən). Large body of salt water north of the Arctic Circle. p. 7.

Arkansas River (är′ kan sô riv′ ər). River that begins in central Colorado and flows into the Mississippi River north of Greenville, Mississippi. pp. 354–355.

Asia (ā′ zhə). The earth's largest continent. p. 7.

Aspen (as′ pən). Skiing resort in Colorado. (39°N/107°W) p. 263.

Atacama Desert (ät ə käm′ ə dez′ ərt). Dry area in Chile. Major source of sodium nitrate. p. 120.

Atlantic City (ət lant′ ik sit′ ē). City on the Atlantic Ocean in New Jersey. The most popular resort in America. (39°N/74°W) p. 19.

Atlantic Coastal Plain (ət lant′ ik   kōs′ təl plān), Large plain located along the Atlantic Ocean from Maine to Florida. p. 177.

Atlantic Ocean (ət lant′ ik   ō′ shən). Large body of salt water separating North America and South America from Europe and Africa. p. 7.

Atlas Mountains (at′ ləs moun′ tənz). Mountains located along the northern edge of the Sahara. They are in Morocco, Algeria, and Tunisia. The highest peak is Djebel Toubkal, at 13,665 ft (4,165 m). p. 360.

Australia (ô strāl′ yə). The earth's smallest continent. Also the name of the country located on the continent. p. 7.

Balkan Peninsula (bôl kən   pə nin′ sə lə). Peninsula in southeastern Europe between the Adriatic and Ionian seas to the west and the Aegean and Black seas to the east. Usually thought to include the countries of Greece, Albania, Bulgaria, Romania, and part of Turkey. pp. 366–367.

Baltimore (bôl′ tə mōr). Most populated city in Maryland. Located on the Chesapeake Bay. One of the busiest seaports in the United States. (39°N/77°W) p. 208.

Barstow (bär′ stō). City in the Mojave Desert. Located along the Mojave River. (35°N/117°W) p. 149.

Basel (bäz əl). City in Switzerland. Located on the Rhine River north of the Jura Mountains (48°N/8°E) p. 300.

Baton Rouge (bat′ ən   rüzh). Capital of Louisiana. Located on the Mississippi River. (30°N/91°W) p. 216.

Battle Creek (bat′ əl krēk). City in Michigan. Famous for producing breakfast cereals. (42°N/85°W) p. 15.

Bayamón (bī ə mōn′). City in Puerto Rico. (18°N/66°W) p. 88.

Belgrade (bel′ gräd). Capital of Yugoslavia. Located where the Sava River joins the Danube River. (45°N/21°E) p. 293.

Bering Sea (bir′ ing sē). Part of the North Pacific Ocean bounded on the east by the mainland of Alaska and on the south and southeast by the Aleutian Islands. p. 55.

Bering Strait (bir′ ing strāt). Narrow body of water connecting the Arctic Ocean and the Bering Sea. Separates Asia from North America. p. 55.

Bern (bərn). Capital of Switzerland. Located on the Swiss Plateau. (47°N/7°E) p. 300.

Bethesda (bə thez′ də). City in Maryland. (39°N/77°W) p. 208.

Big Diomede Island (big dī′ ə mēd ī′ lənd). One of two islands located in the Bering Strait. This island, which is part of the Soviet Union, is only 2 miles (3.2 km) from Little Diomede Island, which is part of the United States. p. 55.

Black Sea (blak sē). Large sea located on the southern divide between Europe and Asia. pp. 366–367.

Blue Ridge (blü rij). Mountains in the eastern part of the Appalachian System. They stretch from Pennsylvania to Georgia. pp. 354–355.

Boston (bô′ stən). Capital of and most populated city in Massachusetts. Located on Massachusetts Bay. (42°N/71°W) pp. 356–357.

Boulder (bōl′ dər). City in Colorado. It has an elevation of 5,350 ft (1,630 m). (40°N/105°W) p. 263.

Brisbane (briz′ bən). Capital of the Australian state of Queensland. Port city located on the eastern coast of Australia. (27°S/153°E) p. 245.

Brooks Range (brůks rānj). Northernmost part of the Rocky Mountains. Located in northern Alaska. p. 55.

Buffalo (bəf′ ə lō). Second most populated city in New York. Located on the shore of Lake Erie and the Niagara River. (43°N/79°W) pp. 356–357.

Cairo (kī′ rō). Capital of Egypt. Most populated city in Africa. Located on the eastern side of the Nile River. (30°N/31°E) p. 361.

Calvert Cliffs (kal′ vərt klifs). Sand and clay cliffs along the Chesapeake Bay. Fossils have been found in these cliffs. (38°N/76°W) p. 208.

Canberra (kan′ ber ə). National capital of Australia. Located in southeastern Australia. (35°S/149°E) p. 245.

Canyon de Chelly National Monument (kan′ yən də shā nash′ ə nəl mon′ yə mənt). Area in Arizona set aside by the national government so that people can see houses that were built into the cliffs by Native Americans hundreds of years ago. p. 129.

Caribbean National Forest (kar ə bē′ ən nash′ ə nəl fôr′ ist). National forest located near San Juan, Puerto Rico. p. 88.

Caribbean Sea (kar ə bē′ ən sē). Part of the Atlantic Ocean bounded by South America to the south, by Central America to the west, and by Cuba, Puerto Rico, and other islands to the north and east. p. 352.

Carson City (kär′ sən sit′ ē). Capital of Nevada. Located near Lake Tahoe. (39°N/120°W) pp. 356–357.

Cascade Range (ka skād′ rānj). Mountains that extend from northern California through Oregon and Washington and into Canada. The highest peak is Mount Rainier, at 14,408 ft (4,392 m). pp. 354–355.

Caspian Sea (kas′ pē ən sē). Largest totally inland body of water in the world. Except for its southern shore, which borders Iran, the Caspian Sea is completely within the Soviet Union. pp. 362–363.

Caucasus Mountains (kô′ kə səs moun′ tənz). Very high mountains in the Soviet Union. They form part of the southern divide between Europe and Asia. Highest peak is Mount Elbrus, with an elevation of 18,481 ft (5,633 m). pp. 362–363.

Central Plains (sen′ trəl plānz). Large plains area in the middle of the United States, between the Appalachian and Rocky mountains. p. 177.

Chattanooga (chat ə nü′ gə). City in Tennessee. Located along the Tennessee River. (35°N/85°W) p. 275.

Chesapeake Bay (ches ə pēk bā). Inlet of the Atlantic Ocean in Virginia and Maryland. It is about 190 miles (306 km) long. p. 208.

Chicago (shə käg′ ō). Third most populated city in the United States. Located in Illinois on the southern tip of Lake Michigan. (42°N/88°W) p. 193.

Chihuahuan Desert (chə wä′ wän dez′ ərt). Desert that extends from western Texas to eastern Arizona. Large part of this desert also extends into Mexico. The Rio Grande passes through this desert. p. 134.

Cleveland (klēv′ lənd). One of the most populated cities on the Great Lakes. Located on the shore of Lake Erie in Ohio, at the mouth of the Cuyahoga River. (42°N/82°W) pp. 356–357.

Clingman's Dome (kling′ mənz dōm). Highest mountain peak on the Appalachian Trail. Located in the Great Smokies of Tennessee. Has an elevation of 6,642 ft (2,025 m). (36°N/84°W) p. 275.

Coast Ranges (kōst rānj′ əs). Mountains along the Pacific coast of North America. They stretch from Alaska to California. pp. 354–355.

Colorado Plateau (käl ə rad′ ō pla tō′). Large, high, hilly area west of the Rocky Mountains. pp. 354–355.

Colorado River (käl ə rad′ ō riv′ ər). Starts in Rocky Mountains in northern Colorado and flows into the Gulf of California in Mexico. pp. 354–355.

Colorado Springs (käl ə rad′ ō springz). City in Colorado. The United States Air Force Academy is located here. (39°N/105°W) pp. 356–357.

Columbia (kə ləm′ bē ə). City in Maryland. (39°N/77°W) p. 208.

Crowley (krou′ lē). City in Louisiana. It has many rice mills. (30°N/92°W) p. 216.

Cuba (kyü′ bə). Largest of all the islands in the West Indies. Located about 90 miles (145 km) south of Key West, Florida. p. 353.

Cumberland River (kəm′ bər lənd riv′ ər). Starts in Kentucky and flows into Tennessee and then back into Kentucky, where it joins the Ohio River. p. 275.

Danube River (dan′ yüb riv′ ər). Second longest river in Europe. It begins in the Alps and flows into the Black Sea in Romania. p. 366.

Darling River (där′ ling riv′ ər). Starts in the Great Dividing Range of Australia and flows into the Murray River. p. 245.

Davos (dä vōs′). Resort town in the Alps of Switzerland. (47°N/10°E) p. 300.

Dawson Creek (dôs′ ən krēk). City in British Columbia, Canada. Located at one end of the Alaska Highway. (56°N/120°W) p. 55.

Death Valley (deth val′ ē). Very low valley located at the northern edge of the Mojave Desert. p. 149.

De Kalb (di kalb′). City in Illinois. (42°N/89°W) p. 193.

Denver (den′ vər). Capital of and largest city in Colorado. Located at the base of the Rocky Mountains where they join the Great Plains. It has an elevation of 5,280 ft (1,609 m). (40°N/105°W) pp. 356–357.

Detroit (di troit′). One of eight cities in the United States with a population of more than 1 million. Located on the Detroit River in Michigan, near Lake Erie. It is the center of the United States automobile industry. (42°N/83°W) p. 15.

Duluth (də lüth′). Port city in Minnesota. Located at the western end of Lake Superior. (47°N/74°W) pp. 356–357.

Eastern Hemisphere (ēs′ tərn hem′ ə sfir). The half of the earth east of the Prime Meridian. It includes Australia and most of Europe, Africa, and Asia. p. 13.

East Gulf Coastal Plain (ēst gulf kō′stəl plān). One of three regions in Louisiana. Includes the land east of the Mississippi Alluvial Plain. It has swamps in the south and west and has rolling hills in the north. p. 216.

East Tennessee (ēst ten ə sē′). One of three regions of Tennessee. Very mountainous. p. 274.

El Paso (el pas′ ō). Fourth most populated city in Texas. Located along the Rio Grande in the Chihuahuan Desert. (32°N/106°W) pp. 354–355.

Equator (i kwā′ tər). A line drawn on maps that circles the earth halfway between the two poles. It is labeled 0° latitude. p. 12.

Erie (ir′ ē). City on Lake Erie in northwestern corner of Pennsylvania. (42°N/80°W) pp. 354–355.

Escanaba (es kə näb′ ə). City in southern Michigan. Located on Little Bay de Noc. (46°N/87°W) p. 15.

Europe (yùr′ əp). The earth's second smallest continent. p. 7.

Fairbanks (far′ banks). Town in central Alaska. Located on the Tanana River. (65°N/148°W) p. 55.

Flint (flint). City in Michigan. Located about 60 miles (97 km) from Detroit. (43°N/84°W) p. 15.

Fort Collins (fôrt käl′ ənz). City in Colorado. Located on the high plains. (41°N/105°W) p. 263.

Fort McHenry (fôrt mə ken′ rē). Fort in Baltimore that was attacked by British warships during the War of 1812. During the attack, Francis Scott Key wrote the words for "The Star-Spangled Banner." (39°N/77°W) p. 208.

Four Corners (fôr kôr′ nərs). Only place in the United States where boundaries of four states—Arizona, Colorado, New Mexico, and Utah—come together. (37°N/109°W) p. 129.

Galena (gə lē′ nə). City in Illinois. Located on the Galena River. (42°N/90°W) p. 193.

Gary (gar′ ē). Large industrial city in Indiana. Located on southern end of Lake Michigan. One of the most important steelmaking centers in the United States. (42°N/87°W) pp. 356–357.

Gatlinburg (gat′ lin bėrg). Tourist city in Tennessee. Located in the Great Smokies. (36°N/84°W) p. 275.

Geneva (jə nē′ və). City on the Swiss Plateau in Switzerland. Located on the southern tip of Lake Geneva and on the Rhone River. (46°N/6°E) p. 300.

Gobi Desert (gō′ bē dez′ ərt). Dry area located in Mongolia. p. 120.

Grand Canyon (grand kan′ yən). Largest and best-known canyon in the United States. Located along the Colorado River in Arizona. p. 129.

Grand Rapids (grand rap′ ids). City in Michigan. Located on the Grand River. (43°N/86°W) p. 15.

Great Basin Desert (grāt bās′ ən dez′ ərt). Largest desert in the United States. Covers parts of nine states between the Rockies to the east and the Cascades and Sierra Nevada to the west. p. 126.

Great Dividing Range (grāt də vīd′ ing rānj). Mountain area of Australia. It extends from north to south near most of the eastern coast. It forms the western limit of the coastal plain. Highest peak is Mount Kosciusko, at 7,305 ft (2,226 m). p. 245.

Great Lakes (grāt lāks). Five large lakes located in North America, most of them along the border between Canada and the United States. p. 353.

Great Lakes Region (grāt lāks rē′ jən). Region made up of the eight states that border on the Great Lakes. p. 184.

Great Plains (grāt plānz). High plains area in the western part of the Central Plains. It stretches from Montana and North Dakota to Texas. pp. 354–355.

Great Salt Lake (grāt sôlt lāk). Located in Utah. It is an inland lake with no streams flowing out of it. pp. 354–355.

Great Salt Lake Desert (grāt sôlt lāk dez′ ərt). Part of the Great Basin Desert. Located just west of the Great Salt Lake. p. 122.

Great Smoky Mountains (grāt smō′ kē moun′ tənz). Part of the Appalachian Mountains in western North Carolina and Tennessee. p. 275.

Great Smoky Mountains National Park (grāt smō′ kē moun′ tənz nash′ ə nəl pärk). One of the most visited national parks in our country. Located in the Great Smoky Mountains between Tennessee and North Carolina. p. 275.

Greeley (grē′ lē). City in Colorado. (40°N/105°W) p. 263.

Greenland (grēn′ lənd). Largest island in the world. Located between Europe and North America. p. 353.

Greenwich (gren′ ich). Place in London, England, designated as 0° longitude. The Prime Meridian runs from the North Pole through Greenwich to the South Pole. p. 13.

Gulf Coastal Plain (gulf kōs′ təl plān). Large flat area located along the Gulf of Mexico from Florida to Texas. p. 177.

Gulf of Alaska (gulf ov ə las′ kə). Part of the Pacific Ocean east of Kodiak Island. p. 55.

Gulf of Mexico (gulf ov mek′ si kō). Body of water surrounded by the United States, Mexico, and Cuba. p. 352.

Hana (hän′ ə). Small village and port on the island of Maui in Hawaii. (21°N/156°W) p. 78.

Hawaii (hə wä′ ē). Largest of the Hawaiian Islands. Also the name given to the state that includes all of the Hawaiian Islands. p. 78.

Himalayas (him ə lā′ əz). World's highest mountain system. Located in Central Asia. Mount Everest—at 29,028 ft (8,848 m), the highest peak in the world—is located in the Himalayas. pp. 362–363.

Hispaniola (his pən yō′ lə). Second largest island in the West Indies. Located between Cuba and Puerto Rico. Two countries, Haiti and the Dominican Republic, are located on this island. p. 352.

Honolulu (hän əl ü′ lü). Capital of and most populated city in Hawaii. Located on the island of Oahu. (21°N/158°W) p. 78.

Houston (yü′ stən). City in Texas. Located near the Gulf of Mexico. The fourth most populated city in the United States. (30°N/95°W) pp. 356–357.

Hwang Ho (hwäng′ hō). Chinese river that starts in the mountains of Tibet and flows into the Yellow Sea. Sometimes called the Yellow River. Pronounced "Hwang He" in China. pp. 362–363.

Illinois River (il ə noi′ riv′ ər). Formed by the joining of the Des Plaines and Kankakee rivers. Flows into the Mississippi River. Connected to Lake Michigan by a canal. p. 193.

Imperial Valley (im pir′ ē əl val′ ē). Located in the Sonoran Desert in southeastern California. One of the most productive farm areas in the world. Most of the land is below sea level. p. 134.

Indian Ocean (in′ dē ən ō′ shən). Large body of salt water between Africa and Australia. p. 7.

Inn River (in riv′ ər). River in Switzerland. A tributary of the Danube River. p. 300.

Interlaken (int′ ər läk ən). Resort town in the Alps of Switzerland. (47°N/8°E) p. 300.

Juneau (jü′ nō). Capital of Alaska. Located on the Alaskan panhandle. (58°N/134°W) p. 55.

Jura Mountains (jür′ ə moun′ tənz). Mountains along the border between France and Switzerland. p. 300.

Kailua (kī lü′ ə). City on the island of Oahu in Hawaii. (21°N/158°W) p. 78.

Kalahari Desert (kal ə här′ ē dez′ ərt). Dry plateau region located in southern Africa. p. 120.

Kauai (kou′ ī). Fourth largest island in Hawaii. p. 78.

Ketchikan (kech′ i kan). Seaport town in southeastern Alaska. One of the world's largest pulp mills is located here. (55°N/132°W) p. 55.

Kiev (kē′ ef). Large city in the Soviet Union. Located in the Ukraine on the Dnieper River. (50°N/31°E) pp. 364–365.

Knoxville (näks′ vil). City in Tennessee. Located along the Tennessee River. (36°N/84°W) p. 275.

Kodiak Island (kōd′ ē ak ī lənd). Island in the Gulf of Alaska. The first European settlement in Alaska was started here in 1784. p. 55.

Lake Baikal (lāk bī kôl′). World's deepest lake. It is 1 mile (1.6 km) deep. It is located in the Soviet Union. p. 102.

Lake Charles (lāk chärls). City in Louisiana. It has one of the largest oil refineries in the state. (30°N/93°W) p. 216.

Lake Constance (lāk kän′ stəns). Located in the eastern part of Switzerland. The Rhine River flows in and out of this lake. p. 300.

Lake Erie (lāk ir′ ē). Located along the border between Canada and the United States. Second smallest of the five Great Lakes. Its coastline is in Michigan, Ohio, Pennsylvania, and New York. p. 184.

Lake Geneva (lāk jə nē′ və). Located in western Switzerland. The Rhone River flows in and out of this lake. p. 300.

Lake Huron (lāk hyür′ ən). Located along the boundary between Canada and the United States. Second largest of the five Great Lakes. The United States portion of the lake is in Michigan. p. 184.

Lake Lucerne (lāk lü sərn′). Lake in central Switzerland. p. 300.

Lake Michigan (lāk mish′ i gən). Located in the United States. Third largest of the five Great Lakes. Its coastline is in Michigan, Wisconsin, Illinois, and Indiana. p. 184.

Lake Ontario (lāk än ter′ ē ō). Located along the border between Canada and the United States. Smallest of the five Great Lakes. The United States portion of the lake is in New York. The only one of the Great Lakes that does not have a coastline in Michigan. p. 184.

Lake Superior (lāk sù pir′ ē ər). Located along the boundary between Canada and the United States. Largest of the five Great Lakes. Its coastline is in Minnesota, Wisconsin, and Michigan. p. 184.

Lake Victoria (lāk vik tōr ē ə). Second largest body of fresh water in the world. Located in eastern Africa. Kenya, Uganda, and Tanzania all have coastlines on this lake. p. 360.

Lake Zurich (lāk zùr′ ik). Lake in northern Switzerland. p. 300.

Lanai (lə nī′). One of the islands of Hawaii. Famous for growing pineapples. p. 78.

Lansing (lan′ sing). Capital of Michigan. Located on the Grand River. (43°N/85°W) p. 15.

Las Vegas (läs vā′ gəs). Resort city in Nevada. (36°N/115°W) pp. 356–357.

Leningrad (len′ ən grad). Second most populated city in the Soviet Union. Located on the Gulf of Finland. (60°N/30°E) pp. 364–365.

Little Diomede Island (lit′ əl dī′ ə mēd ī′ lənd). One of two islands located in the Bering Strait. This island, which is part of the United States, is only 2 miles (3.2 km) from Big Diomede Island, which is part of the Soviet Union. p. 55.

London (lən′ dən). Capital of and most populated city in the United Kingdom. Located on the Thames River. (52°N/0° long.) p. 367.

Los Angeles (lô san′ jə ləs). City in southern California. Located along the Pacific Ocean. It is the second most populated city in the United States. (34°N/118°W) pp. 356–357.

Madagascar (mad ə gas′ kər). Island in the Indian Ocean off the southeastern coast of Africa. Also the name of the country located on the island. p. 360.

Manaus (mə nous′). City in the rain forest of Brazil. Located on the Rio Negro, a branch of the Amazon. (3°S/60°W) p. 106.

Marquette (mär ket′). City in northern Michigan. Located on shore of Lake Superior. (47°N/87°W) p. 15.

Maryville (mar′ ē vil). City in Tennessee. A large aluminum plant is located here. (36°N/84°W) p. 275.

Matterhorn (mat′ ər hôrn). Famous mountain peak in the Alps. It is located in Italy along the border between Italy and Switzerland. It has an elevation of 14,701 ft (4,481 m). (46°N/8°E) p. 300.

Maui (mou′ ē). Second largest island in Hawaii. The city of Lahaina located on the island was the first place in Hawaii settled by people from Europe. p. 78.

Mecca (mek′ ə). City in Saudi Arabia. Holy city for Moslems. City where Mohammed was born. (21°N/40°E) pp. 364–365.

Mediterranean Sea (med ə tə rā′ nē ən sē). Large body of water surrounded by Europe, Africa, and Asia. It is the largest sea in the world. pp. 362–363.

Melbourne (mel′ bərn). Capital of the Australian state of Victoria. Located near the coast, in southeastern Australia. (38°S/145°E) p. 245.

Memphis (mem′ fəs). Most populated city in Tennessee. One of the 20 most populated cities in the United States. Located along the Mississippi River. (35°N/90°W) p. 275.

Mexico City (mek′ si kō sit′ ē). Capital of Mexico. The most populated city in North America. (19°N/99°W) p. 353.

Miami (mī am′ ē). Large city in Florida. Located along the Atlantic Ocean. (26°N/80°W) pp. 356–357.

Middle Tennessee (mid′ əl ten ə sē′). One of three regions of Tennessee. Region of low rolling hills. p. 274.

Minneapolis (min ē ap′ ə ləs). Most populated city in Minnesota. Located on the Mississippi River. (45°N/93°W) pp. 356–357.

Mississippi Alluvial Plain (mis ə sip′ ē ə lü′ vē əl plān). One of three regions in Louisiana. Includes the land along the Mississippi River. It stretches from the northern border of Louisiana to the Gulf of Mexico. p. 216.

Mississippi River (mis ə sip′ ē riv′ ər). Second longest river in the United States. Starts in northern Minnesota and flows into the Gulf of Mexico near New Orleans, Louisiana. pp. 354–355.

Missouri River (mə zùr′ ē riv′ ər). The longest river in the United States. Starts in western Montana and flows into the Mississippi River near St. Louis, Missouri. pp. 354–355.

Mojave Desert (mə häv ē dez′ ərt). Desert in California. Located about 300 miles (483 km) west of the Painted Desert and between the Sierra Nevada and the Colorado River. p. 149.

Mojave River (mə häv ē riv′ ər). Starts in the San Bernardino Mountains and flows into the Mojave Desert, toward the city of Barstow. Part of the river flows underground. p. 149.

Mombasa (mäm bäs′ ə). Seaport city on the eastern coast of Kenya. (4°S/40°E) p. 235.

Monte Rosa (mänt ē rō′ za). Group of ten mountain peaks in the Alps near or on the border between Switzerland and Italy. The highest peak in the group is Dufourspitze, with an elevation of 15,203 ft (4,634 m). (46°N/8°E) p. 300.

Monument Valley (mon′ yə mənt val′ ē). Area in the Navajo reservation where rocks rise straight from the desert floor. Located on the border between Arizona and Utah. p. 129.

Moscow (mäs′ kaù). National capital of the Soviet Union. The most populated city in Europe. (56°N/38°E) p. 367.

Mount Everest (mount ev′ rəst). Highest mountain peak in the world, at 29,028 ft (8,848 m). Located in the Himalayas. (28°N/87°E) pp. 362–363.

Mount Kenya (mount ken′ yə). Located in central Kenya. Second highest point in Africa, with an elevation of 17,058 ft (5,199 m). (0° lat./37°E) p. 360.

Mount McKinley (mount ma kin′ lē). Highest mountain peak in North America. Located in Alaska Range in Alaska. Its elevation is 20,320 ft (6,194 m). Also known as Mount Denali. (64°N/150°W) pp. 354–355.

Mount Mitchell (mount mich′ əl). Highest peak in the Appalachians. It has an elevation of 6,684 ft (2,037 m). Located in the Black Mountains of North Carolina. (36°N/82°W) pp. 354–355.

Mount Rainier (mount rə nir′). Located in the Cascade Range in central Washington. It has an elevation of 14,408 ft (4,392 m). Became part of a United States National Park in 1899. (47°N/121°W) p. 25.

Mount Triglav (mount trē′ gläv). Highest peak in Yugoslavia, with an elevation of 9,393 ft (2,863 m). Located in the Julian Alps in the Interior Highlands. (46°N/14°E) p. 293.

Mount Waialeale (mount wī äl ā äl′ ā). Peak with an elevation of 5,080 ft (1,569 m). Located on the island of Kauai in Hawaii. One of the rainiest places in the world. (22°N/160°W) p. 78.

Murray River (mər′ ē riv′ ər). Most important river in Australia. Starts in the Great Dividing Range and flows west into the Indian Ocean near Adelaide. p. 245.

Nairobi (nī rō′ bē). Capital of and most populated city in Kenya. (1°S/37°E) p. 235.

Nashville (nash′ vil). Capital of Tennessee. Located on the Cumberland River. (36°N/87°W) p. 275.

Navajo Indian reservation (nav′ ə hō in′ dē ən rez ər vā′ shən). Land, mostly in Arizona, set aside for the Navajo. p. 129.

Newark (nü′ ərk). Most populated city in New Jersey. Located on Newark Bay. (41°N/74°W) pp. 356–357.

Newcastle (nü′ kas əl). Port city on the eastern coast of Australia. Center of Australia's coal-mining area. (33°S/152°E) p. 245.

New Orleans (nü òr′ lē ənz). Most populated city in Louisiana. Located on the Mississippi River. One of the busiest ports in the United States. (30°N/90°W) p. 216.

New York City (nü yôrk sit′ ē). Most populated city in the United States. Located at the mouth of the Hudson River in the state of New York. (40°N/74°W) pp. 356–357.

Nile River (nīl riv′ ər). Longest river in the world. Flows into the Mediterranean Sea at Alexandria, Egypt. p. 360.

Norco (nòr′ kō). City in Louisiana. It has one of the largest oil refineries in the state. (30°N/90°W) p. 216.

North America (nôrth ə mer′ ə kə). The earth's third largest continent. p. 7.

North China Plain (nôrth chī′ nə plān). Large plain located in the eastern part of China. pp. 362–363.

Northern Hemisphere (nôr′ THərn hem′ ə sfir). The half of the earth that is north of the Equator. p. 12.

North European Plain (nôrth yùr ə pē ən plān). Large area of flat land stretching from southwestern France through Belgium, the Netherlands, West Germany, East Germany, and Poland, and into the Soviet Union. The southeastern part of the United Kingdom is also part of this plain. pp. 362–363.

North Pole (nôrth pōl). Most northern place on the earth. p. 11.

North Sea (nôrth sē). Part of the Atlantic Ocean between Great Britain and Europe. pp. 362–363.

Oahu (ə wä′ hü). Third largest island in the state of Hawaii. Honolulu is located on this island. p. 78.

Ocean City (ō′ shən sit′ ē). Resort city in Maryland. Located along the Atlantic Ocean. (38°N/75°W) p. 208.

Ohio River (ō hī′ ō riv′ ər). Formed at Pittsburgh by the joining of the Allegheny and Monongahela rivers. Flows into the Mississippi River at Cairo, Illinois. Forms part of the boundary of five states. pp. 354–355.

Olympia (ō lim′ pē ə). Capital of Washington. Located on Puget Sound. (47°N/123°W) pp. 356–357.

Pacific Ocean (pə sif′ ik ō′ shən). The earth's largest body of water. It stretches from the Arctic Circle to Antarctica and from the western coast of North America to the eastern coast of Asia. p. 7.

Painted Desert (pānt′ əd dez′ ərt). Small desert located mostly in northeastern Arizona. Part of the Navajo reservation is in the Painted Desert. p. 122.

Palm Springs (päm springz). Resort city in Sonoran Desert in southern California. (34°N/116°W) p. 134.

Pampas (pam′ pəz). Fertile plain area in Uruguay and Argentina. p. 358.

Peking (pē′ king). National capital of China. One of the most populated cities in the world. Also called Beijing. (40°N/116°E) pp. 364–365.

Perth (pərth). Capital of the Australian state of Western Australia. Located on the western coast of Australia. (32°S/116°E) p. 245.

Philadelphia (fil ə del′ fē ə). One of eight cities in the United States with a population of more than 1 million. Located at the point where the Delaware and Schuylkill rivers join. (40°N/75°W) pp. 356–357.

Phoenix (fē′ niks). Capital of and most populated city in Arizona. The ninth most populated city in the United States. Located in the Sonoran Desert along the Gila River. (33°N/112°W) pp. 356–357.

Piedmont (pēd′ mänt). One of five regions in Maryland. It is an upland area of rolling hills. p. 208.

Pikes Peak (pīks pēk). Located in Colorado on the edge of the Great Plains. It has an elevation of 14,110 ft (4,300 m). (39°N/105°W) pp. 354–355.

Pittsburgh (pits′ bərg). Second most populated city in Pennsylvania. Located at the point where the Monongahela and Allegheny rivers join to form the Ohio River. An important United States steel-manufacturing center. (40°N/80°W) pp. 356–357.

Polynesia (päl ə nē′ zhə). Large group of small islands in the central and southeastern Pacific Ocean. pp. 350–351.

Ponce (pôn′ sā). Large city in Puerto Rico. (18°N/67°W) p. 88.

Portland (pōrt′ lənd). Most populated city in Oregon. Located on the Willamette River near the point where it joins the Columbia River. (46°N/123°W) pp. 356–357.

Prime Meridian (prīm mə rid′ ē ən). 0° line of longitude. It divides the earth into the Eastern Hemisphere and the Western Hemisphere. p. 13.

Prudhoe Bay (prəd′ hō bā). Small bay on Beaufort Sea. Located in northern Alaska near the mouth of the Sagavanirktok River. p. 55.

Pueblo (pü eb′ lō). City in Colorado. Located on the Arkansas River. (38°N/105°W) p. 263.

Reno (rē′ nō). Second most populated city in Nevada. Located on Truckee River near Lake Tahoe. (40°N/120°W) pp. 356–357.

Rhine River (rīn riv′ ər). Starts in the Alps of Switzerland. Flows into the North Sea. Most important river in Europe. It passes through or borders on six countries. p. 300.

Rhone River (rōn riv′ ər). Starts in the Alps of Switzerland. Flows south through France to the Mediterranean Sea near Marseilles, France. p. 300.

Rio Grande (rē′ ō grand′). Starts in the Rocky Mountains in Colorado and flows south through New Mexico to Texas. Then it flows southeast, emptying into the Gulf of Mexico near Brownsville, Texas. It forms the boundary between Texas and Mexico. pp. 354–355.

Riyadh (rē yäd′). Capital of Saudi Arabia. (25°N/47°E) pp. 364–365.

Rocky Mountains (räk′ ē moun′ tənz). Longest and highest mountain chain in the United States. It stretches from Canada to Mexico. Highest peak is Mount Elbert, with an elevation of 14,431 ft (4,339 m). pp. 354–355.

Sahara (sə har′ ə). Largest desert in the world. Located in North Africa. p. 120.

St. Moritz (sānt mə rits′). Resort town in Switzerland. Famous for winter sports. Located along the Inn River. (47°N/10°E) p. 300.

Salt Lake City (sôlt lāk sit′ ē). Capital of and most populated city in Utah. Located near the Great Salt Lake. (41°N/112°W) pp. 356–357.

Salton Sea (sôlt′ ən sē). Salty, below-sea-level lake located in Imperial Valley in southeastern California. p. 134.

San Bernardino Mountains (san bər nər dē′ nō moun′ tənz). Mountains in southern California. The Mojave River starts in these mountains. p. 149.

San Juan (san wän′). Capital of and most populated city in Puerto Rico. Founded in 1521. (18°N/66°W) p. 88.

San Luis Valley (san lü′ əs val′ ē). Vegetable-growing area in Colorado. p. 263.

Sarajevo (sär′ ə ye vô). City in Yugoslavia. Site of the 1984 Winter Olympics. (44°N/18°E) p. 293.

Seattle (sē at′ əl). Most populated city in Washington. One of the 25 most populated cities in the United States. Located on the eastern shore of Puget Sound. (48°N/122°W) pp. 356–357.

Seoul (sōl). Capital of South Korea. One of the most populated cities in the world. (37°N/127°E) p. 326.

Shanghai (shang hī′). One of the most populated cities in the world. Located on the delta of the Yangtze River in China, on the East China Sea. (31°N/122°E) pp. 364–365.

Shreveport (shrēv′ pōrt). City in Louisiana. Located on the Red River. (33°N/94°W) p. 216.

Siberia (sī bir′ ē ə). Part of the Soviet Union covering much of the area between the Ural Mountains and the Pacific Ocean. pp. 362–363.

Sierra Nevada (sē er′ ə   nə vad′ ə). High mountain range located mostly in eastern California. Mount Whitney, with an elevation of 14,495 ft (4,418 m), is located in this range and is the highest peak in the United States outside of Alaska. pp. 354–355.

Smyrna (smər′ nə). City in Tennessee. A large automobile plant is located here. (36°N/87°W) p. 275.

Sonoran Desert (sə nōr′ ən dez′ ərt). Desert located in southern Arizona and southeastern California. Much of it also extends into Mexico. p. 134.

South America (south   ə mer′ ə kə). The earth's fourth largest continent. p. 7.

Southern Hemisphere (sᴜᴛʜ′ ərn   hem′ ə sfir). The half of the earth that is south of the Equator. p. 12.

South Pole (south   pōl). Most southern place on the earth. p. 11.

Sparrows Point (spa′ rōs   point). City in Maryland. A large steel factory is located here. (39°N/76°W) p. 208.

Spring Hill (spring   hil). City in Tennessee. A large automobile plant is located here. (36°N/87°W) p. 275.

Swiss Plateau (swis   pla tō′). Region of hills, lakes, and small plains located in Switzerland between the Alps and the Jura Mountains. p. 300.

Sydney (sid′ nē). Capital of the Australian state of New South Wales. Most populated city in Australia. Port city located on Tasman Sea, which is part of the Pacific Ocean. (34°S/151°E) p. 245.

Tennessee River (ten ə sē′   riv′ ər). Formed near Knoxville, Tennessee, by the joining of the Holston and French Broad rivers. Flows into the Ohio River at Paducah, Kentucky. pp. 354–355.

Tientsin (tē en′ sin). Large city on the North China Plain. Also known as Tianjing. (39°N/117°E) pp. 364–365.

Tokyo (tō′ kē ō). Capital of Japan. Located on the island of Honshu on Tokyo Bay. One of the most populated cities in the world. (36°N/140°E) pp. 364–365.

Tongass National Forest (ton′ gəs   nash′ ə nəl   fôr′ ist). Large national forest located in southern Alaska. p. 55.

Towson (taὐs′ ən). City in Maryland. (39°N/77°W) p. 208.

Trenton (trent′ ən). Capital of New Jersey. Located on the eastern side of the Delaware River. (40°N/75°W) pp. 356–357.

Tucson (tü sän′). City in Arizona. Located on the Santa Cruz River. (32°N/110°W) pp. 356–357.

Ukraine (yü krān′). Part of the Soviet Union. Wheat grows well in the rich black soil of this area. pp. 364–365.

Ural Mountains (yùr′ əl   moun′ tenz). Located in the Soviet Union. They form the east-west dividing line between Asia and Europe. Highest peak is Mount Narodnaya, with an elevation of 6,214 ft (1,894 m). pp. 362–363.

Vail (vāl). Ski resort in the Rocky Mountains in Colorado. (40°N/106°W) p. 263.

Vineland (vīn′ lənd). City in southern New Jersey. Important farming center. (39°N/75°W) p. 19.

Washington, D.C. (wôsh′ ing tən   ᴅᴄ). National capital of the United States. Located on the Potomac River. (39°N/77°W) pp. 356–357.

Western Hemisphere (wes′ tərn   hem′ ə sfir). The half of the earth west of the Prime Meridian. Includes all of North America and South America. p. 13.

West Gulf Coastal Plain (west   gulf   kōs′ təl   plān). One of three regions in Louisiana. Includes all the land in Louisiana west of the Mississippi Alluvial Plain. Has many swamps. Salt, natural gas, oil, and sulfur are found under the swamps. p. 216.

West Indies (west   in′ dēz). Group of islands stretching about 2,500 miles (4,023 km), from near Florida to near Venezuela. These islands separate the Caribbean Sea from the rest of the Atlantic Ocean. pp. 352–353.

West Siberian Plain (west   sī bir′ ē ən   plān). One of the largest plains in the world. Stretches from the Ural Mountains west to the Yenisei River. Drained by the Ob and Irtysh rivers. pp. 362–363.

West Tennessee (west   ten ə sē′). One of three regions in Tennessee. Part of the Gulf Coastal Plain. p. 274.

White Sands National Monument (whīt sandz nash′ ə nəl mon′ yə mənt). Located in the Tularosa Valley. Famous for its high sand dunes that consist of white sand. p. 134.

Willow (wil′ ō). City in Alaska selected in 1974 to be the site of the state capital. (60°N/152°W) p. 55.

Yukon River (yü′ kän riv′ ər). The third longest river in North America. Formed in Yukon Territory, Canada, and flows into the Bering Sea. p. 55.

Zagreb (zäg′ reb). Second most populated city in Yugoslavia. Located along the Sava River. (46°N/16°E) p. 293.

Zermatt (ser mät′). Resort town in Switzerland. Located near the Matterhorn. (46°N/8°E) p. 300.

Zurich (zùr′ ik). City on the Swiss Plateau in Switzerland. (47°N/9°E) p. 300.

GLOSSARY

The page reference in each entry tells where the term is first used in the text.

aborigines (ab ə rij′ ə nēz). The first people to live in a country. p. 242.

adobe (ə dō′ bē). A mixture of clay and straw used as a building material by Indians of the Southwest. p. 265.

Aleut (a lüt′). An Indian who lives on the Aleutian Islands. p. 66.

alfalfa (al fal′ fə). A green plant used for cattle feed. p. 126.

ally (al′ ī). A friend or helper. p. 295.

Appalachian Trail (ap ə lā′ chən trā əl). A 2,000 mile (3,200 km) hiking trail that runs from Georgia to Maine. p. 275.

Arab (ar′ əb). A member of a group of people who live in Egypt and other Middle Eastern lands. p. 163.

Arctic Circle (ärk′ tik sėr′ kəl). A special line of latitude located at 66½° north of the Equator. p. 53.

arroyo (ə roi′ ō). A dry streambed. Also called a dry wash. p. 141.

assembly line (ə sem′ blē līn). A row of workers and machines along which work passes until a product is finished. p. 323.

astronaut (as′ trə nôt). A person who journeys in outer space. p. 6.

avalanche (av′ ə lanch). A large amount of snow falling down a mountainside. p. 302.

axis (ak′ sis). An imaginary line running through the earth between the North Pole and the South Pole. p. 38.

barbed wire (bärbd wīr). Two or three steel wires twisted together with sharp points called barbs about every 12 inches (30 cm), used by farmers to fence land and protect crops from animals. p. 190.

barge (bärj). A flat-bottomed boat used to transport goods. p. 183.

bar graph (bär graf). A graph that shows information by means of bars. p. 30.

barking drum (bär′ king drum). A large container in which log sections are rolled and moved about to remove the bark from the logs. p. 60.

basin (bā′ sən). A region drained by a river and its tributaries. p. 105.

bauxite (bôk′ sīt). The ore from which aluminum is made. p. 108.

Bedouin (bed′ u̇ in). A wandering Arab herder. p. 159.

bituminous (bə tü′ mə nəs). Soft coal, which is used in making steel. p. 193.

blizzard (bliz′ ərd). A snowstorm with high winds. p. 185.

borax (bôr′ aks). A soft white mineral mined, among other places, in Death Valley. It has many industrial uses. p. 150.

border (bôr′ dər). To touch; an outer edge or boundary. p. 9.

boundary (boun′ dər ē). A line that separates one state or country from another. p. 9.

broiler (broi′ lər). A young chicken that is good for cooking. p. 210.

bucking (buk′ ing). Sawing the trunk of a tree into logs. p. 59.

cacao (kə kā′ ō). A tropical tree, the seeds of which are used in making cocoa and chocolate. p. 108.

cactus (kak′ təs). A desert plant of many varieties and sizes that can store water in its leaves. p. 136.

Cajun (kā′ jən). A person related to the early French Canadian settlers in Louisiana. p. 221.

camel (kam′ əl). A desert animal used for carrying goods and people, pulling plows, supplying milk, and other purposes. p. 157.

canopy (kan′ ə pē). The upper layer of a forest, formed by the top branches and leaves of the tallest forest trees. p. 76.

canyon (kan′ yən). A very deep valley with steep sides, formed by running water over thousands of years. p. 34.

caravan (kar′ ə van). A group of people traveling together and carrying loads of goods. p. 164.

cash crop (kash krop). A crop grown mainly for sale and not for use by the growers. p. 238.

cassava (kə sä′ və). A tropical plant, the root of which is used to make pudding and flour. p. 112.

Chilean (chil′ ē ən). A person who lives in Chile. p. 167.

clan (klan). A group of people who are related to each other and live together. p. 111.

climate (klī′ mit). The combination of a region's precipitation, wind, and temperature over a long period of time. p. 54.

coast (kōst). The land next to a large body of water. p. 34.

coastal plain (kōs′ təl plān). Flat land that lies along a coast. p. 204.

collective farm (kə lek′ tiv färm). A smaller government-owned farm in the Soviet Union, on which a variety of crops and animals are raised and workers are paid partly in money and partly with a share of the products. p. 102.

colony (kol′ ə nē). A place that is settled by people who leave their own country but remain citizens of that country. p. 211.

communism (kom′ yə niz əm). Belief in the common ownership of land and industry by all the people. p. 98.

Communist (kom′ yə nist). A person who believes in communism; a member of the group that controls the government of a country such as the Soviet Union or China. p. 98.

compass rose (kum′ pəs rōz). A drawing that shows where north, south, east, and west are on a map. p. 11.

Congress (kong′ gris). The group of people who meet in Washington, D.C., to make laws for our country. p. 287.

continent (kon′ tə nənt). A very large body of land. There are seven continents—Asia, Africa, North America, South America, Europe, Australia, and Antarctica. p. 7.

continental climate (kon tə nen′ təl klī′ mit). A climate in which the summers are hot and humid, and the winters are cold and snowy. p. 185.

Continental Divide (kon tə nen′ təl də vīd′). The line of mountain ridges that separates drainage areas on a continent. The Continental Divide in North America runs along the highest land of the Rocky Mountains. p. 264.

contour lines (kon′ tùr līnz). Lines on a map connecting points of land that are equal distance above sea level. p. 22.

copper (kop′ ər). A reddish-orange metal used to make electric wire, pots, pans, lamps, jewelry, and other things. p. 168.

core (kôr). The inner layer of the earth, below the mantle. p. 259.

creeper (krē′ pər). A ropelike vine in a tropical forest. p. 76.

Creole (krē′ ōl). A person related to the early French and Spanish settlers in Louisiana. p. 221.

creosote bush (krē′ ə sōt bùsh). A small plant that grows in orderly rows, found in some deserts. p. 143.

crude oil (krüd oil). Oil in the form that comes from the earth, before impurities are removed. p. 164.

crust (krust). The outer layer of the earth. p. 258.

dam (dam). A wall built across a river or stream that stops the flow of water. Lakes and reservoirs are created by dams. p. 281.

delta (del′ tə). A piece of land formed by mud and sand that settles from water flowing out of the place where a river ends. p. 34.

depression (di presh′ ən). An extended period of time when very many people are out of work and there is very little buying and selling of goods. A depression is longer and more severe than a recession. p. 325.

derrick (der′ ik). A tall tower used to hold oil-drilling machinery. p. 164.

desert (dez′ ərt). A region with very little rainfall and few plants. p. 124.

diagram (dī′ ə gram). A special kind of drawing that explains how something works or why something happens. p. 38.

dike (dīk). A bank of earth built along a river to keep water from flowing onto the fields. p. 228.

dinosaur (dī′ nə sôr). An animal that lived on the earth many millions of years ago. p. 265.

dry farming (drī fär′ ming). A way of growing crops on land where there is little water. p. 129.

dry lake (drī lāk). A low place in the desert where rainwater has evaporated. p. 142.

dry wash (drī wosh). A streambed that has no water. Also called an arroyo. p. 141.

east (ēst). The main direction from which the sun seems to rise each morning. p. 10.

elevation (el ə vā′shən). Distance or height above sea level. p. 25.

Equator (i kwā′ tər). The imaginary line on the earth halfway between the North Pole and the South Pole. It is represented on a map or globe by the latitude line numbered 0°. p. 12.

erosion (i rō′ zhən). The wearing away of the earth's surface by wind, ice, running water, or waves. p. 89.

Eskimo (es′ kə mō). An Indian who lives in the northern or western part of Alaska. p. 66.

estimate (es′ ti māt). To judge or figure out something, such as distance or location on a map or globe. p. 14.

ethnic group (eth′ nik grüp). People who have the same language and customs and often the same religion and country of origin. p. 97.

evaporate (i vap′ ə rāt). To change from a liquid to a gas, as water does when heated. p. 125.

Fall Line (fôl līn). A line of small waterfalls and rapids that separates the Atlantic Coastal Plain from other regions. p. 207.

famine (fam′ ən). A very great shortage of food. p. 231.

felling (fel′ ing). A term that loggers use to describe cutting a tree down. p. 59.

fishery (fish′ ə rē). A place for catching fish. p. 63.

food processing (füd pros′ es ing). Preparing farm products for sale in stores by means of canning, freezing, and so on. p. 193.

fossil (fos′ əl). The hardened remains of a plant or an animal that lived many years ago. p. 208.

game reserve (gām ri zėrv′). An area set aside by the government where animals are protected from hunters. p. 240.

geography (jē og′ rə fē). The study of how people use the earth. p. 8.

ghost town (gōst toun). A community from which people have departed but where buildings still stand. p. 266.

glacier (glā′ shər). A large body of slowly moving ice. p. 299.

globe (glōb). A model of the earth. A globe shows the shapes of the earth's land and water. p. 7.

gold rush (gōld rush). The act of many people hurrying to a region where gold has been discovered. p. 144.

grid (grid). A system of crossing lines that form boxes. p. 14.

grinder (grīn′ dər). A machine that wears logs down into tiny pieces. p. 60.

groundwood pulp (ground′ wùd pulp). The finished product after pieces of wood are mixed with water and bleach and are passed through screens. p. 60.

growing season (grō′ ing sē′ zən). The time of the year when crops can be grown. p. 209.

gulf (gulf). A part of an ocean or a sea that pushes inland. p. 35.

harbor (här′ bər). A protected body of water. p. 35.

hardware (härd′ wār). Things made of metal, like tools, locks, nails, and screws. p. 195.

headquarters (hed′ kwôrt ərz). The center of a business. p. 320.

helium (hē′ lē əm). A gas that is lighter than air. p. 132.

hemisphere (hem′ ə sfir). Half of a sphere, or ball. Half of the earth. p. 12.

high technology (hī tek nol′ ə jē). The use of up-to-date tools and machines that do jobs that were once done by people. p. 233.

historical document (his tôr′ ə kəl dok′ yə mənt). A written record of the past. p. 335.

historical marker (his tôr′ ə kəl mär′ kər). A sign that tells about something important in history. p. 335.

historical source (his tôr′ ə kəl sôrs). Something or someone that tells about the past. p. 335.

history (his′ tər ē). The story of what happened in the past. p. 8.

hogan (hō′ gôn). A one-room Navajo dwelling made of logs and clay. p. 130.

humid (hyü′ mid). Very damp. p. 77.

hurricane (hėr′ ə kān). A violent storm with heavy rain and high winds. p. 217.

hydroelectric power (hī drō i lek′ trik pou′ ər). Electricity produced by the power of falling or rushing water. p. 56.

igloo (ig′ lü). A small dwelling made out of blocks of ice. p. 67.

independence (in di pen′ dəns). A country's or people's freedom to rule itself or themselves. p. 211.

insulin (in′ sə lən). A liquid taken from cattle and hogs that is used as a medicine to help control diabetes. p. 192.

irrigation (ir ə gā′ shən). The bringing of water to crops or other plants by pipes, canals, or ditches. p. 90.

Islam (is′ ləm). A major world religion whose followers are called Moslems. p. 160.

island (ī′ lənd). A body of land that has water all around it. p. 35.

jazz (jaz). A kind of music developed in New Orleans, Louisiana. p. 223.

Joshua tree (josh′ ù ə trē). An evergreen tree with long, sharp leaves that grows in some deserts. p. 142.

jungle (jung′ gəl). A place where trees and other plants grow in thick tangles, usually in the tropics. p. 105.

Kaaba (kä′ bə). A Moslem shrine in Mecca, the holy city for Moslems. p. 160.

kerosene (ker′ ə sēn). A fuel made from crude oil. p. 166.

key (kē). The part of a map that tells what the symbols stand for. p. 16.

laborer (lā′ bər ər). A worker. p. 326.

lake (lāk). A body of water with land all around it. p. 35.

landlocked (land′ lokt). Not bordering a sea or an ocean. p. 299.

latitude (lat′ ə tüd). Distance north or south of the earth's Equator measured in degrees. The lines that measure latitude run east and west on a map or globe. p. 12.

lava (lä′ və). Melted rock that is very hot. p. 80.

leeward side (lē′ wərd sīd). The side opposite the windward side. p. 79.

limestone (līm′ stōn). A rock used in making cement. p. 150.

line graph (līn graf). A graph that shows information by means of a line. A line graph usually shows how things change over a period of time. p. 31.

llama (ä′ mə). An animal related to the camel but smaller and humpless, found only in South America. p. 169.

local history (lō′ kəl his′ tər ē). The history of a community. p. 334.

logger (lôg′ ər). A person who cuts trees for lumber and gets them out of the forest. p. 58.

longitude (lon′ jə tüd). Distance east or west of the Prime Meridian measured in degrees. The lines that measure longitude run north and south on a map or globe. p. 13.

loom (lüm). A frame used for weaving threads to make cloth. p. 130.

lumber (lum′ bər). Trees that have been sawed into boards, beams, and other forms of wood. p. 56.

manganese (mang′ gə nēs). A mineral that is mixed with metals to make them stronger. p. 108.

mantle (man′ təl). The thickest layer of the earth, found under the crust. p. 258.

map (map). A special kind of drawing that can show different parts of the earth. p. 9.

meadow (med′ ō). A piece of grassy land mainly used as a pasture for animals. p. 304.

Mediterranean climate (med ə tə rā′ nē ən klī′ mit). A climate in which the summers are hot and dry, and the winters are mild and rainy. p. 294.

metropolitan area (met rə pol′ ə tən är′ ē ə). A large city and surrounding towns, smaller cities, and other communities. p. 137.

mineral (min′ ər əl). A valuable substance found in the earth, such as gold, copper, or iron. Minerals are mined and used for various purposes. p. 103.

monument (mon′ yə mənt). Something that is built to honor a person or an event. p. 334.

Mormon (môr′ mən). A member of a religious group centered in Salt Lake City, Utah. p. 127.

Moslem (moz′ ləm). A person who practices the religion of Islam. p. 160.

mosque (mosk). A Moslem place of worship. p. 160.

mountain (moun′ tən). A piece of land that rises steeply from the land around it. p. 36.

national monument (nash′ ə nəl mon′ yə mənt). A place of interest set aside by the government for the public. p. 147.

natural resource (nach′ ər əl rē′ sôrs). Something useful to people that is supplied by nature, such as land, minerals, water, and forests. p. 53.

natural rubber (nach′ ər əl rub′ ər). Rubber made from the sap of the rubber tree. p. 110.

neutral (nü′ trəl). Not taking sides in a dispute. p. 307.

nomad (nō′ mad). A person without a fixed home who wanders from place to place. p. 159.

north (nôrth). The main direction that is toward the North Pole. p. 10.

North Pole (nôrth pōl). The northern end of the earth's axis. It is located in the Arctic Ocean. p. 10.

oasis (ō ā′ sis). A place in the desert where there is enough water for some plants to grow. p. 156.

ocean (ō′ shən). A large body of salt water. There are four oceans—the Atlantic, Pacific, Indian, and Arctic oceans. p. 7.

oil refinery (oil ri fī′ nər ē). A big industrial plant that makes crude oil into oil products. p. 166.

oil tanker (oil tang′ kər). A large ship with big tanks used for shipping oil. p. 64.

oil well (oil wel). A hole drilled in the earth, from which oil is obtained. p. 164.

open-pit mining (ō′ pən pit mī′ ning). Mining carried out by stripping the soil from the surface rather than by tunneling into the earth. Also called strip-mining. p. 151.

oral history (ôr′ əl his′ tər ē). Information about the past that is gathered by talking with people who remember events in the past. p. 336.

orchid (ôr′ kid). A flower cultivated for its beauty and found growing wild in some tropical forests. p. 88.

ore (ôr). A material containing one or more minerals. p. 108.

Parthenon (pär′ thə non). An ancient Greek temple, a full-size copy of which stands in Nashville, Tennessee. p. 285.

peasant (pez′ ənt). A person, usually poor, who farms as a small landowner or as a laborer. p. 98.

peat (pēt). Decayed moss and plants used to make fuel and fertilizers. p. 194.

peninsula (pə nin′ sə lə). A strip of land with water nearly all the way around it and connected to a main body of land. p. 36.

permafrost (pèr′ mə frost). A permanently frozen layer of land found in the colder regions of the earth. p. 54.

physical map (fiz′ ə kəl map). A map that shows mountains, plains, and other forms that land and water take. p. 338.

pictograph (pik′ tə graf). A graph that shows information through symbols or drawings. p. 28.

picture dictionary (pik′ chər dik′ shə ner ē). A reference tool that gives pictures or drawings and written descriptions of things. p. 32.

pie graph (pī graf). A graph in the form of a circle, used to show the parts of a whole. p. 29.

plain (plān). A large piece of grassy land that is almost level and is often treeless. p. 36.

plantation (plan tā′ shən). A large farm on which only one kind of crop is usually raised. p. 82.

plateau (pla tō′). A raised, level piece of land that covers a large area. p. 37.

political map (pə lit′ ə kəl map). A map that shows such things as national and state boundaries and the names and locations of towns and cities. p. 338.

pollution (pə lü′ shən). The act of making the air, land, and water dirty. p. 151.

population density (pop yə lā′ shən den′ sə tē). The number of people per unit of area, as a square mile or square kilometer. p. 66.

poverty (pov′ ər tē). The state of being very poor. p. 130.

preserve (prə zərv′). To protect from change. p. 196.

Prime Meridian (prīm mə rid′ ē ən). The line of longitude from which other lines of longitude are measured. The Prime Meridian is numbered 0°. It passes through England. p. 13.

pueblo (pweb′ lō). An Indian village in the southwestern United States. Also a dwelling in such a village. p. 129.

pulp mill (pulp mil). A place where logs are turned into pulp, which is used to make paper. p. 59.

pyramid (pir′ ə mid). A carefully built stone structure with four triangular sides built to hold the body of an Egyptian ruler. p. 163.

rain forest (rān fôr′ ist). A forest with a thick growth of trees in a place with heavy rainfall, often in the tropics. p. 76.

ranch (ranch). A large farm with grazing land for raising cattle, sheep, or horses. p. 126.

reaper (rē′ pər). A machine used to harvest crops. p. 190.

recession (ri sesh′ ən). A period when many people are out of work and the sale of goods drops. A recession is less severe and is shorter than a depression. p. 325.

refine (ri fīn′). To improve or make pure. p. 64.

refuge (ref′ yüj). A place that protects people or animals. p. 54.

relief maps (ri lēf′ maps). Maps that use different colors to show the range between contour lines. p. 25.

renewable resource (ri nü′ ə bəl rē′ sôrs). A material created by nature that is valuable and can be replaced. Trees are one example. p. 60.

representative (rep ri zen′ tə tiv). One chosen to act for others. In our government, each state sends people to represent it in the House of Representatives in Washington, D.C. States with larger populations have more representatives in this lawmaking body than do states with smaller populations. p. 344.

republic (ri pub′ lik). In Yugoslavia, a state with its own laws and government. p. 295.

reservation (rez ər vā′ shən). Land set aside by the government for a special purpose, such as for the use of Indians. p. 130.

reservoir (rez′ ər vwär). A collection and storage place for water. Reservoirs look like little lakes. p. 271.

resort (ri zôrt′). A place where people go for recreation or entertainment. p. 137.

restore (ri stōr′). Bring back to an original state. p. 199.

river (riv′ ər). A long, narrow body of water that flows through the land. p. 37.

river mouth (riv′ ər mouth). The place where a river reaches the ocean. p. 106.

ruling class (rü′ ling klas). A group of educated, well-to-do people who are in control of a country, as in Russia before 1917. p. 98.

sandalwood (san′ dəl wůd). A tropical tree with a fragrant, oily wood used for the carving of ornaments and decorations. p. 79.

sand dune (sand dün). A hill made of fine sand. p. 147.

sandstorm (sand′ stôrm). A desert windstorm that fills the air with sand. p. 147.

scale (skāl). A way of showing size or distance on a map. p. 16.

sea (sē). A large body of salt water, smaller than an ocean. p. 37.

sea level (sē lev′əl). The base from which the elevation of all the earth's land is measured (0 feet). p. 22.

seedling (sēd′ ling). A small tree or other young plant grown from seed. p. 60.

senator (sen′ ə tər). A person who represents his or her state in the United States Senate, one of the lawmaking bodies in Washington, D.C. Each state has two senators. p. 344.

service industry (sėr′ vis in′ dəs trē). An industry that offers people a service. p. 284.

shaft mine (shaft mīn). A mine that is entered by a passage dug straight down to the level of the material that is to be removed. p. 278.

shrine (shrīn). A holy place. p. 160.

silt (silt). A mixture of soil, sand, and ground stone deposited by a river. p. 215.

skidding (skid′ ing). Dragging logs to a loading area. p. 59.

slave (slāv). A person who is owned by another person. p. 221.

sodium nitrate (sō′ dē əm nī′ trāt). A mineral used to make fertilizers and explosives. p. 169.

solar energy (sō′ lər en′ ər jē). Energy that comes from the sun. p. 263.

south (south). The main direction that is toward the South Pole. p. 10.

South Pole (south pōl). The southern end of the earth's axis. It is located on the continent of Antarctica. p. 10.

sphere (sfir). An object that is round like a ball. p. 7.

station (stā′ shən). In Australia, a big sheep or cattle ranch. p. 244.

steel plow (stēl plou). A farming tool used for turning over the soil and preparing it for planting. p. 190.

steppe (step). A grassy, treeless plain found in southeastern Europe and Asia. p. 101.

strait (strāt). A narrow strip of water that connects two larger bodies of water. p. 53.

sugarcane (shŭg′ ər kān). A plant whose stalk provides juice that is made into sugar. p. 82.

surplus (sèr′ plus). More of something than is used or needed. p. 317.

swamp (swomp). Low ground often covered with water. p. 205.

symbol (sim′ bəl). Something used on a map to stand for a real thing or place on the earth's surface. p. 16.

synthetic rubber (sin thet′ ik rub′ ər). Rubber made from oil and chemicals. p. 110.

Tennessee Valley Authority (ten′ i sē val′ ē ə thôr′ ə tē). A group set up by the federal government in 1933 to build and run dams and hydroelectric plants and control floods on rivers in the Tennessee Valley. Commonly known as TVA. p. 280.

territory (ter′ ə tôr ē). An area of land. In Australia, a region that has not been developed enough to become a state. p. 243.

tideland (tīd′ land). Underwater land lying just off a coast. p. 206.

timberline (tim′ bər līn). The point at which trees no longer grow on the slope of a mountain. p. 263.

tornado (tôr nā′ dō). A very strong wind that sweeps across the land in a narrow path, often causing great destruction. p. 185.

trade wind (trād wind). A wind that blows over the ocean in one direction, usually toward the Equator. p. 78.

Trail of Tears (trāl əv tērz). The forced journey of the Cherokee from their homeland to reservations in Oklahoma. p. 286.

Trans-Alaska Pipeline (trans ə las′ kə pīp′ līn). A large and long pipe through which oil is transported from Prudhoe Bay to Valdez, Alaska. p. 64.

tribe (trīb). A group of people that form a community under a leader or leaders. p. 286.

tributary (trib′ yə ter ē). A stream or river that flows into a larger stream or river or into a lake. p. 106.

tropics (trop′ iks). The region extending on either side of the Equator from about 23° north latitude to about 23° south latitude. p. 76.

tundra (tun′ drə). Lowlands with low plants, found in far northern regions. p. 54.

unemployed (un em ploid′). Without a job. p. 324.

unemployment (un em ploi′ mənt). A lack of jobs. p. 346.

uranium (yu̇ rā′ nē əm). A metal that is used to make electric power. p. 132.

valley (val′ ē). A long, low place between hills or mountains. p. 37.

volcano (vol kā′ nō). An opening in the earth, usually at the top of a cone-shaped hill, out of which steam and other gases, stones, ashes, and melted rock may pour from time to time. p. 78.

volunteer (vol ən tēr′). A person who does something of his or her own free will. p. 287.

west (west). The main direction in which the sun seems to set each night. p. 10.

windward side (wind′ wərd sīd). The side or direction from which the wind is blowing. p. 79.

yucca (yuk′ ə). A desert plant with swordlike leaves and beautiful flowers. p. 134.

INDEX

CREDITS

B C D E F G H I J—RRD—97 96 95 94 93 92 91 90